Great Jewish Thinkers
of the Twentieth Century

The B'nai B'rith History of the Jewish People
was first published during the years 1959–1964
as the B'nai B'rith Great Book Series.
The present edition, in five volumes,
has been selected to be part of the B'nai B'rith Judaica Library.
The Library is sponsored by the
B'nai B'rith International Commission on Adult Jewish Education
in an effort to promote a greater popular understanding
of Judaism and the Jewish tradition.
The volumes in the series are:

Creators of the Jewish Experience in Ancient and Medieval Times
Creators of the Jewish Experience in the Modern World
Concepts that Distinguish Judaism
Great Jewish Thinkers of the Twentieth Century
Contemporary Jewish Thought

The B'nai B'rith History of the Jewish People

GREAT JEWISH THINKERS OF THE TWENTIETH CENTURY

Edited with introductory notes by
Simon Noveck
Annotated bibliographies by
Steven T. Katz

B'nai B'rith Books
Washington, D.C.

Jerusalem • London • Paris • Buenos Aires • East Sydney

Library of Congress Cataloging in Publication Data

Great Jewish thinkers of the twentieth century.

Bibliography: p.   Includes index.
1. Rabbis—Biography. 2. Zionists—Biography. 3. Philosophers,
Jewish—Biography. 4. Judaism—20th century.
I. Noveck, Simon.
BM750.G68 1985   296'.092'2   85-72297
ISBN 0-910250-06-5   ISBN 0-910250-07-3 (pbk.)

Contents

Introduction

The towering achievement in publishing by the B'nai B'rith International Commission on Adult Jewish Education has been, to this date, the B'nai B'rith Great Book Series edited for four volumes by Simon Noveck and for the fifth by Abraham Ezra Millgram. These books, as Rabbi Noveck described, presented "the inner-content of Jewish tradition, the great personalities and thinkers, the ideas, beliefs and religious movements of Judaism." In short, they are a *History of the Jewish People*. The nearly fifty scholars, teachers, and rabbis who contributed original essays to these volumes were a preponderant majority of the great interpreters of Jewish civilization at mid-century. Twenty-five years after they began to appear, the freshness and vigor of each essay is undiminished.

The continuing demand for each of the volumes by colleges and universities, synagogues and day schools, is being met by this revised edition. The essays are presented as they originally appeared, though for greater clarity the volumes themselves have been retitled and the series renamed. It was my belief that this new edition would enjoy a greater utility if each of the essays were supplemented by annotated bibliographies that reviewed the literature relevant to the subjects of the essays. Three distinguished scholars and teachers have joined me in the preparation of these bibliographies: Steven T. Katz of Cornell University, Reuven Kimelman of Brandeis University and Arthur Kurzweil, the noted author and lecturer. Each of us benefitted as students from this series, and the opportunity to enhance its value has brought us much satisfaction.

The American journalist George Will recently wrote of the growing rootlessness of our lives, our failure to connect to our past and our neglect of our legacy of a shared and valuable civilization. He was addressing himself to the inadequacies of the American educational system as it teaches the essence of Western civilization, but his point applies with a special urgency to the demands of a sound Jewish education. He chose, quite fortuitously, a Biblical example to illustrate his argument:

> In 1940, a British officer on Dunkirk beach flashed to London a three-word message, "But if not..." It was instantly recognized as a quotation from the Book of Daniel, where Nebuchadnezzar commands Shadrach, Meshach and Abednego to worship the golden image or be thrust into the fiery furnace. They reply defiantly; "If our God whom we serve is able to deliver us, he will deliver us from the fiery furnace, and out of thy hand, O king. But if not, be it known unto thee, O king, that we will not serve thy gods, nor worship the golden image which thou hast set up."

The message from Dunkirk is stirring evidence of a community deriving cohesion, inspiration and courage from a shared history. The question this story raises is how many of us today could either receive or transmit such a message from the rich legacy of Jewish civilization?

B'nai B'rith International through its Commission on Adult Jewish Education is sponsoring the republication of these volumes in the belief that they can play a large role in stimulating a desire to learn about Judaism, Jewish history and Jewish civilization, and that of themselves they are superb examples of the living Jewish tradition.

The joy of being a Jew is not derived from books. It is a product of a rich family life wherein Judaism radiates a happiness and contentment that passes beyond the ability of language to describe. It is the product of partaking of the company of other Jews. Yet for the connectedness of one Jew to his religion and peoplehood there is a need for the passion to be grounded in understanding and knowledge. These essays can play an important part in awakening and satisfying a desire to learn and comprehend.

There is nothing obscure in these volumes. They have been written with an enviable clarity, and they will inform the non-Jewish reader as fully as the Jewish reader. In presenting these volumes to the public, B'nai B'rith looks forward to a full engagement of the ideas presented therein with the wisdom and curiosity of men and women everywhere.

The B'nai B'rith Commission on Adult Jewish Education continues to enjoy the support, advice and commitment of its founder Maurice A. Weinstein, and the then B'nai B'rith International President who worked diligently to establish the Commission's work at the center of the B'nai B'rith—Philip M. Klutznick.

This new edition has benefitted from the encouragement of B'nai B'rith International President Gerald Kraft and key members of the Board of Governors. Mr. Abe Kaplan, the immediate past chairman of the Commission, and Dr. A.J. Kravtin, the current chairman have been effectively energetic in promoting this work. Executive Vice President Dr. Daniel Thursz and Associate Director Rabbi Joel H. Meyers provide the leadership and environment necessary for a Jewish educational program of quality to flourish, and within the Commission my patient secretary Mrs. Edith Levine does the same. My collaborator on this project has been Mr. Robert Teitler, a devoted B'nai B'rith member and a creative publisher.

> Michael Neiditch, Director
> B'nai B'rith International Commission
> on Adult Jewish Education

Washington, D.C.
July 24, 1985
5 Av 5785

Foreword

One of the unique characteristics of the Jewish people has been its ability to meet the intellectual challenges with which it has been confronted in every age. In ancient Alexandria, during the Hellenistic period, Judaism was often derided for what was described as its crudeness and primitiveness in comparison with Greek philosophy. The anthropomorphic expressions in the Bible, the accounts of miracles and other literal expressions were criticized as incompatible with Greek thought.[1] The Jews of Alexandria, however, created a new type of literature in which Judaism was defended against pagan attacks, and Philo, philosopher and theologian, through his allegorical interpretations of the Bible, undertook the task of reconciling Judaism with Greek thought.

Eight centuries later the Jews in the Arab speaking world were again faced with the impact of the Greek spirit. This time the challenge was more direct and widespread than it had been in Alexandria. Arab controversialists questioned the authenticity of the Jewish revelation, ridiculed Jewish doctrines or tried to demonstrate the inferiority of the Jewish to the Muslim tradition. Some Muslims even accused Jews of lacking a purely monotheistic faith.[2] The effect of these criticisms was to create doubts in the minds of many Jews. A number of philosophers and theologians then arose from tenth to the twelfth centuries, including Saadia Gaon, Judah Halevi and Moses Maimonides, who defended the traditional faith of Judaism. They demonstrated the rationality of such beliefs as divine providence, freedom of the will, immortality and other cherished doctrines and thus were able to resolve the perplexities of their time.

The modern period of Jewish history, which began at the end of the eighteenth century, has again presented the Jew with challenges to his religious outlook and way of life. In the Middle Ages, which preceded the advent of modernism, although Jews lived under constant threat of persecution, they subscribed almost universally to the traditional Jewish outlook. This meant belief in God and his revelation, in the chosenness of the Jewish people, the coming of the Messiah and the doctrine of immortality. It included the discipline of Jewish law, the love of study and the practice of charity—all of which gave meaning to their lives.

There were occasional challenging spirits, particularly during the sixteenth and seventeenth centuries, who denied some religious tenet or broke with the accepted discipline. In Amsterdam Uriel Acosta (ca. 1585-1640), a descendant of a Marrano family who converted to Judaism, denied such Jewish tenets as belief in the immortality of the soul and in the resurrection of the dead;[3] and the philosopher Baruch Spinoza (1634-1677) expressed doubts about the divine origin of the Torah and developed a system of philosophy which though based in part on Jewish sources, in the opinion of many scholars lies outside the mainstream of Jewish tradition.[4] In Italy Azariah de Rossi (1514-1578) questioned the Biblical chronology and rejected the view that the Talmud was a binding authority on science and history.[5] But on the whole, until the end of the eighteenth century, almost all Jews had the security of a religious way of life.

However, as the walls separating Jews from non-Jews broke down at the end of the eighteenth century, the Jew emerged from the ghetto and came into contact with contemporary ideas. The new philosophy—which had begin with Descartes; the scientific contributions of Galileo and Newton; the impact of the age of reason; the development of the social sciences—all these brought about a transformation in intellectual outlook which aroused doubts in many believing Jews. As a result, a whole series of questions arose, presenting religious dilemmas to which nineteenth century Jews sought answers: What is Judaism? What makes a man a Jew? What is the meaning of revelation? The purpose of prayer? Can modern man believe in immortality? Are Jews really a chosen people? What is the relation of Judaism to Christianity?

Aside from these theological questions involving doctrine and belief, contact with Protestant and Catholic thinkers led some Jews to question the value of Jewish rituals, the meaning of the Sabbath and holidays and the use of Hebrew in religious services, and to ask whether modern Jews should continue to live under Jewish law.

For the past two centuries Jewish thinkers have concerned themselves with many of these issues. Moses Mendelssohn (1729-1786), philosopher of enlightenment, in his finest work, *Jerusalem* (1783), examined the character of Judaism and described it as a religion of reason. To him, theological tenets such as the unity of God, the moral law and the immortality of the soul, were rational concepts which could be demonstrated by logic and therefore should have been acceptable to men of all religions. The Jew was a bearer of revelation and Judaism was distinguished not by dogmas but by the network of revealed laws and ceremonies which were obligatory only for Jews.[6]

In the 1820's and 1830's Nahman Krochmal (1785-1840) in Galicia attempted a philosophy of Jewish history in the spirit of German philosophy.[7] However, neither Mendelssohn nor Krochmal presented a comprehensive or adequate reinterpretation of Judaism which could help the modern Jew reconcile his Judaism with contemporary thought. Leaders in the three religious camps in Germany, Abraham Geiger (1810-1874) for Reform Judaism, Zechariah Frankel (1801-1875) for the historical school, and Samson Raphael Hirsch (1808-1888) for Orthodox Judaism, formulated their views on many of these issues and won many followers.[8] But each left unanswered many questions, and none furnished a guide that is still acceptable to all segments of world Jewry.

During the past seven decades most of the issues which have confronted Jewish thinkers since the time of Moses Mendelssohn have continued to be of interest to contemporary Jewish thinkers. However, in the twentieth century, new emphases and new orientations to the old questions have emerged. The period beginning with the last decade of the nineteenth century marked a new era in the history of Jewish thought, characterized by increased concern with the problems of Jewish survival and the question of nationalism, a deepening quest for religious understanding and a search for Jewish identity.

Several factors made the twentieth century a distinct period in the development of Jewish thought. First, there was the failure of the science of Judaism *(Wissenschaft des Judentums)* to develop an adequate rationale for Jewish living through investigations of the Jewish past. Beginning in the 1830's a series of notable scholars such as Leopold Zunz (1794-1886), Solomon Rapoport (1790-1867), Heinrich Graetz (1817-1891), and Moritz Steinschneider (1816-1907), began to trace the origins of Jewish law and literature. Influenced by the new historical sciences, they composed biographies of past Jewish leaders, catalogued libraries and compiled bibliographies. It was believed that Judaism could be saved by this scholarly research. But *Judische Wissenschaft* soon lost its sense of direction when it allowed archival research to take precedence over considerations of the meaning of Judaism. Contemporary problems were left to apologetic literature, and no adequate philosophy emerged. By the end of the century it had become clear that there was need for something more than a historical orientation, if the issues of Jewish living in the modern world were to be clarified.[9]

Secondly, by 1900 it became apparent that emancipation had failed to solve the Jewish problem. The dream of *Haskalah,* based on the belief that the broadening of the intellectual horizons of Russian Jewry would bring them political and social rights, was shattered by the pogroms of 1881, in which the educated classes joined the peasants and police in attacking the Jews. The subsequent dillusionment and the return of many alienated Jews to Jewish life accentuated the need for a new interpretation of Jewish tradition. The rise of racialist theories and of anti-Semitism in Germany in the 1880's and in France in the 1890's again impelled many Jews to explore the meaning of their Jewish policy. Such rights did not give to Judaism a spiritual content nor did they settle the question of Jewish identity in the non-Jewish world.

Most important of all was the rise of Jewish nationalism in the 1880's followed by the dramatic convening in 1897 of a World Zionist Congress, the first in Jewish history. Although the Zionist movement had to overcome great opposition, particularly in western Europe, its appearance marked a turning point in Jewish life. Though Jewish nationalism did not completely dominate Jewish life during the twentieth century, most activities directly or indirectly related to this idea.

Thus new areas of interest emerged which became increasingly important in twentieth-century Jewish thought. Beginning in the last decade of the nineteenth century, a number of thinkers began to express their views on these areas.

In Russia theories of Jewish nationalism, both secular and religious, dominated the thought of the community. Jewish thinkers were particularly concerned with the purpose of Zionism, the question of language, the role of religion, and the relationship of Palestine to the Diaspora. In Germany the reorientation of Jewish theology away from its framework of Hegelian philosophy began. In America there were attempts to formulate rationales for the new religious movements which emerged in the modern period—Reform and Conservative Judaism and, particularly in recent years, expositions of the ideals of "modern" Orthodoxy.

The purpose of this book is to present the views on the basic issues of Judaism of ten of these twentieth-century thinkers. To our knowledge no book exists, authentic in scholarship and popular in approach, which includes these ten figures under one cover. The essay on Soloveitchik is the first systematic presentation of his ideas in English.

We begin with the philosophy of three exponents of Jewish nationalism: Ahad Ha-am, the brilliant essayist whose new interpretation of Judaism and theory of spiritual Zionism exerted a great influence on his generation; Aaron David Gordon, philosopher of the modern labor movement in Palestine and inspiration of many present day leaders of Israel; and Abraham Kuk, Chief Rabbi of Palestine, modern-day mystic and leader of Orthodox Judaism.

We turn next to the four outstanding German Jewish thinkers who helped to reorient Jewish theology in Germany: Hermann Cohen, founder of the Marburg School of philosophy and the intellectual spokesman of German Jewry during the first two decades of the twentieth century; Leo Baeck, spiritual leader of German Jewry during the Nazi era; Franz Rosenzweig, modern-day saint and philosopher of Jewish existentialism; and Martin Buber, intellectual leader of west European Jewry after the death of Hermann Cohen, and interpreter of *Hasidic* thought.

The volume concludes with three Americans: Kaufmann Kohler, president of the Hebrew Union College and philosopher of Reform Judaism; Mordecai Kaplan, professor at the Jewish Theological Seminary and founder of the Reconstructionist movement; and Joseph Soloveitchik, rabbinic authority and interpreter of *Halakhah* as a way of life.

It is regrettable that limitations of space prevented the inclusion in this book of an essay on the thought of Simon Dubnow, outstanding Russian Jewish historian and proponent of the theory of Diaspora nationalism, and on Abraham Heschel, whose neo-*Hasidic* thought has made such an impact on American Judaism. Fortunately, a first-rate exposition of Dubnow's ideas and a collection of his major theoretical writings are now available.[10] Solomon Schechter, who merits inclusion in this book, appeared in the previous volume.[12]

The great thinkers of the twentieth century inevitably represent a variety of viewpoints and approaches to Jewish life and thought, reflecting not only differences in temperament, background and personal conviction, but also the rapidly changing character of the twentieth century. The century opened with a decade of comparative calm and serenity, characterized by optimism, confidence and personal security. In those years the cruelties of violent revolution and dictatorship were inconceivable and the spread of democracy throughout the world seemed inevitable. Then came the tragedies of the First World War, the rise of totalitarianism, the years of false optimism between the two wars which were climaxed by the emergence of racialism in Germany and the holocaust of the Hitler years. For the Jew, the annihilation of six million Jews was followed by the dramatic rebirth of the State of Israel. In general the period since the Second World War has been described as an "age of anxiety" in which little of the optimism of the early part of the century remained.

During these turbulent years, the philosophical climate also underwent a change. The main current of nineteenth-century thought, rationalism, gradually gave way to philosophies which put less emphasis on intellect; and the past decade has seen the increasing impact of existentialist thought.

The thinkers in this book reflected the various events and the changing state of mind of the century. They differed in their interpretations of many aspects of Jewish tradition and in their answers to many of the basic issues of our time.

Heterogeneous and diverse as the thinkers discussed in this book were in philosophic background and outlook, all of them were united in their desire for an understanding of the uniqueness of Judaism and the meaning of Jewish existence. All were deeply versed in Jewish traditional sources—Bible, Talmud and medieval philosophy. Most of them were familiar with modern Jewish scholarship and history. They were all children of the twentieth century who recognized that Judaism does not exist in a vacuum and must be understood in the perspective of modern civilization. They understood that the challenges of the modern era must be met by Philo, and those of the Arabic period by Saadia and Maimonides.

Because of this, familiarity with the men in this book should be helpful to all who are in search of a philosophy of Jewish living or who are trying to find some solution to the intellectual perplexities and challenges of our time. Perhaps some readers may discover a clue to the solution of a deep personal problem, or a clarification of theological or community issues which confront modern-day Jews. This book can also serve as an introduction to a systematic study of twentieth-century Jewish thought.

Every effort has been made to make this book as useful as a learning tool as possible. Though written by ten authors, all the essays have a common frame of reference. In consonance with the plan of the book, most of the writers indicate at the outset the significance of the thinker being discussed as well as some of his lasting contributions. This is followed by a somewhat detailed biographical sketch enabling the reader to become acquainted with the life of each thinker and his personality. Each essay concludes with a summary of his thought, with special reference to his views on some of the contemporary issues to which we have referred.

As far as possible we have tried to minimize in this book the use of technical vocabulary and a discussion of the more abstract philosophical concepts of some of the thinkers. Our aim in each case has been to make available the thinker's views on specific Jewish issues, rather than to present his opinions on general metaphysical or epistemological questions.

It is hoped that the essays will be read in conjunction with the original writings of these men which can be found in Volume IV of this series. Wherever possible the reader should, after each chapter, turn to the appropriate selections in the anthology.

For those who prefer to go directly to the complete works of a thinker or to read further about a particular figure, there is a bibliography at the end of each chapter. For those who want to delve more deeply into the historical background or into specialized aspects of a thinker's works, there are references in the footnotes to the editor's foreword and introductions. As in the first two volumes, some of the contributors have submitted footnotes, while others felt that in an adult education volume such notes were unnecessary. All of the chapters, however, are authentic in scholarship and are based on research in the original writings.

A project of this scope could not come into being without the cooperation of many colleagues and friends who have been helpful in various ways. It is a personal joy to express my appreciation to each of them for his help.

I am grateful to Dr. Oscar I. Janowsky, Chairman of the Publications Committee of the B'nai B'rith Department of Adult Education and to Dr. Ira Eisenstein, a member of the Committee, who very carefully read the entire manuscript and made a number of valuable suggestions. Each of them was also personally helpful in a variety of ways. Dr. Harry Orlinsky, also a member of the Committee, read most of the volume and made several suggestions. Rabbi Harry Essrig read several sections of the book from an adult education point of view and gave me the benefit of his insightful criticisms.

I have derived great stimulation and benefit from conversations with several colleagues and friends—Dr. Jacob Agus, Professor Israel Knox, Rabbi Ludwig Nadelmann, Rabbi Steven S.

Schwarzschild and Rabbi David Silverman—each of whom generously gave of his time and shared his specialized philosophical knowledge with me. In London, several years ago, Sir Leon Simon was personally helpful in working out some aspects of Ahad Ha-am's thought. The writing of the sketch of A.D. Gordon's life was facilitated by the help of Joseph Baratz, Shmaryahu Barhon and the librarian of Bet Gordon in Degania, Israel, who made available source materials on Gordon's life. Throughout the preparation of this book I have enjoyed the ready help and fine spirit of cooperation of Abraham Berger and the staff of the Jewish Division of the New York Public Library.

Individual chapters were read by Rabbi Alexander J. Burnstein, Joseph and Margot Dembo, Dr. Norman Drachler, Dr. Ira Eisenstein, Professor Marvin Fox, Bernard Frank, Rabbi Norman Frimer, Dr. Alfred Jospe, Dr. Louis L. Kaplan, Rabbi Abraham Karp, Rabbi Arthur Lelyveld, Rabbi Harold Schulweis, Professor Lou Silberman, Maurice Weinstein, Rabbi Walter Zenner and Rabbi Arthur Zuckerman. Their critical reactions were most helpful to the contributors in revising their original drafts. Professor Marvin Fox was also very helpful in revising one of the chapters.

I am grateful to Rabbi Simcha Kling, Tuviah Preshel, Sefton Temkin, Professor Harold Weisberg, and Rabbi Walter Zenner for various acts of helpfulness and friendship. My warm thanks go particularly to Dr. Emanuel Rackman and Isaac Toubin whose personal interest in this project helped to overcome obstacles which stood in the way of publication.

The original idea that B'nai B'rith sponsor such a series of books for adult education purposes came from Professor Mordecai Kaplan. While the project has taken a different form from that which he had suggested, his original inspiration was in part responsible for this series of books.

I am also indebted to the officers and leaders of B'nai B'rith for granting me freedom to plan and launch these books; to Lily Edelman for her skillful and valuable editorial assistance during my association with B'nai B'rith, and to Joan Merrill for subsequent editorial help.

In the final stages of preparing this book during the spring and early summer of 1961, I benefited greatly from the help of my wife who participated in the research, and made many suggestions for improving the manuscript in style and in content. She also prepared the glossary which appears at the back of this book. Credit for the final copy-editing goes to Vera Zabelle.

SIMON NOVECK

EAST EUROPEAN JEWISH THINKERS

EDITOR'S INTRODUCTION
The Idea of Jewish Nationalism

Jewish thought in Russia during the last decade of the nineteenth and the first two decades of the twentieth century was dominated by the idea of Jewish nationalism. The central problems on the agenda of Russian Jewish thinkers during this period were the meaning of Jewish nationalism, the relationship of the Jewish people to its historic land, the question of language, the role of religion in Jewish culture, and the future of the Jews in the Diaspora. Rarely had Jewish life been so replete with ideas and programs as at this time. Books, essays and pamphlets as well as the poetry and *belles lettres* of the period reflected these concerns.

This emphasis on nationalism represented a basic change from the nature of Jewish thought in the previous century. From Moses Mendelssohn to Hermann Cohen, the major German Jewish thinkers were all concerned with the reconciliation of Judaism as a religious faith to modern culture. Their interest was in the universal aspects of Judaism, its ethical ideals, its principles of faith, and the character of the Jewish mission. To nineteenth-century liberal thinkers, systems of law and ceremony were hindrances to the expression of the unique spirit of Judaism.

In Russia, where the *Haskalah* (enlightenment movement) dominated Jewish thought during the 1860's and 1870's, the primary concern was with the introduction of European culture into Jewish life and the broadening of the intellectual horizons of the Jew. It is true that the novels of Abraham Mapu (1808-1867) depicted the glories of ancient Judea, and awakened thoughts of Zion, as did some of the poetry of the *Haskalah* period.[1] But on the whole, *Haskalah* literature in the nineteenth century was practical in character, stressing scientific knowledge, European languages and the value of manual labor. It also emphasized the role of aesthetics and beauty in life, the importance of reason and social progress.[2] During the twentieth century, however, Jewish thought in Russia turned to problems of Jewish survival and to the meaning of Jewish nationhood.

Many factors contributed to the national awakening of the Jewish people. Nationalism, as a dynamic force in Europe during the nineteenth century, induced demands for national self-determination by many subject peoples and actually led to the independence of some, like the Greeks, Serbians and Rumanians. These political struggles inspired a number of early Jewish leaders and thinkers. If the Serbians, Poles and Ukrainians could develop national aspirations, why not the Jews? The Jewish people in Russia dwelt in compact masses in the Pale of Settlement. They spoke a common vernacular and maintained their own cultural and religious institutions. Their homogeneity made these aspirations very plausible.

While some exponents of nationalism insisted on territory as a basis for nationalistic hopes, in the last quarter of the century the persistent demand for national rights by the diverse ethnic groups of the Austro-Hungarian Empire, gave rise to a new, non-political concept of nationalism.[3] In this concept a nationality consisted of a group having common memories and common aspirations for the future. Patriotism meant "not love of the soil, but love of the past, reverence for the generations which have preceded us." [4] This cultural emphasis encouraged advocates of Jewish nationalism, who sought, for the most part, cultural rather than political rights for the Jews.

The pogroms of 1881 and the subsequent May Laws deepened the sense of insecurity of Russian Jews, and the rise of anti-Semitism in western Europe shook their faith in the efficacy of the western type of emancipation. These were, perhaps, the most important factors contributing to the emergence of the national aspirations which flowered in the wake of disillusion and despair. Faith in *Haskalah* declined and a spiritual vacuum developed.

Large numbers of Jews, convinced that there was no future for them in Russia, began to emigrate to America. Others joined the revolutionary movement whose aim was the overthrow of the Czar. Their hope was that the problem of the Jew would find solution when the general social question was resolved.[5] Concurrently with this approach, several theories and political ideals emerged, based on the concept of Jewish nationalism.

One theory, which received wide support among Jewish middle class as well as proletarian groups, was that of Diaspora nationalism. This concept was propounded by the distinguished historian, Simon Dubnow, who saw the Jewish people as the supreme representative of the highest stage of nationalism in which the connection between state and nation had disappeared. In his now classic *Letters on Old and New Judaism*, published in book form in 1907, he advocated a form of cultural nationalism or socio-cultural autonomy wherein Jews would participate in the civic life of the country in which they lived, and would also sustain their "national rights," to speak their own language, use it in their social institutions and regulate their own internal, communal existence. Although he regarded Hebrew as the most important of the national languages of the Jews, he was opposed to "linguistic chauvinism." To him, Yiddish, too, was a strong bastion against assimilation. In his view, communal autonomy characterized the history of Jewry in the Diaspora and should be reestablished; the Jewish nationality in Russia should have the sanction of public authority with the right to organize Jewish education and culture.[6]

Reluctantly, Dubnow admitted to his friend Ahad Ha-am that "a full and complete national life" in the Diaspora was not possible.[7] But he felt that such a plan would make the best possible national life, not only in eastern Europe, but with certain changes, throughout the world.

The idea of cultural autonomy was likewise championed by Chaim Zhitlovsky (1865-1943), one of the founders of the social revolutionary movement in Russia. Zhitlovsky saw in a secular, progressive Jewish nationalism, separated from religion, the legitimate heir to the former Jewish way of life. While he was critical of Dubnow's theory because it failed to put the Jewish community on a solid economic foundation, he urged Jewish national rights along similar lines. He placed an even greater emphasis on the role of Yiddish than did Dubnow. To him, Yiddish was the most effective tool for Jewish survival.[8]

In 1905, the Bund, the general organization of Jewish socialist and trade union groups in Russia, adopted the idea of national rights. Though its primary interest was in the general political aspirations of the socialist movement, it recognized that the Jewish worker had special interests and could not separate himself from his people.[9]

For most Russian Jews, however, the idea of Jewish nationalism meant a return to Palestine. Shortly after the pogroms of 1881, the *Hoveve Zion* (Lovers of Zion) movement arose among middle class Russian-Jewish intellectuals and university students. Its goal was the establishment of colonies in Palestine. The movement spread to Rumania, Austria-Hungary, Germany, England and the United States, and during the next fifteen years was responsible for the emigration of twenty to thirty thousand Jews to Palestine.[10]

Members of the first wave of immigrants, or *aliyah*, flocked to the cities of Jerusalem, Jaffa, Haifa and Hebron. They laid the foundations for the colonies of Petach Tikvah, and Rishon Le-Zion, southeast of Jaffa; Zikhron Yaakov in Samaria, and Rosh Pinnah, east of Safed. Conditions were hard. The settlers were inexperienced at farming, and raids by marauders caused them much suffering. Only through the assistance of Baron Edmond de Rothschild of Paris were the colonies put on a stable foundation.[11]

Despite the Baron's aid, the movement could not develop a dynamic Zionism. Its methods were slow and haphazard; its organization too small to undertake major projects.

It was Theodor Herzl who gave Jewish nationalism dynamic impetus and brought the Jewish problem to the attention of the world. In a few, feverish days of writing in 1896, he composed his famous tract, *The Jewish State*. The following year he organized the first Congress from which evolved the World Zionist Organization as the instrument for political and financial action to realize the dream of nationhood. Herzl's incessant quest for a charter did not succeed. But, as Herzl himself recognized, the Congress laid the groundwork for a Jewish state that was to become a reality half a century later.

In 1904, at the age of forty-four, Herzl died. For more than a decade little political progress was made. However, the Second Aliyah, comprised of young, idealistic pioneers, established the principle of Jewish self-labor and initiated the remarkable network of cooperative colonies which have given the Palestinian community its unique character. When the Balfour Declaration was issued in November 1917 and the mandate over Palestine was given to Great Britain after the war, the idea of Jewish nationalism was on the way to becoming a reality.

What was the purpose of Jewish nationalism? Was it to build a state which would make Jews like other nations? Or did it have some higher ideal? What attitude should Jews have toward the Arab people? What kind of economic system should be established in the new land? What was to be the role of the Jewish worker? What status was religion to have in the new community? These were some of the questions with which the theorists of Jewish nationalism were confronted as the Zionist idea began to take on reality.

Four basic philosophies of Jewish nationalism emerged in the twentieth century and vied with each other for adherents. We refer briefly to these differing approaches as background to the thinkers in the first section of this book.

First was the theory of political Zionism advocated by Herzl, Nordau and their followers. Herzl believed in the "restoration of a Jewish state," achieved through political negotiations as accomplished by other modern European national movements. He was opposed to infiltration of Jews into Palestine. For Jews to "steal into the land of their fathers" seemed to him futile, for the immigration could be stopped at any time and all the efforts lost. Zionism insisted

on a publicly recognized home in Palestine for the Jewish people.
The idea for establishing the Jewish state was propelled by the
"gravity of the Jewish situation" which Herzl recognized was daily
becoming more intolerable. He saw no hope that this situation would
improve.

Herzl's concern was not primarily with the cultural or spiritual
problems of the Jewish nation, nor with the practical work of
colonization. To him, Zionism had to concentrate on a diplomatic
and political solution for the Jewish problem. In his program a great
exodus of the Jews from Europe would take place over a period of
decades until the majority of the Jews would dwell in their "unforgettable homeland." Those who remained behind would eventually become absorbed among the peoples in their native lands.[12]

In opposition to Herzlian Zionism was the philosophy of Ahad
Ha-am with which we shall deal in detail. In essence, Ahad Ha-am
was interested in the "plight of Judaism" rather than the "plight of
the Jew." All about him he saw the signs of the progressive disintegration and decay of Jewish cultural life. To overcome the challenges which confronted the Jew in modern times, Palestine would
have to become a "spiritual center" from which would come new
cultural influences to revive the spirit of the Jewish nation in the
Diaspora. This cultural emphasis of "Ahad Ha-amism" was accepted
by many twentieth-century Jewish writers and thinkers, who had
little faith in the diplomatic approach of the political Zionists. They
felt that "practical" work in building colonies and the establishment
of a Hebrew university to encourage a "renaissance of Israel's intellectual life" were more important.

A third philosophy that soon won many followers and has been
a paramount influence on the character of the present state of Israel
was that of labor, or socialist Zionism. The ideological founder of
labor Zionism was Nahman Syrkin (1867-1924) who in his writings, and in the *Poale Zion* movement he helped to organize, effected
a synthesis between socialist and Zionist trends in Jewish life. Two
years after Herzl's *Jewish State* appeared, Syrkin, at the age of
thirty, published *The Jewish Problem and the Socialist Jewish State*.
In this brochure he demonstrated a realistic understanding of the
role of the worker in the new state but argued that socialism alone
would not end Jewish suffering.

To Syrkin it was inconceivable that a Jewish state should be established on a basis of inequality, and class distinctions. Stressing the
economic hazards of colonizing Palestine under terms of private
property, he warned that wages would become depressed and many
settlers would leave the country if Palestine were turned into a busi-

ness venture. A Jewish state founded on capitalism would also be impossible for technological reasons. For the Jewish state to come into being, he insisted, it must from the very beginning "avoid all the ills of modern life . . . its guidelines must be justice, rational planning and social solidarity." [13]

Finally, there was the theory of religious nationalism associated with the Mizrachi, the religious group within the Zionist movement. At the fifth Zionist Congress in 1902, when the problem of cultural activities came up, the religious Zionists, unwilling to sanction a secular system of education, organized a separate group.[14] Actually the ideals of Mizrachi pre-dated the formation of the first Zionist Congress. Rabbi Samuel Mohilever (1824-1898) of Bialystok, who had been chosen honorary president of the first international conference of *Hoveve Zion* societies in 1884, was a seminal figure in the development of this approach. During the 1880's Mohilever undertook to win support for the new movement among the Orthodox, urging cooperation with non-observant Jews on the basis that all those who came to rescue Judaism should be welcomed. "Our attitude towards those among us who do not observe the religious precepts," he wrote, "must be, as it were, as if fire had taken hold of our homes, imperiling our persons and our property. Under such circumstances would we not receive anyone gladly and with love who though irreligious in our eyes, came to rescue us?" [15]

Yehiel Pines (1824-1912), who had come to Palestine in 1878 to administer the fund created in honor of the ninetieth birthday of Sir Moses Montefiore, also contributed to the theory of Orthodox religious Zionism. Pines was very critical of the theories of Ahad Ha-am, who saw the essence of Judaism in the national ethic rather than in religion. To Pines the idea of a secular nationality was an "alien implantation." There might be value in such a theory for the assimilated Jews who would have a "new bond to reinforce their attachment to their people." But he was opposed to disseminating such a doctrine among the Jewish people as a whole. Other groups could perhaps have national aspirations divorced from religion, but for Jews "the thought-image of Jewish nationality lay in the unity of the Jewish people with its Torah and its faith." [16]

While both Herzl and Syrkin for a time considered the possibility of creating a national home in territory other than Palestine, Pines and the Orthodox adherents of Zionism were completely devoted to the Palestine ideal. To them only this exalted goal could overcome all the obstacles and hardships that settling in the Holy Land entailed.

From among these four schools of nationalist thought, we have chosen three outstanding figures, each of whom made a distinctive contribution to the theory of Jewish nationalism. In their concepts of nationalism, in their approach to religion and in their attitude toward the Diaspora, each saw the national ideal in different terms. Ahad Ha-am, for example, as Martin Buber has pointed out, was a true "lover of Zion" that is the state of hoped-for perfection, while A. D. Gordon, more than anyone else, recognized the unique relationship between the people and the land. Abraham Kuk stressed the holiness of the land and its deep spiritual power.[17]

But transcending these differences are many common features. All three were born and grew up in the Russian Ukraine and brought the folk background of Russian Jewry to bear on their interpretations of Judaism. None of them wanted Palestine to become a nation like all other nations. All three were spiritual Zionists to whom a Jewish state was a means to a higher moral goal. All believed that Judaism possessed certain distinctive values and ideals which ought to be preserved.

These three exponents of Jewish nationalism were neither scholars nor philosophers in the technical sense of the word. They did not attempt a systematic exposition of their ideas nor were they interested in purely theoretic speculation. Their aim was to clarify issues and to point the way to a new spiritual era in Jewish life.

The life of each served as an example of his ideas and each won followers through the strength of his personality and moral leadership, as well as through his writings. Each demonstrated that it is possible to be a strong Jewish nationalist without giving up universal ideals. It is to these twentieth-century theorists of spiritual nationalism that we now turn.

1. Ahad Ha-am
[1856-1927]

SIMON NOVECK

A m o n g the outstanding Jewish thinkers from the end of the nineteenth century until today, no one has exerted greater influence nor is more important to an understanding of the issues of contemporary Jewish life than Asher Ginzberg, better known by his pen name of Ahad Ha-am (one of the people). His penetrating and cogent essays have become part of the classics of modern Jewish thought and have provided a new, nationalistic and secular interpretation of Judaism for a generation unable to accept the traditional religious approach.

While Herzl was the great political leader whose vision made possible the Jewish state, Ahad Ha-am was the philosopher and teacher who analyzed the crisis confronting Judaism in the modern world and furnished a rationale for the Zionist movement. His central idea that Palestine should not be established solely to resolve the economic plight of the Jew or to alleviate the problem of anti-Semitism, but should serve as a spiritual center which would revivify Jewish life in the Diaspora, provided a balance to the political and diplomatic emphasis of Herzl. The spiritual or cultural approach with which his name is linked has helped to determine the character of the emerging Jewish state.

Asher Ginzberg was not a bold dynamic leader of men. Small in stature with a large bald head which seemed disproportionate to the size of his body, he was quiet and reserved in manner and lacked the confidence and aggressiveness of the political leader.[1]

But through the cogency and clarity of his ideas, his concern with the problems of Jewish survival, and the deep integrity of his own character, he became a guide to the perplexed of his time.

The great poet Bialik regarded him as his mentor; Chaim Weizmann paid tribute to him over and over again in his autobiography.[2] Solomon Schechter described him as "one of our finest intellects and most original thinkers" and invited him to come to America to head the new Dropsie College of Hebrew and Cognate Learning which was established in 1905.[3] His essays were translated in his lifetime into several European languages and were eagerly read by writers and publicists as well as by the Hebrew-reading public both in eastern Europe and in America. In our time, Mordecai Kaplan and other American Jewish thinkers have expressed their indebtedness to him.[4]

In a sense, Ahad Ha-am is also the father of modern Hebrew style. As a writer and editor he taught his generation to express itself with force and clarity, to eliminate slovenliness and unnecessary phraseology, and to see Jewish problems in the perspective of modern European thought. Hebrew creativity since the end of the last century bears the stamp of his life and work. To understand Judaism in the twentieth century, particularly its national and cultural aspects, we must begin with the life and thought of Ahad Ha-am.

Early Years

Asher Ginzberg was born on the eighteenth of August 1856 in the small town of Skivira in what he later described as "one of the darkest corners of the *Hasidic* district" in the Russian Ukraine.[5] His father, a prosperous merchant of scholarly interests, was one of the most important members of the Sadagora *Hasidim*, who looked askance upon any form of secular learning. Isaiah Ginzberg therefore insisted on educating his son entirely along traditional Jewish lines. At the age of three, little Asher was taken to the local *heder* where he began to study Hebrew and Bible with the Rashi commentary. Though his parents were well-to-do, Asher had to endure the same hardships as the other boys in town. Before dawn he was taken to the cold one-room apartment of the *melammed* (teacher) and only after several hours of lessons and prayers would breakfast be brought from the boy's home. Nevertheless, young Asher excelled in his studies and became known for his intellectual abilities in spite of a lack of self-confidence and a tendency toward shyness. After a few years at the *heder* he advanced by stages to several higher Hebrew schools until, at the age of ten, he was given the privilege of studying Talmud and its commentaries under a special teacher of his own.

The only general knowledge he enjoyed before the age of twelve was that of mathematics, secretly acquired from some of his older classmates. At the age of nine he also began to learn the Russian alphabet by studying the signs on the shop windows on the way home from school. But when he came home later and later each evening, an investigation was made, his secret was discovered and the study of "foreign letters" was prohibited.[6]

From Hasidism to Haskalah

When Asher was twelve, the Ginzberg family moved to the small village of Gopitshitza where he was to spend the next eighteen years of his life.

Shortly thereafter, Asher was taken by his father to the rabbi of Sadogora to receive the rabbi's blessings before his Bar Mitzvah. He was introduced to the rabbi's son and his friends, but as he wrote years later the coarse language and vulgarity of the *Hasidim* and their sudden shift to religious fervor so repelled him that, though the *Zaddik* personally made a deep impression on him, he lost his respect for *Hasidism*.

On his return home Asher declared himself an opponent of *Hasidism* (*Mitnagged*) and refused to observe many of the *Hasidic* religious customs he had followed until that time. His father greatly regretted the change which had come over his young son and tried unsuccessfully to bring him back to the "right path." But Asher, though he continued to live in the environment of the *Hasidim* and remained a practicing traditional Jew, had no real identification with them.[7]

The home in which he lived was a fifteen room mansion situated on a large estate, leased by his father, which offered ample opportunities for many diversions, but Ginzberg showed

little interest in the beautiful surroundings and in the carefree
life of childhood. There were few young people in the village,
and withdrawing into himself, he devoted himself to his studies
with the same intensity as before.

Unlike most east European children Asher Ginzberg never
attended a yeshivah and his deep knowledge of Jewish thought
was entirely the result of his own wide reading among the volumes in his father's well-stocked library. In addition to Hebrew
grammar, the Spanish Jewish commentaries on the Bible, and
Jewish ethical literature, he began to read in a haphazard and
piecemeal manner the philosophical works of the medieval
period which developed in him a tendency to abstract thoughts
on all matters, particularly religious questions. By the time he
was sixteen or seventeen he had completed the entire Babylonian
Talmud, was proficient in Codes and Responsa and had gained a
reputation as an expert in Jewish ritual law.

Meanwhile, because of his great learning, several families were
anxious to have him as a son-in-law. As was the custom, they
sent scholars from other cities to check on the rumors about his
unusual abilities. Asher Ginzberg passed their tests without difficulty and at the age of sixteen was married to a girl of good
family with an "illustrious pedigree on both sides." Despite his
fears, the young lady turned out to be a "normal Jewish girl,"
religiously brought up, who "knew her prayers and all the other
things that a Jewish girl should know." [8]

After his marriage, Ginzberg continued to live in the seclusion
of the village with ample time to study and read.

He soon became interested in the new *Haskalah* literature of
the 1870's, including the books of Kalman Shulman, from which
Asher Ginzberg gained his first knowledge of general history,
and the magazine of Abraham Gottlober (1811-1899), a contemporary Hebrew writer in Warsaw. A friend who came to
the village frequently to do business with his father also brought
him the poetry of Abraham Dov Lebensohn (1794-1878) and
his son Micah Joseph (known as Michal) (1828-1852). Asher
read deeply in this literature and through it his perspectives
were broadened. While his wife's family intervened and tried
to stop him from reading these "heretical books," his young
bride sided with him and gave him moral support. Gradually,
he obtained the works of Moses Mendelssohn, Samuel David

Luzzatto (1800-1868), Nahman Krochmal (1785-1840), Abraham Geiger (1810-1874) and other nineteenth-century thinkers which he read with great interest. However, the Jewish thinker who had the greatest influence on him was the great medieval philosopher Maimonides (1135-1205), whose rational approach to Judaism he found very attractive.[9]

From Haskalah to Love of Zion

For many of the *Haskalah* writers of the period a knowledge of Hebrew literature was important primarily as a stepping stone to European culture, and soon young Ginzberg, like the other *maskilim*, began to study Russian and German. Though he had no teacher and few books, by frequent re-reading of whatever came his way and by his great powers of concentration, he soon mastered these languages sufficiently to read their literature. While he did not respond to the abstract philosophies of the German thinkers, Hegel and Kant, he read with great interest the British philosophers, particularly Locke, Hume and John Stuart Mill in German translation. He also read volumes on mathematics, the natural sciences, history, psychology, literature and philosophy, studying each field according to his ability without any outside help.

Asher Ginzberg's enthusiasm for *Haskalah*, however, did not last very long. At the age of twenty-two, on a visit to Warsaw he met some of the outstanding *maskilim* of the period including Gottlober, and "either young Nahum Sokolow or David Frischman" [10] but found himself repelled by their negative attitude toward religion. While he himself was no longer religious in outlook, he nevertheless retained a sentimental and nostalgic attitude toward Jewish traditional customs. The men he met, however, were for the most part scornful of religious tradition which, in their eyes, represented a reactionary force. Ginzberg found this negativism disappointing and when he returned to his village *Haskalah* had "gone down several steps" in his eyes.

For a few months Asher Ginzberg, like so many in his time, found himself intellectually without any guiding principles. Later that year on a visit to Odessa where his wife had fallen ill, he met a young man who lent him some of the writings of Pisarev, the intellectual idol of the younger generation in Russia at that time. Pisarev's critical essays made Ginzberg feel that he had found "the last word of that modern culture" for which he was all athirst. While Ginzberg was not able to accept the complete philosophy of Pisarev, he was impressed with his objective critical analysis of social and moral problems. He was also attracted by the idea of the "love of the people" advocated by Pisarev and by his emphasis on the importance of improving the condition of the masses.[11] This idea was one of the factors which contributed to his own "love of Israel" which gradually evolved into his concept of Jewish nationalism.

Meanwhile, the series of pogroms which broke out in 1881 in the wake of the assassination of the Czar, and the subsequent oppressive May Laws imposed on the Jews, for a time put him in a state of consternation. Like so many others during this period his world was shaken to its foundations and more and more new ideas began to take the place of those which had been shattered. Gradually he arrived at the concept of cultural Zionism which became the cornerstone of all his subsequent thinking.

In the interim, through the friend in Odessa who had introduced him to Pisarev's writings, he was encouraged to enter a university to fill the gaps in his education. In 1882, at the age of twenty-six he left for Vienna with the intention of entering the university there. But he remained in the Austrian capital only two or three weeks and becoming discouraged, returned home. During the next two years he made several other attempts to attend a university, going in turn to Berlin, Breslau and then to Vienna again, each time returning with nothing accomplished. Critical letters from home, the need to study with men and women younger than he and above all a "defect in my own character, a lack of confidence in my own capacity and abilities" discouraged him and prevented him from carrying through his resolve. Throughout his life this lack of self-confidence was to plague Asher Ginzberg and undoubtedly was an important factor in his later reluctance to assume positions of leadership which were offered to him.

In retrospect, he described this formative period as the worst years of his life. Had he been born to more understanding parents, he lamented, who would have "strengthened my faith in myself and helped me to try my strength, then the spirit of doubt would have left me and I would have been successful." [12]

Whatever the merit of his own interpretation, Ginzberg remained isolated and withdrawn in the village with his family until the age of thirty. Unknowingly, however, he was preparing himself for his life's career as a writer and Jewish thinker. For at the end of this period, he had independently worked out the philosophy of Jewish nationalism which he was to put forth so forcefully during the rest of his life.

Odessa

After it became apparent that he was not to realize his dream of studying at a university, Asher Ginzberg decided to leave the little village where he had been a "prisoner" throughout his youth and to move to some big city where he could engage in business and live among enlightened men. Accordingly, in the spring of 1884, he left with his wife and five-year-old daughter for Odessa, but after a few months in that Black Sea port he returned to the village for some unexplained personal reasons and remained there for another two years. However, in 1886 the entire family, including his mother and father, left the village of Gopitshitza forever and moved to Odessa.

Odessa at that time boasted of the most enlightened Jewish community in Russia and offered Asher Ginzberg many advantages and a new way of life. Here, he could complete his education, learn English and French and read their literature. In Odessa there was a group of well-known Jewish writers who either made their permanent home in the city or sojourned there from time to time in connection with their scholarly work. These included Shalom Jacob Abramowitz, better known as Mendele Mocher Sephorim (1836-1917), Moses Leib Lilienblum (1843-1910), who had become an ardent Jewish nationalist after several years of alienation, and J. H. Ravnitzki (1860-1937), writer and publisher, who became one of his closest friends and associates. A few years after Ginzberg's arrival in Odessa, young Hayyim Nahman Bialik (1872-1934) joined the group, and in the nineties Simon Dubnow (1860-1941), who was to become the great historian of Russian and Polish Jewry, made his home there for a decade. Asher Ginzberg liked the congenial surroundings with like-minded Jews and looked to this circle of writers and scholars for stimulus and companionship.[13]

Odessa was also the center of the new *Hoveve Zion* (Lovers of Zion) movement which had sprung up in the wake of the pogroms and which was spark-plugging efforts to resettle Palestine. The outstanding leader of the society and head of its central committee was Dr. Leo Pinsker (1821-1891). A physician, Pinsker was stirred to his depths by the manifestations of mass psychopathology in Russia's anti-Jewish riots of 1881. In *Auto-Emancipation*[14] he brilliantly analyzed the psychological bases of anti-Semitism and the hereditary character of the hatred of the Jew. He came to the reluctant conclusion that only a complete abandonment of assimilation, which he had formerly espoused, and the formation of a self-governing Jewish nation on its own soil would furnish the necessary relief to the disease of anti-Semitism.

At the meetings which took place in Pinsker's home, Ginzberg was very shy at first, considering himself a mere rustic, and listened carefully to what the others had to say. Gradually he lost his nervousness and came to realize that even so humble a person as himself might sometimes have a useful contribution to make and that the townsmen did not necessarily talk sense. Just before the Kattowitz Conference, Pinsker read to the group the draft of his opening speech as president of the Conference. He indicated that his intention was to stress the purely humanitarian aspect of Palestinian colonization and play down its national aim in order to attract the Jews of western Europe who were wary of nationalism. Ginzberg, the exponent of a Jewish national revival, objected to this tactic. He felt that the *Hibbat Zion* movement should not be made a matter of charity for the sake of appearance but that its national aspirations must be clearly articulated. Ginzberg's strong convictions, faultless logic and deep knowledge of both Jewish and general European culture, together with his innate modesty, made a profound impression on the group.

First Essays

The thought of putting his ideas on the national revival into writing, however, had never entered Asher Ginzberg's mind. His entry into the field of literature came purely by accident in 1889, when he was thirty-three years old. The *Hibbat Zion* group of which he was a member needed a letter of congratulation on the seventieth birthday of a Hebrew writer, and Ginzberg's version was judged the best and published in the Hebrew daily *Ha-Melitz.* This led the editor, Alexander Zederbaum (1816-1893), to invite Ginzberg to present his views on *Hibbat Zion* for the newspaper. After some persistence on the part of Zederbaum, Ginzberg finally submitted an article which appeared in the spring of 1889 under the title *Lo Zeh Ha-Derekh* (The Wrong Way). In this epoch-making essay, Ginzberg attempted to answer the question of why the new idea of a Jewish national rebirth was having so little success and why the initial enthusiasm had waned. In his view, blame could not be placed either on the *Halukkah* system which doled out charity to many of the settlers in the Holy Land, or on the high-handed methods of Baron Rothschild's agents who administered the new colonies. Ginzberg believed that the lack of success of Palestinian colonization was a result of the fact that its basis was an appeal to the economic interests of the individual Jew rather than to his national sentiments. The task of *Hoveve Zion* was not to solve Jewish economic need but rather to strive toward "the revival of the spirit, to enlarge the love for the collective life and to glorify the desire for success." An appeal to economic self interest could not win the hearts of the people since their hopes for material advantage would be disappointed and inevitably, disillusionment and loss of interest would follow. More important than the number of colonists in Palestine was the revival of the national spirit upon which colonization must be based.[15]

This article, which gave Ginzberg an opportunity to crystallize his years of study and inner travail, was a compact presentation written in the precise and balanced style for which he was soon to become famous. He signed the article "Ahad Ha-am" (one of the people) to indicate that he was not a professional writer but "just a visitor in the tent of literature." [16]

This initial essay shook the Zionist and Hebrew world and aroused criticism in the ranks of the *Hoveve Zion.* Ahad Ha-am soon found himself the center of controversy and a target of abuse as the champion of a new philosophy of Zionism. While many of the *Hoveve Zion* were not yet ready for this spiritual and cultural approach, there were some who became enthusiastic followers and who urged him to put his ideas into practice. A plan to establish a specially dedicated group within the broader movement had been put forward by a member of the Jaffa *Hoveve Zion*, and Ahad Ha-am, against his own better judgment, was persuaded to become its head.

Thus, there was founded in the spring of 1889 the *Bene Mosheh* (Sons of Moses), a secret society whose purpose was more or less to implement the ideas of Ahad Ha-am.[17] The society, which did not number more than two hundred members scattered in various countries, was divided into local groups of no less than five members each. Only those who knew Hebrew could belong and a high level of discipline was expected. Each member was to dedicate his choicest material possessions and spiritual endowments to Palestine.

It soon became evident, however, that the society would not be able to live up to the high ideals which Ahad Ha-am had set for it. It suffered from ideological differences and from a lack of idealism among some of its members, from opposition within the *Hibbat Zion* movement as well as from attack by fanatics of the *Halakhah* to whom *Hibbat Zion* was anathema. Moreover, Ahad Ha-am was not temperamentally suited to serve as leader of such a group and soon gave up the presidency. Though many years later he summed up the story of *Bene Mosheh* as "an experiment that failed," actually in its eight brief years of existence it made several contributions to the Jewish revival: it established the first modern Hebrew school in Palestine, the great publishing house Ahiasaf, and helped found the colony of Rehovot.[18] Most important of all, it contributed a number of gifted leaders and teachers to the Zionist movement such as Menahem Ussishkin and Chaim Weizmann.

At the Crossroads

In February 1891, Ahad Ha-am made his first trip to Palestine to see with his own eyes the "land of my longing and waking dreams." He spent eighty-two days visiting the old ruins and the new colonies such as Rishon Le-Zion, Rehovot and Mikveh Israel, and tried to evaluate the possibilities for the future. The report which he published under the title *Truth From Palestine* was outspokenly critical, and with characteristic courage he exposed the inefficiency and short-sightedness of the leaders. Ahad Ha-am predicted that the Turkish government would place increasing difficulties in the way of the settlers, that the Arabs would not easily give up their holdings to the Jews. He warned that it was economically unsound to build up the country exclusively on viticulture and that greater preparation was necessary, if the colonists were to become self sufficient. He saw the solution to these problems neither in individual philanthropy nor in the devoted efforts of East European Jewry, whose condition would not allow for large scale action, but in the creation of a national society for Palestine settlement, centered in western Europe.[19]

Two years later in May 1893, he made a second trip to Palestine, this time remaining for six weeks. At the suggestion of several friends, he decided to settle permanently in the land but was unable to obtain the necessary permit. His second report which he sent to the Hebrew periodical *Ha-Melitz* from Palestine again stressed the pitfalls which stood in the way of the development of the *yishuv,* and he urged that whatever was to be done on behalf of the colonists must be done openly, not by infiltration.

Instead of sailing directly to Odessa, Ahad Ha-am returned via London, hoping to obtain support from British Jewry for the colonization work in Palestine. He also thought of making some business connection which would allow him to settle in England. But his efforts in both directions were fruitless, and he returned to Odessa somewhat disillusioned.

Meanwhile, during the years since the appearance in 1889 of his first article, and his reports on conditions in Palestine, Ahad Ha-am had been contributing five or six essays a year to various Jewish journals, each written with the clarity and depth for which he had by then become known. Some of these essays dealt with current problems, while others concerned themselves with philosophical themes in which he put forth his concept of Judaism and of Jewish nationalism, of the dangers to Jewish survival confronting modern Jewry and of his concept of a spiritual center. He was at his best in these pieces, many of which have become the classics of modern Hebrew literature.

In 1895, Ahad Ha-am published these essays in one volume.

It was his hope that collected in this manner, they might have greater influence than when scattered through several journals.[20] He called the volume *At the Crossroads* to indicate the character of the era and the importance of choosing a proper philosophy of Jewish life.

Ha-Shiloah

Ahad Ha-am's literary activities did not end with the publication of this volume. Through the generosity of K. Wissotsky, a wealthy Moscow merchant of scholarly interests, he was now offered the opportunity of launching a new monthly periodical in Hebrew that would lift the cultural level of Russian Jewry. This had been his dream for many years. Although dailies existed, such as *Ha-Tzefirah* and *Ha-Melitz*, there was as yet no publication on a level equal to that of the great European monthlies. Ahad Ha-am, in spite of his reluctance to earn his livelihood through the Jewish community, accepted this opportunity to devote himself to editing and writing.

The purpose of the journal, as he made clear in the opening statement (October, 1896), was not to spread enlightenment and general knowledge, as was true of many *Haskalah* publications, but to improve knowledge of Jewish life, the status of the Jew and the development of the inner Jewish spirit through the ages.[21]

As the title of the magazine he chose the name *Ha-Shiloah*, which he took from the Biblical river whose "waters go slowly." Thus he indicated his faith in slow and steady progress, as opposed to precipitous revolutionary change.

To carry out his aims, however, he had to overcome many difficulties, and his letters are full of references to the problems he faced. Aside from the restrictions of Russian censorship, there were few competent Hebrew writers and those who contributed often had shoddy standards. He found that in many of the articles submitted, he had to work on every line, struggling with loose thinking and slipshod writing, and had to get rid of "stupidity, *batlanut* (slovenliness) and tactlessness."

He found it difficult to obtain a sufficient number of subscribers. Ahad Ha-am regarded it as an insult to Hebrew literature to promote the magazine by sending it to anybody who had not asked for it. As a result of these various problems Ahad Ha-am also felt a sense of personal frustration about his own lack of growth and development. "I neglect my own work and waste most of my time and energy in correcting what others write . . . this work is ruining me intellectually and in the end will kill my soul." [22]

In spite of these discouragements *Ha-Shiloah* became under Ahad Ha-am's guidance the most notable Hebrew magazine ever to have been published. He trained a generation of writers from Hayyim Nahman Bialik to David Frischman. The imprint of his personality and style remained even when the publication had passed into other hands.

Herzl and Political Zionism

Shortly after Ahad Ha-am had agreed to be editor of *Ha-Shiloah*, Theodor Herzl published his brochure on the *Jewish State*, and the following year issued his call for the first Zionist Congress to be held in Basle, Switzerland on August 3, 1897. Unlike many of his friends Asher Ginzberg was not swept away by the general enthusiasm which Herzl engendered among the Jewish masses in Russia as well as in some circles in the West. He instinctively mistrusted the art of diplomacy on which Herzl was relying and refused to put much confidence in the activities of what was to him a semi-assimilated westerner who had come back to his people through the back door of anti-Semitism rather than through an understanding of the spiritual character of Jewish nationalism. Just before the Congress opened he had a brief conversation with Herzl in Basle and gained the impression of a "feuilletonist spirit running through his ideas and opinions." [23]

Ahad Ha-am followed the proceedings of the Congress in his own peculiarly critical fashion. He was deeply moved like everyone else by Max Nordau's "unforgettable speech" full of prophetic passion on the situation of the Jews, but his overall reaction to this historic gathering was negative. He felt like a "mourner among the bridegrooms." [24] When he returned to Odessa, he expressed his views in an article in *Ha-Shiloah*. The aim of Zionism, according to Ahad Ha-am, must be a moral one, "to liberate ourselves from inner slavery, from feelings of inferiority and to strengthen our national unity until Jews will be ready for a new life." After thousands of years of historical experience, he felt that Jews could not be satisfied with becoming "a small lowly nation whose state is like a football in the hands of its mighty neighbors and cannot survive except by diplomatic intrigues." Ginzberg warned against the false hopes and the disillusionment that would follow when the promises of Herzl were not fulfilled. "The salvation of Israel will come through prophets and not through diplomats," he wrote. This article attracted wide attention and, as happened after his report on Palestine, aroused a storm in the Hebrew press.[25]

Although Ahad Ha-am agreed that "active participation in the Zionist movement may be more useful than an attitude of passive discontent," he did not join the organization, for he felt that as editor of a publication, he ought not to be bound by organizational rules. "I must always be free to say exactly what I think without the restrictions which the rules of discipline would impose." [26] Ahad Ha-am held on to this freedom throughout his life.

He was most critical in his review of Herzl's utopian novel *Altneuland*. In that book the Zionist leader, inspired by his trip to Palestine in 1899 to meet the Kaiser, attempted to forecast conditions in the land twenty years later. *Altneuland* is the story of an embittered Jewish intellectual from Vienna and a wealthy Prussian aristocrat, who after two decades in happy isolation in the South Sea Islands, return to take one more look at the world. They learn that the Palestine which they had visited in 1903 is no longer a desolate country, but a flourishing community founded on the basis of a charter granted by the Turkish government.

Ahad Ha-am was deeply disturbed by several features of Herzl's vision of the future Jewish state. The return to Palestine was pictured as taking place in an impossibly short time. There was an excessive emphasis on the idea of tolerance and an exaggerated concern for non-Jews in Herzl's projected state. Worst of all, there was virtually no reference to the development of a Jewish cultural life nor to Hebrew as the national language. The masses in *Altneuland* speak Yiddish and the enlightened Europeans, German. The Jewish Academy in Herzl's vision would devote itself primarily to general, not Jewish culture.[27]

It was, therefore, inevitable that Ahad Ha-am became almost completely disillusioned with the Zionist movement, particularly when in 1903 the Sixth Zionist Congress agreed to a Commission of Inquiry to investigate the British government's offer of an autonomous territory in East Africa. What was done at this Congress, he thought, was "equivalent to a public act of apostasy." He saw this as the culmination of a long development in which Zionism gave up its ideal, and he urged friends to put an end to the "confusion of ideas and policies and to part company with the political Zionists." [28]

However, soon thereafter came the tragic death of Herzl and at the following Congress the British offer was officially declined. Many Zionists now began to emphasize the need for practical work in Palestine without waiting for political guaranties. These "practical Zionists" waged a protracted struggle with the "political Zionists" until eventually they dominated the Zionist movement.[29]

London

Long before these political developments, Ahad Ha-am had resigned as editor of *Ha-Shiloah* and had accepted a position with the Wissotsky tea firm as inspector of its outlying branches in Russia. He planned to give up writing on current problems and to concentrate on some subject of importance, work at it for a few years and leave something worthwhile for posterity. But he was not sure he would succeed. "Perhaps I am not suited for a long and difficult work," [30] he wrote. However, the necessity for constant travel, often to outlying regions like Tiflis and Baku, taxed his strength and gave him much less opportunity to study and write than he had expected.

In 1903, Volume II of *At the Crossroads* appeared. It contained several articles on political Zionism, reports on the third trip to Palestine which he made in 1899, together with essays on Jewish ethics, on the question of Jewish culture and the relationship of Nietzsche to Judaism. The following year, volume III was published and included a series of articles on the various Zionist Congresses and other current topics. In addition, Ahad

Ha-am wrote three outstanding essays during his last years in Russia. In *Moses*, usually regarded as his greatest piece, he retells the story of this Jewish leader, interpreting his role not as a law-giver but as a prophet whose constant concern was an uncompromising passion for justice. *Flesh and Spirit* is a philosophical discussion of the Jewish attitude toward asceticism. *The Supremacy of Reason* is Ginzberg's only venture into pure scholarship. It describes in detail the thought of Maimonides, his emphasis on reason and his underlying concern with Jewish nationalism.

On the whole, however, his last years in Russia did not constitute a very creative period. His health was not good and in the winter of 1907, at the suggestion of his doctor, who urged a complete rest, he left Odessa for Palestine and spent three weeks with his married daughter in Haifa. Reaching Constantinople on his return, he found a telegram from friends warning him not to return immediately to Odessa, since the police had searched his home in connection with his part in encouraging Jewish self-defense two years earlier. Ahad Ha-am, therefore, proceeded to Vienna and Carlsbad and did not return home until the end of the summer. Fortunately, there were no further repercussions.[81]

In the autumn of 1907, the Wissotsky tea firm asked him to take charge of its recently established London office. After a trial period of several months, though he found himself lonely and depressed, he decided to accept the offer. Perhaps economic circumstances offered him no alternative. Thus in 1908, Ahad Ha-am settled with his wife and two of his children in a comfortable suburban home in Belsize Park in northwest London where he was to spend the next fourteen years.

From the outset, Ahad Ha-am was unhappy in this big metropolis. "There are meetings here, Zionist or simply Jewish; there are literary societies, and even Hebrew speaking societies," he wrote to Dubnow when he first arrived in London. "But there is no life in all these things, and you feel at once that the whole thing is only an exotic plant which has been brought from abroad and artificially stuck in the ground without any deep roots. If I have to settle here, I think that I shall always feel myself to be in a world which is not mine." [32]

This sense of alienation persisted throughout his stay, both in his relations with the official community and also in a personal sense. He had little in common with the assimilated section of Anglo-Jewry and not much more with the Russian Jews whom he found to be "either ignoramuses with a smattering of jargonized (i.e. Yiddishist) socialism or 'observant' Jews of the driest Lithuanian type." [33]

Nor did Ahad Ha-am find the London environment very conducive to his mental or physical health and he was, therefore, unable to do the creative work he had planned. The climate did not agree with him and the noise and gloom of the city ruined his nerves and made adjustment difficult. After a day in the city he was so "tired and limp" that he found brainwork impossible.

A few of his friends urged him to settle in Palestine and several positions were made available to him. But he insisted on living by the old Talmudic principle that one must sacrifice everything for independence. In spite of these obstacles the years until the eve of the First World War were not without creative expression. During this period he wrote several important essays in which he developed his attitude toward Judaism in the Diaspora and explored the difference between Jewish and Christian ethics.

In the summer of 1911 he decided to make his fifth trip to Palestine and to stop enroute at the tenth Zionist Congress in Basle. It was fourteen years since he had attended a Congress and twelve years since he had witnessed the condition of the colonies. He spent ten days in Basle and fifty in Palestine and out of this trip came the essay *Sakh Ha-Kol* (The Summing Up) in which he surveyed what he had seen and heard. He was grateful for the trend opposing "Zionism based on anti-Semitism" and for the adoption of the program of the practical Zionists. He came to the conclusion that the Congress was an institution of great educational value from the national point of view. It was pleasant for him to see Zionism moving more and more in what he regarded as the right direction.

The same positive aim appeared even more clearly in Palestine. Despite the mistakes of the past he could see emerging "a fixed centre for our national spirit and culture" and the goal was already visible on the distant horizon. He was not optimistic about the attempt to develop a class of Jewish agricultural workers, which was underway at this time. "The Jew can become an upper class farmer of the type of Boaz in the Bible," he wrote, "but he wants to live like a civilized human being without the land absorbing all his time. While the existing colonies depend entirely on non-Jewish labor, they are so many little 'generating stations' in which there is gradually being produced a new type of national life unparalleled in the exile." [34]

After concluding his report, Ahad Ha-am compiled the essays he had published in the previous decade into a single book and brought out volume IV of the work he had begun twenty-four years before. This publication marked the end of his literary creativity.

Several factors explain the decline of his literary output. In 1912 the inter-marriage of his daughter, Rachel, to a Russian fellow-student in Switzerland profoundly affected him. The proud nationalist, who had written so strongly against inter-marriage as a blow to Jewish survival, was unable to reconcile himself to this event.[35] In the winter of 1913, possibly as an aftermath to his domestic tragedy, he became severely ill and never fully recovered. The outbreak of the war had a crushing and disillusioning effect upon him. As a result, except for a translation into Hebrew of Pinsker's brochure *Auto-Emancipation* and a short contribution commemorating the twenty-fifth anniversary of Pinsker's death, Ahad Ha-am made no further literary contributions during his stay in England.

Balfour Declaration

While the war practically put an end to his literary career, it led ironically to his participation for the first time in Zionist diplomacy and political work. With the outbreak of hostilities, the Zionist world was divided into three parts, the Allied Countries, those of the Central Powers, and the neutral countries. The headquarters of the movement, located in Berlin, soon found itself cut off from Palestine with the elected officials scattered in all directions. There was no member of the Zionist executive committee in London to represent the movement.

At this juncture, Chaim Weizmann, a member of the Greater Actions Committee who was then a lecturer in chemistry at the University of Manchester, began a series of interviews with the British leaders Lloyd George and Arthur Balfour, to win sympathy for the Zionist cause. Ahad Ha-am was in his confidence from the outset. At Ahad Ha-am's suggestion, Weizmann arranged for representatives of official Zionist leadership to come to London and, in the beginning of 1915, Nahum Sokolow and Dr. Tschlenow made their way from Berlin to the British capital.

Ahad Ha-am was chosen a member of the political committee that was established in 1917 to help Weizmann and Sokolow obtain an official declaration from the British government. The Zionists had to overcome the opposition of anti-Zionists like Lucien Wolf (1857-1930) in England, and Salomon Reinach (1858-1932) in France, who tried to use their influence in government circles against such a declaration. Early in 1917, however, the government appointed an emissary, Sir Mark Sykes, who was in charge of the Middle-Eastern Department of the Foreign Office, to enter into negotiations with the Zionist leaders. Ahad Ha-am, together with Weizmann, Sokolow, Herbert Samuel and Lord Rothschild, participated in these conferences with Sykes. His letters from this period contain many references to the events of "those days of great hopes and preparatory work for a proclamation by the British government." [36] He served on the committee which was to present a draft of the declaration to the British government. The Balfour Declaration was issued in November, 1917, after several modifications resulting from opposition by the anti-Zionists as well as from within the Cabinet. Before its publication to the world, Weizmann came to Ahad Ha-am's home at midnight, shortly after receiving it, and showed it to his friend and advisor.

Ahad Ha-am rejoiced at this great achievement, gratified that Britain and the other allied nations had acknowledged the reality of the Jewish people and its historic right to build a home in the land of its fathers. But he did not share in the frenzied enthusiasm of many Jews to whom the Balfour Declaration marked the end of the Jewish exile and the fulfillment of Biblical prophecies. He sensed how many obstacles still had to be overcome before the goal of Zionist aspirations would be reached.

In the preface to a new edition of his collected works, which appeared in 1920, he acknowledged the "widening of the horizon of our work in Palestine through the Balfour Declaration," but he warned against those who were already building "castles in the air, without regard to the realities of this earthly life." [37]

Though he was able to participate in the diplomatic events which led to the Balfour Declaration, Ahad Ha-am's health during the war years continued poor. At the end of 1919 he fell seriously ill with arteriosclerosis and spent several months in a hospital in Montreux, Switzerland. Thereafter Ahad Ha-am remained virtually a semi-invalid.

Having reached the age of retirement on pension with the Wissotsky firm, he decided, at the urging of his doctor, who knew what Palestine meant to him, finally to settle in the "place where my heart has been all my life." He hoped that the congenial atmosphere of Palestine, and the companionship of some of the old Odessa friends such as Bialik and Ravnitsky, who had already preceded him, might stimulate him once again to creative work. At the end of 1921 Ahad Ha-am, his wife and son sailed for Palestine.

Palestine

The family settled in Tel Aviv, a new town on the outskirts of Jaffa with a population of less than twenty thousand, rather than in Jerusalem. Ahad Ha-am recognized the historic importance of the latter city but was reluctant to live there because of its "fanatical religious groups." In Tel Aviv there were enlightened Jews and he believed this new city would become the cradle of Hebrew culture. It was not good, he thought, to concentrate all the cultural forces in one place, particularly since other religions also looked to Jerusalem as an important city.[38]

In Tel Aviv, Ahad Ha-am was treated with great respect. The municipality provided a home for him next to the Gymnasium Herzliah, which he visited each day during the noon hour. Every afternoon while he rested, the street was roped off so traffic would not disturb the old philosopher of Zionism.

But his illness made it impossible for him to undertake any original work that demanded great mental effort. Some of his close friends among the Hebrew writers in Palestine, however, hit upon the idea that he should prepare his correspondence for publication. They had worked with him in Russia and knew that these letters contained material of significance to the history of Hebrew literature and to the Jewish national movement. They convinced him that he was better qualified than anybody else to select what was most worth preserving. Ahad Ha-am allowed himself to be persuaded, particularly since the work fitted in with his circumstances and gave him something he was able to do in "these evil days of old age and infirmity." Some seventeen-hundred letters were chosen, covering the years from 1896 until he settled in Palestine. They appeared between 1923 and 1925 in six volumes. Subsequently, some of his correspondence in Palestine was published, together with his reminiscences, as a separate volume of memoirs and letters.

In 1926 the entire Jewish world celebrated his seventieth birthday and for a brief time there seemed to be an improvement in his health. But his physical condition was beyond repair. Those who visited him in his last year found him thin and shrunken and in a state of nervous exhaustion. He died on Sunday, January 2, 1927 and was taken to his final rest in the old cemetery of Tel Aviv where he was buried next to Max Nordau whose ideas he had opposed throughout his life.

THOUGHT OF AHAD HA-AM

Ahad Ha-am's Zionism stemmed from his original philosophy of Jewish history and interpretation of Judaism. Unlike several of the other thinkers dealt with in this book, he was not a systematic philosopher and had little interest in speculative philosophy or theological questions. He refused as he put it to "follow the philosophers into the deep waters of metaphysics." [39] Underlying his commentary on the topics of his time was an approach to Jewish tradition which had particular meaning for Jews who wanted to return to Judaism for nationalistic rather than religious reasons.

One of the dominant schools of philosophical thought of the nineteenth century, positivism, was developed by Auguste Comte (1798-1853), the founder of the science of sociology. It was this positivism which greatly influenced Ahad Ha-am. Contrary to the metaphysical dialectics of the German idealist philosophers Fichte and Hegel, positivism concerned itself with the implications of scientific method for the social sciences. According to Comte, the historian of ideas can observe a law of three stages in every field of thought: theology, in which all problems are explained by the will of some deity; metaphysics, which explains everything in abstract theory; and finally, positive science, which rejects the propositions of traditional theology and metaphysics and refuses to accept as worthy of belief any statement which cannot be verified by the methods of empirical science.

Darwin's (1809-1882) theory of evolution, with its biological, developmental approach to man, and the works of Herbert Spencer (1820-1903) also had a strong influence on the development of Ahad Ha-am's thought. He accepted their basic approach to social phenomena and to the physical universe. Thus he rejected supernaturalism in all its aspects, was indifferent to metaphysical abstractions, and assumed that all human ideas and institutions, including religion and morality, could be explained by man's will to survive and his reactions to changing external circumstances.

Essentially, Ahad Ha-am was a rationalist. He possessed a critical, analytic mind and a passion for logic which manifested itself in the clarity and architectural structure of his essays. He recognized, however, that reason cannot explain all of human life. "The human mind is not guided by reason alone," he wrote. "There is another force at work below the surface, a force which quietly assumes control of the mind's movements, and directs them whither it will, giving to its commands the semblance of reason and truth." [40]

In part at least, these feelings explain his own warm attachment to Jewish tradition, his nostalgia for the old religious customs which he could not logically accept, and the sentimentality which at times crept into his writings.[41] Indeed, the motto for his collected works, a passage written by the French author Montesquieu, emphasized that "there are certain truths for which it is not sufficient to persuade, but which one must feel."

Thus, despite Ahad Ha-am's positivism and his acceptance of evolutionary thought, his loyalty to Judaism was rooted more deeply than any doctrine that he encountered in later life, and he managed to hold on to many of the values and principles of traditional Judaism.

Concept of Nationalism

To Ahad Ha-am, the basis of Judaism was the concept of Jewish nationalism. The Jewish nation, he held, had existed since ancient times and the Jewish group had never relinquished this central aspect of its existence. The Reform view that Judaism had been, or could be, merely a religious differentiation, he felt, could not be justified. While he maintained that it was possible to be a Jew in the national sense without accepting many things requiring religious belief, he believed that it was not possible to be a religious Jew without accepting Jewish nationality.

From the Middle Ages to modern times, Jews had possessed all the characteristics of a national group except a territory of their own: a common language and religion, past memories and future aspirations. But no adequate formulation of Jewish nationalism had been developed. In the middle of the nineteenth century, Nahman Krochmal (1785-1840), the Galician scholar, had advanced a philosophy of Jewish history which centered around the concept of a Jewish nation. His work, however, was written in the framework of German idealist thought and he did not work out the implications of his theory.

It was Ahad Ha-am who, for the first time, made nationalism the basis for a complete philosophy and presented an analysis of the psychology of Jewish nationalism.

He expanded the idea of nationality beyond that of Giuseppe Mazzini, with whom he has often been compared. It was Mazzini's opinion that a people must have a territory, a country of its own, before it can become a member of the brotherhood of nations. "Without a country," he wrote, "you have neither name, voice, nor rights, no admission as brothers into the fellowship of the peoples. You're the bastards of humanity—Ishmaelites among the natives." [42] Ahad Ha-am, however, theorized that the material and political bases of nationality were subordinate to its spiritual and moral foundations. Following the approach of the French thinker Renan and of the British liberal, John Stuart Mill, he viewed the essence of nationalism as "a combination of past and future, a combination, that is, of memories and impressions, with hopes and desires, all closely interwoven and common to all members of the nation." [43]

The Spencerian view of society which looked upon a nation as an organism with its own unique character, and not merely an aggregate of individuals, also had its influence on Ahad Ha-am. According to this view, the organism is held together by a group feeling, a sense of solidarity; it possesses a will to survive

and a desire for self-preservation (*hefetz ha-kiyum*) and struggles to maintain the life of the group and to perpetuate its values.
This desire for self-preservation is instinctive, a biological drive,
in the Spencerian view—"a natural force . . ." inherent to the
heart of a nation. It is this natural drive, according to Ahad
Ha-am, which explains Jewish survival. This will to live stems
from the subconscious regions of the soul and is an irrational
and primary force which like every instinct finds the means
necessary for its fulfillment. Judaism, as it emerged during the
Second Commonwealth and after the destruction of the Second
Temple, represented, he believed, the means by which the will to
live insured the survival of the Jewish people.[44]

Every nation had its own individuality, a "national spirit"
(*ruah leumi*) which found expression in the national culture
and distinctive values of the group.

Ahad Ha-am saw no conflict between the values of humanity
as a whole and those of any one nation. Nationalism was the
concrete form in which universal human values were expressed
according to the conditions, needs and history of the nation.
Each nation attempts to embody in its own particular fashion
the ideals which are common to humanity. Specifically, what are
these basic values which reflect the national spirit and help it to
survive?

Role of Language

One of them is the language of a people. There is an intangible
bond between a people and its language. Language is born with
a nation, even before a national consciousness has fully developed, and accompanies it through all the stages of its history. It
bears the imprint of the spirit of a people and is inseparable from
the people and its national characteristics.

A national language, however, is not necessarily expressed in
the speech of the masses, but rather is the one in which the spiritual treasures of a nation have been written. Yiddish, for example, was considered by some writers at the turn of the century
to be more important than Hebrew. But Ahad Ha-am believed
that although it was used in daily life, it could not become the
national language of the Jew. That had to be Hebrew, which

for successive generations had been the historic medium by which the sacred feeling, the joys and sorrows of the Jewish people were conveyed.

Ginzberg recognized that the majority of Jews would continue to speak Yiddish for the next few generations and did not display that fear of the "jargon" which some of the other Hebraists did. To him, Yiddish was "an external and temporary medium of intercourse, a passing phase and would disappear." Hebrew, on the other hand, although no longer a spoken tongue, had been the language of the Jew since the beginning of his history. "Hebrew alone is linked to us inseparably and eternally as part of our being." [45]

Religion and Nationality

Together with language, he believed religion must be included among the aspects of culture which reflect the national spirit. A positivist, Ahad Ha-am did not personally accept a religious orientation to life in its traditional sense. Like many of the enlightened of his day, he felt that religion had fulfilled its historical role and would eventually disappear. Faith, like philosophy, was a form of "spiritual disease" which kept man from concerning himself with the problems of this world.[46]

Ahad Ha-am recognized, however, that religion still had its role in the life of a nation—not through speculative theology but in the customs and rituals which had become national symbols. One can be religious, he felt, even though one is not a believer. "At bottom religion is a matter of feeling, not of views," he wrote. "A man's views may change completely, but his feeling remains." [47] Although he described himself as a "free-thinker," [48] Ahad Ha-am believed that Jewish nationalists should keep traditional observances for their survival value and should look upon the "sacred things of the nation" with love and respect.

In his own behavior there were countless illustrations of this reverence toward traditional religious practices. In Odessa, for example, he attended the synagogue from time to time, and occasionally delivered a talk on Saturday afternoons.[49] When his parents died he recited the *kaddish* daily for the traditional period of eleven months. He would not begin a journey during the intermediate days of Passover lest he find himself traveling on the holiday itself.

Most of these practices grew out of his own deep feelings of Jewish identity; others were a matter of practical compromise with the realities of life. While he opposed intellectual compromise, which he felt was never justified, he agreed that practical compromises were desirable in order to avoid offending the Orthodox members of *Hibbat Zion*.

When Salomon Reinach, a leading French Jew, urged East European Jews to become emancipated from ceremonial law (observance of the Sabbath and the dietary rules), Ahad Ha-am defended these institutions which have been "sanctified by the blood of our people, and have preserved it for thousands of years from spiritual degeneration." [50] Similarly, when Max Nordau wrote that he saw no national values in observance of the Sabbath, and as a free spirit he must rest whenever it was possible for him to do so, Ahad Ha-am felt called upon to defend the Sabbath as a historic institution of the Jewish people. "He who feels a true bond with the life of his people," he wrote, "cannot visualize the existence of the Jewish people without 'Queen Sabbath.' More than the Jew kept the Sabbath, the Sabbath has preserved the Jew." [51]

Primacy of Ethics

What seemed to Ahad Ha-am the most important index to the national spirit of a people is to be found in its ethics, the ways it has developed to distinguish between good and evil and the basis it has evolved for personal and social relationships. Though many in our time are accustomed to think of ethics as a part of religion, to Ahad Ha-am the two were separate disciplines, each responding to a different need in man, each the result of a separate historical development.[52] Ahad Ha-am did not agree with Schechter that in Judaism ethics were subordinate to religion and that moral law had its origin in revelation. On the contrary, to him "religious development has followed moral development." [53]

He held that although there are general principles which are universally accepted among all peoples, there is a distinctive ethic which each nation develops in terms of its own national spirit, its character and its needs. What is considered good by one nation is regarded by another as bad; what elicits sacrifice from one is not considered essential by another. If this is true among nations with similar backgrounds, how much more does it apply to the Jewish people who from the beginning of their history have been separated from other nations by a unique way of life. Inevitably the Jewish group developed a unique morality based on the character of its own national spirit.[54]

To Ahad Ha-am, the essence of Jewish ethics is "the predominance of the spiritual life over physical force, the search for truth and justice in thought and deed, and an eternal struggle against falsehood and wickedness." Unlike Christianity, Jewish ethics are oriented to the salvation of the group rather than to that of the individual and are based, not on a subjective view of sentiment and mercy, but on an objective standard of justice which must be applied impersonally to all alike. Judaism condemns all forms of selfishness, but it does not ask the individual to substitute the "other" for the self in his individual life and to practice what he calls "an inverted egoism."

Ahad Ha-am does not suggest that Jewish ethics are superior to those of Christianity. They are, rather, a unique and distinctive product of the national Jewish spirit which derives from the Jewish predilection for the abstract. He insists, however, that Jewish ethics are better suited to serve as a basis for international relations than is the altruism of the gospels.[55]

This ethical ideal, with its emphasis on the superiority of the spirit and on the "universal dominion of absolute justice" was developed by the Hebrew prophets, who represented to Ahad Ha-am the highest type of personality which Jews have produced, the truest expression of the Jewish national spirit.

The prophets were universalists, who transcended in spirit political and national boundaries and preached a message of love for the whole human race. But they were also nationalists who remained true to Israel, and regarded it as the "chosen people." They knew that scattered individuals could not do the necessary work and that a whole community was needed which would be the standard-bearer of the forces of righteousness throughout the generations.[56]

In these ethical ideals of the prophets, Ahad Ha-am saw the

essence of Judaism. Critics, like the Hebrew writer Berdichevsky, however, influenced by Nietzsche and his doctrine of the
superman, censured the excessive concern of prophetic Judaism
with spirituality and called for a reversal of Jewish values in
favor of the select few. In rebuttal, Ahad Ha-am emphasized
the possibility of "spiritual supermen" within the framework of
Judaism, who like the prophets would be uncompromising in
their ethical demands. Before there could be such supermen,
however, there must be a super-nation whose characteristics
would make it superior to other nations in moral growth and
whose way of life would be governed by a moral law which sur-
passed ordinary morality.[57]

How Judaism Survived

How were these prophetic teachings perpetuated through
exile and the subsequent hardships which befell the Jewish
people? It was inevitable that such absolute ideals had to undergo
modification if they were to influence the new conditions of life
which followed the Babylonian Exile. This adaptation was undertaken by the priests who, after the decline of prophecy, dominated the Jewish scene. The priests were men who could not
rise to the elevation of the prophets, and who held no sympathy
for extremism. Nonetheless, they were nearer to the prophets
in spirit than were the masses. They fostered prophetic ideals
but were willing to compromise with the exigencies of reality.[58]
Concern for the national welfare gave way to a state of mind in
which the individual became preoccupied with his own personal
fate. Unchecked, this tendency might have resulted in the total
disintegration of the people of Israel. At this juncture the Pharisees became the heirs of the prophets and developed the doctrines of reward and punishment, and of personal immortality in
place of national immortality, and satisfied the longing of the
individual for personal happiness. As the nation gradually lost
its political power, religion came more and more to the fore-
ground of Jewish life.

Prophetic Hebraism gave way gradually to rabbinic Judaism
which Ahad Ha-am viewed as an imperfect, truncated expression of the original Hebrew spirit. The center of Jewish life
shifted from the temple to the synagogue; prayers replaced sacri-

fices and poetic works gave way to legal compilations and collections of folklore. Hebrew became less of a living language and more of a literary idiom. The new religious emphasis became a protective bulwark set up by the will to live for the maintenance of national identity. It constituted what Ahad Ha-am called the "weapons of exile" to help the people in their battle to survive.[59]

Thus, the original Hebrew spirit was put into a form which would accompany the people in their wanderings and would serve to maintain a national existence through the long, black years of exile. It was a meager existence. The creative spirit of the nation was almost crushed, but the hope of restoration gave the nation strength to endure its martyrdom. The national spirit was kept intact for all to see and until the end of the eighteenth century, with the advent of modernism, there was no doubt that Jews constituted a distinct nation with its own special character.

Modern Plight of Judaism

With the advent of emancipation, however, rabbinic Judaism began to break down. The Jew achieved political rights in western Europe, but at the price of accepting a Judaism restricted to the sphere of religion. The solidarity of the Jewish people was broken; many began to doubt that the national aspirations of the Jewish people had any meaning. In the ghettos of eastern Europe, "Hebraism" was saved from extinction but at the expense of a one-sided development and the danger of petrification. The ghetto did not provide scope for the free activity of the national spirit.

Thus, as Ahad Ha-am saw it, Judaism in his day was undergoing a progressive disintegration and decay which was evident in all areas of the national life.

The Hebrew language, so intimately tied up with the national spirit, was not encouraged to develop because Hebrew writers were too concerned with *belles lettres* rather than with an acquisition of knowledge and an exposition of ideas. When the great works of Jewish philosophical literature had appeared in the Middle Ages, philosophical terms had been lacking and the Hebrew vocabulary expanded in response to the need. In modern times, however, writers were concerned first with the restoration of the beauty of the Hebrew language and disinterested in the depth or originality of the thought expressed. The literature of *Haskalah*, therefore, was intellectually sterile.[60]

Ahad Ha-am found, too, that the books of the times consisted mostly of translations or imitations of work in other literature. This was the result of the abandonment of Jewish culture by the most gifted sons of the Jewish people in favor of a life devoted to the service of other peoples. What remained, therefore, was "a barren field for dullards and mediocrities." To him, the only literature of the modern period which contained a shadow of originality was that of *Hasidism*. Though the content and form of *Hasidic* writings were often open to censure, this literature was the genuine product of the Jewish spirit and expressed the inner life of the nation.[61]

Nor was the cultural level of the people as high as it might be. There was a dearth of books in Hebrew on many subjects and it was impossible to find information on many aspects of Jewish life and thought. For example, there were no books on the Bible, which Ahad Ha-am considered "the source of our national spirit." Nor was there an encyclopedia of Jewish knowledge in Hebrew which would make Judaism accessible to the Hebrew reading public. Ahad Ha-am urged that such a work be created, designed for the interested public rather than for scholars, and devoted to an understanding of the Jewish people and their national spirit in all aspects. In his opinion, only a Jew who had such knowledge could have a basis for his Judaism and such a work would be the weapon which would assure survival of the Jewish nation.[62]

Together with the decline of Jewish scholarship, religion had become "more or less a spent force" in modern times. Ahad Ha-am was very hostile to Reform Judaism which had arisen in the West. He felt that it did not represent a natural growth or satisfy a spiritual need, but was superimposing changes in an artificial and mechanical fashion. To him, religion was based on a belief in the Divine source of truth, and an overly critical approach to "the holy things of a nation" indicates the loss of religious faith.[63] He was particularly critical of Reform because it wanted to "strip the shell of practical observance from our religion and retain only the kernel, the abstract beliefs." In one of his best known essays, *Sacred and Profane*, he drew the distinction between profane things in which the shell or external form is preserved only for the sake of the kernel, and soon discarded, and sacred things like the parchment scroll, in which the external form is raised to the dignity of the belief. The attempt of Reform to eliminate the external forms, or ceremonies, was the negation of one of the important aspects of Judaism.[64]

But while Ahad Ha-am opposed the idea of Reform, he believed in "development in religion"—in the natural, imperceptible changes which take place slowly when external conditions make them necessary. Traditional Judaism did not accept the idea of development in religion and artificially preserved outworn beliefs and practices which might have been expected to disappear. Ahad Ha-am was equally critical of this rigidity. To him, Orthodox Jews were "people of the book" who surrendered the soul to the tyranny of the written word. They did not allow for spontaneity, for free expression, for the natural play of the heart and mind. Without this range for natural feeling, Orthodox Jews were unable to retain contact with the actualities of life.[65]

With the disintegration of modern Judaism there was a psychological problem—the feelings of inferiority and self-hatred of western Jews, particularly in France, where the façade of freedom masked the inner spiritual slavery of the Jew. The constant need of French Jewish writers to affirm their French patriotism, their insistence that Judaism is simply and solely a religion; their justification of Jewish religious practices on the ground that Christians also practice such customs, were, to Ahad Ha-am, evidences of "moral slavery."

But this enslavement was only half of the price western Jews were paying for emancipation. Their need to resort to the antiquated theory of mission was evidence to Ahad Ha-am of a further intellectual servitude. In his view, they were compelled to do so because they could find no other way to reconcile Judaism and emancipation.[66]

Another aspect of the plight of modern Judaism was the threat of fragmentation which resulted from the innate tendency of one group to imitate another. Because of this tendency, there was the possibility that Jews living in various countries would evolve different forms of Judaism, eventually splitting into many fragments, each group with a different language and separate characteristics.[67]

This breakdown of modern Judaism was based on the waning of Jewish national hope. All that was left was a "negative awareness" that Jews are different from other people, and this approach was not enough to assure the survival of the Jew.

Doctrine of Spiritual Center

To Ahad Ha-am the way to overcome the atrophy of language and culture, and to cope with the danger of fragmentation with its weakening of the national spirit, lay in the establishment of a spiritual center in Palestine.

The idea of a spiritual center did not originate with Ahad Ha-am. Moses Hess, the bold forerunner of modern Zionism, referred to a "spiritual nerve center" in his book *Rome and Jerusalem* (1862), which would quicken Jewish life in the Diaspora. In his plan, this center would be a model for social action rather than culture and would mark the renewal of the great social ideals of Israel.[68] Smolenskin, in his magazine, *Ha-Shahar*, expressed similar views to those of Hess and Pinsker, and in conversation spoke of a "spiritual national center in Palestine." In *Auto-Emancipation* Pinsker did not commit himself to the "Holy Land." What was needed, Pinsker felt, was "a land of our own, a territory as far as possible continuous in extent and uniform in character, either in North America or in Asiatic Turkey." [69]

To Ahad Ha-am, however, only Palestine could house such a center since this land was sacred to all Jews and because it was "the soil on which was developed the ancient Jewish culture." Only in Palestine could "our spirit become strong and pure and our inner powers awake."

What did Ahad Ha-am mean by the term "spiritual center"? There was much criticism and misunderstanding of this concept. To many readers, the word "spiritual" meant a denial of the material aspects of colonization. He was accused of wanting to establish a "heavenly Jerusalem" in Palestine, where "unpractical idealists would sit and bask in the radiance of the Divine presence." [70] In a special article, written in 1907, Ahad Ha-am tried to make clear that the center would consist, not only of "spiritual institutions" but would also be concerned with practical and material matters. It would work out a system of economics which would include farmers, laborers, craftsmen and merchants.[71]

Moreover, the spiritual center could not be achieved without a Jewish majority in Palestine. While Ahad Ha-am saw insurmountable obstacles to an immediate large-scale migration to Palestine, in the course of time he felt the land could support a population of a million. Eventually, he hoped, some degree of autonomy would be established in Palestine but, in his credo, this would be at "the end of things" and not at the beginning.

When Jews became a majority of the population and owned most of the land, automatically they would control the institutions that shape the culture of the country and impress their own spirit and character on the whole of its life. Thus, there would be created a "new pattern of Jewishness, which we need so desperately and cannot find in the Diaspora." It would develop a "new genuine kind of Jew whether he be rabbi or scholar" and lead to greater cultural creativity.

Ahad Ha-am did not go into details about the future settlement of Palestine. Primarily, his concern was with the impact of the center on the Diaspora and the quickening of Jewish life wherever Jews lived. He differed from Herzl and the political Zionists on the future of Judaism in the Diaspora. Herzl expected Jews outside the Jewish state to become absorbed within the nations where they lived. Ahad Ha-am could not accept this "negation of the *golah*." Even after the establishment of a center in Palestine, the majority of Jews would remain outside of Palestine since the natural increase in the countries of the Diaspora would offset the exodus to Palestine.

Nor could he accept the theory of national autonomy as advocated by Dubnow. In Ahad Ha-am's view, the possibilities of national life for Jews in the Diaspora were very limited. To him the Diaspora could never satisfy our demands so far as to enable us to say that we are living as a nation in the fullest sense, and that there is ample scope for the Jewish spirit to develop and express itself in original creative work up to the limit of its capacity. To Ahad Ha-am there was no purpose to Diaspora work unless Jews simultaneously tried to obtain a "really free national center in our historic land." This center would exert a "spiritual" influence on Jews throughout the world. By this, he meant that it would have a psychological, as well as a cultural and intellectual impact. It would strengthen Jewish morale, increase the feeling of unity among Jews and restore the national consciousness which had atrophied. It would overcome the threat of fragmentation and serve as a "purifying fire and connecting link" for the scattered sections of world Jewry. The intellectual and moral servitude which characterized the western Jew would be eliminated. In a word, the challenges confronting the modern Jew would be transcended through the spiritual center, and his spiritual plight would be alleviated as Judaism was revitalized and teaching once more emanated from Jerusalem.

FOR FURTHER READING

Books about Ahad Ha-am

AVINERI, Shlomo, *The Making of Modern Zionism* (New York: Basic Books, 1981). A fine introduction to the main figures in the history of Zionist thought. Contains a valuable chapter on Ahad Ha-Am.

KOHN, Hans, editor, *Nationalism and the Jewish Ethic: Basic Writings of Ahad Ha-Am* (New York: 1962). A good introduction to Ahad Ha-Am's own writings.

KORNBERG, Jacques, editor, *At The Crossroads: Essays on Ahah Ha-Am* (Albany: SUNY Press, 1983). A valuable collection, by distinguished scholars, covering all aspects of Ahad Ha-Am's career and creativity.

NASH, Stanley, *In Search of Hebraism* (Leiden: E.J. Brill, 1980). A valuable study of the arguments and issues surrounding the rebirth of modern Hebrew, a debate in which Ahad Ha-Am was a central figure.

VITAL, David, *The Origins of Zionism* (New York: Oxford University Press, 1975). (See next entry).

VITAL, David, *Zionism: The Formative Years* (New York: Oxford University Press, 1982). This and the volume above form the most sustained and detailed general review of early Zionist history in English. It provides, as part of its tale, an extensive analysis of Ahad Ha-Am's role and ideology in this larger story.

2. Aaron David Gordon

[1856-1922]

JACK J. COHEN
and SIMON NOVECK *

I. LIFE OF GORDON

A A R O N David Gordon was the interpreter of Jewish nationalism who symbolized the social idealism of the new Palestinian
community. Gordon was the outstanding personality to emerge
from the Second Aliyah, the wave of idealistic pioneers from
eastern Europe who emigrated to build the land from 1904 to
the beginning of the First World War. Among his contemporaries were Ben Gurion, Ben-Zvi, Moshe Sharett and Berl
Katzenelson.[1]

His doctrine of a return to nature was opposed to all forms
of parasitism and exploitation in Jewish life. He emphasized the
blessings of labor and helped to mold the thinking of Jews
in Palestine during the formative years of its new development.
His theory of religion was based on a world view which has
been receiving increased attention in recent years.[2]

Gordon and Ahad Ha-am came from similar backgrounds.
Both were born and grew up in the Russian Ukraine, but there
were many differences in their outlook and approach to Jewish
life. Ahad Ha-am was a clear, logical thinker who stressed
the "supremacy of reason"; Gordon wrote his essays from the
heart, pouring forth his ideas without order or system. Ahad

* Part I on the life of A. D. Gordon was prepared by Simon Noveck;
Part II entitled the "Naturalism of Gordon" by Jack J. Cohen.

Ha-am saw Palestine as the center from which new teachings would radiate to the Diaspora; Gordon stressed the importance of the individual and the contributions of the land. Ahad Ha-am had little hope for the building of Palestine by Jewish labor; Gordon was optimistic about such a development and devoted himself to bringing about this ideal.

Their personalities may also be contrasted. Ahad Ha-am, as we have seen, was aloof and aristocratic, primarily a man of ideas. Gordon had warmth and spontaneity, influencing young and old alike through personal guidance and inspiration. While Ahad Ha-am stimulated and aroused his readers, he was not a practical leader of men. The Jews of Palestine not only read Gordon's essays, but looked to him as a spiritual leader and personal guide. This white-bearded man standing in the fields, hoe in hand, exemplified his own philosophy. His pure faith and original ideas, his joy in work and his dedication left their imprint on a whole generation. In his last years he became almost a legendary figure. In Degania, where he spent these last years, he is still a living force.

Early Years[3]

Aaron David Gordon came from an old and eminent Vilna family noted for its piety and learning. The grandfather, after whom he was named, was a famous author of Talmudic commentaries who refused to serve as a rabbi because he would not use his learning to earn a livelihood. His grandmother also had a reputation for wisdom and, unlike most Jewish women of that period, knew Hebrew and German.

Gordon's father, Uri, though a pious scholar, was not a fanatic and did not oppose his son's learning the wisdom of the world. His mother, Deborah, a truly religious woman, was respected for her kindliness, high moral qualities and wisdom. Uri Gordon had accepted a position offered by his relative, the noted Baron Joseph Günzburg, to manage a liquor tax concession, and moved to Podolia in southern Russia. Later he gave this up to manage a large farm in the village of Troyano in Southern Podolia.

It was in Troyano that Aaron David was born on *Shavuot* in 1856, the year of Asher Ginzberg's birth. Four children who had preceded him died in infancy. An only child, Aaron David was raised with exceptional care by his parents. He was not very strong and his education was delayed until he was seven. He studied with a private tutor for several years. At fourteen, although his parents were reluctant to let him go, he was sent to a *yeshivah* in Vilna and, after a year, to the town of Haschovato to study with the local rabbi.

When he was seventeen, Gordon returned home and continued his religious studies with a tutor. He was also permitted to study languages and sciences by himself. With the help of a soldier, stationed in the area, he learned the Russian alphabet and rudiments of Russian grammar. By dint of unflagging industry, sometimes at cost to his health, he became proficient in German, French and Hebrew. His parents wished him to enter a university to study medicine, but he refused.

Meanwhile, the lease on the farm managed by his parents had expired, and the Gordons went into the timber business and lived in the middle of the Ukrainian forest. Gordon therefore lived in close contact to nature and developed a love for the soil and the natural life which was later to be the basis of his doctrines.

When he was fifteen, Aaron David became engaged to be married to his cousin Feigel Tartakov. Two years later, on his return from Haschovato, his parents wanted the marriage to take place. Gordon, however, refused to marry before passing the tests for military service. His anxious parents were willing to bribe the officials (as was frequent in Russia) so that their son would not be called. Gordon, however, knowing that if he were excused, someone else would have to take his place to make up the necessary quota for the district, insisted on presenting himself for the draft. However, he was found medically unfit for military service.

On the Baron's Estate

Six months after this episode Gordon married. He lived for two years at Obodovka and then moved to Mohilna where his father was employed as an overseer on Baron Günzburg's estate.

In Mohilna Aaron David became an official in the office of the Baron's estate and remained in this position for nearly twenty-three years. While outwardly tranquil, he was full of sadness and frustration during this period. Seven children were born to the Gordons, but five died in infancy, and each death caused the father great pain. Only a son and daughter grew to maturity. The daughter remained devoted to her father throughout his life, but the son, having become extremely Orthodox, left home for a *yeshivah* despite his father's objections.

The humiliating May Laws of 1881, which restricted the Jews' right of domicile, prevented Gordon from residing in his place of work. He was, therefore, compelled to travel each day to a neighboring town or else to stay away all week and return home only for the Sabbath.

Moreover, Gordon was not happy with his colleagues on the estate. The other officials were snobbish, petty, and unable to appreciate his uncompromising sense of integrity. However, since he had no alternative other than commerce, which he intensely disliked, Gordon remained in his position.

He found satisfaction only in his contact with young people. Being a natural pedagogue, he taught his children and their friends. Young people came to his home to read books and newspapers, to hear lectures and to participate in debates. Gordon organized a choral society for them, and established a library. He encouraged the young people to speak Hebrew and educated his own children to use the national language. He made no distinction between boys and girls in his educational philosophy and made certain that his daughter received the same training as his son.

He also concerned himself with the education of adults and frequently spoke in the synagogue on Sabbath on "The Love of Zion" and other subjects of public interest. After the pogroms of 1881, he joined the *Hoveve Zion* movement about which he frequently spoke when he addressed adult as well as youth groups.

Many *Hoveve Zion* members, considering Palestine as the only solution to the Jewish problem, opposed the project launched by the philanthropist, Baron Maurice de Hirsch (1831–96), to settle Jews in the Argentine. Hirsch was so moved by the plight of his fellow Jews and so certain that their troubles could be alleviated only by resettlement in South America, that in 1891 he founded the Jewish Colonization Association, and contributed large sums of money for this purpose.[4] Though an ardent member of the *Hoveve Zion* movement, Gordon did not object to the Argentine drive. To him, the idea of *Hibbat Zion* was a long-range project, which would ultimately bring about a fundamental change in the Jewish condition. Since Argentina promised an immediate solution to the plight of the Russian Jew, he saw no objection to the plan. He himself, however, when offered the opportunity to emigrate, refused to do so, although he continued to be interested in the movement.

Throughout this period of his life, Gordon devoted a great deal of time to reading. But at first he was repelled by modern Hebrew literature because of the defects of style and thought which characterized it during the nineteenth century. "This literature was to me the symbol of our shame and degeneration," he said, "and sick at heart I drew away from it." [5] One day, however, one of his friends persuaded him to read an article by Ahad Ha-am in the *Ha-Shiloah*. As he read, he realized his mistake and excitedly exclaimed, "Has our literature indeed been so revolutionized while I have been sleeping the sleep of *Honi Ha-Meagel*, and remained ignorant?" [6] When he came home that day he immediately took out Ahad Ha-am's *Al Parashat Derahim* (*At the Crossroads*) and read it from cover to cover during the next two days. He gained respect and admiration for Ahad Ha-am and realized that not only this master stylist, but also other contemporary Hebrew writers had something pertinent to say. As a result of this reading, his efforts on behalf of *Hoveve Zion* were intensified.

In 1903 the Mohilna estate was sold, and though he could have obtained another Günzburg appointment, he was not pleased with the prospect of continuing dependence on wealthy kinfolk or on working with their clerks and officials. He wanted to work with his own hands, to be in direct contact with nature and to get away from the hated Czarist government. He yearned to migrate to Palestine, to begin life anew, but this meant a shirking of his responsibility toward his family. For a time he was torn by an inner struggle between duty to his family and the realization of his spiritual dream. The decision was made more difficult by the objections of his parents and his wife's relatives. For several months he wavered in painful indecision. However, when both his parents died within a short period of each other, he decided finally to emigrate to Palestine. His son was at the *yeshivah* and no longer financially dependent on him. His daughter opened a school and his wife was able to support herself on a small legacy which Gordon turned over to her. With her consent, he bade Russia farewell and left for Palestine, in the spring of 1904.

Arrival in Palestine

When Gordon came to Palestine at the age of forty-eight, he hoped to earn enough for his support and to send a little money home to his wife. However, he was not interested simply in finding a job. Gordon sought physical work because he felt that only through labor could the Jew find his salvation. He believed that Jewish labor is the foundation of the national re-birth, just as it is the foundation of national redemption. He rejected offers to become a teacher or an official in an institution. But it was not easy for a Jew to find work as a laborer in Palestine in 1904, certainly not for a frail, middle-aged man. Those of the First Aliyah who had remained in Palestine had by this time lost their idealism; they preferred cheap Arab laborers to idealistic, inexperienced Jewish workers.

Also, the system of administering the colonies, while established with good intentions, was not sympathetic toward Jewish labor. Baron Edmond de Rothschild loved the Holy Land and contributed vast sums to help the Jews to colonize it. However, to insure the efficient use of these funds, he appointed administrators who controlled the management of the colonies. Unfortunately, these administrators were not idealists interested in a rejuvenated Jewish Palestine. Many were petty tyrants who harassed and humiliated those who depended on their good graces.

Gordon, and those who arrived during these years, would not accept these humiliating conditions. If they could not earn enough to live by European standards, they would live by the standards of the Arabs. But they were determined that Jewish labor was to build the land. Their slogan was *Kibbush Ha-Avodah*, the conquest of labor, all labor, no matter how difficult, and they would not surrender any of their principles.[7]

Gordon succeeded finally in obtaining work as a day-laborer in the groves of Petach Tikva. This work, however, did not enable him to support himself and send money home. He decided to go to Rishon Le-Zion[8] where Rothschild had established the now-famous wine cellars, and where he was able to get a job. He wrote glowing letters home, expressing his enthusiasm about his new work. In one of them he said, "I have been born anew. The work is backbreaking but it gives much to the soul." [9]

Gordon did not stay long in Rishon. He left as the result of an incident caused by tension in the colony. The Jewish farmers there were not Zionists. They felt that some other territory than Palestine should become the Jewish homeland. The administrative officials shared these sentiments and used their power to elicit support from the workers. *Shekalim* were sold in Palestine and among the subscribers were many workers in the wine presses. On one occasion a laborer in the wine cellar rebuked one of the non-Zionist farmers for intimidating the workers to buy *Shekalim* and one of the officials hit him. Gordon and another worker resigned in protest and left Rishon.

By this time, Gordon had worked far beyond his physical endurance and was unable to resist the disease which plagued so many of those who had come to work the land—malaria. He was hospitalized for three weeks but remained so weak that he was unable to work for three months. Palestine did not yet have a *Kupat Holim* or workers' sick fund, and one of the laborers, named Rutchik, took him into his home and cared for him, a kindness which Gordon never forgot. After his recovery, Gordon failed to find employment in Petach Tikva, and went to work at Rehovot. During this period he was waylaid by three masked Arab horsemen who shot and stabbed him as he was walking to Jaffa. It was not the physical pain which caused him suffering, as much as the moral pain that fellow humans could act so inhumanely.

For Gordon, the moral issue was always paramount. This was reflected in his reaction to the attempt by the settled farmers of Petach Tikva to boycott Jewish labor in 1905. The friction between the farmers and workers was aggravated by the religious issue. The colonists, on the whole, were Orthodox; the workers, mostly irreligious. The tension reached a climax when one of the workers mocked the wearing of *tefillin*. When this was reported, the village council was incensed and declared a boycott against the employment of Jewish workers, and against renting them apartments. The workers met in Gordon's room to discuss the situation. He warned them against any acts of violence, but also stated, "We will not budge. . . . They cannot drive us out either by force or by starvation." What grieved Gordon more than the deprivation of the workers was the moral degeneration of those who would use such a weapon. The boycott, he felt, was a disgraceful attempt to starve those who disagreed. He told the workers that they were wrong in flaunting religious sancta, but he regarded the idea of a boycott as a sin against the ideal of a national renaissance.

Ein Ganim

Three years after Gordon came to Palestine, his wife and daughter joined him. They found him a different person. His daughter, Yael, later recalled that she was astonished at his physical appearance, "He had become older, his hair had become white and his clothes worn. But his whole manner and bright eyes made me forget the first impression." [10]

Gordon rented a small house for his family in a new settlement outside of Petach Tikva called Ein Ganim. This was an agricultural workers' settlement established on Jewish National Fund land. Those who lived there were kindred spirits. Gordon, too, worked in the colony, returning home to spend his evenings in writing or discussion. He loved the plot of grass at the back of his house. He considered it his parlor and welcomed his guests there.

His domestic happiness did not last long. Four months after their arrival, his wife and daughter became seriously ill. Mrs. Gordon soon died, but Yael recovered and took care of her father for a few years until she left for the Galilee.

Some of Gordon's associates in Ein Ganim were among the foremost personalities of the *yishuv*. The writer, Yosef Hayyim Brenner (1881-1921) lived there and he would engage Gordon in animated discussions. The young poet, David Shimoni (Shimonowitz) (1886-1956) worked in the same orchard with Gordon. These people and the other workers would gather in Gordon's grassy "parlor" to debate the burning issues of the day. Nearly every evening, the back yard was full of people. Brenner was a pessimist, despairing of the future of his people because of its spiritual decay. Gordon, also, was pained by the degeneration of Jewish life, but he was full of faith in the vitality of the Jewish people and its eventual regeneration.

In 1911, a conference of the Judean agricultural workers was held in Ein Ganim and Gordon participated actively in all the sessions. One of the subjects which led to heated discussion was how to use Jewish National Fund money that was at their disposal. Many wanted to build a workers' center in Petach Tikva; others, Gordon among them, thought it improper to use the money allocated for buying land to construct a building. The majority, however, voted to build the center. Characteristically, Gordon was not offended; he abided by the decision, insisting that, in the place where the workers were, there was his place.

In 1911, Ahad Ha-am visited Palestine and stopped briefly at Ein Ganim. The workers were incensed at him because he had recently written an article in which he expressed doubts that a Jewish working class could be created in Palestine. Ahad Ha-am accepted as natural the situation in which Jewish farmers supervised Arab workers in their fields. After meeting with Ahad Ha-am, Gordon invited ten colleagues to his home to discuss the situation. He was very grieved because he admired and respected Ahad Ha-am and considered him a great man. He suggested that a letter be sent to Ahad Ha-am explaining the views of the workers and signed by all. This was agreed to and Gordon wrote the letter, respectfully pointing out Ahad Ha-am's errors and stating his conviction that the realization of Zionism depended on the Hebrew worker. Unfortunately, the letter made no impression on Ahad Ha-am, which hurt Gordon deeply.[11]

Another issue of the Ein Ganim days reveals a further aspect of the high standard of Gordon's ethics. The Zionist Labor Party outside of Palestine initiated a fund to help the workers in Palestine. The party affiliated with it, *Poale Zion*, wanted to accept this financial help. However, *Ha-Poel ha-Tzair*, the group with which Gordon was identified, considered such contributions as charity and was opposed to accepting it. A decision was to be made at the second conference of the Judean agricultural workers held in 1912. After an intensive campaign, it became clear that *Ha-Poel ha-Tzair* would win by one vote. However, when voting time came, Gordon could not be found.

The next day he explained that he had felt it would be wrong to determine such an important issue on the basis of one vote, even though he favored the outcome.

Galilee

In 1912, about a year after Yael had gone to work in the Galilee, Gordon decided to join his daughter. He did not remain very long in any one place. For a time he lived in Migdal where Yael was working, but when the administrator insulted one of the workers, Gordon rebuked him and resigned. He stopped for a period at Tel Adashim, the settlement of the *Shomrim* (organization of Jewish guards) who undertook to protect Jewish lives and property.[12] It is of interest to note that Gordon, too, served as a guard for a while, but he refused to bear arms and carried only a whistle. Whenever he suspected thieves, a blast of the whistle would awaken his sleeping comrades who rose to investigate.

Wherever Gordon went he was regarded as the spiritual father of the workers. Young men and women enjoyed being in his company and came from all parts of the country to consult him about their problems. One of them later recalled:

> We would at times assemble in his room, a group of the youth, without previously planning to meet there, whenever our hearts were heavy and there was need to talk or to listen to the voice of a great believer. He loved to listen to what young people had to say and, with the goodness and wisdom of his eyes, would encourage them with a warm smile to speak whatever was in their hearts. There were no refreshments in the room, nothing to drink was on A. D. Gordon's table, but deep joy would at times overcome those in his presence to such a degree that we felt as if we were the happiest of human beings by being workers in *Eretz Yisrael*.[13]

These young people loved to walk with him and talk, always departing with renewed confidence. One girl wrote of her conversation with him, "This was my true university." Another commented, "We who are forging a new way drew from the well of his faith in man." [14]

Gordon was not interested in political organizations which set up rigid dogmas, and he did not belong officially to any group. He was drawn to the *Ha-Poel ha-Tzair*, because it had no written program, and allowed free speech and conscience. He was its representative at the Eleventh Zionist Congress in Vienna in 1913. While in Vienna, he met with the delegates of *Ha-Poel ha-Tzair* and another group very close to it in its aims —*Tzeire Zion*—and helped to unify the two.

Degania

In the spring of 1919, Gordon came to live in Degania.[15] He had visited this cooperative colony in 1912, shortly after it had been founded, and had remained for three months. He returned for short periods in 1913 and 1915. But now he accepted the invitation from one of the founders in the name of the community to make his permanent home there. Gordon never became a member of the *kevutzah*. Though he was a socialist, he did not believe that any specific form of society had virtue in itself, not even the *kevutzah*.[16] In his view, nothing can change man but man himself. The source of happiness lies in man's relationship to the universe and to nature. Gordon spent the remaining few years of his life in this settlement on the Jordan. He shared a room with three other men and worked, as did everyone else in Degania. He would not permit his age nor his frailty to serve as an excuse for being assigned lighter tasks.

Gordon spent a great deal of time writing his essays and corresponding with friends in Europe and Palestine. He would get up at midnight or early in the morning, take his lamp to the hayloft or the shower room, and put his thoughts on paper. However, important as his writing was to him, he never felt that literature was a substitute for physical labor. In his view, writing should be a by-product of the day's work. Gordon refused all remuneration for his writings except for translations, which he considered labor. When, on one occasion, he received a check from Europe for one of his treatises, he turned it over to the *Ha-Poel Ha-Tzair*. He considered it a "dishonor" to receive compensation for creative writing.

Gordon was happy at Degania and as in the past, people would come from all directions to be with him and hear him talk. He had an enthusiastic joyousness about him, which was contagious. He never tolerated gloomy faces and always insisted on gaiety. He participated in the dancing, constantly encouraging everyone and brightening the mood by his own joy.[17] Singing and dancing to him were holy tasks, a form of religious ecstasy.

One event cast a great shadow over his last years. His son, Yehiel Mihel, had planned to join his father and sister in Palestine. When the war broke out in 1914 correspondence with him was cut off. Gordon worried about his son and tried unsuccessfully to obtain news of him. In 1920, while eating lunch in the communal dining hall, Gordon was handed a letter. He paled as he read it, sat silently for a few moments and then quietly arose and went to his room. He lay there for a while, then picked up his hoe and went to the fields to work. The letter had informed him that his son had died of typhoid the previous year. He showed no open signs of mourning, but he did not sleep for several nights and was heard walking back and forth in the meeting room of Degania.

In the same year Gordon became ill and gradually grew weaker. He attributed this to old age, but finally agreed to go to a doctor in Safed. The doctor diagnosed his illness as cancer, and suggested that Gordon be sent to Vienna for X-ray treatments. Though Gordon was reluctant to have Degania spend money on him, he finally agreed to go. In Vienna, realizing that nothing could be done for him, Gordon accepted the news of his incurable illness calmly and stoically. He did not fear death which he regarded as a part of nature. His only desire was not to burden his comrades. "If I could work until my last day," he said, "I would go to meet death joyously." [18]

Gordon returned to Degania where he died a few weeks later in his sixty-sixth year. He was buried in the little cemetery near the place where the Jordan flows into the sea of Galilee. There he lies alongside the well known Zionists Arthur Ruppin, Otto Warburg and other members of the kibbutz. On his simple tombstone are inscribed the words: *Oved Ha-adam Ve-ha-tevah*, THE SERVANT OF MAN AND OF NATURE.

II. THE NATURALISM OF GORDON

Aaron David Gordon occupies a place all his own in the history of the Zionist movement. He was a unique personality, as his biography clearly indicates, and we should not be surprised to find that his uniqueness is reflected in his writing. Gordon was not, strictly speaking, a writer. He wrote in those late hours of the night after a day of backbreaking work in the fields because he had to express to others how he felt about nature and work and man, and the regeneration of his people. But it was just as important to him that he communicate his philosophy through the example of his life. He was incapable, in other words, of trying to influence his generation as a professional intellectual. Therefore, he never developed a systematic exposition of his ideas. He never produced a book but confined himself to correspondence and scattered essays and the spoken word.

Yet there is no mistaking what Gordon tried to say. Nor is it possible to escape the passion of his concern for the moral quality of human life. What Ahad Ha-am was able to communicate by his incisiveness, Gordon transmitted by his lyric earnestness and ethical purity.

Our task will be to put into a logical framework the ideas scattered throughout Gordon's emotion-laden prose. For it would be a mistake to underestimate what Gordon was trying to say and to give way only to the spell of the attractive personality revealed in his published letters, essays and lectures.

The Regeneration of Man

Despite the fact that Gordon was addressing himself primarily to his fellow settlers in Palestine, his philosophy is in essence a hymn to universal man and to his perfectibility. There is much in that philosophy which is merely an expression of faith, unfounded in any empirical study of how human character actually develops; Gordon was no social scientist. But no one can gainsay the inspiration of his wisdom. If he cannot be said to have solved the problem of the education of man, he has at least held out for us a magnificent picture of what man should and could be like.

Let us begin by contrasting Gordon's view of the origin of man with that of traditional Judaism. In the tradition, man is described as having been created in the image of God, a creature molded from the dust and into whom God breathed the breath

of life. Man was made of the same stuff as other earthly substances but somehow stands apart as a unique product of divine
creativity. Man is lord of nature, and in his highest form, as
described by Maimonides and other medieval philosophers, he
may even have the power to dominate nature in miraculous
fashion. This power over nature is conferred on man in order
to enable him to carry out his function as "the partner of God
in the act of creation."

In contrast, Gordon sees man as a creature of nature. Man
is a product of the natural process which eventuates in the
myriads of living and lifeless substances. Nature is depicted by
Gordon as a vast sea of motion, and man is "the bubble on
the upper surface, beyond which there is no further com-
motion." There is nothing particularly startling in Gordon's
imagery. Ever since Darwin's *The Origin of Species* was written
it has been quite impossible for the modern mind to deny the
gradual emergence of man in the evolutionary process. The
biblical description appeals to us, at best, as a metaphorical expression of the divine potentialities in man, but no longer commands respect as a literal description of his origin. Indeed, as
some geneticists inform us, it may very well be that contemporary man is only a precursor of a superior posterity, the pro-
genitor of a being who will advance far beyond the half-animal,
half-divine creature he now is.

What distinguishes Gordon's description of man, however,
is his keen awareness that although man is a creature of nature,
he runs the constant danger of losing contact with it, thereby
depriving himself of the very force which gives him life and
power. He writes, "You find that the more man takes from
nature, the farther he moves away from it. The more wealth he
acquires the more industrious are his labors for building a thick
barrier between himself and nature. He withdraws into his
walled cities as a turtle within its shell, until he has accustomed
himself to find this a first principle: life and nature apart."

How is this possible? How does man, born of nature, rise so
far above it as to lose contact with it? Gordon's response is
that once consciousness and intelligence emerge in man, he
builds for himself a world apart. This world, made up of ideas
and values, takes on a reality all its own—a reality so powerful
that it, in turn, becomes more compelling to man than contact

with physical reality itself. Indeed, by means of these abstractions, man actually reconstructs nature—to his own hurt.

If we apply some examples from our contemporary life, Gordon's contention becomes clear. We block out the stars with city lights; our very ability to abstract the principles of electricity and use them to illuminate our cities causes us to lose the experience of nocturnal sublimity. We build machines for man to operate; thereby we unwittingly curtail man's desire and capacity to create with his own hands. We manufacture automobiles; but by mastering the techniques of locomotion we weaken man's physiological structure and make him susceptible to troubles of the spinal column. All these inventions, of course, result from man's power to comprehend nature, to abstract experience, and to fashion from it materials, ideas and values that soon take on an existence apart from nature. More correctly, they become unnatural, in that they distort the harmonious order of things or prevent that order from coming into existence.

Gordon was the first Jewish thinker to wrestle with the problem of man and his alienation from nature. Other Jews before him and in his own day spoke of the hurt of their people in having been forced off the soil. Abraham Mapu, the novelist, had written idyllically in the early nineteenth century about the pastoral heroes of the Biblical period. His historical reminiscences, set forth in Biblical Hebrew, clearly delineated a longing for a return to the land. And at the end of the century, Bialik put into verse the yearning of his people to be restored to the land "where flourish almond tree and palm." The Mapus and the Bialiks, however, merely articulated the pain of the Jewish people at its uprootedness from nature and particularly from the soil of *Eretz Yisrael*. Gordon reacted to this uprootedness with a new philosophy of man and society.

The regeneration of man can take place only when the direct connection between him and nature has been restored. For the Jew this involved the additional problem of finding a locale where such a connection could be effected. It is at this point that Gordon's humanism and nationalism meet.

Man—Nation—Nature

There had been many attempts before to restore man to his natural stature. But the problem had always been: what is natural? The Eastern religions are replete with passages calling on man to turn his back on the illusions of his material existence and to seek out his true self, his *atman*, as the Hindus called it. Even high culture has about it an aura of artificiality, of unnaturalness. As Laotse, on whose thinking Taoism was based, put it, "Those who seek to satisfy the mind of man by hampering it with ceremonies and music and affecting humanity and justice have lost the original nature of man." On the other hand, Confucius found in humanistic culture the very essence of what is natural to man.

In the first century B.C.E., Cicero summarized the Stoic view of man's chief good as consisting "in applying to the conduct of life a knowledge of the working of natural causes, choosing what is in accordance with nature and rejecting what is contrary to it." But still, what is natural? And to this question there have been many answers in every generation.

Gordon makes two distinctive contributions to the understanding of man's relationship to nature. One is his theory of Jewish nationhood, and the other is his theory of work.

For Gordon, the nation is one of the bridges between man and nature. Gordon's call for a return to nature was no mere echo of similar movements in previous ages. For example, Gordon was no follower of Rousseau; civilization could not be advanced by restoring society to a prior, primitive state. Gordon accepted the fact that human nature was a cultural product; and he firmly believed that the treasures of the spirit could not be preserved in the human personality by setting the clock back too indiscriminately on social invention. For the same reason, he would not have followed Gandhi in his call to revive the economy of the spinning wheel. No, Gordon's plea was for the profound dedication of nations to the creative employment of science and art as indispensable to man's perfection. Civilization had to be built on the heritage of the past and not on its elimination.

Thus Gordon saw that man's social nature inevitably leads him to form groups and to be molded, in turn, by the very social organisms he creates. The nation is a funnel through which "at its wide receiving end endless existence is poured in, while through its concentrated, restricted end the funnel empties its contents into the soul of man." When the nation is so

constituted as to encourage the employment of individual talent
and initiative, and when it conceives of work idealistically, as
man's method of sharing with God in the process of completing
the unfinished business of Creation, then it becomes a force
"which creates the spirit of man. It is the link which unites the
life of the individual to the life of mankind and to the world
at large."

The nation, then, is the funnel through which nature pours
its meaning into human consciousness. It is the nation which
established the manner of interaction between its members
and nature. If it maintains an agricultural economy, it pre-
serves a relatively stable and static concept of nature. If it
operates with a high degree of industrialization, it introduces
many social forms which separate man from nature but which,
at the same time, spur him to a never-ending exploration of
new sources of natural power. Gordon, as has been stated, did
not call for an abandonment of industrialization. He merely
wanted the nations to become aware of the dangers for human
growth inherent in a complicated economy. If the nation is to
be a medium between man and nature, it has to keep the
channels of communication clear of artificial obstructions.

What does all this mean for the Jewish people? In an essay
entitled "Fundamentals," Gordon said to his fellow pioneers:

> We who belong to a people that has suffered more than any other,
> that has been uprooted from its soil, and alienated in unique
> fashion from nature, and that, on the other hand, still maintains
> the strength to survive despite two millennia of oppression—we
> understand, that in our striving for complete regeneration, we
> have no choice but to base the life we seek wholly upon its natural
> foundation. We must return fully to nature, to work, to creativ-
> ity, and to a sense of order and spirituality characteristic of family-
> nationhood. More than others we must be concerned, indeed we
> are charged with the responsibility for the regeneration of our
> nation and for directing its attention to the development of the
> human spirit and the search for truth and righteousness in its rela-
> tions with other peoples and with all mankind.

Gordon was addressing himself to men and women who had
come largely from an East European society in which the Jews
were outcasts, in which they had for centuries been forced to
live an unnatural existence, away from the soil and permitted

to engage only in those economic pursuits which constituted no threat to the master groups. To Gordon, the over-concentration of Jews in commercial enterprises constituted not only economic distortion but warped the whole character of the Jewish people and of the individual Jews themselves. Perhaps with exaggeration, but without some of the bitterness of his younger contemporary, Yosef Brenner, Gordon saw the Jewish role in the world's economy as essentially unproductive. Therefore, he felt the Jewish people had descended from its ancient standing as a spiritually creative entity. The place to begin, then, was with the soil itself. Jews must learn to find in physical work, and particularly in farming, a source of personal fulfilment. And the nation had to regenerate itself through a recapturing of its ancient contact with the soil of *Eretz Yisrael*.

From the foregoing, it should readily be seen that Gordon saw the problem of the redemption of man in all its complexity. He realized that the individual can be perfected only in a social setting which supports his growth. There is no individual road to salvation. Yet peoples and nations are themselves imperfect, and man cannot wait passively to be saved by his group.

Other Jews had been won over to the Marxian philosophy of class struggle to a thorough upheaval of the whole world economic order. But Gordon opposed Marxism because he firmly believed that no political or economic evolution could succeed in redeeming men and women who themselves were corrupt. He wrote,

> There is no improvement and no elevation of life unless it be through the improvement and elevation of man. Nor can there be improvement and elevation of the group, unless it come through the improvement and elevation of the individual; neither can there be improvement and elevation of the individual unless it come through the improvement and the elevation of the whole. This is mutual interaction, but also a magic circle.

The answer for Gordon was thus a process of interaction between the individual and his society, but an interaction which was rooted in a common dedication to "the natural." Gordon no more than anyone else has been able to put the finishing touches on the meaning of this term, but he has taught us the important idea that when we speak of man, we must always speak of him as in society and in nature. Even man's solitariness is a social affair, because his thoughts in moments of introspection are socially learned.

It was this conception of the individual and the nation which Gordon brought to Zionism. Like Ahad Ha-am, he looked upon the movement as a means to an end, that end being the ethical and spiritual elevation of the Jew and the Jewish people. He belongs in the stream of cultural Zionism, but it is interesting that it was his ethicism which supplied the inspiration on which a viable Jewish community was built in Palestine. It was men like him, the practical idealists of the *kevutzot* and *kibbutzim*, whose agricultural efforts actually provided the backbone of the modern *yishuv*. When we evaluate Gordon's own idealism, therefore, we must acknowledge its historic role in the creation of modern Israel. The idealist was, indeed, a political force.

On Work

While the nation is the funnel through which nature impinges on man, work is the means whereby man takes hold of nature and elicits from it the power that makes for his own growth and that of his people. But work, in turn, is not what it is conceived to be in the thinking of so many of us who live in a modern industrial economy. For us, work is the way we earn a living. For some of us it is a way of serving society. But for few of us is it the source of character, and of fulfilment. Yet it is precisely this conception of work which Gordon sought to convey to his fellow Jews, a conception which has led others to describe his philosophy as "the religion of labor."

Our own society offers ample proof that there is an intimate correlation between the creative opportunities which a job affords a person and the happiness and sense of fulfilment which that person achieves. It is probably true that there are millions of men and women who look upon their jobs as drudgery, as necessary means of earning a livelihood so as to enjoy life in their hours of leisure. The losses of human potentiality and creativity which result from this condition are immeasurable. And yet there is little that can be done to make work a source of genuine joy unless we can establish clearly, in the very image of what society must become, a conception of work as a force for the spiritual elevation of man.

The labor movement has, of course, given workers a heightened sense of dignity. But that dignity most frequently arises not from work itself but from the new status of the laborer who shares in the decisions that concern the conditions and rewards of his toil. The labor unions have succeeded in establishing humane conditions of work, but they are not equipped, obviously, to help a man find the kind of job that suits his capabilities and interests. It is utopian to dream of an economic order in which every man can always be happy in his work. However, it is not utopian to look forward to the type of society in which every man would find in work a spiritual or ethical purpose which would be important to his own personality. It was this which Gordon sought to emphasize in his own theory of work.

To conceive properly the purpose of work, it is necessary to relate it to the other creative activities of man; namely, science and art.

What is the function of science? It is to seek out the order which exists objectively in nature—what we have come to call the laws of nature. Science may be said, therefore, to be synonymous with discovery; in Gordon's terms it is the search for that which is revealed in nature. If man is to benefit fully from his contact with nature, his work must not be in violation of its laws. He cannot abuse nature and expect it to flourish; he cannot misuse the soil and avoid famine. Nor can he manufacture and put on the market destructive products without their taking a toll of public health and safety. If man wants nature to respond beneficially to his dealings with it, he must harmonize his work with the laws of nature's operation.

On the other hand, the laws of nature do not automatically compel man to behave in a certain way. Science is not ethics; what is, is not necessarily what ought to be. Therefore, work must be conceived as the way in which man puts science to use to enhance or to lower the quality of nature and human nature. Neither man nor any of the other entities of nature is static; all of nature is in flux. Work is the peculiar activity of man whereby nature, having arrived at the level of self-consciousness, transforms itself.

But what determines whether work will be constructive or destructive? This is the function of art, defined by Gordon as the search for what is concealed in nature. Art is the means whereby men draw new entities out of the natural order, ideas and objects which could have no existence unless men create them. The sun, moon and stars exist whether or not man sees them through the telescope or orbits them with artificial ester-oids. Law of gravitation operates whether man attempts to transcend it or not. But a symphony can be composed by man alone. The works of art, however, are not apart from nature in the sense of having their origin in another realm of being. They are as natural as the findings of science, but they differ from the latter in that they are invented rather than discovered. There are no laws of art by means of which we can predict a symphony or a painting.

What is the bearing of art on work? Art is the vision of life which determines the social purpose of work and the method of its organization in each polity. For the Jewish people, as we have seen, Gordon saw work in terms of the ancient conception of man's partnership with God in the process of creation. The world is unfinished; man must help to complete it. But he can succeed only if the means he employs are in accord with the divine order of things. How does man know what is divine? By studying and using nature with artistic imagination, tempered by the discipline of science. When man works with a view to perfecting himself, then he must steep himself in nature and the natural; for without that contact he loses the sense of partnership and suffers the delusion that he alone is the master of his fate.

Gordon's close association with the collective movement should lead no one to underestimate his awareness of the need for a varied economy. He looked forward to a balanced society of village and city, of farming and industry. That balance could be achieved only under the impact of a conception of work as a source of a new life and creativity.

The spirit of the new life, of new creativeness, must penetrate labor and industry. The builder, the carpenter, the tailor, the factory worker, and so on, must first of all realize that he is a living being whose spiritual needs are as vital to him as his physical demands. He must feel that he and the others for whom he is working are bound not alone by economic ties, but by a spiritual, human bond. Like us, the farmers, he must strive toward the goal wherein the important thing for him must be not the wage he receives for his work, but the work itself—the product of his labor. For this product is created to fill a vital need, physically, spiritually. Do we not see that while he is producing his wares for others that those others are laboring to fulfill his needs?

We can begin to understand now why "the religion of labor" is so apt a designation for Gordon's philosophy of work. It is based on the conception that man is destined to a life of creativity in the midst of a natural order that lends itself to his creative, artistic powers. In this conception the humanity of man is perceived as the resultant of his efforts to discover that which is natural in the world about him and to enhance nature by working on it with artistic vision. Gordon's faith in man, his profound belief that this universe of ours is what the term itself implies—a single, well-knit and orderly set of interactions among the entities that constitute his hopes for the sense of community in and among nations, his profound ethicism—all these bespeak the essentially religious perspective of his thought.

On Religion

We should not misconstrue Gordon's intention. He did not seek to make a religion of labor—although he undoubtedly saw in work an opportunity for enhancing the meaning of religion and for deepening the religious experience. His point was that through a proper understanding of the social role of work, the Jewish people could take another step in its career of religious creativity. It was, for him, an ardent prayer.

We have bequeathed to the nature of our land the expression: man created in the image of God. The phrase has gained significance in the life of mankind. We are on the point of giving new expression to the spirit which lives within us, for we say: "A nation created in the image of God." This expression, too, will come into its own; it will produce more than any power of the mailed fist.

A Jewish people dedicated to the regeneration of man—that is Gordon's view of the essence of Jewish religion. The centrality of Israel, not an Israel as the passive recipient of God's Word, but Israel, the active agent of divinity—that is the core of his religious naturalism. As did Leo Baeck some years later, Gordon identified the basic difference between Judaism and Christianity in the passivism and non-opposition to evil of the latter, and activism and the prophetic ethics of the former.

Christianity holds that "only the passive will, in sight of the Supreme Will, can influence for good the doer of evil." Since only God knows what is good and what is evil in their ultimate sense, human activism in behalf of good may be an expression of the sin of pride rather than of genuine piety.

In contrast, "Judaism teaches that man is primarily an active force, that is—his human form, and not a force acted upon. Man, all mankind, creates the world in the image of God and fulfills his mission in life by exalting his essence to the highest degree. As the purpose of man does not lie in self-renunciation, but in the exaltation of this self, so also is the purpose of life. This purpose of life, then, is neither monasticism nor asceticism, but purification, naturalness and sanctification."

Gordon conceived religion, of course, in idealistic terms. It was the kind of values which a people imparts to its members which is important. As he put it, "Religion, in the final analysis, is the tie by which all personalities of the nation are united into one collective personality. And since the progress of thought and the purification of the human spirit in general come primarily through individuals, religious content is apt to go hand in hand with the advance in thought and in spirituality, to renew itself and to rise with these attributes in proportion to their growth."

Gordon gave much thought to the problem of spiritual growth. As far as he was concerned, man had entered a new era of religious feeling, the age of naturalism. If the Jewish religion is to function effectively it must be transposed into this new key; and the idea of God as well must be reinterpreted. Only thus could the spiritual power inherent in the Jewish people be put to work for the benefit of mankind. "Pure, natural life, a life amid nature and with nature, a life expressing the sense of higher unity and higher responsibility—this is true religion. This living expression; this expression in practice, in life, is an acknowledgment of God—a deeper knowledge than an intellectual one."

Gordon sought to overcome the stagnant attitude of his generation toward the concepts of God and religion. He criticized severely the laziness of mind which permitted the Jews of his day to overlook the changes that regularly occur in religious ideology. Nietzsche had declared that God is dead, but "it is only the outmoded, passive concept of God that is dead, not God, the Unseen, whom he (man) meets in everything he thinks and feels, whom he cannot grasp, nor overtake, with whom he deals in all he senses, thinks, speaks, yet does not know what He is or whence He came." The call to rethink the meaning of God, and most important, to feel His reality, was truly an amazing sentiment to come from the mouth and pen of an early twentieth-century socialist.

In like manner, Gordon would have us "conclude that religion, too, will not die while there is a human soul in the world, a sense of human responsibility, and a longing for human life."

For Jews who today have lost their spiritual anchor, Gordon's message has a particular poignancy. For here was a man who literally took on a new way of life well after the age when most men have fallen into an unchangeable pattern of thinking and acting. He lived his philosophy. It may, therefore, be pertinent to add this footnote to the foregoing brief account of his views on religion. It must have occurred to the reader to ask what role, if any, Gordon assigned to ritual. Polity, ethics and ideology—these seem to be enough. Is there anything of value in the ritual tradition of Judaism?

Admittedly, Gordon left very little on this subject, but there is an incomplete statement of his on *Yom Kippur* which indicates the path he might have chosen. Gordon would bid us reinterpret the tradition in order to make it live in our minds. And so he comments concerning *Yom Kippur*, "If the day will cease being what it is, and will become an ordinary day like other days, will it not involve a great human and national loss, a decline that will entail no elevation for us, for all of us, sons of this nation?" The direction is clear; we cannot lightly discard tradition. Our only recourse, therefore, is to wrestle with it and to force it to bless us, as it did our ancestors, with its life-giving power. How can *Yom Kippur* and all of our religious heritage be reinterpreted in a naturalist key? That is the problem to which Gordon bids us address ourselves.

Jews and Arabs

Devotion to a people and identification of its religion with its national tradition, interests and aspirations could result in blindness to the needs of other peoples. But when such devotion is animated by a sense of ethical responsibility and subjected to the demands of a universal and humane morality, it eventuates in a prophetic mentality. It is no surprise, therefore, to find Gordon's essays dotted with passages in which he expresses his concern about the Arabs. His Zionism was founded on a recognition of Arab nationalism and of the needs of the Arab masses. He cautioned his fellow colonists to appraise realistically the strength and validity of the Arab cause. He wrote:

> The Arabs have all the traits and accoutrements of a living nation, albeit one not free. They dwell in the land, live in it, work its soil, speak their unique national language, and the like. Therefore, their claim to the land has a form and value merited by a living people on its natural soil—even if the claim is expressed in an unseemly and uncultured manner. . . . While we debate whether there is an Arab national movement or not, life takes its course. The movement sprouts and grows, because all the conditions necessary for its development and spread are present. It is dangerous for us to close our eyes to this living fact, to fool ourselves by saying that before us are nothing more than the acts of effendis.

Alert to the Arab potential and sympathetic to the rights and aspirations of the Arabs, Gordon urged his fellow Zionists to strive for a society in which Jews and Arabs could work together for their common good. It should be sobering to note that the growth of Arab nationalism was early predicted by Ahad Ha-am and Gordon, both of whom have sometimes been dismissed as unrealistic by more political-minded Zionists. But it is sad, too, to reflect that even had the Jews made no ethical slips in their relations with the Arabs, they could have achieved neither independence nor a status of bi-national equality with the Arab community. Goodness cannot move without power. It seems obvious in retrospect that a saintly *yishuv* could not have provided a haven for hundreds of thousands of homeless Jews. And yet, after one has introduced this word of realistic criticism of Gordon's views, his ethical position is impregnable. "We must be men of truth for *ourselves* and not because of *them.*" Somehow morale and morality have gone hand in hand in Jewish history. Should the *yishuv* ever lose its ethical spark, it is fair to say that it would lose whatever power it has achieved.

Gordon's Message to Us

Assessing Gordon's actual influence on Jewish life is partly a matter of recalling the impact he had on the ideology of the kibbutz movement. He was the spiritual mentor of the *yishuv's* youth. He taught them the meaning of spiritual nationalism and provided them with the patience and courage to work at the back-breaking job of reclaiming the worn-out soil of Eretz Yisrael. He and others like him gave a soul to a political movement and kept alive the vision of Jewish ethical Messianism. He articulated the best in Zionism.

It is that articulation which we urgently need today, both in Israel and in the Diaspora. If the Jewish people has the wisdom to read Gordon afresh, it will find a rich mine of inspiration.

For Zionism and the State of Israel, Gordon can supply a realization of their spiritual purpose which is needed by Jews in Israel and outside it and by non-Jews throughout the world who continue to ask what purpose the Jewish people has in mind in reasserting its national existence. Gordon's conception of spiritual nationalism is badly needed in our era of rivalry between states and the struggle for power.

For all mankind, Gordon's call for a new conception of the spiritual values to be discerned in nature and to be elicited from ethically motivated work could constitute a veritable revolution in prevailing theories of man, religious ideology, ritual, and ethics. The church and synagogues, were they to take a man like Gordon seriously, would become alive to the real challenges of art and science. Religious institutions would change their static pose and try to achieve a harmonization with the process of dynamic change going on all around them. Scientists would not look upon religious faith as a realm apart, and religionists would no longer fear science as a threat to faith. Each religion would develop in accordance with its own genius, but it would deem its main function to be the elevation of its own adherents to true humanity rather than the conversion of outsiders.

By attending to Gordon's message the Jewish people would be able to take a long stride toward making of itself a people made in the image of God. Jewish youth would be challenged by a call to spiritual greatness and a challenge to its moral responsibility for the improvement of the Jewish heritage. It would experience that sense of community that alone can break through the barriers that have made of modern society a collection of isolated individuals and alienated men and women. Gordon's concept of work as the builder of society and community is a needed antidote to the careerism that warps the soul of our generation.

Is it too much to hope that in an age when vision is so scarce a commodity, the figure of the white-bearded Jew working the soil of *Eretz Yisrael* and dreaming of a brighter future for man can be a source of universal inspiration?

A rich world lies before us, wide vistas, great depths, infinite boundless, unquestionable light. Plunge, O Man, into the depths of your heart to these currents of light and of life. Live! live in every atom of your being! Live and you will see that there is still room for love, for faith, for idealism, for creation; and perhaps, who knows, there may yet be worlds still undreamed of.

FOR FURTHER READING
Books about Aaron David Gordon

AVINERI, Shlomo, *The Making of Modern Zionism* (New York: Basic Books, 1981). Contains a brief, intelligent, synthetic overview of Gordon's Labor Zionist ideology.

BUBER, Martin, *On Zion* (New York: Schocken Books, 1973). In the concluding chapter Buber draws out the meaning and historical significance of Gordon's understanding of Zionism. Written in Buber's unique style.

LAQUEUR, Walter, *A History of Zionism* (London: Weidenfeld & Nicolson, 1972). Provides a helpful introduction to Gordon in the context of what Laqueur terms "left-wing Zionism."

ROSE, Herbert, *The Life and Thought of A.D. Gordon* (New York: Bloch Publishing Company, 1964). An elementary, unsophisticated, biography. Contains the basic information.

ROTENSTREICH, Nathan, *Jewish Philosophy in Modern Times* (New York: Holt, Rinehart & Winston, 1968) pp. 239-253. Provides one of the few sustained expositions and critical analyses of Gordon's theoretical outlook available in English.

3. Abraham Isaac Kuk

[1865-1935]

JACOB AGUS

R A B B I Abraham Isaac Kuk is a legendary figure in both Israel and the United States. The first Chief Rabbi of Palestine, though one of the leading authorities of Orthodox Judaism in the modern period, towered above ideological differences and the fires of partisanship, and concerned himself with all groups within the Jewish community. A philosophical and literary mystic of scope and profundity, he belonged to that company of rare souls for whom religion is not merely faith and conviction but direct experience and the essence of life itself. He drew his inspiration from Jewish sources though he was not unfamiliar with the vision and sweep of classical and modern thought.

More than any of his contemporary colleagues, Kuk was aware of the need for adapting the tradition of Judaism to the temper of the new age, of endowing ancient doctrines and concepts with fresh life and relevancy to the problems of the day. To achieve this goal, however, he did not deem it necessary to compromise with Orthodoxy. On the contrary, he felt that what was needed was not the trimming down or streamlining of Jewish theory or practice but rather its emotional vitalization and intellectual reinterpretation. Kuk also made a unique contribution to the development of modern Zionism by giving to the spirit of nationalism a more honored place in the divine scheme of things than any of his predecessors had done. He interpreted the whole range of Jewish religious practice from the prohibition of shaving to the observance of the Sabbath in terms of the nationalist ideology of Zionism.

All of his attitudes and ideas can be understood in reference to his deep and genuine mysticism. Contrary to the general impression, a mystic is not a monk, living in an isolated cell and guarding his soul in a shaded retreat so as to keep it "unspotted of the world." The great mystics were men of action. Certainly, Kuk took an active part in the major concerns and most important controversies of modern Jewish life. He emerges as a religious nationalist, and one of the most luminous personalities in twentieth-century Orthodox Judaism.

Early Years and Study

Abraham Isaac Kuk, born in 1865, was reared in northwestern Russia in the little Jewish community of Grieve, a typical self-enclosed *shtetl* isolated from the broad stream of history. The son of the local rabbi, a *Hasid*, and of a devout mother, herself descended from *Mitnagged* rabbis, he was plundered almost from birth into a God-centered pattern of life with piety and love of learning as its two central pillars. The great figures of Jewish history and legend were more real to him than the leading political and military figures of his time, and the past of his people was more alive than the present. Among his early memories were tales of his paternal great-grandfather, Rabbi Isaac, reputed to have been one of the first disciples of the Baal Shem Tov, the founder of *Hasidism*. Despite this illustrious ancestry, however, the dominant tradition in the Kuk home was not the emotional and gentle piety of the *Hasidim* but rather the stern austerity of his maternal antecedents, the *Mitnaggdim*.

The ideal of Torah was intense, and Kuk was plunged at a very early age into the "sea of Talmud." From then on, his intellectual fare was restricted to the law and lore of that complex storehouse of Jewish learning. A phenomenal student, by the age of nine the boy had already earned the name of *illuy* or child prodigy, and was no longer required to attend *heder*. Instead, he studied entirely on his own, in a corner of the ancient synagogue, and was soon recognized as a *matmid*, i.e., an unusually diligent student. At fifteen, he went to study in Lutzin, in keeping with the traditional principle of being "an exile to a place

of Torah." In that distant city, free from any family interference, he could give single-minded devotion to learning. An
account of young Kuk's life in Lutzin by a classmate describes
him as "an exceedingly diligent student, whose diligence was
not the same type as that described by Hayyim Nahman Bialik
in his famous poem, 'The Matmid.' Bialik's *matmid* studied
Torah in order to attain the scholarly level of an *illuy* or a *gaon*,
but the diligence of Abraham Isaac derived entirely from a sense
of piety; therefore, his ardor was all the more remarkable. If he
failed to study Torah for a short period of time, he would feel
genuine sorrow, real physical pain."

Until now Kuk's world was circumscribed, and his sense of
religious consecration so intense that he barely deigned to cast a
glance beyond the recognized limits of Orthodox studies. He
lived the life of Torah and dreamed of serving as a priest in the
reestablished Holy Temple on the sacred mountain in Jerusalem.
He did not apparently miss the larger world of secular studies
and he allowed his soul to respond to the stringent disciplines of
the Talmud with utter abandon. But when, after a few years, he
left the quiet little town of Lutzin and moved to the metropolis
of Smargon, he came into contact with *maskilim* (students and
lovers of secular learning), university students and men of the
world. During this period young Kuk joined the *musar* movement, founded by Rabbi Israel Lipkin of Salant, which held that
the path to faith was long, winding, and narrow as the edge of
a knife. "Sinfulness" was the inevitable state of the human soul,
sorrow was the only proper mood of a sensitive person, salvation
in the hereafter the only worthwhile goal. His aim was to ward
off the corrosive effects of the modern spirit by fortifying himself with the fundamental motivations and teachings of Judaism.

From Smargon, the young scholar went on to the famed Academy of Volozhin, then under the leadership of the aged scholar
Rabbi Naphtali Zvi Yehuda Berlin. This great institution was
then the foremost center of Talmudic learning in the world,
with a student body of close to five hundred. Kuk's piety, scholarship and arduous manner of praying soon won him a place as
one of the outstanding scholars of the academy. "Every prayer
that was uttered by Abraham Isaac," commented a former room-
mate, "was thoroughly soaked with tears."

During his stay in Volozhin, Kuk developed a predilection for speaking Hebrew to his friends instead of employing the Yiddish vernacular. Since the revival of Hebrew (as the basic vehicle for secular nationalism) was one of the ideals of the *maskilim*, his comrades suspected him of being infected with the virus of *Haskalah*. Their suspicion was only partly justified; actually his use of Hebrew was an early manifestation of Kuk's way of meeting the manifold challenges of modernism by deepening his piety and incorporating into it the new values. He saw nothing strange in accepting Hebrew as part of his pattern of Jewish loyalties. Under the influences of his teachers, he was becoming more and more interested in Zionism, which was then a new movement, and in Palestine as the Land of Israel. He paid Rabbi Berlin the great compliment of saying that he felt at Volozhin "as if (he) were living in the Holy Land."

While still a student at Volozhin, Abraham Isaac was married to the daughter of Eliyahu David Rabinowitz-Tomin, the rabbi of Ponivesh. This marriage was not so much an affair of love, but, as in the case of Ahad Ha-am, a recognition of the scholarly achievements of the young *yeshivah bahur*. Subsequently, his father-in-law preceded Kuk to the Holy Land where he became the head of the *Bet Din* (religious court) of Jerusalem. He was to be a great influence on his young son-in-law and was later largely responsible for the fact that Kuk was invited to become the rabbi of Jaffa.

After his marriage, Kuk, in the fashion of the day, lived with his bride's parents at Ponivesh, where he continued his Talmudic studies with even greater zeal than before. As was his habit, he wore *tallit* and *tefillin* all day while he studied, feeling that these holy objects helped to inspire within him the mood of consecration to the word of God. All this time, Rabbi Kuk was becoming increasingly aware of the intense spiritual crisis confronting Judaism during the latter half of the nineteenth century. For the first time in his life he was venturing beyond the limited sphere of the Talmud and attaining an acquaintance with the secular culture of his day. He read the literature of *Haskalah* in Hebrew and also the works of Kant and Schopenhauer in German. As far as we know, his faith did not seem to falter even for a moment. His was a peculiarly selective mind which intuitively drew from Western philosophy and literature only those elements that enriched and deepened his religious beliefs. Appalled by the apathy and utter lack of responsiveness to the burning issues of the day on the part of the official leaders of Russian Jewish Orthodoxy, he embarked on a one-man crusade to rouse public opinion. Certain that the truth was contained in the Torah and tradition of Israel, Kuk believed that the inroads of heresy into Jewish life could be stemmed only if an aggressive literary campaign were undertaken by the leaders of world Jewry. He himself, at twenty-three, sought to voice his opinions by publishing a rabbinical periodical called *Itur Sofrim*. Its purpose was to discuss not only "problems of ritual sanctity, *Halakhic* questions, and Midrashic interpretations, but also those problems which stand at the zenith of the world of Torah and Judaism; to clarify the multitude of great and important questions that concern the present life of our people, to discuss and to establish the right policy and the proper path for the solution of the great problems, upon which depend the honor of the nation, its fortunes and its revival." Though this bold venture into rabbinical journalism proved abortive, the young editor was able to enlist the cooperation of some of the leading rabbis of the time. His own reputation as a scholar had already spread far; in some quarters, despite his youthfulness, he was referred to as a *gaon*.

Spokesman for Orthodoxy

For some time, Kuk had rejected the advice of his father-in-law to become a practicing rabbi, and had sought to engage instead in some kind of commercial enterprise that would give him financial independence and at the same time leave him free to pursue his studies. During this period he studied Talmud with Rabbi Israel Meir of Radin, better known by the name of his book *Hofetz Hayyim*. This saintly personality also urged him to enter the rabbinate, which he considered more important even than studying Talmudic law. He told him that a position was open in the town of Zoimel and persuaded Kuk to accept it. Since pastoral and preaching obligations in Zoimel were few and unexacting, Kuk was able to continue his studies with only minor interruptions. From time to time he would go out on preaching tours to plead for more conscientious observance of the *mitzvah* of *tefillin*. Perhaps the outstanding event in his life during the six years he served in Zoimel was his acquaintance with Rabbi

Solomon Eliashev of Shavell, the great *Kabbalist*, in whose company he stayed up many a night, poring over the books of Lurianic *Kabbalah*, the ancient lore of Jewish theosophy and mysticism. It was under the aegis of *Kabbalah* that his own philosophy was formed.

At the age of thirty he became rabbi in the comparatively large city of Boisk, situated close to the border of the province of Kurland and within the sphere of German culture. Here Rabbi Kuk was brought closer than ever before to the challenge of modernism. His brilliant sermons and essays on current problems, published in his rabbinical periodical *Ha-Peles*, brought him national recognition and fame. While his unquestioned piety and vast Talmudic erudition won him the reverence of the Orthodox, his original ideas and eloquent style were expertly attuned to the modern ear. In a short time, he became known as the outstanding spokesman for an awakened Orthodoxy.

Concept of Zionism

Kuk was also gaining notice at this time by his defense of Jewish nationalism as a mystical current of thought and sentiment that issued out of the sacred source of divine inspiration. It was his belief that along with the Books of the Torah, God has given the people of Israel certain unique endowments as well as the feeling of mutual solidarity. Divine revelation was in part the letter of the Law and in part the living spirit of the Jewish people. It followed for Kuk that all which is truly and genuinely Jewish was by the same token also truly divine.

Kuk's ascription of a high dimension of holiness to the sentiments and products of Jewish nationalism won for him the name of "the Orthodox Ahad Ha-am," leader of the Orthodox "lovers of Zion," in distinction from the secularist or cultural Zionists who followed the leadership of Ahad Ha-am. Kuk, however, never joined the Mizrachi (Orthodox branch of the World Zionist Organization) because he could not accept the secular interpretation of the nature of Jewish being, which lies at the base of the world Zionist movement. But he labored mightily to obtain the cooperation of the Orthodox masses toward the practical tasks involved in the upbuilding of the Holy Land.

Kuk's concept of Zionism was developed in his essay, *The*

Mission of Israel and Its Nationhood, which saw the dynamic creative urge of the Jewish people, that perpetually assumes new forms and creates new values, as holy in the highest sense of the word. While other Orthodox leaders regarded the new secularistic Hebraic art and literature emerging in Palestine as an impudent attempt to supplant the religious culture of Judaism, Kuk recognized it as a divine phenomenon and set the seal of divine approval on these products of the enlightenment and the national renaissance. As he saw it, secular nationalists like Ahad Ha-am and Berdichevsky, who proclaimed their "liberation from the precepts of the Torah of Israel," were in reality doing the work of God, though unwittingly.

All the while, Rabbi Kuk, of course, remained unimpeachably Orthodox, accepting the traditional conception of divine revelation. But at the same time, he showed an unusual willingness to assimilate modern ideas in a genuinely Orthodox frame of reference. He provided nationalistic reasons for the precepts of Torah. He transcended the nationalists by exalting nationalism to the rank of a sacred principle, a divine creative ferment growing out of the inner mystical bond between Israel and Torah. Zionism emerged as the most important religious obligation of Orthodox Jews. "There is no doubt," Kuk wrote, "that we cannot fulfill our all-embracing mission unless we settle in the Holy Land, for only there can the spirit of our people develop and become a light for the world." In his view, nearness to God could in some measure be attained through the intensification of national feeling, which restores to the Jew the sense of being rooted in God's world and encourages him to be true to the deeper springs of his own soul.

The Holy Land

In keeping with his Zionist philosophy, Kuk decided to settle permanently in Palestine, where, as he was to write later, the soul of a Jew regains its roots and vital force. Calls from such prominent communities as Vilna and Kaunas came to him, and some of the leading rabbis appealed to him to remain in Russia where the vast majority of the world's Jews were concentrated. But he preferred to accept the call to the city of Jaffa in Palestine, the Ashkenazic Jewish population of which was then scarcely larger than that of a village. He felt strongly that Palestine would eventually become the center of world Jewry. In the summer of 1904, therefore, in full awareness of the difficulties that would confront him, Kuk began the career that subsequently earned him the title "High Priest of Rebirth." He took up his post as the religious leader of Jaffa and the surrounding agricultural colonies.

It was not long before he was accepted as a man above all party differences. While the Orthodox were impressed by his profound piety and Talmudic learning, *maskilim* were elated by the fact that he spoke fluent Hebrew, the language of national rebirth. Unlike other Orthodox leaders who decried the atheism of the colonists, he praised the *halutzim* on the collective farms, most of whom had little or no use for Jewish ritual.

After only a few weeks in Palestine, he undertook to visit each of the *kibbutzim* or colonies on a preaching tour. The colonists, many of whom were former students of Russian universities, sophisticated intellectuals who scorned the morals as well as the rites of religion, became acquainted with a new type of rabbi, one who wore *tallit* and *tefillin* all day, but who spoke and thought in thoroughly modern terms. These first *halutzim* had come to the fields and swamps of Palestine out of European classrooms, impelled by the desire to build a new life for themselves and lay a new foundation for the life of the Jewish people. They felt that the circumscribed little world of Orthodox Judaism was totally irrelevant to their problems and their vision of days to come. Rabbi Kuk was, therefore, a complete revelation to them, impressing them as a saint who did not dwell in the mental atmosphere of the past, and who was human enough to join them in dancing the *horah*. Though they disagreed with his Orthodoxy, they could not ignore his sincere interest in their problems and his Zionist principles.

However, Rabbi Kuk was severely criticized by other Orthodox leaders for his friendliness toward the *halutzim*. When challenged to explain why the Lord should allow atheistic laborers to lead the way, if the upbuilding of Palestine is truly a divine undertaking, he answered that in ancient Israel there were degrees of holiness within the Holy Temple. The holiest portion, he said, was the so-called Holy of Holies, which only the high priest was allowed to enter. And even the high priest was permitted to do so only on the holiest day of the year, *Yom Kippur*, the Day of Atonement, after a week-long period of preparation supervised by members of the *Sanhedrin*. Yet, when the Holy Temple needed to be rebuilt, ordinary workmen in working clothes were allowed to enter and do their jobs. The present time, he declared, was one of building, when the entrance of workmen into the Holy of Holies was altogether in order. In the future, pietists and priests would come.

Rabbi Kuk's interest in the colonies was not confined to religious and educational matters. In a short time, he came to be recognized as their advisor and godfather. To improve their financial position, for example, he encouraged the colonists to plant *etrogim* (citrons used in the ritual of the Feast of Tabernacles), and he campaigned for the sale of the ritualistic fruit among Jewish communities the world over. He made strenuous efforts to get the rabbis of Russia to urge the use of Palestinian citrons in preference to those that were then being imported from the Greek Island of Corfu. In the same vein, he conducted an active correspondence with his colleagues in order to stimulate the sale of Palestinian wine.

As the religious authority for the colonists, Rabbi Kuk was on one occasion confronted with the task of rendering the final decision on a question that had occupied the greatest *Halakhic* minds in the past generation—the question of *shemittah*, the law prohibiting agricultural work every seventh year. If the colonists were to be required to cease all work on their lands for a whole year, the infant settlements would be thrown into bankruptcy. Following the precedent of such earlier pro-Zionist rabbis as Mordecai Eliashberg and Samuel Mohilever, Kuk, despite opposition from many quarters, took the initiative in suspending the law. While he himself did not eat any of the products of the Sabbatical year, it was his hope, as it had been of his predecessors, that by granting this permission during these early years, the colonists would be strengthened and the time would come when they would be able to observe the law. His argument was subtle enough, proceeding in the approved pathways of *pilpul* (Talmudic casuistry) and involving the subterfuge of "selling" land to a Gentile for the duration of the seventh year, but his real motive was to permit no obstacle to stand in the way of the progress of reconstruction of the Holy Land. Through activities of this sort, he gradually won the affection and esteem of all the colonists, who knew that in Rabbi Kuk they had a friend who would procure whatever help was necessary.

Indeed, Rabbi Kuk responded warmly to every aspect of life in Palestine, finding his every contact with it an exalted and ineffable religious experience.

He wrote:

> The difference between Torah in Palestine and that of other lands is mighty and powerful. In Palestine, the flow of the Holy Spirit bursts forth, ready to invade the minds of the scholars who seek to study Torah for its own sake . . . the kind of sweetness and light of holiness that it offers in Palestine to scholars who seek God is not found at all in other lands. I can testify to this fact out of my own experience.

In this spirit, Rabbi Kuk made all the problems of the community his intimate concern, seeing them in a total religious context. Less than a year after his arrival, he found it necessary to publish a circular letter criticizing the nationalistic atheists who clustered around the Hebrew enthusiast Eliezer Ben Yehuda, editor of the periodical *Ha-Shkafah*. In a special pamphlet addressed to the *yeshivah bahurim* and other Talmud scholars, Kuk urged them to widen their horizons so as to meet the challenge of modern free thought. "It is our duty," he wrote, "to work with the living and for the living in order to sanctify life." He delivered daily lectures on the Talmud and the *Kuzari* in the local *yeshivot*, and founded a special trade school in which students might continue their Torah education while preparing themselves for the practice of a chosen trade.

European Interlude

In 1914, Rabbi Kuk traveled to Germany to attend the second conference of *Agudat Israel*, the non-Zionist Orthodox organization. When it was first organized in 1912, Rabbi Kuk had hoped that it would subscribe to his own bold philosophy of nationalism and that it would be a unifying force in world Jewry. Though greatly disappointed in the organization's initial tendencies, he nevertheless decided to attend its second convention. Arriving in Berlin just a few days before World War I broke out, he was interned, at first, as an enemy alien, since he was a Russian citizen. Through efforts of several German rabbis, he was later given the opportunity to travel to Switzerland, where he attempted unsuccessfully to procure return passage to Palestine. After two years in Switzerland, he went to London, where he was able to help mobilize public opinion in favor of the Balfour Declaration. During these years, Kuk continued to write philosophical reflections on the nature of the religious consciousness, a work he had begun in Switzerland. A collection of these reflections, centering around the mystical significance of the Hebrew letters, vowel signs, and musical notes, and entitled *Resh Millin*, was published in London. This *Kabbalistic* little book, conceived and written in the intoxication of mystical ecstasy, was particularly precious to its author, who considered its conception an "undeserved gift from God."

Following the war, Rabbi Kuk launched the "Banner of Jerusalem" (*Degel Yerushalayim*) movement of Orthodox Jews, dedicated to the upbuilding of Palestine. Detached from the official World Zionist movement, of which many observant Jews disapproved, this organization carried on an active campaign for the maintenance and growth of the spirit of religion in the Holy Land.

In 1919, after normalcy returned to Palestine following World War I, Rabbi Kuk received and accepted an invitation from the Jewish community of Jerusalem to become its Chief Rabbi. He returned to the Holy Land and subsequently, in 1921, became Chief Rabbi of all Palestine.

Chief Rabbi of Palestine

The period of Kuk's leadership, 1919-1935, coincided with the formative stage of the emergent Jewish commonwealth in the Holy Land. During that comparatively brief epoch, Palestine's Jewish population increased from 90,000 to 400,000, and the "old *yishuv*," formerly the dominant element, was reduced to a lesser position. The new settlements, consisting of young, idealistic pioneers, seethed with spiritual unrest and bristled with intellectual and physical energy. Palestine became the scene of a new birth, the re-emergence on the political and cultural stage of history of one of the oldest peoples in the civilized world. In this drama, Kuk played the role of revered godfather.

The Chief Rabbi's first great achievement was the organization of the rabbinate of the Holy Land. A united and effective rabbinate was obviously essential if the religious character of the rapidly growing Jewish community was to be maintained. As it happened, the initial suggestion for its organization and possible unification came from the British government in Palestine, the office of which was then headed by Sir Herbert Samuel, the High Commissioner. Chief Rabbi Kuk responded to this challenge with great enthusiasm, seeing in it a long-hoped-for opportunity to introduce order and discipline in the inner life of the Jews residing in Palestine.

Subsequently, the Jewish community of Palestine, the so-called *Knesset Yisrael,* was organized with Chief Rabbi Kuk at the head. The vast majority of Jews in Palestine were thereby rallied behind this beloved spiritual leader, who became the most respected rabbinic authority in world Jewry as well as the official representative of the Jewish religion before the Mandatory Government. The Orthodox and the secularists were brought to a common meeting ground and made to realize that the bonds of kinship between them were more significant than the doctrinal differences which kept them apart. On the one hand, the Orthodox were compelled to agree that non-observant Jews were also entitled to the name and destiny of Israel. On the other hand, the secular nationalists had to concede that membership in the Jewish community entailed the obligation to respect the authority of the Torah and the rabbinate, though only in limited areas.

Despite this superficial harmony, however, Jewish Palestine was rent by differences, and the Chief Rabbi encountered many problems and conflicts. A group of ultra-Orthodox extremists, for example, headed by the Hungarian Rabbi Sonnenfeld, refused to recognize Kuk as Chief Rabbi or to abide by his religious authority. His supposed leniency in the interpretation of the Law was offensive to them, and his friendly attitude toward the secularists seemed to them sinful.

Party tension and strife reached its apex in Kuk's last years, when he found it more and more difficult to endure or harmonize the turbulent partisanship of Palestinian politics. During the notorious Stavsky trial, the Chief Rabbi was sorely abused. Hayyim

Arlosorof, leader of *Histadrut*, the general Jewish workers' union, had been assassinated, and the murderers could not be found. Suspicion fell upon a small Revisionist clique, headed by Stavsky, who was arrested and brought to trial. The evidence presented at the trial was extremely meager, but the organs of the *Histadrut*, in the blind fanaticism of bitter partisanship, campaigned for conviction. Though the majority of Palestinian Jews prejudged the accused Revisionist, Chief Rabbi Kuk regarded the whole trial as a mockery of true justice and the result of Palestine's unhealthy and poisonous politics. Accordingly, he took the side of the accused in a most forthright and crusading spirit. Daring the displeasure, abuse, and alienation of the Jewish workers and "leftists," he did not leave a stone unturned in his efforts to save the accused. A storm of protests descended upon the aged saint, but, when the dust kicked up by the bitter clamor of fratricidal strife cleared, there were few indeed who did not recognize the justice of his position.

As Ashkenazic Chief Rabbi of Palestine, Kuk had the opportunity to speak for the whole people of Israel during the trying days which began in 1929 with disputes over the Wailing Wall and a series of bloody riots. During all that troubled period he represented his people with courage and dignity. Though many Zionists were willing to compromise regarding the Wailing Wall, he insisted that no Jewish individual or group had the right to sign away any part of the eternal possessions of the nation, and least of all the Wailing Wall, the symbol and remnant of the grandeur of ancient Judaism.

When, in spite of all the efforts of Zionist leadership, the Passfield White Paper was proclaimed in 1930, the Chief Rabbi urged the Jews throughout the world not to lose hope nor to despair, but to remember that Israel's strength lay in the spirit which is eternal.

In the dark days of the thirties, when cynicism and despair enveloped Jewish communities, the Chief Rabbi was an inexhaustible fountain of faith. His home became a haven for worried and distraught Jewish leaders, and included Hayyim Nahman Bialik and M. M. Ussishkin as well as less famous figures of Palestine Jewry. The non-observant as well as the Orthodox felt that his spirit was an inspiration to weary souls, radiating faith and hope in the future of Israel.

From every corner of the Jewish world, questions in Jewish law and thought were addressed to him. His replies comprise four big volumes, covering every aspect of Jewish life, including the right of workers to strike. Regarding himself as a servant of his people, he attended personally to a multitude of requests, large and small. He could be seen at all hours, walking in the fur hat and long gown, the dress of the East European religious Jew, which he always wore, visiting the sick and ministering to the diverse concerns of the community. As his son Zvi Yehudah Kuk recalled:

He was always overburdened with the needs of the community. Everything was referred to him. A call from the High Commissioner asking his intervention in keeping the Jews from blowing the *shofar* at the Wailing Wall, or someone asking for help in getting a visa. And everything he liked to do personally. Even when he was sick in the last months of his life, I can remember his running through the streets to the Consulate to arrange some papers for somebody . . . the water bottles, which he carried to relieve his pain (he was afflicted with cancer), flapping about his body as he hurried. He always wanted to do things with his own hands.

Kuk, for example, always insisted, in spite of his inhumanly heavy load of work, on copying his own manuscripts to prepare them for the press, and on doing his own proofreading for his books. His reason was that since the *halutzim* had to do so much "black work" in building the land, he also felt obliged to do some "black work" in order to be one of them.

In the field of Jewish education Kuk cooperated with the *Mizrachi* organization in founding a network of religious elementary and high schools through the length and breadth of the Holy Land. He headed a group of prominent rabbis in 1924 in a tour of the United States on behalf of the *yeshivot* in Jerusalem and Poland.

According to his own view, Kuk's greatest educational achievement consisted in the founding of the *Yeshivah Merkazit, Merkaz ha-Rav*—a Talmudic academy which still functions in Jerusalem today and is known as "The Center of the Rav" or the Universal *Yeshivah*. In the winter of 1921 at the laying of its cornerstone, the Chief Rabbi outlined its curriculum and philosophy. While including the usual close study of the Talmud and analysis of Jewish law in all its minutiae, the *yeshivah*, Kuk stipulated, was also to teach secular and scientific subjects. "For how can a teacher communicate and inform his people," he said, "unless he be acquainted with the ideas that set the style of the generation?" Kuk called for a creative approach to the study of the Talmud, an approach which would make it the basis for a renaissance in Orthodox Judaism. His dream was that great minds, in approaching Torah with fresh genius, would enrich Judaism. One of his much-quoted expressions, fervently uttered on the occasion of a visit from one of Palestine's great but non-religious scientists, was "May the day come when the great of the Jews will also be Jewishly great." His subsequent lectures at the *Merkaz ha-Rav* on the classic works of Jewish philosophy attracted wide attention in Jerusalem, because they served as a bridge from the long-isolated world of Orthodox thought to the great, restless battlefield of modern philosophy.

Last Years

Despite the opposition of the ultra-Orthodox to Kuk's leniency in the interpretation of the law and his friendly attitude toward the secularists, the Chief Rabbi enjoyed the love and admiration of the entire Palestinian Jewish community. Rabbi Kuk is particularly remembered for his love toward his ideological opponents, especially the young people, so clearly shown in his devotion to the *halutzim*. In one of his liberal decisions, through which he incurred the wrath of some Orthodox elements, he permitted young people in Tel Aviv to play football on the Sabbath provided that admission tickets were sold in advance.

An aura of saintliness gathered about him even before his declining years, and many legends about his unique piety circulated in the streets of Jerusalem. One writer told of an evening's visit to the Chief Rabbi. Since it was time for the religious service, the visitor asked to accompany him to the synagogue so that they might take part in public worship. The Chief Rabbi is reported to have replied, "I cannot go with you. I am all afire with the love of God. If I should now go to the synagogue, I might be completely consumed. . . ."

There were two occasions each year when the citizens of Jerusalem were enabled to glimpse their Chief Rabbi's religious ardor. On the first night of *Shavuot* the doors of his house were thrown wide open while he preached from nine o'clock in the evening to dawn the following day. On the night of *Simhat Torah*, he would dance for hours with a Torah in his arms, surrounded by young *halutzim* and *yeshivah* students.

To the last day of his life, while suffering from cancer, Kuk labored for the strengthening of the united community of Palestine, remarking with the last ounce of his strength, "there is nothing which justifies and permits division in Israel." On the last Friday evening before his death, he urged participation in the 19th World Zionist Congress, observing, "How can one not be a Zionist, seeing that the Lord God has chosen Zion?"

His Religious Ideas

Abraham Kuk was not a systematic thinker. "My father didn't organize his writings," his son relates. "He wrote and wrote. He would take up his pen whenever he had a moment, and everything, poems, legal observations, philosophy, commentaries on the prayers, he wrote swiftly, and would rarely rewrite or cross out."

Clearly, Kuk lacked order or the metaphysician's urge for analysis, consistent definition, and the rigor of pure abstract thought. But he was a philosopher in that he loved all forms of wisdom and sought constantly an intimate knowledge of the substance and purpose of all existence. Many of his writings still remain in manuscript, but those that have been published reveal the sources of religious consciousness which guided the thought and life of this outstanding personality.

Kuk Essentially a Mystic

Kuk, as has already been noted, was essentially a mystic. Daring as some of his ideas appear to be, they never break out of the charmed circle of mystical experience and contemplation. His many published and unpublished writings are but a series of variations on the basic melody of his life, his yearning for and discovery of the nearness of God, his awareness of the mystery of eternity, hovering above and beyond the temporal world. He was among the "seers" of religion, sensing keenly the reality of the existence of God, which most men glimpse only faintly and at rare exalted moments.

> I thirst for truth, not concepts of truth.
> Lo, I ride above the heavens,
> Wholly absorbed within the truth
> Wholly pained by travail of expression;
> . . .
> I see those flames arising,
> Bursting through all firmaments.

Together with this soaring mysticism and his yearning for eternity, Kuk at the same time was always concerned with the details of Orthodox ritual law. All of this formed for him parts of the whole—the visible evidences of the great invisible truths whose totality man cannot grasp.

The starting point of Kuk's thought is the conviction that reason is incapable of revealing truth. In one of his books he exclaims:

> Expanses, expanses,
> Expanses divine, my soul doth crave.
> Enclose me not in cages,
> Or matter or mind.

It is beyond the ken of dialectics to envisage the amorphous, unifying, ever-changing substance that underlies the whole of experience. He frequently refers to the "call" that wordlessly transmits a message to the mystic. Thus he defines the basic attitude of the mystic as being that of absorbed, whole-souled listening:

> The higher waves beat upon our soul increasingly. The inner movements of our spirit are products of the notes which the violin of our soul sounds in its rapt exaltation. Though we cannot know what it is all about, nor give a rational summary of it, nor define the topics of the higher sounds, nevertheless we listen with a total listening. The voice of words do we hear . . .

In accordance with his mystical approach, Kuk is not concerned with formal proofs for the existence of God. He accepts the testimony of faith as entirely sufficient and asserts that the attributes of the Deity are directly implied in the intuitive "feeling" of religion. Kuk actually says very little about the nature of God in his voluminous writings. The subject of all his pietistic speculation is rather a certain emanation, or product, or phase of the Deity—His sight, His wisdom, His will.

Influence of Kabbalah

Kuk's concept of God and, indeed, most of his views, were shaped by *Kabbalah*, of which he was a faithful disciple, and from which he derived much of the poetic imagery that recurs in his utterances. The basic premise of *Kabbalah* is the utter dependence of the visible world upon the invisible realm of spirit, the rational upon that which is beyond reason. The *Kabbalists* carried to its ultimate conclusion the Maimonidean hesitation to apply to God any but negative attributes. They thought of God as essentially un-knowable, even though they claimed detailed and exact knowledge of the manner in which His power was manifested in the real world. Their God, though nameless and inscrutable, is the vital center toward whom all energies and thoughts are directed.

The word *Kabbalah* means tradition. More specifically, it refers to a vast body of literature and doctrine within Judaism, a complex system of ideas not proved by reasoned argument but based on a series of revelations supposedly granted to great Jewish personalities. Its most important book is the *Zohar*, traditionally attributed to Rabbi Simeon bar Yohai, a second-century Palestinian rabbi, but actually composed (according to most contemporary scholars) in Spain in the thirteenth century by Rabbi Moses de Leon. Among the Orthodox of eastern Europe, the authority of *Kabbalah* was unquestioned, and, in theory, an Orthodox thinker even today cannot venture into the domain of philosophy and metaphysics without accepting its ready-made answers. In practice, however, an intellectually vigorous personality is likely to be selective in appropriating *Kabbalistic* ideas because, along with its keen insights, it abounds also in superstitions and quasi-magical devices amassed over the centuries.

The following *Kabbalistic* ideas or doctrines came to form an integral part of Kuk's thoughts:

(a) The world is viewed as a perpetual battleground between the ideal forces deriving from God—the forces of holiness—and those deriving from Satan. All real power is from God; in the end, the evil power will be completely overcome and the Messiah will appear in all his glory. Whatever happens within this world reverberates in the "upper worlds," affecting the *shekhinah* (Divine Presence) and determining the drama of human redemption. Every thing and every event of this world is "rooted" in those higher worlds, like a tree turned upside-down whose roots cannot be seen but whose trunk and branches are visible on earth. Kuk's expressions of "lifting the soul" upward in order to "go up to the roots" and "see things from above" stem directly from this poetic *Kabbalistic* imagery.

(b) God is both very remote and very near. In His true being, God is the Inconceivable or the Infinite (*Ein Sof*). But He also issues out of His true Being in order to assume more concrete shapes. In His lower manifestations, God is in direct immediate contact with man's divine soul.

(c) The Jews have been given a divine soul partially encased within their personalities, and partly "rooted" in the Divine Being. They are thus obliged to live in perpetual tension between good and evil, between their divine souls and their non-divine general human souls.

(d) The Torah is a concrete expression of the Divine Will on earth. In the "upper worlds," the Torah exists in the form of "lights" but, here on earth, the Torah takes the form of specific commands and doctrines.

(e) The *mitzvot* or divine commands are also earthly manifestations of an ideal reality. It is through the *mitzvot* that fresh accessions of divine redemptive energy are poured into the world. The flow of divine grace and blessing is thus dependent upon continuous performance of the *mitzvot*.

(f) The people of Israel play a cosmic, redemptive role in *Kabbalah*. They are united in soul with the Divine Being, the source of all blessings, but their superiority is potential, not actual, and is dependent on their piety. If their life is governed by loyalty to Torah and *mitzvot*, the redemptive light of the Messiah is generated. Their sorry state of exile is a reflection of the "exile" of God's "sparks of holiness," and conversely, the redemption of Israel will bring about the redemption of all humanity.

Personal Mystical Experiences

This structure of *Kabbalistic* concepts was transmuted in Kuk's thought by the living fire of his mystical experiences. While *Kabbalists* generally studied their sacred lore in isolation from the teeming world around them, Kuk actually lived through profound psychical upheavals which lit up the complex fantasies of *Kabbalah* with fresh meaning.

In truth, the central fact in Kuk's life was his actual attainment of genuine mystical experiences, through which the dry abstractions of *Kabbalah* took on the flesh and blood of reality. He arrived at states of mind when he knew himself to be one with the inner current of reality, "tasting and seeing" the redemptive power in the heart of the universe.

> Through heavenly vastness my soul doth soar
> Unfenced by walls of heart
> Or walls of deed,
> Of ethics, logic or mores,
> Above all these it soars and flies
> Above all the expressible and nameable,
> Above delight and beauty.
> Exalted and ethereal.
> Lovesick am I,
> I pant, I pant for my Lord,
> As a deer for river banks.

In the light of his inner vision, Kuk expanded the meaning of holiness beyond the borders of dogma and ritual. No longer determined exclusively by the words of the Torah and by the occult tradition of the "inner wisdom," holiness was for him a present reality, a thing felt and apprehended, a quality universal and uplifting. The holy was the forward thrust of the divine power, an upward, ceaseless impetus toward perfection. In his exalted moments, Kuk believed he "tasted" the reality of holiness and its power as a dynamic impetus in the heart of the universe, driving toward perfection and redemption.

The drive toward perfection found in the universe and in

society is a phase of the Divine Will. The inventions of the scientists, the visions of the statesmen, the conscience of the masses are somehow related and made possible by the worship of the saints and their mystical experiences. In this way, Kuk bridges the gap between the "religious" and the "secular" realms, maintaining that there is no such dichotomy. The entire universe is one in essence. Out of the worship of such saints, creative energy is generated for the advance of society in all fields, in science, art, and human welfare.

Every traditional concept is broadened and deepened in the world-view of Kuk. Torah and *mitzvot* are no longer the special concern of the Jewish people; the whole progress of mankind depends upon their observance. On the other hand, science, art and statecraft are not alien or irrelevant studies to the mystical saint. In essence, every effort for the improvement of society is worship in action. In this view, the Messiah is no longer a person but a symbol of the horizon of perfection. Kuk writes of "the lights of the Messiah," rather than the Messiah himself, which appear whenever any forward step is taken in the advance of mankind toward perfection.

Kuk's Religious Nationalism

With all his universalism, Kuk did not surrender the special position which the Jewish people occupy in the *Kabbalistic* scheme of salvation. Here is where the renewed fervor of Jewish nationalism in modern times came to the rescue of his Orthodox faith. Sustained by the rising wave of ethnic pride, he did not deem it unreasonable to assert that the soul of the Jew was metaphysically different from the souls of the rest of mankind; that the Jewish soul was alone suited for the "channeling" of the divine striving for human society; that the Land of Israel was, similarly, different metaphysically from the rest of the globe, and that only there would the Jewish people regain that unique endowment in its perfection which enabled them to "draw down" divine help for the advance of mankind toward the goals of redemption.

Kuk esteemed highly every form of nationalism, but Jewish nationalism he regarded as a sacred phenomenon, a kind of fluid and dynamic supplement to the Torah. While the national loyalties of many Jews appear on the surface to be purely secular, the true currents of national feeling run deep. In its deeper currents, nationalism is the yearning by the national Jewish soul for fullness of expression. And the national soul of the Jew is oriented inexorably toward the service of God.

If the Zionist movement is inwardly holy in spite of its superficial secularism, then all the manifestations of the new Hebraic renaissance must also be regarded as holy. Indeed, Kuk followed the policy of saying "yes" to every action of the builders of Zion, befriending the atheistic pioneers even when they sinned against the most basic principles of what they were pleased to call "bourgeois" morality.

Kuk's acceptance of Jewish nationalism and his emphasis on its beneficent effect upon religious faith are important aspects of his view of Judaism. He regarded as untrue the paragraph in the official constitution of the united Zionist organization which proclaimed that "Zionism has nothing to do with religion." He was convinced that the secularists were working for the revival of prophetic Judaism despite their conscious selves. Palestine was the Holy Land, the land set apart by God. Like Halevi before him, Kuk taught that the highest level of piety cannot be reached by a Jew anywhere in the Diaspora; the revival of prophecy and the enjoyment of the holy spirit are possible only in the Holy Land. Like Ahad Ha-am he believed in the spiritual character of nationhood.

Nationalistic Value of Ritual

This religious nationalism is the essence of Kuk's message. The re-awakened instincts of nationalism, he believed, would bring fresh life to universal religion, widening its scope and restoring to it the vigor of pristine youth. The nationalistic motive constituted for Kuk the rationale for his Orthodox ritual observances. He believed that the Torah as formulated in the Talmud, the Codes, and the *Kabbalah* were the genuine national culture of Israel, and that a Jewish nationalist was in duty bound to observe its precepts. In the all-embracing plan of God for the achievement of the eternal destiny of Israel, the national motive performs the function of cementing Jewish loyalty with the force of a national instinct. The Jewish religion was weakened and robbed of the vital forces of originality and creativity when the pious Jews of previous generations completely ignored the feelings and demands of Jewish nationalism. To restore Judaism to its pre-exilic vigor, it is imperative that the nationalist motive be reintegrated into the pattern of Jewish piety.

Kuk undertook to reinterpret Jewish ceremonials and rituals and to reveal their profound significance to modern Jews. In this endeavor the basic maxim was, "as there are laws to poetry, so there is poetry in laws." He expounded the whole regimen of pious Jewish practice as a kind of symphonic variation on the central themes of the love of God, the love of humanity, and the love of Israel. He appealed to those who shared these loves to accept the total historical symphony on the ground that emotions cannot be abstracted from the forms of their expression.

The Legacy

Though it is still too early to estimate Kuk's place in the history of Jewish life and thought, it is certain that he belongs among those personalities whose stature and influence grow with the passage of the years.

As a defender of Orthodoxy, Kuk more than any of his contemporary colleagues was aware of the need for clarifying the traditions of Judaism and relating them to the temper of the new age. To achieve this goal, he did not deem it necessary to compromise with the Orthodox faith. On the contrary, he felt that the more deeply Jewish tradition is searched, the more its essential modernity will become manifest.

Kuk, however, does not seem to have concerned himself in detail with the historical challenges to Orthodox Judaism. In his overwhelming enthusiasm for every part of the Jewish heritage, he could find no flaws in it. He hated and therefore left to the attention of other men the business of detailed critical investigation.

More than any of his predecessors he accorded to the spirit of nationalism an honored place in the divine scheme of things. Loyalty to Israel, however, was according to Kuk wholly in accord with the modern doctrine of humanism, since Israel was "the ideal essence of humanity." With all his intense nationalism, he never allowed himself to forget that the ultimate justification of nationalism consisted in the good that it might bring to the whole race of mankind. But the love of humanity does not imply the levelling of all peoples to the monotony of dead uniformity. Every nation has its own characteristics and talents, and in the economy of human civilization, Kuk felt, Israel has the mission of being "a people of priests and a holy nation."

But above all, it is Kuk's mysticism that is of particular importance in the history of Jewish philosophy. He was practically the first Jewish literary mystic. His persistent emphasis on the current of vitality perceived in the mystical state is especially worthy of note. In this respect Kuk is true to the life-affirming character of Jewish piety, in which holiness is not a thing "other than life" but an intensified form of life itself, transmitting and sanctifying all that is coarse and earthy. It was this purity of religious feeling that Kuk brought to bear on his daily life and thought, and in his approach to Zionism. Holiness was the essence of his being and his most important legacy for our times.

FOR FURTHER READING
Books about Abraham Isaac Kuk*

BOKSER, Ben Zion, *Abraham Isaac Kook* (Ramsey, NJ: Paulist Press, 1978). A valuable English collection of some of Rav Kook's more available, if still highly difficult, mystical ideas. Ben Zion Bokser's Introduction is one of the most intelligent and sustained decipherment's of Rav Kook's Kabbalistic world-view we have in English.

EPSTEIN, I., *Abraham Yizhak Hacohen Kook: His Life and Times* (1951). A helpful, introductory work.

HERTZBERG, Arthur, *The Zionist Idea* (New York: Doubleday and Herzl Press, 1959) pp. 416–427. Provides a brief but wise introduction to Kook's thinking on Zionism, as well as selections from Kook's own corpus.

METZGER, Alter B.Z., *Rabbi Kook's Philosophy of Repentence: A Translation of "Orot Hateshuvah"* (New York: Yeshivah University Press, 1968). A readable translation of one of Rav Kook's basic works.

ROTENSTREICH, Nathan, *Jewish Philosophy in Modern Times* (New York: Holt, Rinehart & Winston, 1968) pp. 219–238. Provides a synoptic, coherent, picture of Kook's primary concerns.

WEINER, Herbert, *9½ Mystics* (New York: Collier Books, 1971) ch. 10. A very popular, easily assimilable recounting of Rav Kook's approach to Kabbalah.

*Surname is frequently spelled· Kook

GERMAN
JEWISH
THINKERS

The character of Jewish thought in twentieth-century Germany stands in dramatic contrast to that of Russia during the same period. Although German Jewry made contributions to Zionist theory (Martin Buber was an outstanding philosopher of Jewish nationalism), the dominant interests of its intellectual spokesmen were in Jewish philosophy and theology. While Russian Jewish thinkers were concerned with problems of group survival and the meaning of national consciousness, German Jewish thinkers were more interested in the "spiritual community" and the meaning of religious consciousness. The former were agitated over the role of language in Jewish survival (Yiddish vs. Hebrew); the latter did not consider this question important and recorded their thoughts in German. Russian theorists, in many instances, were secularists to whom Judaism was a nationality and not merely a religious commitment. German Jewish thinkers interpreted tradition in religious terms, emphasizing the Jewish concept of God and man.

In Eastern Europe there was a difference of opinion on the question of the future of Jewish life in the Diaspora; in central Europe, except for the extreme political Zionists, it was taken for granted that Judaism was completely compatible, not only with German nationality, but with the spirit of the German *Volk*.

The preoccupation of German Jewish thought with philosophical and theological issues began early in the nineteenth century. It stemmed, at least in part, from the general interest of the German mind in abstract, idealistic philosophy and its engrossment with metaphysical speculation and system-building.

Throughout its history, Judaism has not put great emphasis on theology. While the books of Job and Ecclesiastes in the Bible deal with issues which may be called philosophical, and the *Aggadic* portions of the Talmud contain speculations about man and the universe, neither the Bible nor the Talmud contain any systematic Jewish philosophy or theology. In most periods of their history, Jews took their concepts and beliefs for granted and felt no need to organize them logically or philosophically. The first systematic attempt to create a Jewish theology was made by Saadia, Judah Halevi and Maimonides during the tenth to twelfth centuries in response to the attacks of Muslim apologists and the criticism of the Karaites, a sect within Judaism which emerged in eighth-century Babylon.[1]

Similarly, the attacks of German philosophers, who proclaimed the superiority of Christianity over other faiths, forced Jewish thinkers such as Abraham Geiger, in Germany, to reformulate Jewish beliefs and demonstrate their uniqueness and worth.[2] The example of the German Protestant church with its opposition to Catholic ritual led some Jewish thinkers to re-evaluate their own ritual practices.[3] The new status of the Jew in the era of emancipation necessitated new interpretations of Jewish tradition which would allow him to practice his faith within a modern environment.

Thus, there arose in Germany in the 1840's and the ensuing decades, a number of men who devoted themselves to speculation on Jewish theology. These men attempted to reformulate Jewish thought to demonstrate that Judaism was not an obscure, oriental sect, but was congruent to the ideas of Europe's leading intellectual community. What Aristotle had been to the philosophers of the Middle Ages, German philosophers became for Jewish thinkers of the nineteenth century. Jewish thought of this period was essentially a Jewish application of the philosophical idealism of Kant, Hegel and Schelling.

These exponents of Jewish theology were, for the most part, rabbis of the new type that emerged in Germany in the middle of the nineteenth century. They were not formal philosophers, but for the most part, under the influence of the metaphysical systems of the period, they were seeking a basis for their own interpretations of Judaism.[4]

The scholars of the time made few contributions to Jewish theology. The three rabbinic seminaries founded in Germany during the nineteenth century (one in Breslau, headed by Zachariah Frankel, and two in Berin, the *Hochschule für die Wissenschaft des Judentums*, where Abraham Geiger taught and the Orthodox *Lehranshtalt* to which Dr. Asriel Hildesheimer came as head), were all dedicated to the scholarly study of Judaism. None of the three, however, had more than a minimum concern with the theological implications of its program. Kaufmann Kohler, looking back on this era in which he had grown up, wrote: "We look in vain among the writings of Rappaport, Zunz, Jost and their followers, the entire Breslau school, for any attempt at presenting the contents of Judaism as a system of faith . . . a system of Jewish theology was wanting." [5]

It was not until the twentieth century that Jewish theology came into its own in Germany. During the years before the First World War and in the following decade, a return to Judaism took place which included many Jewish intellectuals and stirred a spiritual awakening among some segments of German Jewry.

Several reasons account for this deeper concern with Jewish issues and the reorientation of Jewish thought which occurred at this time.

First, the rise of anti-Semitism in Germany at the end of the nineteenth century led to the gradual realization by many assimilated Jews that equality of rights did not furnish the Jew with spiritual contentment nor settle the problem of the relationship between Jews and Germans. During the course of the nineteenth century, the majority of German Jews had become almost completely assimilated in their environment. Secular, and even Christian customs gradually replaced old Jewish ceremonies. The collective consciousness of the Jew was submerged. In contrast to the intensive identification of Eastern European Jews, the Jews of Germany were essentially removed from Judaism.

The emergence of the anti-Semitic propaganda of Adolph Stöcker and his Christian Socialist party in the 1880's and the spread of the new theory of racism expounded by Arthur Gobineau and the English writer, Houston Stewart Chamberlain, led inevitably to disillusion on the part of Jews in Germany.[6] Faith in the efficacy of emancipation to solve the Jewish problem declined and an intensified interest in Judaism resulted. A whole generation of Jewish writers and artists who had remained on the periphery of Jewish life became aware now, for the first time, of many of the basic issues of Jewish living and began to express their views on these aspects of Judaism.

Jewish thought in Germany was also directed to the rise of Jewish nationalism. In the middle of the nineteenth century no representative German Jew would have admitted the nationality of Jews. The apologetic literature of the period attempted to prove that Judaism was a religious denomination, different from Christianity only in customs and beliefs. Zionism, however, stressed the national aspect of Judaism. Youth groups evolved with a lively interest in Jewish issues. Discussions were held on the role of the homeland and the importance of Jewish culture.[7]

The twentieth century also witnessed a lessening in the estrangement which had existed between East European and German Jewry. German Jewish soldiers during the First World War who served on the eastern front came into contact with Polish Jews and saw for the first time, a richer, more organic Judaism. The several hundred East European students at German universities, particularly in Berlin and Munich, had an impact on their fellow students. Increasing contact was established between Eastern Jewish poets and writers, and German Zionists. *Der Jude*, the monthly founded and edited by Martin Buber, regularly printed articles on East European Jewry.[8] The deep impression made on Franz Rosenzweig by the Polish Jews during his visit to Warsaw in May 1918, and the impact of Russian Jewry on Hermann Cohen in 1912, are described in the pages to follow. All this helped to modify the feelings of superiority held by German Jews toward their eastern brethren and narrowed the gap between the two communities.

As a result of these developments a new sense of spiritual vitality became evident in the twentieth century. During the ensuing four decades in German Jewish history there was a renaissance marked by a return to Jewish life among youth groups as well as adults, and a reorientation of Jewish religious thought. For the majority of German Jews, Jewish loyalties were limited to the struggle against anti-Semitism, but an increasing number underwent a slow but conspicuous transformation.

This transformation was manifest in several ways. First, there was evident among German Jewish scholars a desire to relate their research to contemporary needs. The *Wissenschaft des Judentums* was criticized because it had not "penetrated into the underlying ideological and emotional motives" of its subject. For the first time statements were made about the "creative energies of present-day Jewry," of the "new Jewish purpose." Twentieth-century scholars saw the role of research not merely as "objective scholarship," but to "show us a way to the sources of Jewish life." [9]

Contemporary interest injected new impetus which brought greater respect for Jewish scholarship in university circles. After the First World War, sixty leading non-Jewish German theologians petitioned the Ministry of Education to establish a chair for Jewish scholarship at a university. In 1923 the first such chair for Jewish religious thought was created at the University of Frankfurt. Martin Buber joined the faculty as professor of Jewish ethics and religion, remaining in this post for ten years.

Secondly, the period saw a greater interest in the sources of Jewish tradition and in its various religious forms. *Hasidism*, for example, had been looked down upon throughout the nineteenth century by Western Jews as an obscurantist movement. Graetz, in his history, described the *Hasidim* as ignorant and superstitious, and did not consider them worthy of extended attention. To him, they represented a spiritual retrogression in the inner development of Judaism.[10] It remained for the twentieth century to rediscover the teachings of *Hasidism* and their relevance to the modern Jew. One of the great contributions of Martin Buber was to make the inner world of the *Hasidim* accessible to German-speaking Jewry. The character of Buber's work and the reception of his *Tales of the Hasidim* are described in detail in the chapters that follow.

This interest in the sources of Jewish faith also helps to explain the impact of Buber's and Rosenzweig's new and unique translation of the Bible. To Franz Rosenzweig, Biblical literature was the source and the foundation of everything that is living in Judaism. Unlike Buber, however, he also stressed the study of rabbinic writings, medieval philosophers and the prayerbook.

This emphasis on the original sources of Jewish tradition was sustained in the curricula of various adult educational institutes (*Lehrhäuser*) established in the 1920's in Stuttgart, Cologne, Mannheim and Frankfurt. In Frankfurt, where Franz Rosenzweig assumed the leadership, there were eleven hundred students. Rosenzweig succeeded in uniting the different Jewish organizations—Orthodox, liberal, Zionist, neutral—into one educational endeavor for adults. The courses offered included Bible, Jewish history, Talmud, *Hasidism*, etc. The lecturers included Martin Buber, Ernst Simon (who played a major role in the Jewish renaissance in Germany before he emigrated to Palestine in 1928), Rabbi A. N. Nobel, the saintly teacher of Rosenzweig, the Hebrew writer, S. Y. Agnon, Erich Fromm, then a student of Jewish thought, and Nahum Glatzer.[11]

Finally, underlying these trends were the theological strivings of the period. Jewish thought as well as the general intellectual world reacted against the historical emphasis of the nineteenth century. What was needed was a theological, rather than a pure historical approach. Baeck, Rosenzweig and Buber are the outstanding, and most profound representatives of this new theological emphasis.

Each of these thinkers had his own unique approach to Judaism. Baeck emphasized the psychological, stressed the primacy of ethics in Judaism, and concerned himself with the dialogue between Judaism and Christianity. Rosenzweig was less interested in ethics than in the religious experience of revelation. Buber's great concern was with the subterranean currents of Jewish tradition—the Rechabites, Essenes and *Hasidim*, who represented to him the authentic Jews. In addition, their attitudes differed on Jewish law and the importance of ritual in Judaism. Nor were they united on the question of Zionism and Jewish nationalism.

But they were united by many common features. They were interested in questions of personal faith, the meaning of prayer, the authority of revelation and the relation of Judaism to Christianity. All three were concerned with the core of Jewish religious experience and with the great issue of how to live before God. Together they created a classical era in the history of Jewish religious thought during which Jewish theology attained a sublimity of expression.

Each, in his own way, was a spiritual leader as well as a thinker whose own life as well as doctrine inspired a whole generation. When the great crisis of the Nazi era came, the Jews of Germany were able to face their tragedy with greater dignity because of their teachings. These German Jewish theologians must be included, alongside the Russian theorists of nationalism, among the great Jewish thinkers of the twentieth century.

4. Hermann Cohen

[1842-1918]

EPHRAIM FISCHOFF

O v e r four decades have passed since the death of Hermann Cohen, one of the most distinguished European philosophers of recent times, and one of the most famous of alienated Jews who returned to Judaism. An eminent figure in the general intellectual world, he was the founder of the neo-Kantian school of philosophy, possibly the most influential stream of thought in western Europe in the closing years of the nineteenth and beginning of the twentieth century. He became, especially in his later years, profoundly Jewish in his interests and intellectual activity, producing significant interpretations of Jewish thought and a philosophical theology of Judaism. In his unique position as a professional philosopher who was at the same time a committed and deeply learned Jew, he was able to bring to western thought a new appreciation of the Hebraic religious and ethical heritage. Interpreting Judaism as a religion in harmony with the spirit of rationalism and idealistic philosophy, Cohen takes his place alongside Philo, Maimonides, Moses Mendelssohn and other classic formulators of Jewish religious thought.

Although Cohen started his philosophical career with an essentially anti-religious position, he gradually evolved a systematic philosophy which assigned to religion prime importance and indeed promulgated a view of God as the guarantor of truth and ethical fulfillment. While he never sought to justify religion by positing any mystical faculty or any specifically religious emotion or intuition independent of reason, the progress of his thought over several decades impelled him to make increasingly great concessions to religion as a unique force in the human enterprise. In his treatment of religious problems, beginning with his systematic work on ethics, Cohen took ideas and motifs from Judaism and made them an integral portion of his philosophic system. He made it clear, however, that his use of Jewish concepts was prompted by scientific and philosophic considerations rather than by ethnic sentiment. As his views on religion matured, Cohen slowly evolved a unique religious philosophy deeply rooted in the tenets of Judaism.

It is impossible to overestimate the influence on modern Jewish thought exerted by this passionate intellectual who, in the latter period of his life, emerged as the greatest exponent and philosopher of liberal Judaism in Germany and western Europe. With his great gift for philosophical analysis for the clarification and systematization of ideas, combined with a memorable fervor of expression, Cohen affected in a crucial manner many distinguished expounders of Judaism. Not only did he make Judaism understandable for modern, scientifically and philosophically trained west European Jews, but he also made it intellectually respectable and defensible. Through his teaching and lecturing, he gave a great impetus to Jewish scholarship and adult education. It was logical then that he came to be regarded as the unofficial intellectual spokesman of his people in Germany and other German-speaking lands. A German Jew himself, he also undertook various missions of defense and propaganda in behalf of his east European brethren of that period. Finally, as a distinguished *Baal Teshuvah* (repentant sinner), Cohen was the first of a series of previously alienated Jews (later to include Franz Rosenzweig, Nathan Birnbaum, Will Herberg and others) who, after many wanderings, gravitated back to their ancestral faith.

Early Studies

Hermann (Ezekiel) Cohen was born July 4, 1842, in Coswig (Anhalt), midway between Wittenberg, the birthplace of Protestantism (where Luther first publicly challenged the power of Roman Catholicism), and Dessau, the native city of Moses Mendelssohn. His family was very devout, and his early years were steeped in religion. His father was a *hazan* and Hebrew teacher of considerable learning as well as exemplary dedication to Judaism. Gerson Cohen began teaching Hermann when the child was three and a half years old and continued this instruction until the boy was in his late adolescence.

Even after Hermann went on to the *gymnasium* in the city of Dessau, where he remained until his sixteenth year, this devoted father would get up at dawn and make the long journey from Coswig to Dessau every Sunday, in order to continue teaching Hebrew to his gifted son. From his father, whose love and enthusiasm for Jewish learning were contagious, the young student derived a deep appreciation of Judaism that was to remain throughout his life, even after he drifted away from traditional Judaism. His exemplary relationship with his father must account, at least in part, for his own subsequent "return" to Judaism, albeit of a liberalized, philosophically idealized type. Cohen later dedicated his great work on the philosophy of Judaism, *Religion of Reason* (*Religion der Vernunft*), to the beloved memory of his father.

His family hoped that Hermann would become a rabbi, and in 1859 enrolled him in the Jewish Theological Seminary at Breslau, a famous rabbinical school with a faculty of great teachers, including Zechariah Frankel, the founder of Conservative Judaism, and Heinrich Graetz, the renowned historian. However, at nineteen, after two years of study at this institution, Cohen withdrew for several reasons, not the least of which was his feeling that his religious beliefs had changed to the point where he could never be a rabbi. Under the influence of Abraham Geiger's liberal interpretation of the origins of Judaism, Cohen went even further in rejecting traditional Judaism than did that apostle of Reform. The ex-seminarian now determined to dedicate himself to philosophy and proceeded to prepare for an academic career in this field. This step must have caused some pain to his parents, but he remained a loving son in other respects. Indeed, when as a university student he would come home for the religious festivals, he would assist his father at the High Holy Day services. Thus publicly he remained a practicing Jew, attending synagogue services occasionally and observing the Sabbath at home, though privately his religious views had changed.

For Cohen at this time, Judaism was, at best, identical with ethical earnestness and moral resolve, which he identified as the core of Hebraic prophecy. Most of the Jewish tradition appeared to him as a network of sentimental memories and observances related to filial piety. That he continued to participate in such ceremonies as the *seder* at Passover, or in the aforementioned synagogal observances, was the consequence of family loyalty rather than religious conviction.

His Philosophical Studies

As Cohen immersed himself in his philosophical studies, his interest in traditional Judaism dwindled. Several years after his enrollment in the Breslau Seminary he was introduced as an "erstwhile theologian, now a philosopher" to the great Jewish scholar Leopold Zunz. Interestingly enough, Zunz is alleged to have countered with the tart observation that "once a theologian, always a philosopher."

In the fall of 1861 he had begun to attend the University of Breslau, where he majored in philosophy, receiving a prize in 1863 for an essay on Platonic and Aristotelian psychology, and completing his baccalaureate training in 1864. He enrolled at the University of Berlin for postgraduate study, and the following year (1865) won his doctorate with a difficult thesis (written in Latin, as was the practice of that time) on causality and contingency in philosophy. He pursued post-doctoral study at the University of Berlin in mathematics and science, supporting himself by tutoring; and he hoped to win an appointment to the University on the strength of some of his work in philosophy which was beginning to appear in print. Cohen's first significant essay—*The Platonic Theory of Ideas*—was published in 1866; five years later this was followed by an important treatment of Kant's *Theory of Experience.*

To the young man's sorrow, however, the authorities at the University of Berlin, allegedly because they felt that his early essays were too radical in some of his interpretations of traditional philosophy, did not extend the teaching invitation for which he was waiting. Actually in that period it was difficult for someone of Jewish background to become a professor in a German university.

Finally, in 1873, a small and at that time (before Cohen came to it), provincial university offered him a post. Professor Friedrich Albert Lange, author of a famous *History of Materialism* (to the ninth edition of which Cohen later contributed a lengthy introduction) and head of the department of philosophy at the University of Marburg, invited Cohen to become an instructor (*Privatdozent*) at that institution.

Lange was an exemplary ethical personality, a liberal and humanitarian, and indeed an idealistic, philosophical socialist. He recognized in Cohen great philosophical ability, and also perceived in the young Jewish scholar a strong ethical drive which reminded him of the moral fervor of the Biblical prophets. In one of their early conversations preliminary to Cohen's being called to the Marburg post, Lange turned the conversation to religion and the ethical witness of Christianity. To the implication in the senior scholar's remarks that only Christianity taught a perfect morality, Cohen replied fearlessly, heedless of the possible effects of such hardihood upon his prospective employment, "What you call Christianity, I call Judaism." Thereupon Lange, impressed by Cohen's integrity and fearless honesty, took out his German Bible, and pointed out the passages in the Hebrew prophets which, he, Lange, who had emerged from a stern Protestant background, had underscored as being very important for an ethical interpretation of religion. By this gesture the older philosopher sought to demonstrate to the younger that he was well aware of the Hebraic contribution to Christian ethics, and indeed to the ethical progress of mankind. As to Cohen's philosophical gifts, Lange thought so highly of Cohen's early essays and inaugural lectures that he regarded him as "teaching them all to start anew from the very foundation."

Cohen was to stay at Marburg for almost forty years. Approximately two years after his arrival at this university, he became an assistant professor, and in 1876, on the death of Lange, with whom Cohen had developed a deep friendship on the basis of shared intellectual and spiritual interests and concern with ethical progress and democratic socialism, the Jewish philosopher was invited to take over his former colleague's chair. In that period of expanding anti-Semitism in Germany, when most Jews in academic life were converts to Christianity, it was no small triumph that Hermann Cohen, a committed Jew and the son of a *hazan*, could rise to so high a position.

The Marburg Philosopher: 1876-1912

For the next four decades Cohen enjoyed a busy, productive and brilliant academic career. He threw himself headlong into his work—writing, studying, and teaching with force and vigor. His name began to be known far and wide as possibly the foremost German philosopher in the last quarter of the nineteenth century, following Nietzsche. He became first the outstanding interpreter of Immanuel Kant, the great German critical philosopher, who in the latter part of the eighteenth century had pointed out both the strength of human thinking and its limitations, and who had investigated the relationships between science, on the one hand, and ethics and religion on the other. Cohen became the undisputed head of the movement in the last third of the nineteenth century to restore the philosophical supremacy of Kant, that "mighty crumbler of all traditional philosophy," as Heine had termed him. Together with his disciples, Cohen then developed Kant's thought to new levels, producing a system known as neo-Kantianism, which in the last third of the nineteenth century and indeed up to World War I was perhaps the most important and influential philosophical school in Germany. These neo-Kantians emphasized in one way or another that Kant's basic and lasting contribution lay in his demonstration of the limits of knowledge, and of the operation of certain innate laws of the mind in the formation of ideas. In general, their position was that any object known by the mind is not a ready-made thing existing out in the world but that the object in question "becomes" what it is perceived to be only in the course of the process of knowing.

This neo-Kantian trend of thought came to clear, full, and learned expression in Hermann Cohen. He produced three distinguished, complex works of interpretation and commentary on Kant's three great philosophical works, each of which bore the term *Critique* in its title, establishing himself as a brilliant interpreter of the revolutionary thinker of Koenigsberg, but with his own unique emphasis.

After producing his masterful exposition of Kant's thought, Cohen worked at the construction of his own systematic philosophy, covering the whole range of human thought—science, ethics, religion and art. It had also been his intention to produce a system of psychology, but he failed to accomplish this.

Cohen's own philosophic theory was developed in several massive works of an abstract and systematic character, which followed in their general organization the model of his great preceptor Kant: *The Logic of Pure Knowledge, The Ethics of Pure Will* and *The Aesthetics of Pure Feeling.* In addition, Cohen wrote and edited numerous other books and articles. By the beginning of the twentieth century, Cohen had established himself as a creative philosopher of stature who had produced an independent system, though one deriving admittedly from the central position of Kant.

As a result of his significant philosophical work, Cohen became the acknowledged head of the so-called Marburg School, an intellectual current which exerted notable academic influence. Among his disciples dating from this period were Ernst Cassirer, the eminent philosopher and perhaps Cohen's most distinguished academic successor in the neo-Kantian tradition, who came to the United States and taught here after the Nazi tyranny drove him from Germany; and Jacob Klatzkin, the author of numerous philosophical works in Hebrew, including a dictionary of philosophical terms. It is of note that Karl Barth, the leader of modern Protestant neo-orthodoxy, and Martin Heidegger, perhaps the most significant figure of contemporary German thought, studied under Cohen but went in other directions. Another disciple of Cohen is Henry S. Slonimsky, emeritus professor of Jewish philosophy and theology at the Hebrew Union College–Jewish Institute of Religion, who has written an eloquent summary of Cohen's life and achievement (in *Historia Judaica,* Oct., 1942).

Cohen Encounters Anti-Semitism

How much of a Jew was Cohen during the early portion of his academic career? Interestingly enough, he kept the Jewish element in his life alive, though it was a minor and apparently submerged concern, even when he was a fervent advocate of assimilation. Thus he was affiliated with various Jewish organizations, particularly those concerned with education and was, like Freud, a loyal and proud member of the B'nai B'rith lodge. Occasionally, he would contribute an article or address on some topic relating to Jewish learning, e.g., *Heine and Judaism* and *The Sabbath in the History of Civilization.*

Aside from these rather peripheral activities, however, Cohen's interest in Judaism was negligible during the early phase of his academic career. He regarded Kant as the acme of German culture, and the latter as the peak of western civilization. Indeed, with the optimism typical of a good nineteenth-century liberal, he looked forward to increasing assimilation of German culture-patterns by Jews.

But in 1880, a few short years after he had become well-established as a full professor at Marburg, Cohen was sharply jolted by an explosion of academic anti-Semitism. He could hardly believe his eyes when one day he saw in a leading German periodical, *Preussische Jahrbücher* (Prussian Year Books), an article by an eminent German historian, Heinrich von Treitschke, attacking Jews for their questionable loyalty as an enclave within a culture. Cohen was infuriated by this because he regarded himself as a fervent German patriot, with a reverence for German *Kultur*, and particularly its contributions to philosophy, art, and social liberalism.

Stirred to his depths by these slurs against Jews and Judaism, he wrote a personal letter to Treitschke remonstrating with him for having written so prejudiced a statement, which hardly bespoke a scholar's temperament or achievement. When Treitschke ignored his letter, Cohen wrote a second time, but the German historian again ignored the Jewish thinker. Treitschke never replied to Cohen directly, but he did allude tartly, in the next issue of the magazine, to the fact that he had heard from a Jewish teacher in a small undistinguished German university who had objected to his animadversions against the Jews, but that he, Treitschke, still held to his position. This experience of academic anti-Semitism exerted a profound effect upon Cohen who had for some years been coasting along as a liberal, animated by the idea of an enlightened society that was moving forward to an era of internationalism, when group differences would be eradicated and a unified mankind would emerge.

To rebut Treitschke's slurs upon Jews, Cohen issued a pamphlet under the title *An Avowal Concerning the Jewish Question*, which in later years he credited with inaugurating his return to Judaism. In this tract, he proclaimed that he was both a Jew and a German, and that there was no contradiction between the two. A man could be both; in fact, each helped the other, since there were congruous elements in the two cultures. Cohen asserted that anyone who questioned the capacity of a Jew to be modern, liberal, German, enlightened and cultured, was virtually an enemy of progress. As for himself, Cohen averred, he had not the slightest intention of abandoning his Jewish heritage because he felt it to be not a relic of the past, but indeed the strongest incentive to modern, civilized living. He was convinced that Judaism, to which the Kantian philosophy had a deep inner congruence, still had a great contribution to make to the religious progress of mankind. Such was the message he delivered to the Fifth World Congress on Liberal Christianity and Religious Progress, held at Berlin in 1910, when he and Rabbi Emil G. Hirsch of Chicago, represented Judaism. Indeed through the years, Cohen continued to defend Judaism against depreciation and denigration by notable figures in German academic life, rebutting the attacks by such eminent personages as Rudolf Virchow, the biologist; Theodore Nöldeke, the orientalist; Gustave Schmoller, the economist; and Paul Lagarde, the orientalist and virulent anti-Semite.

Some years later, when an anti-Semitic secondary school teacher publicly maligned the Talmud, accusing it of being a vicious book teaching hatred of Christians and encouraging Jews to falsify and engage in dishonorable dealings with Christians, and a litigation ensued against these libels, Cohen served as the expert who testified in defense of the Talmud, presenting it as a compendium of Jewish cultural experience and as an ethical document teaching proper relations between Jews and non-Jews. Cohen's appearance at the Marburg court was reported in the *Jüdische Presse* of April 25, 1888 as follows:

> One must have been present, one must have heard with one's own ears, with what earnestness and determination the eminent scholar answered the questions fired at him in rapid succession by the judge and the various participating attorneys. Only then could one understand the incalculable merit of Professor Cohen's achievement, and be in a position to understand fully the profound impression he made upon all who heard him.

Incidentally, the defendant was sentenced to a fortnight in jail and assessed costs. Subsequently when Lagarde, an energetic, academic Jewbaiter who had also participated in this trial as an "expert" on the opposing side, published his testimony in an anti-Semitic sheet, Cohen felt obliged to issue his expertise in a brochure, *The Love of One's Fellow-Man in the Talmud*.

After Cohen's brush with Treitschke there was a serpent in his Garden of Eden at Marburg. He never was quite able to forget this episode, nor were the Germans able to forget that Cohen, the Jew, was a stormy petrel. From 1880 to 1912, his life was really a succession of minor storms. But he continued to teach and write and to enhance the reputation of his institution, bringing world-wide fame to the little University of Marburg. He continued to construct his system of philosophy but at the same time he grew increasingly concerned about the problem of Jewish survival. He became more and more interested in Judaism and the possibility of integrating it with Germanism. For it must be admitted that even his *Avowal*, evoked by Treitschke's attack, had been assimilationist in tone. Thus, for example, Cohen had agreed with the German historian's denunciation of certain allegedly non-German Jewish types, and of interpreters of Judaism like Graetz, who had stressed the ethnic factor in Jewish life (Cohen himself referred contemptuously to Graetz's "Palestinism").

Actually Cohen remained an ardent German nationalist all his life. He celebrated in his writing the glories of German culture —its philosophy and music (he wrote a glowing appreciation of Mozart), its religious freedom, and its economic liberalism. Indeed, so enduring was Cohen's fervent patriotism that when World War I broke out, the seventy-two year old professor was ready to accept a governmental order to journey to the United States to make pro-German propaganda in behalf of his German fatherland. That plan did not materialize, but in 1915 he wrote an article in a New York City German daily, the *Staats-Zeitung*, under the significant title of the Biblical admonition "Thou Shalt Not Go About as a Tale Bearer," in which he appealed to American Jews not to accept anti-German propaganda. During World War I he also wrote a strange piece of patriotic propaganda entitled *Germanism and Judaism* which attempted with rather shrill emotional arguments to establish the dubious

thesis that the two cultures were identical, and that therefore it
was incumbent upon Jews everywhere to respect and support
the German cause.

Retirement from Marburg

For all his Germanism and patriotism, however, Cohen was
increasingly troubled about the Jewish problem. In the 1890's
he had been stirred, as were very few others in Germany, by the
Dreyfus case which was rocking France. He felt that Jewish
security was imperiled, but he placed his hope in energetic political and social liberalism and therefore refused to support
Theodor Herzl's Zionism. He still felt that one day mankind
would progress in understanding and reasonableness with the
result that persecution and war would be abolished. In his view
it was incumbent on Jews not to retreat from the positions they
had achieved; on the contrary, they ought to remain at their
posts and to participate in all ethical endeavors together with
other men of good will, whether in the socialist trade union
movement, the reform of the universities, or the maintenance of
civil liberties.

Personally, Cohen suffered a great deal as a Jew. Despite his
academic eminence, he was never elected to the rectorship of the
University. By 1912, with the intensification of German nationalism, he became aware of a growing anti-Jewish feeling in Marburg among both faculty and students; he felt compelled finally
to withdraw his course on Schiller so as not to expose himself
to slurs of hostile students on his own patriotism. He found himself increasingly isolated and almost without friends at the very
university which he had helped to make famous. Finally, with a
heavy heart—because he still had a great deal of intellectual
energy left—he gave up his position at the University.

Cohen's active return to Judaism really began with his retirement. Increasingly he had become absorbed in the study of the
great Jewish philosophers, particularly Maimonides, and he had
begun to rediscover the profundities of the Bible. Following his
retirement, the culture and philosophy of Judaism became his
primary concern, and he was particularly preoccupied with the
formulation of a liberal philosophy of Judaism.

When Cohen left Marburg, he went on to Berlin. From 1913

to his death in April, 1918, he taught at the *Lehranstalt* (*Hochschule*) *für die Wissenschaft des Judentums* (Institute for the Scientific Study of Judaism) in Berlin, where he had lectured occasionally even before he left Marburg. It was the hope of the aging scholar, still vigorous at seventy, to reach out to a large Jewish following by means of his lectures at the Berlin Academy. Because of his own newly awakened awareness of the significance of Judaism among world religions and in western culture, he seemed animated by a passionate compulsion to arouse German Jews to an understanding of the importance of their faith. Cohen believed fervently that the Jews had a mission in the world, and that his task was to help them discharge it. He felt that if they truly lived as Jews, if they lived deeply committed ethical lives, if they mirrored to the world the one God who is ethical and spiritual, then the Messiah would come even in our lifetime. As God was the guarantor of truth and of justice, it was incumbent upon Jews to exemplify Judaism's requirement of ethical dedication. Indeed, Cohen's own life was distinguished by a lofty moral zeal and an energetic quest for justice in human relations.

The studies and lectures growing out of Cohen's preoccupation with the great sources of Judaic thought provided the materials for a fundamental treatment of the philosophy of religion. Unfortunately, however, although some aspects of his final systematic philosophy of religion were sketched in his lectures and essays, during the closing years, his magnum opus, *The Religion of Reason, from the Sources of Judaism* (1916), remained unfinished at his death. It was published posthumously in 1919 by his widow Martha, with the assistance of some of Cohen's disciples, among them Bruno Strauss who produced the index and subsequently was responsible for the revised edition of 1929.

Though this large, fundamental work, unfortunately remains as yet untranslated into English, and therefore largely inaccessible to Americans, it is unquestionably one of the most important books on the philosophy of Judaism written in the twentieth century. Its contents were heard in part at Cohen's moving lectures by not a few gifted Jews who later were to occupy significant positions in Jewish communal and intellectual life, and decisively influenced their development. Without the magisterial interpretations of Judaism by Hermann Cohen, there might conceivably have been no Buber, no Rosenzweig, and no Leo Baeck, the three great interpreters of Judaism produced by German Jewry. There might also have been no Abraham Heschel, who taught in the school of Rosenzweig, which was founded as a result of Cohen's influence. Nor, to conclude this speculative judgment, might there have been any Will Herberg, who combines certain elements of all of them. Rosenzweig regarded Cohen's work as another *Guide for the Perplexed* and declared that it would remain alive in that remote future when the language in which it had been composed would be read only by scholars.

In her preface to the first edition, Cohen's widow noted that this last great work of Cohen's was composed by him with unshaken confidence in the continued vital force of Judaism, the apex of which he saw as Messianism, through which he felt all his life long a close kinship to the prophets.

During the last six years of his life, Cohen also composed many of the essays which subsequently were gathered into three volumes, and which served as the building blocks for the last great work mentioned above. Over sixty of these essays, which Cohen had intended to dedicate to his mother, were collected and published under the title *Jüdische Schriften* (*Jewish Writings*) (1924). Incidentally the long introduction to the first volume of these collected essays on Jewish themes, by Franz Rosenzweig, one of Cohen's most eminent disciples, still provides an admirable and moving summary of the master's thought and achievement.

Though the Jewish community of Berlin recognized Cohen's worth and on his seventieth birthday celebrated the occasion by publishing anniversary volumes in his honor, disappointingly few students and auditors attended his lectures. He was hurt and embittered by this lack of interest but continued faithfully at his task. Apropos of the apparent lack of far-reaching influence of his efforts as an interpreter of Jewish philosophy, he remarked wryly that he would probably have an impressive funeral (*schöne Levayah*) one day.

Trip to Eastern Europe

Among those attending his lectures were a number of Russian Jews studying in Berlin. Through them, Cohen became vitally interested in the status of Jews in eastern Europe; he was particularly aroused by reports of the misery of Jewish students who were being victimized by discriminatory educational policies. Unlike most German Jews, he was warmly interested in his east European coreligionists. Fired with the idea of establishing Jewish-sponsored academies or universities in that part of the world, Cohen, in his seventy-second year, undertook an arduous journey to Russia and Poland in the spring of 1914.

In setting out on this mission, Cohen wanted to see Jewish life in eastern Europe and to help modernize it. From his experience with Russian-born students at Marburg, he knew that there was an almost impassable gulf between the Orthodox and the religiously indifferent, many of whom became atheists. He hoped to become for his Russian brethren a sort of Mendelssohn, whom he had called the Johanan ben Zakkai of modern Jewry; he wanted to build modern schools and help develop the kind of liberal scientific approach to Judaism which had already evolved among German Jews.

For Cohen this trip proved to be a heartwarming experience as well as a personal triumph. In the enthusiastic crowds which came to hear him in Moscow, St. Petersburg, Riga, Vilna and Warsaw, Cohen saw the traditional Jewish love of learning. He visited various educational and cultural institutions of east European Jewry and was moved again and again by demonstrations of devotion to learning, and "the thrills of Talmudic dialectic." He was also impressed by the many schools in arts, crafts and sciences, as well as by the numerous charitable institutions.

In his essay on the Jews of eastern Europe, Cohen testified to the profound impression made upon him by the rooted and sturdy Jewries he found there in the course of his travels, their vitality, and their potentiality for continued productivity and influence, if suitably modernized. He was fond of telling how, during a visit to a *heder* in Vilna, when he had asked one of the pupils, "What will happen when the Messiah will come?" the lad had replied in a flash, "Why, of course, all the *goyim* will become Jews."

It is not unlikely that Cohen's changed tone in his later writings regarding the ethnic survival of Jews reflected his experiences with Russian Jews. He had found encouragement for his plan to stimulate the organization of a strong liberal religious movement that would foster academies for advancing the scientific investigation of Judaism. Unfortunately, the outbreak of World War I put an end to these plans, but two years later he was still hoping to return to eastern Europe to finish his task. "I could wish for no better conclusion to my life," he stated, "than to have some influence, however transitory, on the life of these coreligionists of mine, whose elevation of spirit as well as equable patience and originality everyone must honor and indeed love, unless his feeling for noble naturalness has been completely dulled."

Academy for Jewish Studies

The duration of the war, however, forced Cohen to confine his educational efforts to his coreligionists in Germany, through his *Hochschule* lectures (he also did some part-time teaching at Marburg as a war-time replacement). During the last months of his life, he also plunged into a new project in Jewish education, the organization of an Academy of Jewish Studies (*Akademie für die Wissenschaft des Judentums*). In 1917, from the trenches of eastern Europe, Franz Rosenzweig had addressed to his fellow-Jews at home and above all to Cohen, as the foremost Jewish savant in Germany, a petition beginning with the words, "It is time," (*Zeit ist's*) in which he pleaded for the necessity of organizing a new movement for the re-education of the Jews in their faith. Cohen gave his full support to this effort, but he did not live to see the actual establishment of the Academy in 1919. Subsequently this learned body, in recognition of Cohen's contribution to Jewish scholarship, established a special division to stimulate the study of his work (*Hermann Cohen—Stiftung bei der Akademie für die Wissenschaft des Judentums*). It undertook the posthumous publication of his *Jewish Writings* and sponsored the publication of his general philosophical and cultural essays under the title, *Schriften zur Philosophie und Zeitgeschichte* (*On Philosophy and Contemporary Problems*). It also made possible a Hebrew translation of selections culled from his *Jewish Writings* and from *The Religion of Reason*.

Last Days

Notwithstanding the tumult and alarums of the First World War and its aftermath, Cohen continued to lecture to a limited number of students on the philosophy of Judaism. He pursued further his great spiritual adventure among the masterpieces of Judaism. He discovered the full importance of the Psalms at this time and interpreted them as decisive for the doctrine of immortality. Similarly, he penetrated to the deepest meanings of the prophet Ezekiel, Cohen's illustrious namesake of Biblical days, whom he credited with the discovery of religious individualism. In the darkest hours of the war, Cohen never betrayed bitterness, desperation or frustration but on the contrary, retained a firm hold on the Messianic idea of Judaism which he construed, in contemporary form, to involve the ultimate victory of an ethical, democratic and socialized society.

Cohen's last lectures dealt with sundry aspects of the Jewish faith and expressed fervently various aspects of his final philosophy of religion. In these discourses on Jewish theology, later assembled in *Religion of Reason,* Cohen pressed forward to new religious insights, sustained by an ardent emotion of faith and a belief in the profound moral power of Messianism. He had gradually come to see that religion is an independent cultural enterprise, not just an adjunct of ethics; and that God is more than a mere concept. Similarly, he had also discovered an infinite task beyond that of the theoretical or practical reason, namely, the unending striving to be worthy of the image of God through the pursuit of holiness.

So Cohen continued his lecturing and teaching labors until his death, dedicated to his self-appointed tasks, as the preceptor of his people in the philosophy of Judaism, the ancient insights of which he strove to make understandable and acceptable to the modern cultivated and liberal Jew, as well as to the Christian of enlightened conscience. But these activities of the period following his retirement from Marburg brought him little recognition. When the end came on July 4, 1918 only the leaders of the Jewish community attended Cohen's funeral, and throngs of Russian Jews, but neither the University of Berlin nor the Prussian Academy of Sciences sent representatives to the obsequies.

Cohen's destiny was certainly less favorable than his greatness as a man and as a scholar warranted, but infinitely worse was that which befell his survivors, whom the horrors of Nazism later engulfed. His widow disappeared without a trace; and his devoted disciple, Dr. Bruno Strauss, who had edited *The Religion of Reason*, was compelled to flee for his life, suffering the additional agony of losing in the course of his flight the collection of Cohen's letters which he had assiduously assembled for the purpose of publication.

The philosopher, F. H. Heinemann, in his German work, *New Ways of Philosophy* has described Cohen as a doughty warrior of massive and powerful temperament, the greatest personality produced by German Jewry since Mendelssohn and possibly the most important Jewish philosophical theologian since Maimonides.

He was at once a believing soul filled with the spirit of Messianic faith, and at the same time he was the great phenomenon of German cultural history, deeply rooted in German humanism, in the music of Beethoven, in the living stream of European exact science, and, not least, in "his" Plato. He was a profound thinker of penetratingly keen mind, but suffused by a glowing love of mankind which peered out frequently from the stern outlines of his doctrine like the warming sun, and occasionally swept by a zeal of fantastic proportions. Hermann Cohen was a great ethical personality in action, who remained until his death strong and vital, a magnificent advocate of the Jews and Judaism.

INTERPRETATION OF RELIGION
AND JUDAISM

Hermann Cohen's approach to Judaism was that of a rationalist. He was unique in that he was the only philosopher by vocation since Philo to have immersed himself in the study of the Jewish culture complex and to have developed a complete philosophy of religion around it. As has already been suggested, Cohen, in his first period, held that essentially it was science that provided the basic knowledge on which a systematic philosophy might be constructed. At that time his view was that religion was a concern that possibly provided satisfaction for certain sentiments but was not a source of ultimate truth; and that the retention of religion was a matter of family loyalty.

Then, in a remarkable shift which developed over a period of forty years, Cohen gradually came to recognize the significance of religion in the human condition and indeed to ascribe to religion a decisive role.

Some of his disciples—including Martin Buber, Franz Rosenzweig and Ernst Simon—believed that Cohen's later ideas about religion went far beyond the framework of his original system. On the other hand, some close to him regarded Cohen's later ideas as merely a modification rather than an abandonment of his fundamental rationalist position. Whether the change in Cohen's approach represents an accommodation or a fundamental transformation, the important thing is that in the course of his later re-examination of the basic problems of religion and Judaism, Cohen produced a learned and ardent interpretation of liberal Judaism.

Concept of God

Cohen's tussle with the complex problem of religion and his ultimate championship of the God concept of authentic Judaism has been compared by the learned Yiddish writer, Abraham Coralnik, to the life work of Rabbi Levi ben Gerson, the fourteenth century Jewish philosopher whose major work was entitled *Wars of the Lord*. In Coralnik's judgment, Cohen, too, had engaged in a lifelong struggle for God, with the difference that Cohen had fought in the arena of modern Western philosophy, and had striven desperately to find a place in his earlier rigid neo-Kantian system for the God of Judaism.

Like his great teacher Kant, Cohen held that there are two sets of problems for the thinking man, one concerned with the understanding of nature—the realm of being—and the other with the understanding of ethics—of values.

What then is the connection between nature and ethics? Are they two worlds which are absolutely separated? Cohen developed the view that they do indeed have a connection, one in which religion is remarkably involved. He saw a parallelism between understanding the nature of the world and understanding the nature of ethical obligations; and he taught that religion is that which helps one to make such a connection, God being the concept that is absolutely required to establish a connection between the two worlds. Without God, the world of fact and the world of obligation or ethical value would be completely separated, with no connection between them. God is the source or origin of both the world of nature and the world of value, and is the force that unifies them.

In the early stages of his philosophizing, Cohen tended to view God as only an idea. He later developed the view, however, that truly to understand this Being was also to love Him because there is something in the nature of man that reacts with enthusiasm and love to the idea of a Being capable of unifying the cosmos. Subsequently, Cohen maintained that Judaism's great contribution to mankind was its ethical monotheism and its unique idea of God. Like Philo and Maimonides, Cohen recognized that in the idiom of the Biblical account, God has been referred to as a person. Thus, for example, He is represented as becoming indignant and then repenting of His anger, quite like human beings. In later Jewish thought, however, the concept of God was spiritualized and great effort was expended to avoid anthropomorphism and anthropathism, that is, the tendency to refer to God as though He had the form, functions or psychological attributes of human beings.

According to Cohen, Judaism emphasizes that what is important for man is not the preoccupation with God's nature, but rather the imitation of His virtues.

For man to approach the divine perfection there is required a zealous fulfillment of the religious virtues enjoined in the systematic moral code comprising the Pentateuchal legislation and prophetic and post-Biblical interpretations thereof. This life-long and continuous ethical aspiration is animated by the hope that by such conduct one would improve the world and hasten the advent of the Messianic period.

Cohen placed great stress on the uniqueness of God as crystallized in the Jewish concept. He felt that it was incorrect to assert that the great contribution of the Jew to the history of religion was the discovery of the unity of God. For such an assertion about God merely constituted a denial of the multiplicity of polytheistic gods; moreover, there were other theories of the cosmos which have affirmed its unity, such as the pantheism of Spinoza. For Cohen, the decisive contribution of Judaism was its doctrine of the uniqueness of God, His incomparable difference from anything available to human experience. This otherness of God precluded the possibility of any intermediary between God and man, such as is represented by the central figure of Christianity; and of course it precluded the possibility of other deities. The Judaistic doctrine of the uniqueness of God implied that nothing could be compared to God, and that any analogy of God with anything save Himself was an absurdity, as He alone possesses singularity.

Creation

Whereas traditional Judaism holds that God created the world at a specific point of time, Cohen, like other liberal interpreters of Judaism, maintained that the creative process is eternal and that there is a constant renewal of the work of creation. Man is a co-author and co-adjutant with God in perfecting the work of creation. In His goodness God renews daily the work of creation through the activity of those who imitate Him by living an ethical life. To believe in God means to assert a relationship of God to the world. The uniqueness of God has as its consequence the creation of the world, the coming into being of nature. Creation is thus a necessary attribute of a unique God, and not a contradiction of reason, nor a mystery the solution of which has to be assigned to a type of knowing different from that pursued in the realm of science. Cohen cited one rabbinical exegesis of the very opening verse of the Bible—the account of Creation, which is apparently oriented to this rationalistic perspective: "In the beginning God created heaven and earth." Now *be-reshit*, the first Hebrew word in this clause and indeed the very first word of the Bible, means "in the beginning" or "at the head." But *be-reshit* may also mean "with perfection." Thus, Cohen points out, the first verse of the Bible may be construed as really affirming that "with perfection God created the world." It is part of the concept of a unique God, utterly transcendent and incomparable, that creation, the sum of things entire, should flow out of His unique essence.

To the reflective mind, therefore, creation does not mean that once upon a time the divine Being had an extraordinary explosion of power, which resulted in the world's coming into being. If God is a unique Being out of whom the world proceeds, then creation is an incessant and infinite process. This idea, Cohen insisted, is actually expressed in the liturgy: "Thou renewest daily Thy work of creation."

Revelation

Another aspect of God's relation to the world is that of the process of revelation. In traditional theology this refers to an historical event on Mount Sinai, a unique disclosure at a definite point in time of God's instruction or direction. In Cohen's view, however, the process of revelation is tantamount to man's total quest for truth, including both scientific and religious or ethical matters. Accordingly in his judgment, that religion is the most profound which does least violence to the total reflective potentiality of man. In this interpretation, revelation may be said to have occurred whenever a new truth has been perceived. So, too, both the beauty and profundity of the Psalms and the harmony and grandeur of the universe bespeak a revelation of the divine.

Messianism and the Jewish Prophets

The culmination of the ethical approach to life is Messianism, which next to the emphasis on the uniqueness of God, is basic in Cohen's systematic philosophy of Judaism. Messianism involves a confidence in the efficacy of human endeavor to approach ever closer to the model of God's perfection; indeed it presupposes faith in the inherent potentialities of man for achieving a more humane world in the future. This amelioration is not expected in the traditional "world-to-come." Rather it is a this-worldly concept similar to the nineteenth-century ideal of humanitarianism, with its emphasis on the reconciliation of the nations and the unification of mankind, as well as on the achievement of inner peace for the individual.

It was such a Messianic faith that made Cohen a fervent apostle of democracy and religious socialism. His socialist outlook, though influenced by the doctrine of progress current in the nineteenth century and by Kant's book on perpetual peace, stemmed from his Messianism.

The Great Achievement of Hebrew Prophecy

In connection with his development of the concept of Messianism, Cohen provided one of the finest expositions of the nature and significance of Hebrew prophecy ever formulated. A liberal in religion, who had been deeply influenced both by Reform Judaism and liberal Protestant theology, Cohen accepted the view that in the evolution of Judaism the prophets played a unique role. They moralized religion and emancipated the life of piety from the incubus of myth. The great religious revolution they wrought resulted in the victory of ethics in religion; and the entire subsequent evolution of Judaism can be construed as a continuous re-affirmation of the pristine doctrine promulgated by the prophets.

The prophets never tired of emphasizing the infinite and eternal responsibility of man to achieve sanctification by emulating the pattern of God. Thus by teaching the recognition of obligations to one's fellow man, be he Israelite or non-Israelite, the prophets enjoined a profound concern for man and set forth a program of practical activity to implement this concern. They were not preoccupied with speculations concerning the ultimate meaning of life and death, but rather with the interpretation of poverty as the primary manifestation of human misfortune, which they construed in a manner designed to enkindle a unique feeling of sympathy for the suffering of one's fellow man.

The prophet, when aroused to such fellow-feeling, became a practical implementer of ethics, a statesman and a jurist, as a consequence of his concern to mitigate or terminate the sufferings of the poor. For the prophet, this sympathy for the hurt of the underprivileged became the primary element of human feeling, that in which he discovered his fellow man. In Cohen's view, prophecy and Messianism brought Hebrew social thought to a level above the highest attained by the Greeks.

The Jewish People and Its Law

Cohen's indissoluble ties to the eternal sources of Judaism appeared very clearly in the high value he attributed to the Jewish community, and in his emphasis upon the linkage between the ethical and religious spirit of Judaism and the Jewish congregation—its law, its prayer and its liturgy—as expressions of Jewish monotheism. This deep rooting in the Jewish spirit made possible his wonderful comprehension of the universal, humane content of Jewish monotheism, as it was expressed in the ideas of the uniqueness of God, creation, revelation, the love of God and the love of man, repentance, atonement, salvation and peace. Through Cohen's love for the eternal verities of Judaism, there was enkindled and fortified a love for the Jewish community in its individuality and its uniqueness, its law and its liturgy, which are manifestations of the Jewish spirit. So Cohen gradually perceived unique existential values in the continued existence of the Jewish people (his quaint term of endearment for it was "this tiny people of tradesmen," *"dieses kleines Handelsvölkchen"*), quite apart from any abstract contribution it might make to the dissemination of the monotheistic idea.

The people of Israel were necessary for the establishment of their religion, and this is the true significance of the election of Israel. It is also patent that the survival of monotheism was linked to the survival of the Jewish ethnic group after its statehood had been lost. Throughout its history, however, the deepest spirits of Israel have regarded nationality not as an end in itself but as an indispensable instrumentality for the maintenance and perpetuation of the religion. Because nationality was always related to religion, it became possible for the national factor to be idealized. Consequently Cohen admitted that nationality must remain the necessary basis for the perpetuation of the Jewish religion, as long as the latter was confronted by other forms of monotheism. Of course for Cohen, the idealistic philosopher, with his supreme confidence in reason and the creative power of mind in the universe, Judaism would theoretically survive (of necessity) in a world governed by rationality, if only one could demonstrate from the great Jewish sources, that it was a religion of reason. But he recognized that there was also a need for practical strategies to insure the survival of Judaism as it existed in the midst or by the side of other forms of monotheism, themselves having a certain measure of rationality. What was required to insure the perpetuation of Judaism was, therefore, a certain isolation, and this was provided by the law, which appeared as indispensable for the maintenance of Israel's unique vision of the divine.

Modernism has eroded much of the traditional law, which by some Jews is observed only on the festivals and by some, indeed, only on the Day of Atonement. Yet this traditional law has served as a bulwark against the leveling down of pure monotheism and its doctrine of the atonement of man before God, and the redemption of man by God. So, too, the devout observance of the Sabbath has provided the Jewish community an index and an emblem of the basic social and ethical doctrines of Judaism. Finally, the traditional pattern of observance has expressed a protest against the transformation of the meaning of the Sabbath into a day commemorating the resurrection of Christ, the basic idea underlying the Christian Sabbath.

The value of Judaism's law, Cohen believed, is by no means exhausted in this negative aspect of isolation. Indeed, in its diverse forms and usages, the Hebraic law actually contains a positive power to stimulate, fortify and deepen religious ideas and feelings. The primary purpose of the law is not to isolate but rather to idealize all earthly activity. The service of God is not confined to the synagogue, for the law fills and penetrates all of life. The unique purpose over-arching life is that of sanctification. The merit of the fathers remains vital, particularly in the law, which is bound to endure as a dynamic and catalyzing factor by virtue of this authority of the past that inheres in it.

In the *Religion of Reason* Cohen assigned considerable value to the distinctive empirical existence of the Jewish people. He held that the concept of Israel's mission and vocation had received concrete expression in the fact of Israel's historic existence. Yet the uniqueness and incomparability of Israel, designated in Holy Writ as a people dwelling apart, had a special and momentous import that went beyond the Jewish destiny. Indeed it became emblematic for all mankind, for the very essence of the election of the Jews was that Israel became the symbol of humanity. God's love for mankind was symbolized by his love for Israel; and the "chosen people" became chosen humanity. The sheer survival, the dedicated self-perpetuation of the Jewish people through its isolation was a correlate of Jewry's involvement with the sacred law, and was a function of Israel's idealization of all terrestrial activity, an idealization that Israel effected by linking all such activity with the divine.

Attitude to Zionism

Cohen made a sharp distinction, however, between the ethnic factor involved in the continued maintenance of the Jewish group, and the re-establishment of the Jewish state advocated by the Zionist program. This advocacy seemed to him to be in contradiction to the requirements of Jewish Messianism. For while the separatism of the Jewish community remained a historic necessity because an ethnic culture group was indispensable for the perpetuation of the Jewish religion, the political and nationalistic isolation involved in the re-establishment of a separate Jewish state would, in Cohen's judgment, negate the Messianic mission of Judaism. Cohen felt deeply that it was necessary for the Jewish people to strive for self-perpetuation only through the form of Diaspora existence as ethnic enclaves within the nations, but not to strive for re-establishment of Jewish nationality or statehood.

Consequently Cohen remained a steadfast foe of political Zionism. It must be recognized that for all his philosophic eminence he was bound to the intellectual climate and illusions of his epoch and in particular that he remained wedded to its liberalism and assimilationism—as far as solutions to the so-called Jewish problem were concerned. Indeed he appears never really to have felt deeply enough the precariousness of the Jewish lot as did Baeck, Buber, or Rosenzweig. Notwithstanding the appeals made to him by Martin Buber and other spokesmen for the Zionist cause, Cohen remained steadfast in his anti-Zionist position and resolutely opposed the renascence of the nationalistic political ideal among Jews.

The Legacy of Cohen

The legacy of Cohen is twofold—his written works and his life of dedication to the cause of Judaism. The former comprises his researches into Jewish philosophy and theology, and the interpretations of Jewish ideas and ideals contained in his lectures, articles and books. Yet the personal qualities of this fervent academic advocate of Judaism, his ardor, his profound religious feeling, his passion and zeal—also are part of the legacy, and by no means the least. That an eminent secular academician and philosopher should, in the cultural and social setting of Cohen's time and place, have remained faithful to Judaism is in itself a rare phenomenon. This commitment of Cohen's was precious and exemplary, and undoubtedly served as a powerful stimulus to the rediscovery of the Jewish heritage on the part of central European Jews. Nowhere can this be seen more clearly than in the influence exerted by Cohen upon Franz Rosenzweig.

As in the case of Mendelssohn, Cohen was more than an academic philosopher, and his influence upon his age is to be explained in good part by the force and ardor of his personality. For all his conceptual sophistication, Cohen's heart remained dissatisfied with the God-idea of the philosophers, and like Pascal he yearned for the warmth and exaltation of the God of Abraham, Isaac and Jacob. It was Cohen's prophetic passion for justice and humanitarianism, and his proud and intrepid espousal of the Jewish cause, that won him the accolade he enjoyed. When the Jewish masses in eastern Europe flocked to hear him lecture it was the faithful and ethical personality that won their reverence, not the *Herr Doktor Geheimrat*, the notable savant of international reputation.

Cohen's great intellectual service to modern Jewry was his demonstration of the viable character of the Jewish faith for a modern, scientifically trained and philosophically oriented Jew. His reaffirmation of what he interpreted to be his ancestral faith of truth, his reacceptance of a religious absolute, and his profound exploration of basic themes or motifs in Judaism such as prophecy or Messianism, reawakened the interest of many alienated Jews and brought about a new respect for the antique tradition, which he interpreted to be the most progressive of religious systems. In his fervent expositions of the ethical and Messianic components of the Jewish prophetic faith, and in his treatment of ethical fulfillment as an eternal task, and of eternity as a transcendent Messianic goal, all couched in the ardent language of the prophet—he was wont to refer to his lectures and essays as homilies—there was disclosed anew the prophetic ardor of classical Judaism.

Franz Rosenzweig perceived that in his final period Cohen, by his formulation of the doctrine of correlation of the realm of being and his emphasis upon the individual's relation to God and his personal commitment, had pierced the scaffolding of Kantianism and was approaching an existential position. This interpretation of Cohen's final philosophical position made him, in Rosenzweig's judgment, a leader in a form of thought no longer determined by the long tradition of European classical philosophy. Rosenzweig saw indices of this particularly in Cohen's interpretation of his own Jewishness and in his evaluation of the Jewish fate. For Rosenzweig himself there were no illusions regarding the anomalous and hazardous character of the Jewish position in the world, and no tendency to idealize the painful reality.

It must be admitted that the spirit of the present age is not overly hospitable to traditional systems of idealistic philosophy. Consequently, at the present juncture of history, Cohen's basic philosophical stance and his specific formulations in the philosophy of religion generally, and Judaism in particular, appear alien to the dominant intellectual atmosphere. Yet insofar as rationalistic interpretations of Judaism are abroad today, Cohen's influence lingers on. The theology of liberal Judaism has never found a deeper and grander formulation. Wherever in Jewish religious thought there is a rationalistic trend, even when the direction and conclusion of the particular intellectual enterprise are different, the influence of Cohen abides, as in the case of Mordecai M. Kaplan. For Cohen was also an admirer of that "dominion of reason" represented classically in Jewish religious thought by Maimonides, Ahad Ha-am, and in a more secularist-naturalist direction by Kaplan. Granted that many of Cohen's specific interpretations of Jewish life, such as his antipathy toward Zionism, his advocacy of nineteenth-century assimilationism, and his pro-Germanism, have been superseded by the passage of time and the changed constellation of the Jewish position, there is still sufficient merit in the corpus of Cohen's work on Judaism to warrant renewed attention and study by the questing Jew of liberal spirit.

In the history of thought there have been oscillations between idealism and empiricism in various forms, and between rationalism and irrationalism. One day there may be expected a recoil from the contemporary depreciations of rationalism, and in that day Hermann Cohen will again receive the attention that his notable philosophical achievement merits. In the meantime any questing Jew who seeks a noble exposition of his faith by a creative philosophical mind which united dialectical acumen with spiritual fervor will find much in the pages of Cohen to guide and sustain him in the quest for a mature and viable faith.

FOR FURTHER READING

Books by Hermann Cohen

Religion of Reason Out of the Sources of Judaism (New York: Ungar Publishing Company, 1972). Cohen's *magnum opus* in a readable, though still difficult, English translation.

Books about Hermann Cohen

BOROWITZ, Eugene, *Choices in Modern Jewish Thought* (New York: Behrman House, 1983). A helpful, well written, popular introduction to Cohen's philosophy and historical significance. A good place to start one's study of Cohen.

COHEN, Arthur, *The Natural and the Supernatural Jew* (New York: Behrman House, 1979, new edition). Contains a thoughtful and provocative summary of Cohen's views.

JOSPE, Eva, editor, *Reason and Hope: Selections from the Jewish Writings of Hermann Cohen* (New York: W.W. Norton & Co., 1971). An excellent, readable, collection of some of Cohen's basic writings on specifically Jewish themes.

KAPLAN, Mordecai M., *The Purpose and Meaning of Jewish Existence* (Philadelphia: Jewish Publication Society, 1964). An important work of summary, translation and critical analysis by one major Jewish thinker on another. Not for beginners.

MELBER, Jehuda, *Hermann Cohen's Philosophy of Judaism* (New York: Jonathan David, 1968). Though a work of broad, exegetical scope, not one of much philosophical depth or profundity.

ROTENSTREICH, Nathan, *Jewish Philosophy in Modern Times* (New York: Holt, Rinehart & Winston, 1968). Remains the most extensive and technical summary of Cohen's philosophical position in English.

5. Leo Baeck
[1873-1956]

HENRY WALTER BRANN

L E O Baeck, rabbi of the once important Berlin Jewish community, stands out as one of the most representative religious
personalities of twentieth-century Jewry. A distinguished theo
logian and an emblem of Jewish courage during the Nazi holocaust, he displayed a complete consistency of thought, teaching,
and action that made him invulnerable to any outward assault.
His greatness lay in his almost unique combination of moral
courage, saintliness, and the profound life-long study and reap-
praisal of the indestructible values of Judaism.

Leo Baeck was born on May 23, 1873, in Lissa, in the Prussian
province of Posen. He grew up in a rabbinical family. His grandfather and great-grandfather had been rabbis, and his mother was
the daughter of the well-known rabbi of Kroman in Moravia.
His father Samuel was famed as rabbi of the congregation of
Lissa from 1864 until his death in 1912, and was also a respected
civic leader and member of the *Waisenrat* (Board in Charge of
Orphanages), taught at Lissa's municipal school, and served as
delegate of the *Deutscher Israelitischer Gemeindebund* (Union
of German Jewish Congregations). In addition, Samuel was the
author of several books in German on the Bible and Talmud and
on the history and literature of the Jewish people; the most noted
was *Geschichte des Jüdischen Volkes und seiner Literatur* (History of the Jewish People and Its Literature).[1]

Thus, young Leo's life was steeped in Jewish religious tradition; in spite of its Orthodoxy, however, the Baeck family did

not remain aloof from the non-Jewish environment but mingled freely with advocates of German nationalism. The Baecks had always managed to be loyal Jews and loyal Germans at the same time; even after the Nazi assault Leo Baeck did not basically alter his attitude as he confided to this writer in an interview in New York in 1949.

Samuel Baeck's Orthodoxy was free of fanaticism; he was broad-minded and always stressed spiritual and ethical values in preference to the mere practice of ritual forms. This does not mean that the father was able to agree with his son's later religious liberalism, but he was at least able to understand and appreciate the reasons for Leo's approval of a modified prayer service.

There is no record of any passionate discussion or argument between father and son, but then debate and controversy seemed out of character for the studious young man. Leo Baeck, early in his life, developed the detached attitude of a scholar who was more interested in explaining the history or genesis of religious institutions than he was in taking sides to evaluate them. Two bloody world wars and several formidable revolutions were needed to modify his basic non-partisanship to any considerable extent.

Studies in Breslau and Berlin

After young Leo was graduated with high honors from the Lissa Gymnasium in 1891, he decided to follow the family tradition and become a rabbi. He could not have chosen a more propitious moment for starting such a career in Germany than at this historic juncture. German Jewry had made enormous strides in social recognition, financial security, and middle-class respectability since the Franco-Prussian War, and had just begun to organize a religious and community life second to none in the world. Since Breslau, capital of the Prussian province of Silesia, was only a short distance away from his home town, Baeck selected its *Jüdisch-Theologisches Seminar* as the natural place for his initial training. The first rabbinical seminary to be founded in Germany in 1854, it was dedicated to traditional Judaism, but, unlike the *yeshivot* of eastern Europe, it permitted "freedom of investigation." When it was closed by the Nazis in November,

1938 and its library of more than thirty thousand volumes con-
fiscated, it had trained some two hundred and fifty rabbis, who
occupied pulpits throughout the world.

Living and studying in Breslau opened new vistas to the fledg-
ling theologian, who eagerly availed himself of its great scientific,
literary and artistic resources. Baeck also took courses in philosophy and history at the University of Breslau.

Nothing impressive or exceptional has been reported about
Leo's concepts and actions at this time. His colleagues describe
him as an extremely industrious student who never missed any
class but who intentionally kept aloof from "extracurricular activities." He was so deeply immersed in his studies and scholarly
pursuits that he did not pay any sizable attention to the world
outside the Seminary, the University, and his own study. Since
his ideas were still in the process of formation, he refrained from
committing himself on any subject of discussion other than those
connected with his Seminary classes. Once, when asked why he
did not put aside certain hours for recreation and relaxation, he
replied: "Where could I find any finer recreation and spiritual
pleasure than in the writings and meditations of the great thinkers of the past?"

After several years at Breslau, Baeck was encouraged by his
teachers to continue his studies at Berlin. In that city he enrolled
at the *Hochschule für die Wissenschaft des Judentums* (Academy for the Science of Judaism), the outstanding institution of
liberal Judaism in Germany, which attracted Jewish students
from all over the world. At the same time, he matriculated at
the equally famed Friedrich Wilhelm University, where he
studied toward a doctorate in philosophy.

The young student from Lissa made great strides in Berlin.
It was a blessing for Baeck that his training period ended before
the turbulent twentieth century, marked by wars and revolutions and, at the same time, by incredible advances in science
and technology. His generation was the last to enjoy an unbroken, unified world view.

In 1897 Baeck received his rabbinical diploma from the *Hochschule* and at about the same time his doctoral degree from the
University of Berlin. His dissertation on *Spinoza's erste Einwirkungen auf Deutschland* (The First Effects of Spinoza's Ideas
on German Thought), which dealt with the influence of Spi-

noza's pantheistic concepts on German philosophy, was well received.[2]

First Pulpit: Oppeln

Shortly afterward, at the age of twenty-four, Baeck accepted the post of rabbi in the Jewish community in Oppeln, Silesia. This was the first test of the scholarly young rabbi's capacity for adjustment to reality. For a man of Baeck's sophistication, who during the past six years had moved in the brilliant intellectual circles of Breslau and Berlin, it was not easy to return to the small-town atmosphere of Oppeln. And yet there were advantages. First of all, since Baeck was the only full rabbi in Oppeln, all religious matters of the community were placed in his hands. Furthermore, the quieter pace gave him time for reflection and writing. He was remarkably self-disciplined, getting up at five o'clock every morning so that he would have time for uninterrupted study. Would such a young man, who had to develop his own ideas on the Jewish religion, ever have been able to develop a theology had he remained in the hustle of Berlin, or among the somewhat arrogant disputants at the Breslau Seminary? The fact is that Baeck stayed in his post at Oppeln for ten years, and by the time he left, he had already published several major works.

In spite of these advantages, the leap from the scholarly life to the ministry in a relatively small community was difficult; in the beginning Baeck suffered heartache and inner conflict. But he did succeed in winning over those congregants who liked his serious approach to problems. Evidently Baeck reached the greatest popularity he was ever to enjoy during his rabbinate in Oppeln. It was certainly the only period in which he tried to adapt his lofty philosophical concepts to the level of the average congregant. He delivered sermons of great simplicity which met the emotional needs of his audience.

In spite of his own Orthodox upbringing, Baeck had early decided to introduce a liberal "Conservative" service, because the latter was more dignified and had a far stronger emotional appeal than did most Orthodox services. This type of service, which the majority of German Jews preferred, differed from the Orthodox by the introduction of the organ, the inclusion of women in the choir, a slight abbreviation of the liturgy, the translation of certain Hebrew prayers into German, and the elimination of a few prayers. It retained, however, the covering of the head and the separation of the sexes, with the women sitting in the balcony. One factor contributing to the beauty of the liberal service was its music based on the great Sulzer-Lewandowsky tradition, which Baeck had enjoyed in Conservative synagogues in both Breslau and Berlin.

Rabbi in Düsseldorf

In 1907, after a decade of service in Oppeln, Baeck was offered the rabbinate in Düsseldorf, a lively but still not too large a city in the Rhineland. In the meantime, he had acquired national prominence among German Jewry by publishing, in 1905, his book *Das Wesen des Judentums* (*The Essence of Judaism*). Appearing as a reply to the liberal Protestant Adolf von Harnack's famed book *What Is Christianity?* this work furnished German Judaism, at a crucial moment in its history, with a lucid explanation and interpretation of Judaism. The man who was able to satisfy this urgent need for such a rationale was bound to emerge, sooner or later, as the intellectual and spiritual leader of the German-Jewish community.

In assuming his duties in Düsseldorf, Baeck, at the age of thirty-four, became acquainted with a quite different type of Jewish congregant from that of the Silesian group he had served so faithfully during the preceding ten years. While Jews in the eastern provinces of Prussia were for the most part the offspring of more-or-less recent immigrants from Poland and Russia, though Oppeln itself boasted a large number of old, well-established families, their coreligionists in the Rhineland belonged to families which had lived there continuously for several centuries. The fact that they enjoyed almost the same civil rights as non-Jews made, of course, for a much greater rate of assimilation; on the other hand, the absence of persecution had allowed Düsseldorf congregants a long, uninterrupted connection with purely religious Judaism, in the long sequence of generations, which they had come to take for granted. Furthermore, he found the Rhinelander to be more of an extrovert with a more cheerful and gregarious character than the rather reserved, serious, and occasionally somber type of the northeast; the Jews did not differ from their neighbors in this respect. Baeck, who felt more akin to the northerners, was astonished, if not somewhat embarrassed, when some of his Düsseldorf congregants came to him with their personal problems. He once confided to a friend: "One day, I saw myself exposed, for the first time in my life, to the emotional outburst of a stranger, which I had great difficulties in restraining and redirecting into objective channels."

Call to Berlin

In 1912, Baeck was called by the Berlin Jewish community to take the place of its venerable senior rabbi, Sigmund Maybaum,[3] whose health had become impaired. This was an unprecedented honor for Baeck, who was not yet forty. His new contract exempted him from any kind of teaching or supervising of religious schools, a chore imposed on all his other rabbinic colleagues. Instead, he was granted permission to teach *Midrash* and homiletics at the *Hochschule für die Wissenschaft des Judentums*, the college in which he had received his own rabbinical training, and where, with the sole interruption of the World War I years, he continued to teach until 1941.

The Berlin Jewish community was run by a centralized official body, with its own democratically elected parliament of representatives from several political parties, its own synagogues, schools, a large library, and a cemetery located in Berlin-Weisensee. This vast organization was administered by professional employees with permanent status in a structure resembling Prussia's civil service. There were no independent congregations; rabbis and cantors, as well as conductors of synagogue choirs were employed directly by the Jewish community and responsible only to its leading administrative officers. Congregations had a religious rather than a social function. Members were worshippers who attended certain synagogues to celebrate religious events at particular times. There were no officers of congregations, and members took turns presiding over services.

When Baeck assumed his post as rabbi of the Berlin Jewish community, he was assigned first to the Lützowstrasse Synagogue, located near Potsdammer Strasse, an important business thoroughfare connecting the distinguished old western district with its center. After the building of the new Fasanenstrasse

Synagogue, erected in 1913 between Kantstrasse and Kurfürstendamm, main avenues of the elegant new western section of
Berlin, that became his main temple. This was a high point of
public recognition for German Jewry. Not only did Reich and
Prussian state government officials participate in the inaugura-
tion ceremonies for the new synagogue building, but even the
Kaiser sent His personal representative with a present of famed
tiles from his estate at Cadinen, West Prussia. With Baeck as its
leader, the Fasanenstrasse Synagogue became a "fashionable"
place of worship, and was frequented principally by upper
middle-class Jews who lived on the nearby Kurfürstendamm
and its adjacent streets. The services were of a modernized liberal type, i.e., with an increasing number of prayers in German.

Though many people have called Baeck the "Chief Rabbi" of
Berlin or even of Germany, such a post did not actually exist.
His position differed in no way from that of the other full-
fledged rabbis of the Berlin Jewish community, and he had no
jurisdiction over any other rabbi or over the religious policy of
the community. Baeck's distinction lay in his great scholarly
reputation, based on his broad theological and philosophical
learning. He rapidly emerged as the outstanding personality in
the German rabbinate.

But Baeck was by no means a popular preacher. In the words
of Fritz Bamberger, he "made heavy intellectual demands upon
his congregation." As soon as he discovered the full meaning of
his calling as an interpreter and analyst of modern Judaism, he
felt an inner urge to communicate his findings to his audiences.
It is true that he did not confuse the pulpit with the rostrum of
the academic lecturer and never delivered in the synagogue the
kind of lecture which was appropriate for his disciples at the
Hochschule; at the same time, he refrained from cheap popularization of complicated ideas and never indulged in hollow pom-
posity. If a train of thought which Baeck tried to impart was
complex, he formulated it in simple and easily understood terms,
but without shallow oversimplifications or collective flattery.
Though he felt compelled to emphasize certain parts of his sermons by distinctive oratorical methods, he never sacrificed intellectual content for rhetorical effect.

Another distinctive aspect of Baeck's preaching was that, unlike the practice of other ministers, who raise their voices in pon-

tifical fashion in order to express even the most banal things, he did not "play-act" but was actually deeply emotionally involved whenever his voice took on an unusual tone. The inability to grasp what happened to Baeck in a moment of emotion or exaltation, which was equal to a genuine religious experience, once led an influential member of the Berlin Jewish community's Board of Trustees to ridicule what he called "Baeck's private conversations with God." But most listeners, even those who did not always understand the rabbi's brilliant formulations, were moved by his deep sincerity and the strength of his ethical convictions.

Endowed by nature with a certain sad, plaintive tone in his voice, Baeck used a strong lamenting pitch whenever he wanted to emphasize sentences. He was not given to express joy, pleasure, or exuberance in his voice even if the contents of the sermon were cheerful. This writer cannot remember one single passage of a Baeck sermon which might have evoked a smile or laughter among the audience. This was not due to lack of a sense of humor but rather to Baeck's serious approach. He never joked or used the word "I" or "me" in public. In his farewell address at Oppeln, in fact, he asserted that "in this pulpit the word 'I' has never been used. The person always recedes behind the cause."

Army Chaplain

The friendly situation which Baeck and the Jewish community enjoyed was to change after the outbreak of World War I in July, 1914. When a wave of patriotic enthusiasm shook the German people after the mobilization of the Imperial Army and Navy, the Jews outdid themselves in their manifestations of loyalty to the Kaiser and the Reich. Thousands of youngsters who had not even reached military age volunteered for the armed forces. Many more were drafted in accordance with the severe German laws which forced every able-bodied man from eighteen to forty-five into military service whether he was a family man or not. Baeck was named Jewish army chaplain by the Berlin Jewish community and immediately received an official nomination by the military authorities of the Reich.

This assignment produced a profound change in the life of

the rabbi. It meant not only leaving his wife and daughter but also giving up his cherished teaching activities and his newly acquired tasks as a rabbi of the Berlin community. But Baeck had an extraordinary sense of duty. During his chaplaincy, he succeeded in instilling in Jewish soldiers the basic tenets of biblical and Talmudic philosophy. He showed them ways and means of concentrating on mental tasks in the midst of turmoil and danger. Whenever he was able to assemble a number of Jewish soldiers for the celebration of the High Holy Days or other holidays, he prepared sermons dealing with the immediate problems of troops at the front, as seen in a broad religious context.

Baeck's views on war in general and the struggle of the Central Powers in particular are difficult to describe. First of all, his view underwent considerable change during the different stages of World War I. Though by nature peaceful and profoundly impressed with the various peace messages of the prophets and the high Messianic ideals of Judaism, the rabbi felt compelled to refrain from any pacifist zealotry as he felt that this war might have providential sanction. Like the majority of German and Austrian intellectuals, Baeck believed fully in the moral superiority and justice of the cause of the Central Powers, at least during the first three years of the war. He shared this political blindness with Sigmund Freud, who rejoiced in the first victories of the German and Austrian armies, and only in 1918 recognized the imperialistic designs of the governments of Berlin and Vienna. In Baeck's case, his position as chaplain attached to the German General Staff made his awakening even slower and more difficult. The revelations contained in Woodrow Wilson's famous fourteen-point message came as a shock to the loyal chaplain of the Imperial German Army; still greater was the impact on him of the November, 1918 Revolution, with the toppling of the throne and the flight of the Kaiser. The total collapse of the German front brought about a chaotic situation for all in charge of military units and their immediate assistants, and it took all Baeck's moral strength to avoid a serious nervous breakdown. He was hospitalized for a time in an army clinic, where he suffered from what we would today call a psychosomatic disorder, and fears were expressed in Berlin circles as to whether he would be able to take up his full rabbinical duties.

The Post-War Years

Yet, in 1919, Baeck recovered from his illness, and returned to his pulpit at the Fasanenstrasse Synagogue and to his lectures and seminars at the *Hochschule*. The thirteen years which followed represented a peak in his spiritual and intellectual development. It was at the same time a period of socio-cultural flowering for German Jewry: in the theatrical world were Max Reinhardt, Victor Barnowsky, and the brothers Carl Meinhard and Rudolph Bernauer, all outstanding stage directors; there were conductors like Bruno Walter, Leo Blech, Otto Klemperer; great singers like Herman Jadlowker, Joseph Schwarz, and Richard Tauber; art was represented by such outstanding painters as Max Liebermann and Leeser Ury, the creator of a deeply moving *Jeremiah*; among journalists were Georg Bernhard and Theodor Wolff, editors of the *Vossische Zeitung* and *Berliner Tageblatt* respectively; there were also the novelist Lion Feuchtwanger and the physicist Albert Einstein. That such great men remained faithful to the basic tenets of the Jewish religion and the intrinsic values of Judaic scholarship was due, in part at least, to Leo Baeck. Einstein made it quite clear that he believed in the existence of a superior being and that he was proud of belonging to the Jewish people who had given the world "the highest code of ethics." Feuchtwanger considered the *shemah* his and every other Jew's "supreme credo" which "no deviation in the observation of external rites could ever tear from his heart."

Baeck soon broadened his Jewish activities far beyond his rabbinical duties and his teaching tasks at the *Hochschule*. Not only did he become president of the *Allgemeiner Deutscher Rabbinerverband* (General Association of German Rabbis) in 1922, but later he was elected grand president of the B'nai B'rith in the German District, a post he held until the dissolution of the Order by the Nazis. He also accepted the position of associate president of Keren Hayesod, an agency of the Zionist movement. This was evidence of his independent spirit, as the majority of the Berlin Jewish community was still anti-Zionist and its rabbis were sometimes sharply censored for active participation in Zionist organizations. A little later Baeck also became a member of the Jewish Agency for Palestine.

Meanwhile, Baeck's reputation as a thinker, philosopher, and independent liberal theologian had spread far beyond Jewish circles. The well-known philosopher Hermann Count Keyserling, head of the "School of Wisdom" in Darmstadt, called on Baeck to lecture at his school, the faculty of which consisted of people of international fame, including Rabindranath Tagore, the Hindu poet and thinker. Baeck accepted the invitation and taught there several times on topics of Judaeo-Christian interest. Though other Jewish thinkers like Martin Buber were frequently invited to participate in lecture-meetings organized by non-Jewish institutions in Germany, such an honor was rarely bestowed upon an officiating rabbi.

Writings on Judaism and Christianity

In Baeck's time, it was considered "tolerant" and "broad-minded" both in Jewish and Christian circles to pay friendly lip service to the "equality" of both faiths, as far as their religious values were concerned. Baeck, however, expressed his own conviction of the superiority of Judaism as a religion. He was one of the first to claim Jesus as a Jew, and to restore his place in Jewish tradition, though he did not make him the equal of the great prophets and reformers of the Jewish faith, as Buber had done. His essay, *The Gospel as a Document of History*, re-established the original life story of Jesus, seeking to clear away the various strata that were added to it in later periods in order to make Jesus conform to the concept of the Messiah.

In his essay on *Romantic Religion*, originally published in 1922, Baeck calls Judaism a classical, and Christianity a romantic religion. The distinctive character of romantic religion is its "ecstatic abandonment"; in it, "thinking is only a dream of feeling." Therefore, Schleiermacher, the theologian of German romanticism, defined religion as "the feeling of absolute dependence." Longing is the main characteristic of romantic Christianity, while in Judaism, a classical religion, "the irrational is the profound truth of life and therefore also the profound source of Law." Romanticism, says Baeck, lacks any strong ethical impulse, any will to conquer life ethically.

In another essay on *Judaism in the Church* (1925) Baeck shows that Jewish ideas have a two-fold life, one within, and another outside of Judaism. The real history of Jewish ideas outside of Judaism is to be found in Christianity. "Every change in the spiritual and religious life of the Church was basically a taking of a stand with respect to those ideas." Baeck follows this development from Paul to modern Protestantism, reaching the significant conclusion: Judaism "can be fought against and (it) can be forced to give ground, but now, as it did then, it will spring back with new vigor."

Baeck's famous book, *Die Pharisäer* (*The Pharisees*), which was republished in 1947 in New York, first appeared in 1927. This work did much to dispel misconceptions connected with the name, activities, and teachings of what Baeck called that "sainthood of exclusiveness and purification." Since the vilification of the Pharisees forms an integral part of Christian dogmatism and its popular interpretation, leaders of German Protestantism and Catholicism immediately felt obliged to enter into a discussion of Baeck's book, which closed with the seemingly paradoxical statement: "Pharisaism was a heroic effort to prepare the ground for the kingdom of God." If this were true, Jesus and the Pharisees had the same goal and the *Perushim* (Pharisees) could never have planned his destruction. Indeed, the true conflict was not between the "Son of Man" and the Pharisees, but between the Pharisees and the Sadducees, who had made a compromise with the state. Though Christian theologians could not accept Baeck's interpretations, Baeck's work became a lively issue which was discussed for many months in Christian theological periodicals and other publications throughout Germany, Austria and Switzerland. Unfortunately, the onrush of Hitlerism brought this discussion to an abrupt end.

Rise of Nazism

In 1929, when the first threats of Nazism began to worry German Jews, Baeck tried to minimize the danger. Like other decent Germans and the majority of the apparently "well-entrenched" German Jews, Baeck dismissed the idea of a Nazi victory as something which "could not happen here." He published an article entitled *Neutralität* (Neutrality) in the *Blätter des Deutschen Roten Kreuzes* (*Bulletin of the German Red Cross*), in which he recommended "moderation" and a "nonpartisan attitude" toward the party strife in the Weimar Republic and states. "Permanent inner tension and permanent determination finally eliminate themselves and defeat their own purpose," he counseled. The essay emphasized "commendable restraint toward facts which cannot be changed and make any action purposeless and senseless." One year later, however, when the Nazi party sent 106 deputies to the Reichstag and became the third largest party, Baeck slowly moved toward a more realistic understanding of the peril. Not quite four years later, in 1933, Hitler seized power and began preparations for the eventual extinction of six and a half million German and other European Jews.

In these evil times, Baeck's leadership and his responsibility for the fate of German Jews was put to the crucial test. The Nazis did their unprecedented work of genocide in cleverly camouflaged stages destined to lull their victims into deceptive security. In order to give their work of annihilation an appearance of respectability and orderliness, Hitler organized the so-called *Reichsvertretung der Deutschen Juden* (Reich's Representative Council of German Jews), of which Baeck was nominated president, and which, in the eyes of naive Germans and Jews outside of Germany, looked like a kind of Jewish parliament. Baeck still hoped that something like a cultural ghetto existence was possible for the Jewish people. But this proved to be an illusion, because the growing terror of the Gestapo, which sent its henchmen, spies, and stool pigeons into every Jewish gathering, from the outset precluded such a development. During the first five years of Nazi rule the *Hochschule* arranged courses in the humanities which were conducted by famous Jewish professors who had been unceremoniously dismissed from their regular university posts. Among the latter were the celebrated economist and sociologist Franz Oppenheimer and the philosopher Fritz Kaufmann.

In 1935, the infamous Nuremberg laws were promulgated. Baeck fearlessly criticized the Nazis, composing a special prayer which was sent to all Jewish congregations in Germany and read during *Rosh Ha-Shanah* services from the pulpit: "With the same fervor with which we have confessed our sins, the sins of the individuals and those of the community, we express our contempt for the lies with which we were accused, and we solemnly say that the calumnies which were raised against our religion and its teachings do not touch our dignity. High do we hold the shield of our venerable religion against all vituperations. We shall answer all attempts to injure us by continuing to walk in the ways of Judaism and to fulfill its commandments."

When the Nazis learned of Baeck's authorship of this prayer, he was summoned to appear at Gestapo headquarters in Berlin and threatened with arrest and deportation to a concentration camp. After being warned, he was released and left unmolested; for the regime was just preparing the spectacular Olympic Games to be celebrated in 1936 in Berlin, and foreign countries had to be led to believe that reports on Nazi horrors were "exaggerated" and even "absolutely untrue." As the persecutions against Jews grew bolder, however, Baeck was repeatedly arrested and his "hearings" at the Gestapo center became more and more dangerous. His friends abroad therefore beseeched the rabbi to leave Germany, as so many other prominent Jewish and anti-Nazi leaders were doing. Baeck rejected all such suggestions with the statement that he considered it his rabbinic and moral duty to stay with his people and comfort them.

Tragic events followed each other at a rapid pace. In November, 1938, the Nazis staged the horrible *Kristallnacht* during which synagogues everywhere in Germany were burned, and in many places members of the Jewish community were rounded up or sent to notorious concentration camps. Even after the economic boycott and the dismissal of Jews from all possible occupations, there remained in cities like Berlin, Hamburg, Munich, and Stuttgart thousands of both religious and purely "racial" Jews who were unable to emigrate. This hard core of the Jewish remnant, among whom were many elderly, sick men and women, was harassed and its members had to put up a daily if not hourly fight for the preservation of their lives. They could not hide from the attacks of their ruthless persecutors because every Jew had to wear a yellow *Magen David* sewn on his clothes.

Call to America Unheeded

Early in 1939, Baeck received a call from the Rockdale Avenue Temple of Cincinnati, offering him the post of associate rabbi. Prominent foreign Jews, who still had access to the rabbi, stressed the absolute necessity of his leaving Germany at the earliest possible moment. Dozens of cables from the United States and telephone calls from all over the world urged Baeck to accept the Cincinnati offer and thus save his life, not only for his own sake, but for the sake of Judaism. Baeck refused to abandon his coreligionists, who, he felt, needed his help and guidance more than ever at this moment. He felt that, like the captain of a sinking ship, he had to stay until all his crew were saved. There were two other reasons why Rabbi Baeck wanted to hold out in Germany to the bitter end. First, he had the impression that the Nazi bigwigs would refrain, at least to a certain degree, from their most ruthless misdeeds as long as he was around as a witness; he could not be removed from the scene without stirring up a world scandal, which would be prejudicial to Hitler's secret war preparations. He felt that once he was abroad, the Nazis would proceed much more quickly with their sinister plans. The second reason was psychological, and Baeck himself was perhaps not fully aware of it. He was now a man of sixty-five, for whom adjustment to a foreign country and environment would be difficult, especially for someone like himself, who was so deeply entrenched in the German language and civilization. He regarded himself as an integral part of German culture, and could not completely overcome the shock of seeing himself suddenly excluded from it.

Baeck therefore stayed on, and for two more years managed to continue his lectures and courses at the *Hochschule.* As he grew older, he won an unfathomable measure of strength from the mere fact that his own life was drawing to its end. This, together with his deep conviction that Divine Providence had charged him with the task of caring for those forsaken Jews who were left in the fortress of the enemy, gave him the inner security and staying power to deal with the Gestapo fearlessly and on equal terms. He even published several essays during this trying period, including *Das Evangelium als Urkunde der Jüdischen Glaubensgeschichte* (*The Gospel as a Document in the History of the Jewish Faith*). A second volume of Baeck's essays entitled *Aus drei Jahrtausenden* (*Out of Three Thousand Years*) was seized and destroyed by the Gestapo. After Baeck's liberation from Theresienstadt, a London publisher brought out his lecture *Changes in Jewish Outlook* (1947). Finally, in 1941, the

Hochschule had to close its doors, and Baeck spent the next two tragic years in his apartment under close Gestapo surveillance, always trying to alleviate the fate of his fellow Jews who were now subject to ever-increasing waves of deportation ending in the gas chambers of Auschwitz and other annihilation camps.

Concentration Camp Rabbi

In January, 1943, it was Baeck's turn to be deported. The rabbi, who was nearing his seventieth year, had been completely cut off from the non-Nazi world and was, for all practical purposes, at the mercy of the Storm Troopers; they spared his life only because they had a vague idea of using him to blackmail world Jewry into paying large sums for the release of small contingents of coreligionists still alive in various concentration camps. He was brought to the camp of Theresienstadt in Czechoslovakia, which the Nazis, as the military tide started to turn against them, tried to build up as a kind of "Potemkin village" in order to persuade world opinion that their treatment of the Jews was humane. During the two years Baeck spent in Theresienstadt, he had the opportunity of showing his courage, leadership, and moral strength, this time under the most terrifying conditions.

H. G. Adler,[4] in his work *Theresienstadt, das Antlitz einer Zwangesgemeinschaft* calls that city of Jewish prisoners the "demoniac caricature of a generally possible, perhaps even real administration." The actual power in Theresienstadt was in the hands of the Nazi S. S. *Kommandatur*, but in order to maintain the semblance of self-government the camp was officially "ruled" by a so-called *Aeltestenrat* (Council of the Elders) consisting of thirteen representatives of Czech, German, and Austrian Jews. Soon after his arrival, Baeck was nominated honorary president of the *Aeltestenrat*. As there were elements of a questionable character in this "governing body," this nomination was a rather dubious honor. Baeck took charge of the administration of the large department that cared for the sick, orphans and old people.

Baeck's role and position in Theresienstadt were unique. In an atmosphere of general fear and despair, on the one hand, and mutual distrust, on the other, he was the one person who was universally respected, loved, and revered by the honest and dishonest, the meek and the ambitious, the dreamers and the cynics, the idealists and the realists. The seventy-year-old rabbi became a kind of *Zaddik*, who was perturbed neither by the crimes and wiles of a ruthless foe nor by the moral deficiencies and dissensions of his own people. The essential teachings of Judaism were firmly rooted in his character, enabling him to reach an inner serenity which could brave even death and destruction. This explained the secret of his immunity even in the midst of hell. According to H. G. Adler, he considered himself a witness for the fact that there was and would be another world than this evil ghetto. Baeck became the embodiment of the conscience of the whole camp, and found himself in the center of a moral resistance movement against the corruption of the Jewish administration.

Liberation and Last Years

When the hour of liberation came, the world at large hastened to pay its respects to the now internationally famous Berlin rabbi, who had dared to oppose, at least by passive resistance, the worst persecutors the Jewish people had ever known, and who had survived half-starvation and the terrifying emotional distress unbroken in body and mind. It was only then that Baeck left Germany forever and went to settle in London, where his daughter and son-in-law had made their home after Hitler's rise to power. Passing through the ruins of Germany and of the city of his main rabbinical and scholarly activities and achievements, he believed that German Judaism was a thing of the past, and that the center of Jewish endeavor had shifted to the United States. When in 1948 he was invited to teach at Hebrew Union College in Cincinnati, the seventy-five-year-old patriarch gladly accepted. He held the position of visiting professor for five years, and was loved and admired by a host of rabbinic and non-rabbinic students.[5]

During that period Baeck frequently came to New York to give lectures in Jewish history before large audiences of Jewish and Christian theologians, philosophers, and other scholars. In one of those lectures, formulated in impeccable English, Baeck discussed the problems raised by the rebirth of Israel. He came to the conclusion that Judaism, for its very survival, needed two main centers, one of which would be able to support Israel morally, culturally, and economically in periods of national stress and difficulties from the outside. In the current epoch, the United States, with the largest Jewish population in the world, was called upon to play the latter role. Even in his old age, Baeck felt the need of active work in the interest of world Judaism. He therefore assumed leadership in the World Union for Progressive Judaism.

Last Work: Dieses Volk

The octogenarian left Cincinnati in 1953 in order to return to England, which had bestowed British citizenship upon him. Indefatigable, Baeck continued vigorously with his studies, publishing in 1955 his last book *Dieses Volk: Jüdische Existens* (*This People: Jewish Existence*), based on Isaiah 43:21: "This people that I have formed, it will proclaim My glory." This book, of which no English translation yet exists, is perhaps the most moving and impressive of Baeck's publications. Bearing the dedication: "To the Life and Memory of My Wife," it was started during the darkest days in Nazi Germany and continued in Theresienstadt. It tries to answer the questions: What is the meaning and uniqueness of Jewish existence? Baeck answered himself:

> The uniqueness of Judaism consists in the fact that a people has found its special origin, its ground, in the One who is the ground and origin of the universe. The world of the beyond has talked here of the beginning and the evolution of the people and made known to it the condition and the goal of its history. Among all peoples the Israelite people alone has experienced this from the earliest days of its existence and preserved it forever.

Baeck points out, therefore, that "to this special nation its very origin has become an idea. It emerged, so to say, from the path of the beyond, as a people of metaphysical existence; it originated as a nation by virtue of God's revelation." The book assigns to Judaism the mission to fight for the highest goals of humanity and explains that just for this reason the Jews have been persecuted throughout the ages. It had a tremendous success in post-war Germany, and Baeck received a great number of personal letters. Shortly before his death Baeck wrote a sequel to *Dieses Volk*, which was to serve as its second part.

His last years were saddened by the untimely death of his son-in-law, who had faithfully served as his companion and "secretary" during his travels between Europe and the United States, and also to and from Israel, where Baeck had spent some time as a guest professor at the Hebrew University. Baeck died in London on November 2, 1956, after a short but severe illness.

Essence of Judaism: Baeck's Interpretation

Baeck emerged as a leader in modern Judaism because of his original approach to Jewish thought and his ability to interpret it in terms of the twentieth century. He always used his vast learning to present original combinations of events and concepts never before put together. He demonstrated a sincerity and an absence of zealotry and fanaticism toward religious and philosophical systems basically different from Judaism.

Through the persuasiveness of his style, Baeck revealed to a generation which had begun to take Judaism as a matter of course, the philosophical and ethical depths of the Jewish religion. Out of his own study of Bible and Talmud, integrated with a broad knowledge of history, philosophy and sociology, he conveyed to his readers a concept of Judaism fit to serve as a guide in the revolutionary vicissitudes of the times.

What, then, did Baeck contribute to contemporary Jewish philosophy? The tremendous advances of science in the machine age forced theologians of all faiths to reformulate the fundamental ideas of their religious beliefs. Baeck followed in the footsteps of Hermann Cohen, the German-Jewish philosopher, by explaining in the language of the man of average education what he called *The Essence of Judaism*. This book has since become a standard work, and has been published in many German and English editions.

For Baeck, the essence of Judaism is the divine command to redeem mankind from evil through justice and love. The basic challenge of this command and the Jewish God-conception is eternal and unchanging, but the ceremonial forms of Judaism are to him transient and modifiable. The moral law, as formulated in the Bible, expounded by the Talmud, and codified by subsequent Jewish philosophers, has guided Jews through the ages in all walks of life and is the culmination of the ethical principle. The Jewish religion comprises the doctrine of the Supreme Moral Being, of man created in the image of God and hence perpetually striving for moral perfection, and, finally, of the divine priesthood of Israel whose duty it is to become the light to humanity by its own moral life and endeavors.

On the other hand, Baeck felt that the forms developed by Judaism in its temporal and historic evolution as an expression of its religious life are to be considered as the religion of the people and the community rather than of the individual, a "fence around the law." The future of religion in general depends on the religious evolution, exemplified, as we have seen, by what he calls the "classical religion" of deeds—Judaism—in contrast to "romantic" and "sentimental" Christianity.

Uniqueness of Judaism

In Baeck's view, the basic principle which distinguishes Judaism from Christianity is the absence of dogmas.

The dominant form of Judaism always remained that of a religious philosophy of inquiry, a philosophy which produced method rather than system. Principles always remained of greater importance than results. There was always tolerance and even indifference toward modes of expression; it was the idea which was held to be central. Judaism, and the Jew as well, retained an unorthodox air; they neither could nor would rest in the easy comfort of dogma. This absence of the supporting crutch of dogma is in the very nature of Judaism, an essential result of its historical development. Jewish religious philosophy had as its purpose the constant renewal of the content of religion, by means of which it was best preserved and protected from the deadening rigidity of formula. It was a religion which constantly imposed upon its adherents new labors of thought.[6]

Another important factor which Baeck stresses, in refutation of modern Bible critics, is the originality of the Jewish religion. The ability of the Jewish genius to absorb the most divergent elements of foreign civilizations with which it has been in contact has frequently been cited as proof of its lack of creativeness. Yet if we look at the tradition a little more closely, just the opposite is true. Judaism has amalgamated these alien influences into its own traditions and has given them an entirely Jewish character; every concept has been recast in specific Jewish terms, and only those ideas which could be fully adapted and modified into such terms became part of the permanent Jewish heritage.

The best proof of the originality of Judaism, says Baeck, is the fact that the Jewish religion alone has kept monotheism in its pure form. Whenever this essential nucleus was threatened from the outside, the Israelites fought and died for its maintenance. But just because this basic nucleus was kept intact, "the doors of interpretation," as Maimonides put it, "were never closed." Jews of the Middle Ages saw in this freedom and right of interpretation a distinguishing mark of Judaism.

Baeck believed that a deeper understanding of Judaism could be gained only through study of the great prophets, whom he considered endowed with "intuitive and practical power of vision," [7] and the ingenious creators of a true Jewishness. The prophets did not set themselves apart in a secluded mysticism, but saw their goals and duties firmly anchored in actual Jewish life, where they acted as guardians of the ethical performance of the community. Such an attitude removed the grounds for conflict between faith and knowledge or between faith and life. To use Baeck's own formulation, "The possibility of conflict between faith and life is removed by the prophets' insistence that religion has to be realized through life, while faith and knowledge are reconciled by the insistence that religion is not to be proved by means of knowledge." [8]

What are the main ideas of Judaism, according to Baeck? They consist of an unflinching faith in man based on faith in God, and subdivided into a three-fold faith in ourselves, in our fellow men, and in mankind.

To observe and explore the world is the task of science; to judge and determine our attitude toward it is the task of religion. . . . Religion measures man's experience in terms of intrinsic values and thereby is able to go beneath the surface of existence to apprehend its inner core. Decisive for religion are the ideas of good

and evil, of truth and nullity, of destiny, and of purpose of life
as experienced by each individual.[9]

Judaism, asserts Baeck, distinguishes itself from Buddhism and
Christianity by virtue of being the religion of ethical optimism.[10]
But this optimism is anything but superficial; on the contrary,
it is based on insight into the wickedness of this world, its sea
of misery and suffering, as was experienced in Jewish history.
"Distinctly audible," says Baeck, "in the voice of Judaism is a
note of contempt for the world—a pessimistic and serious note
that vibrates as a dark undertone of Israel's fundamental optimism." Jewish optimism means that, in spite of the baseness
and depravity which we encounter so frequently, it is our duty
to fight for the forces of good and never to succumb to a
cynical acceptance of evil. It is an optimism steeped in the
"strength of the moral will" and imbued with the "tragic force
of the man who fights, and even in defeat feels that he has
triumphed because he can invoke the future and is certain of
the final victory." [11]

Principal Religious Concepts

The fact that Baeck taught at the Hebrew Union College in
Cincinnati has caused some confusion about his attitude toward
Reform Judaism. Though some have called him a foremost exponent of Reform Judaism, this is incorrect. He officiated at
the Fasanenstrasse and Lützowstrasse synagogues in Berlin,
which were typical Conservative synagogues in the American
sense of the term; the same holds true for the synagogues both
in Oppeln and Düsseldorf. He would have resisted presiding
over any service without *tallit* and head-covering for himself
and the other male congregants, let alone the liturgical ab-
breviations and token readings from the Torah customary in
the Reform service. Nor would he have agreed to the changing
of the Sabbath services from Saturday to Sunday as arranged
in German Reform temples.

As we have seen, Baeck did not consider the observation of
Jewish religious ceremonies and rituals as the principal part of
his personal devotion; they were symbols of faith, but, as such,

they had their fixed place in his religious life. He went along with many reforms of the service, as, for instance, the confirmation of girls; but there were limits to the changes of liturgy and rituals which he would accept.

Ceremonies and rituals, Baeck felt, are significant only as they serve to prepare the mind for inner communication with God. Essential to Baeck's conception of the relation of man to God is "the consciousness of being created." This idea, he underlined, is uniquely Jewish, peculiar to the belief in one God. Man and the world are linked in one certainty of life, a conviction that all life was bestowed, is upheld and will be maintained in safety forever. "The mystery of growth becomes the certainty of origin and life. . . . With this consciousness of being created there enters into man's finite and transient life the feeling of infinitude and conjecture . . . but our life derives from Him (God), so that we are related and near to Him." Herein, the great mystery and paradox of genuine religion is incorporated. Through his intimate union with God, man overcomes the futility of his ephemeral existence. "Though we are 'dust and ashes' (Genesis 18:27), when compared to God, we nevertheless belong to Him; though He is unfathomable and inscrutable, yet we emanate from Him."

In this way, the weaknesses and inconsistencies of mortal life are finally mastered; the loneliness of man is overcome by the assurance of eternal life. Man, "born to create," finds his goal in God and thus reaches immortality. "God receives the man whom he has created." Once man believes that when he passes through the gate of death he is passing into eternity, says Baeck, "then all questions of life are answered and all the paradoxes resolved." Death is the great "return," *teshuvah*. "Man's yearning for perfection is fulfilled and his life completed; death becomes the great revelation."

As for Israel's "election" by God, Baeck underlines its basic ethical character. Here is no mystical act of bestowing upon Jews distinctions that cannot be reached by other people but, on the contrary, the "chosen people" are to be judged by stricter standards. Israel is chosen by God, said Baeck in his *Essence*; therefore God is its judge. And Israel can remain so chosen only, as the prophets teach, if it practices righteousness; sin separates Israel from God, as it frequently has done in Jewish history.

Israel's "only possible existence is religious: either it will live
as God has commanded, or it will not live at all."

Election is a prophetic calling of an entire people. This mission is beyond Israel itself; it is an election for the sake of others.
In *Dieses Volk,* Baeck enlarged on this concept. God has given
many other nations the same opportunities to lead the world
to justice and love; they, too, have had their "exodus" and
liberation from bondage. But Israel alone accepted the challenge.
"To have history," he stressed, "is the task of every nation.
But only if and when a nation discovers in itself a genuine
decisive idea and conserves it forever, then the period of its
great history starts." The Jews, with all their weaknesses and
sins, have decided to live as the people of the covenant.

This concept of "election" has an important bearing on
Baeck's attitude toward the rebirth of the Jewish state in modern
Israel. For him, any national existence for the Jewish people
must be intimately connected with its ethical leadership in the
world. He knew how intimately Jewish religious history was
tied to the land of Palestine, and devoted some beautiful passages
in a special chapter of *Dieses Volk* to that question. He was
never an active Zionist in a political sense; before the rise of
the Nazis, his leadership in the *Keren Hayesod* and the Jewish
Agency was directed toward helping Jews in the *galut* who
had to leave their host countries because of physical and economic persecution. After the destruction of German Jewry,
Baeck's views on Zionism became more positive. But, as we have
seen, in a lecture on Jewish history, he warned Jews not to stake
the whole future of Judaism on the small state of Israel; he
urged keeping America open as a second center of Jewish
cultural and religious endeavor.

Baeck's Influence

A bibliography of the writings of Baeck compiled by Theodor
Wiener and published in 1954 by the Hebrew Union College
lists no fewer than four hundred publications. Actually, however, the influence of his writings was restricted to a relatively
small group of Jewish and Christian theologians and religious
philosophers. Recognized all over Europe as the "great man of
Judaism," he shared the fate of many outstanding thinkers who

are lavishly praised but are actually read only by an élite. Two famous liberal Protestant theologians, Adolf von Harnack and Karl Barth, for example, were especially impressed with Baeck's revolutionary interpretations of both the origin of Christianity, and the Judeo-Christian relationship and crosscurrents through-out the ages.[12] The distinguished Protestant scholar, the historian Ernst Troeltsch, for example, leaned on Baeck's interpretation when he dealt with Jewish religious history.

On the wider plane, several Leo Baeck Institutes have been founded in various countries to further studies in Jewish the-ology and philosophy. The best known of these is the Leo Baeck Institute, of Jews from Germany, in New York City. But Baeck's influence as a courageous spiritual leader is as great, if not greater, than his influence as a theologian.

> It is not ideas which make the man, but rather the man who makes something of his ideas. That is as true for an entire nation as for an individual. In both, the personality which they have de-veloped in adulthood is decisive. Our life is fulfilled by what we become, not by what we are at birth. Endowment and heritage mean much . . . and then again nothing; the essential thing is what we make of them.[13]

These sentences, in the opening chapter of *Essence of Judaism*, describe best what Leo Baeck wanted his legacy to be to future generations of Jews. He showed that Jews have to suffer for their heritage in order to acquire the right to possess it. Both by his life and his works, which represent a total unity of action and thought, Leo Baeck helps us to understand and grasp the essence of Judaism.

FOR FURTHER READING

Books by Leo Baeck

This People Israel (New York: Holt, Rinehart & Winston, 1965). His mature exposition of the "essence of Judaism."

Books about Leo Baeck

BAKER, Leonard, *Days of Sorrow and Pain: Leo Baeck and Berlin Jews* (New York: Oxford University Press, 1978). During the dark Hitler era Baeck was one of the leading figures in the German Jewish com-munities' struggle to survive. Baker chronicles these events in a clear, if not profound, manner.

BOROWITZ, Eugene, *A New Jewish Theology in the Making* (Philadelphia: Westminister Press, 1968). A well-conceived, non-technical introduction to Baeck's theological position.

COHEN, Arthur, *The Natural and the Supernatural Jew* (New York: Behrman House, 1979, revised edition). An intelligent, critical summary of Baeck's neo-Kantian reconstruction of Judaism.

FRIEDLANDER, Albert H., *Leo Baeck: Teacher of Theresienstadt* (New York: Holt, Rinehart & Winston, 1968). The most complete biographical and philosophical study of Baeck to date.

KAUFMAN, William E., *Contemporary Jewish Philosophies* (New York: Reconstructionist Press, 1976). A brief, elementary description, and critique of Baeck's basic theological doctrines.

6. *Franz Rosenzweig*

[1886-1929]

NAHUM N. GLATZER

T H E story of Franz Rosenzweig is the story of a rediscovery of Judaism. It is the dramatic narrative of a young German Jewish intellectual who, though brought up in an assimilated family, broke with his personal past and became a Jew by conviction. He rediscovered the existence of his people and became one of its most articulate modern interpreters. Despite an almost total physical paralysis, he managed to write during the last eight years of his life some of the most important material on Judaism that has been created in modern times.

Youth and Study

Franz Rosenzweig was born in Cassel on December 25, 1886, the only child of Georg Rosenzweig, a respected and successful manufacturer and energetic community leader, and Adele, a woman of charm and a devotée of the arts. The Rosenzweig home was a gathering place for prominent officials, civic leaders and creative artists. Self-respect demanded nominal affiliation with the Jewish community, and the rudiments of religious tradition were carried out. Young Franz had a *Bar Mitzvah* ceremony, the High Holidays were observed, but the Judaism of the Rosenzweigs was lacking in devotion and depth, and exerted no real influence on him. Franz himself did not learn of the existence of the Sabbath eve until after he was in college.

Like most boys of the bourgeoisie, he was sent to the *gym-*

nasium, where at the age of eighteen, he was confronted with the need to choose a profession. He vacillated between science, philology, history, and medicine, and finally selected medicine. Early in his university career, however, he became dissatisfied with his medical studies and, after some hesitation, he threw himself into the study of history and philosophy. By 1912 he completed his doctoral thesis on the political and historical theory of Hegel. For this youth of many talents, this was a period of adventuring in many realms of knowledge and art, of discovering the excitement of thinking and living.

Between Christianity and Judaism

An air of optimism pervaded the universities and other institutions of scholarship during this period. The dominant philosophy was that of Hegelianism, and for a time young Rosenzweig identified himself with the prevailing *Weltanschauung* of progress, science and faith in reason. But gradually, after close examination of the intellectual movements of his day, Rosenzweig and his friends (all in their early twenties) began to be critical of the philosophical trend called "German Idealism," revealing a growing interest in religion. He was meeting daily with Eugen Rosenstock-Huessy, a young philosopher then lecturing at Leipzig where Rosenzweig continued his studies. Together they discussed the problem of contemporary academic philosophy and its failure to satisfy the spiritual needs of the individual. More and more Rosenzweig felt himself drawn toward the "existential" approach that took its starting point in the situation of the individual person. Religion seemed to hold the key. Yet Rosenzweig, trained in the sciences, in logical criticism and in methods of modern historical research, could not conceive of a Western scholar, "accepting religion."

His relationship with Rosenstock-Huessy led to a turning point in his life. Rosenstock-Huessy, though of Jewish origin, had found a personal solution in becoming a Christian. Rosenzweig, whose own Judaism was dormant, or passive, at best, even though he had studied some Hebrew and the Bible, was impressed that a man of Rosenstock's intellectual stature could find satisfaction in Christianity. "The fact that a man like Rosenstock was a conscious Christian at once bowled over my entire conception of Christianity and of religion generally, including my own," he wrote. "I thought I had Christianized my view of Judaism, but in actual fact I had done the opposite: I had 'Judaized' my view of Christianity . . . in this world there seemed to me to be no room for Judaism." His friend's thinking seemed sounder than his own. Rosenzweig could not counter the faith of the Christian with the faith of a Jew, for Judaism, as understood by Rosenzweig, appeared then to be an anachronism. Rosenstock regarded his friend's superficial Judaism as merely a "personal idiosyncrasy, or at best a pious romantic relic," that could not address itself to a modern man in search of orientation in the Western world. Rosenzweig himself felt that a Jewish intellectual in Western Europe had only two choices: Zionism, if he wanted to affirm his Judaism, or baptism, if he turned to religion.

There were other influences too, which led him to consider resolving his own intellectual and spiritual dilemmas by taking the latter step. His cousin Hans Ehrenberg had embraced Protestantism four years earlier. When his family, usually indifferent to matters of religious faith, opposed this break with the ancestral affiliation, Franz had written them that Hans had done the right thing. "It's an excellent thing, after all, to be able to make contact with religion, even somewhat late—if only for the sake of one's children—when one has been robbed of it by early neglect. We are Christian in everything. We live in a Christian state, attend Christian schools, read Christian books, in short, our whole 'culture' rests entirely on a Christian foundation; consequently a man who has nothing holding him back needs only a very slight push . . . I myself counseled Hans strongly in this direction, and would do it again." As for himself, systematically minded and history-conscious, Rosenzweig made only one provision, a procedural one: he wished to enter Christianity as did its founders, as a Jew, not as a "pagan." He decided to attend synagogue services on the High Holidays in preparation for this crucial event. He did not wish to "break off," but deliberately aimed to "go through" Judaism to Christianity.

His Religious Self-Discovery

When Rosenzweig entered the small Orthodox synagogue in Berlin on that fateful *Yom Kippur* in 1913, he joined a community of humble men, women and children who had gathered to confess their sins and to pray for forgiveness. On the Day of Atonement, the Jew, though united with his brethren in prayer, stands utterly alone before his God. The drama of this day begins on its eve, with the *Kol Nidre* in which the Jew frees himself of unintentional commitments. The liturgy of the day leads through psalms and hymns, through the recollection of the ancient Temple service of the Day of Atonement at which the high priest pronounced—this single time in the year—the ineffable name of God, to the reading of the story of Jonah the prophet who tried to flee from God. The hour of sunset nears when the worshipper once more expresses his desire to "enter Thy gate," to experience eternity within the confines of time. Then, in utmost solemnity, the congregation cries out the profession: "Hear O Israel, the Lord our God, the Lord is One!" and finally "The Lord is God," which means, the God of Love, He alone is God! In this profession, followed by the sounding of the ram's horn, the drama of the Day of Atonement finds its resolution.

Rosenzweig left the services a changed person. What he had thought he could find only in the church—faith that gives one an orientation in the world—he found on that day in the synagogue. What the day conveyed to him was, that essential as a mediator may be in the Christian experience, the Jew stands in no need of mediation. God is near to man and desires his unmediated devotion. Rosenzweig also realized for the first time in his life that Judaism is not a religion of bygone ages but a living faith.

The very communicative Rosenzweig, usually eager to discuss and to share problems with others, never mentioned this event to his friends and never presented it in his writings. He guarded it as the secret ground of his new life. In a long letter to his mother, however, he discussed Judaism and Christianity, ending with a reference to his own situation: "You have gathered from this letter that I seem to have found the way back about which I had tortured myself in vain and pondered for almost three months." A few days later he wrote a friend: "After prolonged, and I believe thorough, self-examination, I have reversed my decision. It no longer seems necessary to me, and therefore, being what I am, no longer possible. I will remain a Jew." Rosenzweig, at the age of twenty-seven, was now sure of his ground.

During the following year, having resolved to devote his life to the study and teaching of Judaism, Rosenzweig remained in Berlin, where he attended the lectures of Hermann Cohen at the *Hochschule*, an institute of advanced Jewish studies, and began what he hoped would be a period of intensive study of the sources of Judaism. The influence of Hermann Cohen on Rosenzweig was tremendous. It was Cohen's profound mind that led Rosenzweig to his intensive interest in Judaism:

> With Cohen, you feel perfectly convinced that this man must philosophize, that he has within him the treasure which the powerful word forces to the surface. The thing that, disenchanted with the present, I had long searched for only in the writings of the great dead—the strict scholarly spirit hovering over the deep of an inchoate, chaotically teeming reality—I now saw face to face in the living flesh.

In the Trenches

When World War I broke out, Rosenzweig had to interrupt his studies. He joined the army, and was sent to the Balkan front. The war and the dislocation it brought, however, did not deter him from continuing his writings and from beginning to formulate his thought on politics, European history, and general and Jewish education. He managed to work on his book *Hegel and the State*, and to write a number of essays, among them a critical review of Hermann Cohen's essay on *Germanism and Judaism*.

Looking to the future, Rosenzweig became increasingly interested in a teaching career. He was particularly concerned about Jewish education because his own early training in Judaism had been so inadequate. "As soon as the war is over," he wrote, "I shall look (I feel increasingly sure of this) for some kind of public forum . . . I'll either teach in Berlin at the

Hochschule, or, should the department of Jewish theology at Frankfurt materialize—which seems likely—I'll teach there . . ."

During these years, too, in the loneliness of life at the front, Rosenzweig had a vast amount of time to think through and clarify his ideas on Judaism. At the very beginning of his enlistment, he had begun to collect information on the status of Jewish religious instruction in Germany and to formulate plans for the reconstruction of Jewish education on a broad scale. In a pamphlet called *It is Time,* written in 1917, in the form of a letter addressed to Hermann Cohen, he outlined in detail a system of education which would enable Jewish youth to understand Jewish tradition by the study of its sources. For this, he envisaged the creation of a new type of educator who would combine scholarship with teaching ability. A good teacher, in his estimation, was a scholar actively in contact with the sources of learning, who could go out and transmit his knowledge instead of remaining in his study. The synthesis of scholarship and education so admirably blended in the sages of classical Judaism was, in Rosenzweig's opinion, the path most capable of leading out of the stagnation of Central European Jewry and a precondition necessary for a possible renaissance of Jewish life. The Academy for the Science of Judaism, outlined in *It is Time,* was to be the central agency for putting the plan into action.

Star of Redemption

Rosenzweig's interest in Judaism came to fullest flower in August, 1918, when, struck by sudden inspiration, he began writing *Star of Redemption,* which became his magnum opus. That book was a personal account of the writer's position within the philosophical and religious thought movements of his time, as well as a novel system of religious philosophy.

The "manuscript" was scribbled on army postal cards and letters which Rosenzweig mailed one by one, some to his mother, others to a friend who copied them. After the collapse of the front line and during the retreat of the army, he continued to write, as if in a trance, the work which he called "a theory that grew out of an ardent longing." The longing was to reach the state of a man who is aware of the presence of God, and who lived in this faith. It was this state that Rosenzweig had experienced on the Day of Atonement in 1913, and whose reality was further revealed to him in the Jewish section of Warsaw, where his war duties had brought him on a visit shortly before he wrote the book. Like Hermann Cohen in his visit to eastern Europe, he found the Polish Jews "magnificent." ". . . I felt something I rarely feel, pride in my people, in so much freshness and vivacity," he wrote. "Driving through the town, too, I was impressed by the masses of Jews. Their costume is really very attractive and so is their language . . . I can well understand why the average German Jew no longer feels any kinship with these east European Jews: actually, he has very little such kinship left; he has become philistine, bourgeois; but I, and people like me, should still feel the kinship strongly." Referring with enthusiasm to a service he attended in a Warsaw *steebel* (prayer room), he said: "Never had I heard such praying."

In *Star of Redemption*, Rosenzweig presented his criticism of the philosophical system of Hegel and his own religious philosophy. The book is difficult to read, but it was destined to have an impact. Rosenzweig's description of the inner life of the faithful, deeply moving in its utter simplicity, is a classic of religious writing. But one must realize that Rosenzweig, at this time, saw in Judaism mainly its Biblical traditions, *Midrashic* lore, liturgy, and its sacred calendar.

Only later, after Rosenzweig had completed the *Star*, returned from the war, started to direct the *Lehrhaus* (House of Jewish Studies), and joined the study group of Rabbi Nehemiah A. Nobel, did the "Law" structure of Judaism take on a new importance for him.

Return to Civilian Life

In December 1918, released from the service, Rosenzweig turned his earnest attention to Jewish education. Always a voracious student, he began to study Talmud with his friend, Joseph Prager. "Anyone who knew Franz Rosenzweig in his vigorous days knows that it wasn't easy to have him for a teacher," Dr. Prager later wrote. "Neither was it easy to have him for a pupil, or as more precisely fits the case, for a fellow student. He found no time unsuitable for study. Early in the morning before I went to work, at noon, in the evening, every minute I could spare from my professional work he claimed. The assignments were never large enough for him, the pace was never rapid enough. He rushed forward with tremendous verve, never stopping until the material was wholly assimilated."

The Lehrhaus

Rosenzweig, simultaneously, was devoting a great deal of effort in an attempt to set up the Lehrhaus, a modification of the Academy plan which he had discussed with Hermann Cohen and outlined in his *It is Time*. The death of Hermann Cohen and the breakdown of Germany in 1918 had made it necessary to curtail and revise the original plan of an Academy. An institute devoted solely to research was eventually established. Rosenzweig fought desperately, in numerous committee meetings, against the modification of his project, only to realize in the end that it was a lost battle. Though by the time it had ceased to function in 1934, the Academy had published an important body of academic works and could indeed be looked upon as the crowning chapter in the history of modern Jewish scholarship in Western Europe, Rosenzweig took little interest in it. "A mere academy for the science of Judaism matters as little to me as an academy for the science of Botokudoism," he wrote. He dedicated all his effort to the *Lehrhaus*.

In the seven years of its activity, the *Lehrhaus* offered ninety lecture courses and conducted one hundred and eighty study groups, seminars, and discussion meetings. Sixty-four lecturers had participated in the programs, among them Martin Buber, Gershom Scholem, Ernst Simon, Leo Strauss, Erich Fromm. Enrollment reached its peak in 1922-23, with 1,100 students out of a Jewish population of some 26,000.

Within the very comprehensive program of studies, a central position was given to the Hebrew language; it was the key to sources; translations were used as an emergency measure, necessary in a period of transition. The courses in Hebrew were given by Rosenzweig himself. Owing to Rosenzweig's illness, the regular activities were greatly reduced in 1926 and 1927; however, the study groups and special lectures continued.

In 1933 Martin Buber reopened the Frankfurt institution and

made it a source of spiritual and moral strength in the catastrophic period of European Jewry's history.

Paralysis

At the very peak of his creative efforts on behalf of Judaism, Franz Rosenzweig was stricken with a fatal paralysis. Late in 1921 he began to stumble and fall without apparent cause. This was the beginning of a period of suffering and trial in the life of the thirty-five-year-old scholar. A progressive paralysis attacked first his limbs, then his whole body, including the vocal organs. Rosenzweig knew from the beginning that his days were numbered. This only sharpened his will to make the most of the time that yet remained. He refused to give in, and proceeded to master his affliction and to continue with his intellectual activities. With the aid and devotion of his wife, Edith, whom he had married in 1920, he used the remnants of his physical ability to maintain a semblance of "normal" life. His *Lehrhaus* lectures were transferred to large rooms which his landlord offered for the purpose in his own home. Seminar groups met in Rosenzweig's study. As long as energy sufficed, he wanted to go on lecturing, even though "the effortless flow of words is not possible when one has to concentrate continually on the forming of those wretched consonants." He kept in touch with family and friends, making an effort to allay their concern. By August 1922 writing had become increasingly difficult, speech even less articulate. It became necessary to choose a successor for the administration of the *Lehrhaus*, which by this time, in the words of Buber, had come to be known as "the only distinguished cultural institution today among all of Western Jewry."

A son, Rafael, was born to the Rosenzweigs on September 8, 1922. The circumcision ceremony was held at home. As described by a friend, "Rosenzweig took part in the celebration, silent and immobile but with veritable 'joy in fulfilling a commandment,' although he could hardly move at all or speak intelligibly." A few days later the new father noted in his diary that he wished his library given to his son. "It is a library that will mean something even to an intelligent businessman, lawyer, or doctor; it is certainly not meant merely for a scholar. From these books, my son will learn a great deal about me that he could learn in no other way."

Beginning with *Yom Kippur* services that same year, a *minyan* assembled for private services at the Rosenzweig home. Services on the Sabbath and the festivals were held in the sick man's study up until shortly before his death.

By the end of December, 1922, Rosenzweig had entirely lost his ability to write, following a gradual decline during the previous months. He maintained the ability to speak, however indistinctly, to his wife and those closest to him until the spring of 1923. Up to that time he dictated to his wife, who wrote down his letters and other compositions. "I have a guilty conscience about my long silence, but I must husband my time very carefully," he wrote a friend. "You can scarcely imagine how it is now that I can hardly write by myself any more. It costs me more effort to turn a page than cutting the pages of a whole book does a healthy man."

By 1924 the progressing paralysis left Rosenzweig unable to move. He himself prescribed in detail the methods for his care so as to allow him the maximum possibility for continuing to study and write at specified hours. A special typewriter was constructed to facilitate communication. At first Rosenzweig was able to operate the machine by himself, but later on, he had to point out the characters with his left hand. Arm and hand were supported in a sling hanging from a bar next to Rosenzweig's desk. The key was operated by someone else, usually Mrs. Rosenzweig. Eventually his ability to indicate the characters lessened, so that they had to be ascertained by guesswork.

Despite all these difficulties, Rosenzweig remained until the end the dominant, active center of all domestic affairs as well as of all social contacts. He was never simply a passive object of medical treatment and feminine nursing, but always the master of the house, whose every wish prevailed. When guests arrived, the patient was already sitting in his chair; he liked to drink coffee beforehand to make himself alert for conversation. All conversation was managed through Mrs. Rosenzweig; agreement could be read in his features, or if he disagreed, the typewriter was quickly brought into service so that the conversation never halted but kept moving.

"Whoever stepped over the threshold of Franz Rosenzweig's room," a friend later wrote, "entered a magic circle and fell under a gentle yet potent spell. Behind the desk, in the armchair sat, not as one had imagined on climbing the stairs, a mortally sick, utterly invalid man, almost totally deprived of physical force, but a man, well in the fullest sense, and free of life's pettiness and constriction. Whoever came to him, he drew into a dialogue; his very listening was eloquent in itself."

During hours of relaxation, Rosenzweig listened to a phonograph (after March 1924, there was a radio, and he could also listen in on the telephone). He did not allow illness to darken his life: he insisted in maintaining by every possible means a manner of life consistent with his great gifts and numerous human relationships. To his mother he wrote:

> The words *pain* and *suffering* which you use, seem quite odd to me. A condition into which one has slithered gradually, and consequently got used to, is not suffering, but simply a condition . . . that leaves room for joy and suffering like any other . . . What must appear suffering when seen from the outside is actually only a sum of great difficulties that have to be overcome. Of course there's no telling how things will turn out, once all means of communication fail. And I dare not think how they would be without Edith . . . and despite everything, the three of us, I, Edith, and Rafael, praise the day.

His Scholarly Activities

Despite his paralysis, Rosenzweig continued to study and write. During 1922 and 1923 he had worked on *Sixty Hymns and Poems of Judah Halevi*, in German, a volume of representative selections from creations of the medieval Hebrew poet, faithfully rendered in meter. The book, published in 1924, included an epilogue on the art of translating, and notes to each poem. This work introduced the modern reader to the work of the great twelfth-century Spanish-Hebrew poet and thinker. Rosenzweig's translation faithfully reproduced the contents as well as the rhythmic and tonal quality.

In the early summer months of 1923, Rosenzweig wrote *The Builders*, an epistle addressed to the "hyphenated" Jews who wanted to come back to their heritage in all its fullness.

Rosenzweig also wrote an extensive introduction to the *Jüdische Schriften* (*Collected Jewish Writings*) of Hermann Cohen, tracing the philosophical and the Jewish development which led the founder of the Marburg philosophical school to become, in his old age, an interpreter of the Jewish heritage.

Though Rosenzweig's bodily condition rapidly deteriorated, his creativity continued amazingly. In the spring of 1925 a young publisher, Lambert Schneider of Berlin, suggested to Buber that he undertake a new translation of the Bible. Buber made his acceptance of this large-scale commitment contingent on Rosenzweig's collaboration.

None of the Bible translations then in use did justice to the original, none gave sufficient attention to the style and structure of the source, its use of key words as guides to the intention of a given story, speech or psalm; the primal meaning of a Hebrew root was largely ignored by translators who were more concerned with the smoothness, lucidity, and pleasing surface impressions. The great translation by Martin Luther was, admittedly, guided by the principles and needs of the Christian faith. The translations by the representatives of Bible criticism introduced many changes into the established text, some based on good scholarly evidence, others on conjecture. Buber and Rosenzweig offered a translation both accurate in scholarship (allowing only absolutely necessary textual changes) and true to the stylistic characteristics and spirit of the original. They did not share the Orthodox belief of the Bible as the literal record of divine revelation, but were conscious of the organic unity of the Torah.

"Our method of collaborating was the same to the end," Buber later wrote. "I translated and sent the sheets of the first version, mostly in chapters, to Rosenzweig. His replies comprised reservations, references, suggested changes. I immediately incorporated those that struck me at once as being good. We discussed the rest by correspondence, and whatever remained controversial we discussed during my Wednesday visits."

They completed the translation through the book of Isaiah. "Altogether I am grateful to Buber," Rosenzweig wrote, "for making it possible for me to work and live in the two languages I love."

He found time and energy to edit an anniversary volume for

Buber's fiftieth birthday and to write *The Secret of Form in Biblical Tales,* and other essays.

Last Days

But Rosenzweig could no longer deny the inroads made by his deadly adversary. "I find writing very hard," he confessed. "I could say with Hamlet, 'I have of late lost my mirth.' " "Odd as it may sound," he noted in the middle of 1929, "I have only now come to the point where I would welcome the end. Of course this isn't quite true either, as self-analytical generalities never are. I'm still able to enjoy things; it's only that my capacity for suffering has increased more rapidly than my capacity for enjoying."

On December 8, 1929, after eight years of agony, Franz Rosenzweig's end drew near. After a restless day and night, the doctor found him short of breath, his face pale; he complained of sharp pains in his chest. By the alphabet method he indicated: "I am so worn out from forty hours of gasping." Later that afternoon, slowly, laboriously he communicated to his wife. ". . . And now it comes, the point of all points, which the Lord has truly revealed to me in my sleep; the point of all points for which there . . ."

He died in the night from the 9th to the 10th and was buried in Frankfurt. There was no funeral oration, in accordance with his wish, but Martin Buber read Psalm 73, which contains the inscription Rosenzweig chose for his headstone.

I am continually with Thee,
Thou holdest my right hand.

THOUGHT OF FRANZ ROSENZWEIG

The moving and inspiring story of Franz Rosenzweig's life has become one of the legends of modern times and his name has become known in ever-widening circles, particularly since World War II. However, the contribution of Franz Rosenzweig to Judaism is greater than the example of a great personality who displayed spiritual courage in the midst of adversity. He was without question one of the outstanding creative Jewish thinkers in the present century and his approach to Judaism had a great impact on his generation in Germany and, since the recent revival of interest in Jewish theology in America, his writings are being studied with ever greater attentiveness.

The Background of His Thought

Franz Rosenzweig's approach to Judaism is based on his general philosophical orientation which represents a radical break with the intellectual movements prevailing at the beginning of the twentieth century in Central Europe.

For almost a century Jewish thinkers in the West identified Judaism with humanism and with a religion of reason. They presented Judaism as a particular expression of universal ethical truth, of a religion of reason. Such an identification of Judaism with generally accepted teachings relieved the Jew of the burden of giving a special philosophical explanation of Judaism; this work was considered to have been accomplished by general religious philosophy and the results were valid also for the Jewish thinker. He had only to show that the ideas of Judaism were identical with the ideas of the religion of reason. Jewish thinking, engaged in establishing this identity, naturally lost interest in the more profound theological problems that had absorbed Jewish thinkers before the emancipation regardless of whether or not they ran parallel to what was dealt with in the outside world.

As distinct from this nineteenth-century approach, which betrays strong leanings toward some form of assimilation, Franz Rosenzweig restored the full range of classical theological thought.

Criticism of Hegel's Philosophy

The German philosophic trend known as idealism and chiefly represented by the nineteenth-century philosopher Hegel, believed in the omnipotence of thought. "Thought itself is action; thought itself is reality," said Hegel. The world around us can only be understood as evolving out of thought, out of pure reason. God, world, man are products of thought. Thought precedes being. However, what thought "produces" is not the single individual, the human person, but "the whole" of humanity, man in general. Whatever sets the individual apart from the objective whole is irrelevant. The individual with his anguish and his longing, the self with his consciousness of life and awareness of his finitude, his death, is too insignificant within the context of the universe as conceived in the impersonal, abstract act of thinking.

Rosenzweig belonged to the group of thinkers who, like Nietzsche and Kierkegaard, rebelled against this impersonal aspect in thinking. His criticism of German idealism and the answer to the issue which he advanced is, to a large degree, rooted in classical Jewish thought. The Biblical and the Talmudic concept of man drew him toward the existential philosophy which took its starting point in the situation of the concrete individual human being, whom the philosophers of idealism had so badly neglected.

The New Thinking

According to Rosenzweig, being precedes thought; thought is dependent on being. The speculative philosophical systems which constructed all reality out of abstract "concepts" independent of immediate experience, bypassed the individual living being and ignored his deepest anxiety, his fear of death, the perilous nature of his existence. The "new thinking," as Rosenzweig calls it, starts with the living, suffering, doubting, hoping man, and with what his common sense finds at his disposal when he faces the real world around him. In this view there is not one absolute, one whole, as Hegel taught, but three parts of the whole. These elements are God, world, and man.

God, World and Man

These are factors which cannot be reduced to one another. As separate elements, God, world and man exist in the worldview and in the imagery of pagan religion. There we find the tragic hero alien to the society of men and alien to the gods; we encounter the cosmos which had no beginning and has no end, having no meaningful relationship with the divine and the human; we detect the mythical gods, not concerned with the acts of man. This heathen world-view which, in various forms and guises persists even in our day and age, Rosenzweig contrasts with reality as it was understood by the Biblical religions. Here, God, world and man are no longer isolated elements; they appear in a process of constant interaction. Only mutual contact makes them actual and transforms them into what we call reality.

The processes which establish these relationships between the three original elements of reality, Rosenzweig calls by the names familiar in religious thought in the West: Creation, Revelation, Redemption.

Creation

In Creation, God sets himself in relation to the world. This is no longer a God hidden in the mythical beyond, indifferent to the realm outside him, but a God who, in Creation, had initiated a process of relatedness and had taken the first step toward revelation.

Revelation: The Motif of Love

The relationship between God and man is manifested in the process called Revelation. In Rosenzweig's philosophy this is not a one-time occurrence, although it is the revelation on Mt. Sinai which suggested to him this trend of thought. The contents of the ever-renewed, ever-present Revelation is God's love for man. Man, in becoming conscious of the fact that he is created and loved by God, becomes a Self. God's love awakens in man the faculty to respond, to relate himself to others, to love. God's love for man is the origin of the divine commandments to man and, first among them, of the commandment to love one's neighbor, a created being like himself.

In the realm of Revelation, man's love for God is constantly being translated into his meaningful action in the world. Love is the power which keeps the challenge of the divine commands from becoming stale, rigid, statutes; it is the power which prevents man's response in action from becoming a routine performance. The world in which such action is called forth by love is not a mechanical universe functioning by immutable, neutral, blind laws, but a sacred ground on which God and the human person meet. Neither is any longer isolated, hidden in an impenetrable solitude, but both are manifest, and acting upon a real world.

Revelation signifies the final perfection of the relationships between the original elements, God, world, and man. Creation points to the past, Revelation to the present; Redemption is oriented toward the future.

Redemption

As Creation points to Revelation in which the intention of the Creator is fulfilled, so Revelation and its central theme of love point to Redemption and its central theme—perfection, eternity. Man, in translating his love for God into love for his neighbor, takes part in leading the world toward Redemption, a concept patterned by Rosenzweig after the traditional idea of a Messianic redemption and the "Kingdom of God." It is in the practice of deeds of love in this world that the fleeting moment is permeated with eternity. Death, which is the portion of everything created and most keenly felt by man, is transcended by redeeming love. "For love is strong as death," Rosenzweig quotes from the Song of Songs.

The aspect of future fulfillment, of continuity, of eternal life, implied by the term Redemption, is not something confined to a realm beyond earthly time, to a "Hereafter." According to Rosenzweig, it is in the power of man to experience eternity, the fullness of God's love, in the present moment; man is able to fill the present, fleeting moment with the characteristics of the future, or as Rosenzweig calls it, to "anticipate" Redemption. In the realm of religion, it is the ritual and the liturgy, the institution of the Sabbath and the rhythm of the Holy Days in which Redemption is symbolically represented and in which "eternal life" is "planted in our midst" (to use the phrase from the blessing over the Torah reading).

The Human Person

This "new thinking," as Rosenzweig developed it, assigns to the human person a central position in life. The new thinking concerns itself with each individual, not with men in general, or humanity in general, with which the philosophic system of German idealism had dealt. In Rosenzweig's religio-philosophical thought, man is seen as actively engaged in a life of meaningful responses to God and world, a life spent in the presence of the One who is beheld in his relationship to man and to the world, through the modes of Creation, Revelation, and Redemption..

Philosophy and Theology; Science and Faith

Rosenzweig does not wish to leave this re-interpretation of man and his position in the universe in the hands of theologians. He believes that a new type of thinker is required for this task, "a type that stands between philosophy and theology," combining in himself the discipline of both fields. Also science and religion cannot ignore each other but must come to an ever closer cooperation. True, "the object of science is not God but the world," but "God has created the world, and thus the object of science." However, in using the terms religion, faith, belief, Rosenzweig does not refer to dogmas or to abstract theological principles, but—taking the existential approach—to "having a hold which holds one's entire being."

Judaism and Christianity

The comprehensive view which sees the need of both religion *and* philosophy, science *and* faith, finds expression also in Rosenzweig's attitude to Christianity. As he sees it, both Judaism and Christianity are true and valid interpretations of reality under the aspect of Creation, Revelation, and Redemption. But the differences between them are profound; and the differences originate from two separate and historically necessary destinies. Judaism is understood as the "eternal life," Christianity as the "eternal way."

The Christian is born a pagan; baptism, his inner transformation, makes him a Christian. He is always on his way from the first to the second advent of Jesus, a road that takes him through the ups and downs of history; he is sent out to win the world for the faith, to convert the pagan; he must involve himself in the problems of power, conquest, and expansion. He, too, realizes eternity within fleeting time, but he knows that the goal is forever before him.

The Jew, on the other hand, is born a Jew. He is a member of a community that seeks its inwardness and there finds its peace. Keeping in mind the medieval Jewish community, to a large degree segregated from the surrounding Christian world, Rosenzweig assigns to the Jew the role of living the life of a "remnant," dedicated to worship and learning and deeds of charity, concentrated on the eternal and removed from political activity and concern for world-historical movements. The Jew will render service to the country of his residence, but his innermost concern will not be political but "messianic;" after he lost his earthly Jerusalem and the state, he lives in the reality of the Kingdom of God. "Eternal life is planted in our midst."

Both Judaism and Christianity have only a portion of truth; neither has the whole truth. And man can reach his portion of truth only in realizing it, verifying it by his actions, and, if necessary, sacrificing his life for it. The whole truth is not with men, but with God.

Rosenzweig is perhaps the first modern Jewish thinker to take so broad and liberal a view of the Christian faith; for him, such a perspective was the product not of a shallow display of "good will" but of a realistic view of historical and sociological facts.

How Much Observance of Jewish Law

In the *Star of Redemption*, Rosenzweig outlined the foundations of his view of God, world, man, and of the function of Judaism and Christianity in the Western world. Upon these foundations Rosenzweig constructed his own life as a Jew. Within the framework of Jewish life, he gave much thought to the issue of religious traditions and observance.

In his monumental *Lectures About Judaism*, Martin Buber dealt, among other issues, with the problem of how to study Judaism. He opposed the distinction between what is "essential" and what is "nonessential" in Jewish learning. Much too often the "essential" became that body of ethical and generally human sayings in Judaism. Buber advocated more thorough immersion into the literary sources of Judaism, an endeavor on the part of the student to become "a link in the chain of tradition." Only then would that student be in a position to make an authentic, personal choice from the accumulated knowledge of the centuries. No one can know in advance what in the "vast material of learning" will turn out to be "teaching," that is, the source of immediate, relevant, life-shaping instruction. But to reach this goal, the long, arduous road through "learning" must be taken.

Rosenzweig in his treatise *The Builders,* addressed to Martin Buber, argues that what applies to Jewish studies, the realm of knowing, should apply equally to the other central expression of Judaism, the Law (*Halakhah*), the realm of doing and living. Observance of Jewish law, of custom and ritual, is too easily discarded in the Western world, especially since the critical observer is no longer sure of the Law's divine origin. But the Jewish law does not stand, or fall, with the belief, or disbelief, in the direct, verbal revelation of the laws. These laws are deeply rooted in the spiritual soil of Jewish life, with the growth of Judaism through the ages. They therefore deserve serious reconsideration today.

Rosenzweig does not advocate the Orthodox approach of total commitment to the Law, but a *choice*—a choice based, however, on the actual experience of living under the Law. Only in action (and not before) can we realize the scope of our ability to act and to act meaningfully, just as only in the process of "learning" can we realize what we, personally, can accept as "teaching."

By such reasoning Rosenzweig wished to revive concern with practical *Halakhah,* as one of the documentations of classical Judaism. His own free choice ultimately included the whole wide range of Jewish observance. An outsider looking at the observance in his home—with prayer, benediction, and, on the Sabbath and holidays, a scrupulous abstinence from all proscribed manner of work—would conclude that here was a strictly Orthodox Jew. But for his contemporaries Rosenzweig answers the question "How much?" by asking them to evaluate their own faculties.

Views on Education

The great menace to contemporary Judaism is not the variety of possible viewpoints in the growing secularization of life, nor the intellectual and cultural intercourse with the world at large, but rather ignorance. Rosenzweig knew that to be effective today Jewish ideas must be secularized, that is, brought into living contact with the "worldly" life of man and society. However, Judaism must be known if it is to become a spiritual force of aid to bewildered, confused men today. Such knowledge can be gained only by direct contact with the literary sources of Jewish life and thought. Only men who actively engage in study of the basic documents of Judaism (rather than the reading of shallow condensations and popularized presentations), and who, at the same time, preserve their freedom to examine and to question, can overcome the great cleavage between classical Judaism and modern life. Then and only then, will the potentialities in both realms come to full fruition.

Rosenzweig's goal was a new form of the ancient Jewish "learning," which is not a gathering of information but a dedicated study and interpretation of the great books of Judaism, and an attempt to examine our problems in the light of age-old wisdom. He believed that the sacredness of that pursuit could be restored today. In emphasizing this, he once explained to a Christian minister that "Jewish learning is no theology; in what it means to us it roughly corresponds to your sacrament," adding that if speaking before Jews, the address is something like "your communion."

This liberal and at the same time traditional approach, considered in the beginning as too daring, received ever wider acceptance as the work progressed in Rosenzweig's *Lehrhaus*. There the old and the new met; certain problems, human and Jewish, were recognized as common to all; the experience of a common ground helped to create the unity which Rosenzweig had first found for himself. And as the Frankfurt experiment was imitated in other communities, the best in central European Jewry came to appreciate the value-directed and at the same time the liberalizing power of Jewish "learning."

In contrast to a lecture or even a good university seminar, learning implies a patient examination of sources and a patient consideration of what a book contains. Nothing is known in advance. This attitude, however, only the unprofessional man can manage; only he can regard the naive questions of the other more seriously than his own clever answers. A mixture of boldness and modesty is required for "a pursuit so dangerous and yet so necessary." For, "while this unsupervised learning is indeed dangerous, it is necessary in a time of transition, when the old teachers, the scholars, are no longer recognized as guides, and the new ones have not yet appeared."

The Hebrew Language

Jewish observance, though limited by a Jew's personally conditioned background, was to be based on a knowledge of the literary sources which accompany and demonstrate the way of Jewish tradition through the ages.

Rosenzweig approaches the intricate problem of the Hebrew language with a similar attitude. Is Hebrew a sacred language, confined to the prayerbook and the religious literature, or is it a spoken, living language like the others? It is both, Rosenzweig answers. The two realms of the "sacred" and the "secular" interpenetrate; they act as checks and balances one upon the other. Thus, it comes about that the "sacred" Hebrew language, through its contact with the colloquial Hebrew, is protected against petrification; the spoken language, on the other hand, lives in a constant reference to the long history of the Hebrew tongue.

Rosenzweig discusses this issue of the Hebrew language in a critical review of Jacob Klatzkin's translation into Hebrew of the *Ethics* by Spinoza. Klatzkin, a theoretician of pure Jewish nationalism at the time, conceived modern nationalist Judaism as based only on the Hebrew language and the soil of Palestine, thus denying the relevance for the modern age of Israel's spiritual tradition. Rosenzweig opposed Klatzkin, stressing both the importance of tradition in the Hebrew language and the importance of the Diaspora for the land of Israel. Here again, the key to the issue is a thorough knowledge of the past, a knowledge, by the way, which Klatzkin possessed but refused to be guided by.

His Non-Zionism

Rosenzweig remained outside the Zionist movement, so vigorous a force in Central Europe at the time. That movement seemed to Rosenzweig to overstress the temporal, earthly, historical tendencies of Judaism and to underplay the specifically religious aspects which Judaism was destined to represent in the world. This critical attitude to Zionism did not exclude a deep love for the land of Israel. And as the upbuilding of Palestine progressed, Rosenzweig realized that the practice of Zionism was far more important than its nationalist theory which he had criticized. Without giving up his idea of an eternal *Klal Yisrael,* he admitted that a rebuilt Zion is *one* of the possible, even necessary, ways of fulfilling the task of being a Jew and of establishing the Kingdom of God on earth. It is difficult to say how he would have viewed the establishment of the State of Israel. With all due caution it may be suggested that he would have accepted the reality of the state but would have worked for a close, non-political interrelationship between Zion and the Diaspora Jewish community, and toward a strengthening of the relevance of classical Jewish thought as the guiding forces of life in Judaism.

Evaluation

In reading Rosenzweig's religious philosophy (the present discussion gives only a bare simplified outline) it is not important to ask whether or not his teachings are acceptable this day and in this country as the basis of the Jewish faith or of faith in general. Some may feel attracted by the profound interpenetration of philosophy and religion, by his liberalism and concern for the individual; others may object to what sounds like an abstraction, and dislike the use of theological terminology which at times obscures the rational character of his thought.

What truly matters, however, is the fact that here a modern philosopher and historian, who came to Judaism from the periphery, found in classical Jewish sources (*Midrash,* Talmud, Bible commentaries, medieval philosophy and poetry, prayer book) the material from which to construct a complete system of religious philosophy. Dissatisfied with the shallow definitions and surface performance of modern Judaism, Rosenzweig penetrated into the depth of classical Jewish thinking and demonstrated that it is possible to give it meaning today. Others, approaching the same material, may find different emphases, Rosenzweig himself spoke of this possibility. But no Jewish thinker after Rosenzweig will be able, in clear conscience, to dismiss as dated, the rich, though complicated, thought-tradition of Israel. In the words of Reinhold Niebuhr, "Rosenzweig's thought has the power of creatively renewing what seemed conventional and even dead." Thus Rosenzweig's call to review our sources, the *Lehrhaus* idea, and the example of his own attempt at interpreting the ancient books in the light of present-day needs, are no less important than his actual teachings.

FOR FURTHER READING

Books by Franz Rosenzweig

The Star of Redemption translated by William Hallo (New York: Holt, Rinehart & Winston, 1970). A well-done English translation of Rosenzweig's classic work. Very tough going in any language.

Books about Franz Rosenzweig

BOROWITZ, Eugene, *Choices in Modern Jewish Thought* (New York: Behrman House, 1983). As always, Borowitz is a fair and intelligent guide who is able to make highly complex and abstruse matters available. A good first stop.

COHEN, Arthur, *The Natural and the Supernatural Jew* (New York; Behrman House, 1979, revised edition). Contains an outstanding chapter on Rosenzweig's thought. As Cohen is sympathetic to Rosenzweig he presents his position in its best light.

GUTTMANN, Julius, *Philosophies of Judaism: The History of Jewish Philosophy from Biblical Times to Franz Rosenzweig* (New York: Holt, Rinehart & Winston, 1964). An excellent review and critique, but for advanced students only.

ROSENSTOCK-HUESSY, Eugen, editor, *Judaism Despite Christianity* (New York: Schocken Publications, 1969). The text of Rosenzweig's classic debate with Rosenstock-Huessy over Judaism and Christianity. Rosenstock-Huessy, Rosenzweig's cousin, was a convert to Christianity and a major Christian theologian.

ROTENSTREICH, Nathan, *Jewish Philosophy in Modern Times* (New York: Holt, Rinehart & Winston, 1968). Provides a professional, advanced, technical decipherment of Rosenzweig's views. It will be best appreciated by more advanced students.

7. Martin Buber
[1878-1965]
MAURICE FRIEDMAN

No Jewish thinker has had a greater cultural, intellectual, and religious influence in the last four decades than Martin Buber. "We are all his pupils. The contemporary re-integration of modern Western Jewish writers, thinkers, scientists, with their people, is unthinkable without the work and voice of Martin Buber," Ludwig Lewisohn wrote in 1935.

Buber is significant for Judaism as religious philosopher, translator of the Bible, and translator and re-creator of *Hasidic* legends and thought, but especially as a religious personality who has provided leadership of a rare quality during the time of his people's greatest trial and suffering since the beginning of the Diaspora. After the death of Hermann Cohen, he emerged as a leader of Western European Jewry, wielding a tremendous influence not only upon the youth won over to Zionism, but also upon liberal Jews and even upon the Orthodox, despite his own non-adherence to Jewish law. "It was Buber," writes Alfred Werner, "to whom I (like thousands of Central European men and women devoid of any Jewish background) owe my initiation into the realm of Jewish culture."

Today, in his eighties, Martin Buber is a short man, stockily built, with a remarkably fine head and a white beard that make many think of him as the living embodiment of a biblical prophet. Outstanding and unforgettable are his eyes, brown and gentle, sometimes humorous and twinkling, sometimes penetrating and severe, but always revealing a startling openness, endless

levels of depth which seemingly enable one to look right into
the man and receive from him that great and comforting warmth
that one human soul rarely gives to another. He is marked above
all by simplicity, humor, seriousness, genuine listening, and an
unwavering insistence on the concrete. "Outside of Albert
Schweitzer," a well-known German educator writes of Buber,
"I know no one who has realized in himself a similar genuine,
deep identity of truth and life. . . . He is a living proof of
what this life is capable when it wills to fulfill itself fearlessly
and in responsibility." As Buber says of himself, "I possess nothing but the everyday out of which I am never taken . . . I
know no fullness but each mortal hour's fullness of claim and responsibility."

Early Influences

Martin Buber was born in Vienna in 1878 and, because of the
divorce of his parents, from the age of three until fourteen he
was reared in the home of his Galician grandfather. Solomon
Buber was at once a merchant and wealthy land owner, and an
editor and interpreter of classic rabbinic texts, one of the last
great scholars of the *Haskalah*. From his grandfather young
Buber received his introduction to the world of the Bible and
Talmud together with a lasting love of Judaism. He has described his grandfather as "an elementary Jewish being" who
"did not trouble himself about Judaism," for knowledge dwelled
in him and possessed his whole person; his world of the *Midrash*
was a wonderful concentration of soul and intensity of work.
In his home a pure and eloquent Hebrew was spoken, which
young Martin learned to love and speak fluently.

During this early period, however, he had no real interest in
the Jewish way of life, and soon after his *Bar Mitzvah* he gave
up most of his formal religious observances and stopped putting
on the *tefillin*. At the age of fourteen he returned to live with
his father in Lemberg, entered a Polish *gymnasium*, and in the
summer of 1896 enrolled at the University of Vienna.

Buber studied philosophy and the history of art at Vienna and
later at the University of Berlin, receiving his doctoral degree
from the former University in 1904. Among his teachers in Berlin were the philosopher and psychologist Wilhelm Dilthey

and the sociologist Georg Simmel. Dilthey provided an important bridge to Buber's early philosophy of "realization," for he based his thought on the radical difference between the way of knowing proper to a study of man and that proper to a study of the natural sciences. In the former, the knower cannot be merely a detached scientific observer but must himself participate to discover both the typical and the unique in men. Simmel's vitalist philosophy influenced Buber's emphasis on the superior reality of the life process to the forms to which that process gives rise, hence, of "religiousness" to "religion."

Also decisive for the development of Buber's thought was the socialist theorist and leader Gustav Landauer, who initiated him at the turn of the century into German mysticism and religious socialism. Ten years older than Buber, Landauer represented for Buber the unusual richness and profuse variety which marked the culture of Vienna at this period and which Buber made a part of himself. Landauer's activities extended from translating Shakespeare to making the first translation into modern German of the great mystic Meister Eckhart, and retelling the myths and sagas of various peoples—all of these areas in which Buber himself was to become interested and active. Buber himself edited the Finnish epic *Kalewala,* and wrote his doctoral dissertation on German mysticism from Eckhart to Angelus Silesius. But it was Landauer's religiously based and motivated socialism that had the most lasting effect on Buber's early as well as mature thought. Buber shares with Landauer the rejection of centralized and mechanistic state socialism, such as that which came into being in Russia after the Revolution, in favor of a federalistic, organic communal socialism. Like Landauer he recognizes that no political revolution can be of any value unless it is preceded and prepared for by a social revolution which alters the relations between men. Again like Landauer, Buber sees the possibility of true community as already existing within the depths of peoples through their common language, traditions, and memories.

An important influence on Buber's general philosophy as well as on his approach to Judaism was the German philosopher Friedrich Nietzsche, whom Buber called "the first pathfinder of the new culture." That influence may account, in part, for the dynamism of Buber's philosophy, for its concern with creativity and greatness, for its emphasis on the concrete and actual as opposed to the ideal and abstract, and for its emphasis on the wholeness of being as opposed to detached intellectuality. On the other hand, Buber has characterized Nietzsche's stress on "will to power" for its own sake, a sickness, and his philosophy of the "superman" a self-defeating nihilism.

Probably the strongest influence on Buber at this time, apart from *Hasidism*, was that of the nineteenth-century Danish religious philosopher Søren Kierkegaard, in whose early works are the germs of some of Buber's most important ideas: the direct, reciprocal relation between man and God; the insecure and exposed state of the "single one" in the concrete uniqueness of each new situation; the necessity of becoming a true person; and the importance of realizing one's belief in one's life.

Fyodor Dostoievsky, the Russian novelist, Buber ranks along with Kierkegaard and Nietzsche as one of the three great figures of the nineteenth century. In Dostoievsky, Buber found spiritual intensity, fervor, an understanding of man's inner cleavage, and a world-affirming mystic religion of ecstasy, love and brotherhood which bear a marked resemblance to his own thought.

Introduction to Zionism

In his early twenties Buber associated himself with Theodor Herzl, the "father" of political Zionism, and in 1901 he became the editor of Herzl's journal *Die Welt*. He subsequently broke with Herzl because of the latter's emphasis on purely political Zionism, and became the leader of those Zionists, including Chaim Weizmann, who demanded that the movement be based on a Jewish cultural renaissance. In 1902 this group established the *Jüdischer Verlag*, which later became the publishing house for the most important Zionist literature. They projected a Zionist monthly magazine to be entitled *Der Jude*, which they planned to address not to the limited objectives of the Zionist movement, but to the inner needs and actual situations of the Jew.

Though this magazine did not become a reality until 1916, once it emerged, it served as the central point for the higher spiritual strivings of the Zionist movement. It was in that same year that his famous controversy with Hermann Cohen took place, in which Buber attacked the elder statesman and leader of German Jewry for the anti-Zionism which he shared with the liberal German Jews who regarded Judaism only as a creed and not as a national movement.

The effectiveness of Buber's Zionism was demonstrated by the fact that *Der Jude* soon became the leading organ of German-speaking Jewry. Although Buber soon gave up active leadership in the Zionist movement in favor of his broader religious, philosophical, and social interests, he continued to exert a strong influence on the Zionist movement through his speeches and writings. Through his emphasis on the building of a real Jewish community he became a co-creator of the idea of the *halutzim* or pioneers, joining forces in 1919 with the Palestinian group, the *Ha-Poel ha-Tzair* led by A. D. Gordon. An outstanding historian of modern Zionism lists Buber, Nathan Birnbaum and A. D. Gordon as the three most influential leaders of Zionism after Herzl. The new perspective which Buber gave to Zionism was not understood outside of a narrow circle, and it evoked the most intense enmity of all the nationalistic-political Zionists. Yet, according to Bohm, whoever was able to follow Buber, was freed by his point of view from torturing doubts and inspired to more intensive work. In the whole sphere of Zionist activity, even that of political organization, it was Buber's disciples who accomplished what was essential.

Discovery of Hasidism

Though Zionism had given him new roots in the Jewish community, Buber became aware of its real meaning and content only after his discovery of *Hasidism*, the popular mystical movement that swept through the communities of east European Jewry in the eighteenth and nineteenth centuries. In his essay *My Way to Hasidism* Buber tells how when he was a child his father took him on occasional visits to the *Hasidic* community of Sadagora in Galicia. Although estranged by the conspicuous grandeur of the *Zaddik* (the leader of the *Hasidic* community) and by the wild gestures of the *Hasidim* in prayer, when he saw the *rebbe* stride through the rows of the waiting, he felt that here was a real leader, and when he saw the *Hasidim* dance with the Torah, he felt that here was a real community.

Later he went through a period of uncreative intellectuality and spiritual confusion, living without center and substance—

"without Judaism, without humanity, and without the presence of the divine." The first impetus toward his liberation came from Zionism which restored his connection with the Jewish people and enabled him to take root in the community anew. But Zionism was only the first step. "I professed Judaism before I really knew it," he writes. His second step, consequently, was wanting to know Judaism, and this brought him back to his childhood Hebrew and from there to *Hasidism*. He "read—read, at first ever again repelled by the brittle, ungainly, unshapely material, gradually overcoming the strangeness, discovering the characteristic, beholding the essential with growing devotion." Until one day in 1904, during his twenty-sixth year, on a visit to his grandfather's house, Buber picked up a little book which contained a quotation from the Baal Shem Tov, the Founder of *Hasidism*. In the description of the fervor and daily inward renewal of the pious man, he recognized in himself the *Hasidic* soul, and piety as the essence of Judaism. As a result of this experience he gave up for a time his political and journalistic activity on behalf of Zionism, and spent five years in isolation studying *Hasidic* texts. It was only after he emerged from this isolation into renewed activity that he entered on his real work as a writer, a speaker, and a teacher.

Hasidism played a central role both in the development of Buber's interpretation of Judaism and in the evolution of his general philosophy, and perhaps even more than the Bible it served as the meeting point between the two. Buber found in *Hasidism* the communal embodiment of the major emphasis of his early philosophy of Judaism—creativity, concern for personal wholeness, the realization of truth in life, and the joining of spirit and of basic life energies. He also found in *Hasidism* the most impressive attempt in the Diaspora to fulfill the biblical covenant and make real the Kingship of God by establishing the just community and bringing the love of God into the love between man and man. At the same time, as an affirmative communal mysticism concerned with "hallowing the everyday," a religious teaching concerned with the concrete and the unique situation of the here and now, and an inexhaustible treasury of tales pointing to a direct reciprocal relation between man and man and between man and God, *Hasidism* was uniquely qualified to lend impetus and solid content to the progression of

Buber's thought from his early period of mysticism through his middle period of religious existentialism to his mature philosophy of dialogue, or the "I-Thou" relation.

Throughout the span of more than fifty years of work, Buber has devoted himself to the retelling of *Hasidic* tales and the interpretation of *Hasidic* teaching. By his almost singlehanded labors, he transformed *Hasidism* from a little-known movement, largely unknown to Western culture and despised and neglected by the intellectual leaders of Western European Jewry, into one of the major mystical movements of the world. "Buber's discovery of *Hasidism* was epochal for the West," writes a contemporary author. He "made the thesis believable that no renewal of Judaism would be possible which did not bear in itself elements of *Hasidism.*"

In his earlier writings Buber regarded *Hasidism* as the real, though subterranean Judaism, as opposed to official Rabbinism, which was to him only the outer husk. He has since come to feel that in *Hasidism* the essence of Jewish faith and religiousness is visible in the structure of the community, but that this essence is also present "in a less condensed form everywhere in Judaism," in the "inaccessible structure of the personal life." In his first *Hasidic* books Buber exercised a great deal of freedom in the retelling of the *Hasidic* legends, but his later tales are closer to the simple rough originals. "These legends will remain a permanent possession of mankind in the form he has given them by virtue of that form which has itself become a part of their message and meaning," writes Ludwig Lewisohn. We must distinguish, however, as Buber does himself, between the undue freeness of the early legends and the faithfulness of the later "legendary anecdotes." When the Swiss novelist and Nobel Prize winner, Hermann Hesse, nominated Martin Buber for a Nobel Prize in Literature in 1949 it was particularly to these latter that Hesse pointed: "He has enriched world literature with a genuine treasure as has no other living author—the *Tales of the Hasidim.*" Buber's later *Hasidic* chronicle-novel combines both freedom and faithfulness, and it is this work, according to a noted authority on Greek religion and myth, that has won for Buber a secure place among the ranks of classical writers. It is a remarkable calling to life of the inner world of *Hasidism* and at the same time a profound literary creation comparable with Dostoievsky's *The Brothers Karamazov*, in its insight into the problem of evil. Of his own relationship to *Hasidism* Buber writes:

> I could not become a *Hasid*. It would have been an impermissible masquerading had I taken on the *Hasidic* manner of life—I who have a wholly other relation to Jewish tradition since I must distinguish in my innermost being between what is commanded me and what is not commanded me. It was necessary, rather, to take into my own existence as much as I actually could of what had been truly exemplified for me there.

Despite Buber's inability personally to become a *Hasid*, it is to *Hasidism*, more than to any other single source, that he has gone for his image of what modern man, modern Jewish man, can and ought to become. *Hasidism* is a mysticism which hallows community and everyday life rather than withdraws from it, "for man cannot love God in truth without loving the world." *Hasidism* accordingly rejects asceticism and the denial of the life of the senses. To cultivate joy is one of *Hasidism*'s greatest commandments, for only joy can drive out the "alien thoughts" or fantasies that distract man from the love of God. Conversely, despair is worse even than sin, for it leads one to believe oneself in the power of sin and hence to give in to it. One must overcome the pride that leads one to compare himself with others, but he must not forget that in himself, as in all men, is a unique value which must be realized if the world is to be brought to perfection. Everyone must have two pockets, wrote one *Hasidic* master. In his right pocket he must keep the words, "For my sake was the world created," and in his left, "I am dust and ashes."

According to Buber's interpretation of *Hasidism*, everything is waiting to be hallowed by man, for there is nothing so crass or base that it cannot become material for sanctification. The profane, "for *Hasidism*, is only a designation for the not yet hallowed. . . . Any natural act, if hallowed, leads to God. . . . Hallowing transforms the urges by confronting them with holiness and making them responsible towards what is holy."

Academic and Scholarly Activities

After World War I, in 1923, a Chair for Jewish religious thought, the first at a German university, was created at Frankfurt. Franz Rosenzweig, already paralyzed and too ill to accept the Chair for himself, persuaded Buber to take it. Entering formal academic life for the first time at the age of forty-five, Buber served for ten years as Professor of Jewish Religion and Ethics. When Rosenzweig could no longer take an active part in the Frankfurt *Jüdisches Lehrhaus* that he had started, Buber was also persuaded to take over its administration.

In the spring of 1925, when Buber was approached by a publisher to translate the Hebrew Bible into German, he agreed only on the condition that Rosenzweig undertake this task with him. While working together, Buber visited Rosenzweig once a week, bringing the newly translated material and digesting for him all the critical commentaries of other scholars. The product of these joint labors was a unique and remarkable translation of the Bible—one which retains the idiom of the original Hebrew in a forceful German, and is meant, like the original Bible, to be read aloud. The translation and its new methods of interpretation helped to produce a renaissance of Bible study among German-speaking Jews. Had that generation of Jews that went through the Buber-Rosenzweig school of Bible reading and Bible interpreting been permitted to grow up and remain together, "they would probably have become the most Bible-conscious Jews since the days before the ghetto walls had fallen in Europe." After Rosenzweig's death in 1929, Buber completed the Bible translation, a new and revised edition of which has recently appeared.

That translation had brought Rosenzweig and Buber into close contact. Buber had already become famous in Germany as a Zionist, a mystic and the recreator of *Hasidic* legends and thought before Rosenzweig, younger by a decade, had met him. The distrust which the younger philosopher felt for Buber's thought was strengthened by Buber's famous controversy with Rosenzweig's teacher and mentor, Hermann Cohen. They now found that after the war years, which had had a decisive effect on the thought of both men, they were closer together than they had realized. "My acquaintance with Buber has been epochal in my life," wrote Rosenzweig to a friend. "Even the similarity of thought is very great. But of greater importance to me is the awe-inspiring, almost superhuman genuineness of his being." A few months later he wrote Buber directly:

Our thoughts *themselves* meet and would have met even if you and I had not. . . . A different beginning, different grounds on which one must think, different contents for this thought, differences in what one spares and what one rejects; in a word: different men—and yet there exists between us a community, which is no "objective" one, and a common "goal" to which different "ways" lead.

Buber's concern with *Hasidic* tales and Jewish mysticism was as foreign to the more rationalistic Rosenzweig as Rosenzweig's tremendous philosophical system was to the intuitive and largely unsystematic Buber. Despite his respect for Buber's position, moreover, Rosenzweig never came to see Zionism as other than a final aspect of redemption rather than an immediately attainable goal, while Buber could not follow Rosenzweig in his growing emphasis on the observance of Jewish law. Yet the two men united in breaking away from the dominance of German idealist philosophy to what Rosenzweig called "The New Thinking"— a philosophy of dialogue or speech, at which each arrived independently of the other.

Under the Nazis

During the Nazi persecutions from 1933 to 1938, Buber served as director of the Central Office for Jewish Adult Education in Germany. There he was responsible for the training of teachers for the new schools established for Jewish students, who were now excluded from all German educational institutions. He also lectured and organized adult discussion groups and small groups of teachers and disciples who worked and lived together in work-communities. As many witnesses have testified, Buber saved thousands of Jews from spiritual despair by teaching them to die as Jews down through the ages have died—sanctifying the name of God. "He counselled, comforted, raised their dejected spirits," writes Jacob Minkin. "Perhaps not many of those who listened to him survived the fiendish slaughter, but if they perished, they died with a firmer faith in their hearts and a deeper conviction in their minds of their people's spiritual destiny."

Many of the remarkably sustaining and inspiriting addresses which Buber made in this period were published in Germany in 1936 in the book *The Hour and Its Knowledge.* Buber saw his leadership of the German Jews as "a spiritual war against Nazism," and he carried this war into the heart of the Nazi stronghold, fearlessly lecturing in Berlin until he was no longer permitted to speak in public and had to content himself with his writing. His important philosophical treatise, *The Question to the Single One*, was published in 1936 in Germany. That the Nazis allowed it to be published can only be explained on the assumption that they did not understand its implications, for it is, as Buber himself writes, an attack on the very life-basis of totalitarianism. Finally it became impossible for Buber to teach in Germany either in person or through his writings, and in 1938 he left Germany to make his home in Palestine, the Land to which many German and Central European youth had already emigrated under his influence.

Buber counts himself among "those who have not got over what happened and will not get over it." When he accepted the award of the Peace Prize of the German Book Trade in 1953, he pointed out that less than a decade before, several thousand Germans had killed millions of his people and fellow-believers "in a systematically prepared and executed procedure, the organized cruelty of which cannot be compared with any earlier historical event." "With those who took part in this action in any capacity," Buber said, "I, one of the survivors, have only in a formal sense a common humanity. They have . . . transposed themselves into a sphere of monstrous inhumanity inaccessible to my power of conception. . . ." At the same time, Buber pointed to other Germans who underwent martyrdom rather than accept or participate in the murder of a whole people.

"The solidarity of all separate groups in the flaming battle for the coming to be of one humanity is, in the present hour, the highest duty on earth," he wrote in explanation of why he accepted the Peace Prize. "To obey this duty is laid on the Jew chosen as symbol, even there, indeed just there, where the never-to-be-effaced memory of what has happened stands in opposition to it."

The Holy Land

In 1938, when he was no longer able to be of aid to his fellow Jews in Nazi Germany, Buber went to Palestine where he served until his retirement in 1951 as Professor of Social Philosophy at the Hebrew University in Jerusalem. In 1949 he founded and co-directed until 1953 an Institute for Adult Education which trained teachers to go out to the new settlements to help integrate the vast influx of immigrants into the already established community.

Since then Buber has been Editor-in-Chief of the *Israel Encyclopedia of Education*, and he has taught, lectured, travelled, and written with a vigor that provides an unparalleled exemplification of the psalmist's statement, "or even by reason of strength fourscore years." He has visited America three times—in 1951-1952 under the sponsorship of the Jewish Theological Seminary; in the spring of 1957 to give the Fourth William Alanson White Memorial Lectures at the School of Psychiatry in Washington, D.C.; and in the spring of 1958 as a Humanities Council Fellow at Princeton University. His eightieth birthday, on February 8, 1958, was an event celebrated throughout the world.

In Israel this was marked by a week of celebrations climaxed by a mass meeting at the Hebrew University at which Prime Minister Ben Gurion himself came to do Buber honor. Although in the world at large Buber has long been one of Israel's best-known citizens, the Israeli youth have not come under his influence to the same extent as the Jewish youth of Germany and Central Europe formerly did. For this reason, and because of the unpopular stand which Buber has taken as a leader of the *Ihud* (Union) Association for Jewish-Arab rapprochement, the celebration at the University marked a new phase in the encounter between Buber and the youth of Israel. He is one of the very few ever to have received an honorary doctorate from the Hebrew University and was even approached by some members of the government, and asked to accept the nomination for the Presidency of Israel after the death of his former Zionist coworker, Chaim Weizmann. Thus Buber must be counted among the highly respected minority, influential far beyond its numbers, but nonetheless a minority in respect to the mainstream of political and social thinking of Israel.

During his stay in Israel there has been a remarkable new flowering in all aspects of Buber's work.—His translation and interpretation of the Bible, his philosophy, philosophical anthropology, and philosophy of religion, his interpretation of *Hasi-*

dism—both his *Tales of the Hasidim* and his great *Hasidic* chronicle-novel, *For the Sake of Heaven*, were written in Israel and both of the latter are in Hebrew. In 1946, speaking of his *Tales of the Hasidim*, Buber wrote:

> Along with much else, I owe the urge to this new and more comprehensive composition to the air of this land. Our sages say that it makes one wise; to me it has granted a different gift: the strength to make a new beginning. I had regarded my work on the *Hasidic* legends as completed. This book is the outcome of a beginning.

PHILOSOPHY OF MARTIN BUBER

Martin Buber as a religous thinker and an interpreter of the Jewish tradition represents a synthesis of diverse streams of influence—*Hasidism, Haskalah*, the Bible, mythology and Western culture. Many of his insights into Judaism would not have come to him without his general training in Western philosophy, and his total approach to life itself has grown at every point out of his recreation of *Hasidism*, his study of the Hebrew Bible, and his fresh thinking through of the relation of man to man, and man to God.

For Buber, as for Rosenzweig, philosophy must rise out of thinking done from the personal point of view of the thinker. He rejects any attempts to find the "essence" of things in abstraction from the concrete reality of personal existence. His concern is with man and his relationship to the rest of the world.

The New Philosophy of Dialogue: I-Thou

The new thinking that is forever identified with Martin Buber is dialogical: it uses the method of speech. The classic expression of this new philosophy is Buber's little book *I and Thou*, a masterful poetic treatment of the dialogue between man and man and between man and God. Man's two primary attitudes are "I-Thou" and "I-It." Man's "I" comes into being as he says "Thou," as he enters into a direct, reciprocal relation with another human being. Later he also relates to others as objects to be experienced and used, and his existence alternates between these two kinds of relating. The "I-It" or subject-object relationship is always indirect. It enables man to comprehend and order the world, but it takes place within a man and not between him and the world.

Genuine human dialogue, according to Buber, can be either spoken or silent. Its essence lies in the fact that "each of the participants really has in mind the other or others in their present and particular being and turns to them with the intention of establishing a living mutual relation between himself and them." The essential element of genuine dialogue, therefore, is "making the other present" and "experiencing the other side." To meet the "other," one must be concerned with him as someone truly different from oneself, but at the same time as someone with whom one can enter into relation. It is this action of experiencing the other side that Buber believes to be the essence of genuine ethical responsibility, in which one's response is not to subjective interest or to an objective moral code but to the person one meets. It is also the essence of friendship and love, in which each member of the relation is made present by the other in his concrete wholeness and uniqueness. What counts in true friendship and true love, according to Buber, is the mutual reality which exists *between* the partners and which cannot be reduced to what goes on within each of them. If I am a real friend, I care about the other person for his own sake and not just for my own. I do not try to exploit him or make him over into my likeness.

But it is also possible to treat the other person as merely an object, an "It," to be observed and put into categories according to his capacities, race, religion, or social position. When we know a man in this way, we inevitably regard him as there for our use. Although we may not be aware of it, we are like the propagandist who wishes to mold and influence someone for the sake of his own cause but who does not actually care about him as a person of unique value in himself. We *must* use other people as means to our ends—the waitress in the restaurant, the ticket-taker at the movie, the milkman, and the engineer. But if we only relate to others in terms of how we may know and use them, we are not really human, no matter how much power and fortune we enjoy.

Neither do we become real persons through being concerned with ourselves, as we like to think today; on the contrary, we only become known by entering into genuine relations with others. In order that each person may realize his unique potentialities, he must be confirmed by others as to what he is and what he is meant to become. If we overlook the real "otherness" of the other person, we shall not be able to help him, for we shall see him in our own image and not as he really is. But if we allow him to be different and still accept and confirm him, then we shall have helped him realize himself as he could not have done without us. No amount of knowledge on the part of the teacher and no amount of scientific technique on the part of the doctor and the psychotherapist can make up for the failure to make the other person present and to experience the relationship from his side as well as from our own.

The "I-Thou" relation for Buber exists not only in the relations between man and man but also, in modified form, in man's relation with nature and art. Here the relation is not fully reciprocal, of course, since neither a tree nor a painting can move to meet us and address us, as one person can another. Yet, for all that, they can and do "say" something to us, and in that sense we have a dialogue with them. All things address us and speak to us of themselves if we receive them in their uniqueness and not merely in terms of their relations to other things—how they fit into our categories of knowledge and how we may make use of them. Artistic creation and appreciation does not, like genuine dialogue, mean an answering with one's personal existence of what addresses one, but it does mean a genuine response to nature and to works of art which retains the betweenness, the presentness, and the uniqueness of the "I-Thou" relation.

The fullness of dialogue, however, into which all other dialogue enters, is that between man and God. In contrast to the customary view that monotheism is the major contribution of Judaism to the religions of the world, Buber regards the dialogue with God as the center and significance of Jewish religion, and he sees the real meaning of monotheism as bringing every aspect of life into this dialogue. Many people know how to speak *to* God, writes Buber, who do not know how to speak *about* Him. "To believe in God means to stand in a personal relationship to God." God, to Buber, is the "Eternal Thou," who is met through the meeting with man and nature. The true God can never be an object of our thought. Even the most beloved person must again and again become an "It" for us, but God is always "Thou." He is always present; it is only we who are absent. Man becomes aware of the address of God in everything that he encounters if he remains open to that address and ready to respond with his whole being. God wants to come into the world through our loving relation with the people with whom we live and meet, the animals that help us with our farm-work, the soil we till, the materials we shape, the tools we use. "Meet the world with the fullness of your being and you shall meet Him," writes Buber. "If you wish to believe, love!"

Interpretation of the Bible

This same philosophy of dialogue has been of particular importance in Buber's interpretation of the Bible. In his approach to Scripture he leads us on a narrow ridge between the traditionalist's insistence on the literal truth of the Biblical narrative and the modern critic's tendency to regard this narrative as of merely literary or symbolic significance. The former tends to regard the events of the Bible as supernatural miracles and discounts as illicit the quest for any reality comparable to our own experience. The latter sees them as impressive fantasies or fictions, interesting from a purely human point of view. Between these two approaches Buber sets down a third:

> We must adopt the critical approach and seek reality, here as well, by asking ourselves what human relation to real events this could have been which led gradually, along many bypaths and by way of many metamorphoses, from mouth to ear, from one memory to another, and from dream to dream, until it grew into the written account we have read.

This third way is one which refuses the alternatives of factual history or universal and timeless myth and proclaims the history which gives rise to myth, the myth which remembers history. The saga is the direct and unique expression of the reporter's "knowledge" of an event. Rather, this knowledge is itself a legendary one, representing through the organic work of mythicizing memory the believe-in-action of God on His people. It is not fantasy which is active here but memory, that believing memory of the souls and generations of early times which works unarbitrarily out of the impulse of an extraordinary event. Even the myth which seems most fantastic of all is created around the kernel of the organically shaping memory. "Here . . . myth means nothing other than the report by ardent enthusiasts of what has befallen them. The experience of event as wonder is itself great history."

Buber's third way recognizes the connections of historical celebrations with ancient nature rites but also points out the essential transformation of those rites that took place when they were given a historical character. Moreover, in addition to understanding an event comparatively and in terms of the stages of religious development, it leaves room for its *uniqueness*, "which cannot be regarded as the fruit of thought or song, or as a mere fabrication, but simply and solely as a matter of fact." Important as the typical is in the history of religion, just because it is history, it also contains the a-typical, the unique. This concern with uniqueness is a natural corollary of Buber's belief that the absolute is bound to the concrete and particular: the essence of all religion is that "reality is open and accessible in the lived concrete."

Buber calls his treatment of Biblical history "tradition criticism," penetrating beneath the layers of different interpretations of tradition to a central unity already present in the original, and developed, restored, or distorted in the later editions. The Bible as "literal truth" and the Bible as "living literature" are thus supplanted in Buber's thought by the Bible as a record of the concrete meetings in the course of history between a group of people and the divine. The Bible is not primarily devotional literature, nor is it a symbolic theology which tells us of the nature of God as He is in Himself. It is the historical account of God's relation to man seen through man's eyes. "Miracle," to Buber, is neither an objective event which suspends the laws of nature and history, nor a subjective act of the imagination. It is an event which is experienced by an individual or a group of people as an abiding astonishment which no knowledge of causes can weaken, as wonder at something which intervenes fatefully in the life of this individual and this group.

"There are things in the Jewish tradition that I cannot accept at all," Buber has said, "and things I hold true that are not expressed in Judaism. But what I hold essential has been expressed more in Biblical Judaism than anywhere else in the Biblical dialogue between man and God."

The Biblical dialogue finds its most significant expression, in Buber's opinion, in the concept of the kingship of God. The people of Israel recognize YHVH as their King, and they recognize themselves as chosen by Him. Israel must make real God's kingship by becoming a holy people, a people who bring all spheres of life under God's rule. There can be no split here between the "religious" and the "social," for Israel cannot become the people of YHVH without faith between men. The mission of the prophets arises from the failure of the kings in the dialogue with God, from their tendency to a merely cultic acknowledgment of His kingship. The prophets fought the division of community life into a "religious" realm of myth and cult and a "political" realm of civic and economic laws. Their prophecy was altogether bound up with the situation of the historical hour and with God's direct speaking in it. They set before the people real choice in the present rather than the prediction of any certain future. The Messiah of Isaiah, similarly, is not a divine figure who takes the place of man's turning. God awaits an earthly consummation, a consummation in and with mankind. Through the "holy remnant" of Israel which never betrays its election by God, the living connection between God and the people is upheld, and from their midst will arise the Messiah. Through his word and life, Israel will turn to God and serve as the beginning of His kingdom.

View of Jesus

Faithful to his understanding of the Biblical dialogue, Buber sees the Eternal Thou as an imageless and sometimes hidden God who cannot be limited to any one manifestation and, hence, cannot be understood as having become incarnate in Christ. On the other hand, Buber has recognized and pointed to the tremendous religious significance of Jesus within Judaism, as possibly no Jew has heretofore done, while remaining firmly planted on the soil of Judaism. Buber's forty years of concern with Jesus and his significance for Jewish Messianism have culminated in an important study of Jesus and Paul, *Two Types of Faith*.

Jesus stood in the shadow of the Deutero-Isaiahic suffering servant of the Lord, writes Buber, but he stepped out of the real hiddenness which is essential to the servant's work of suffering. The meaning of the appearance of Jesus for the Gentiles "remains for me the real seriousness of western history," writes Buber. But from the point of view of Judaism, Jesus is the first of the series of men who acknowledged their Messiahship to themselves and the world. "That this first one . . . in the series was incomparably the purest, the most legitimate of them all, the one most endowed with real Messianic power, does not alter the fact of his firstness."

Whatever was the case with his "Messianic consciousness," Jesus did not summon his disciples to have faith in Christ. The faith which he preached was not the Greek *pistis*—faith in a proposition (That God became man in Christ)—but the Jewish *emunah*—unconditional trust in the relation with God. Paul and John, in contrast, made faith in Christ as the only-begotten son of God the one door to salvation. This meant the abolition of the immediacy between God and man which had been the essence of the Covenant and the Kingship of God. Though Jesus demanded a moral perfection necessitated by the imminent coming of the Kingdom of God, whereas Judaism demanded only that man serve God with this full capacity, both saw the Torah as God's instruction to teach man how to direct his heart to Him.

The faith of Judaism and that of Christianity will remain separate until the coming of the Kingdom, writes Buber. The Christian sees the Jew as the incomprehensibly obdurate man who declines to see what has happened, and the Jew sees the Christian as the incomprehensibly daring man who affirms redemption in an unredeemed world. Nevertheless, each can acknowledge the other's relation to truth only when each cares more for God than for his own image of God.

Approach to Zionism

Buber's attitude toward Zionism is integrally related to his conviction that in the work of redemption Israel is called on to play the special part of beginning the kingdom of God by itself becoming a holy people. This election is not an occasion for particularist pride but a commission which must be carried out in all humility. Israel's special vocation is not just another nationalism which makes the nation an end in itself. The people need the land and freedom to organize their own life in order to realize the goal of community. But the political state as such is at best only a means to the goal of Zion, and it may even be an obstacle to it if the true nature of Zion as commission and task is not held uppermost. If Israel reduces Zionism to "a Jewish community in Palestine" or tries to build a small nation just like other small nations, it will end by attaining neither.

One of the means by which Buber exerted the greatest influence on the Zionist movement was through his recreation of *Hasidism*. Through this discovery Buber opened up important new aspects of Jewish experience to the Jews of Western Europe and at the same time helped bridge the growing gap between them and the Jews of Eastern Europe, the hitherto despised "poor relations."

The essence of the essays that Buber has written on Zionism over a period of fifty years is the teaching that Zion must be built *be-mishpat*, with justice. "The use of unrighteousness as a means to a righteous end makes the end itself unrighteous," writes Buber. One of the central emphases of Buber's Zionism, correspondingly, has been his insistence that the Jews in Palestine live *with* the Arabs and not just *next* to them. In 1939 Buber wrote in an open letter to Gandhi: "I belong to a group of people who from the time Britain conquered Palestine have not ceased to strive for the conclusion of a genuine peace between Jew and Arab. By a genuine peace we inferred and still infer that both peoples together should develop the land without the one imposing its will on the other." We cannot renounce the Jewish claim, writes Buber, but we "consider it our duty to understand and to honor the claim which is opposed to ours and to endeavor to reconcile both claims."

Jewish Law and Ritual

If Buber's concern for Jewish-Arab rapprochement has often placed him at variance with official Zionism, his attitude toward Jewish law and ritual makes it impossible to identify him with any of the three American categories of Judaism—Reform, Conservative, or Orthodox. Buber does not stress the observance of

Jewish law, nor does he regard it as essential to the Jewish tradition. The Law, to be meaningful, must be a part of the dialogue between God and man and cannot legitimately be upheld as a separate objective reality. In the last of his *Talks on Judaism*, he contrasts the false desire for security of the dogmatists of the new law with the "holy insecurity" of the truly religious man who does not divorce his action from his intention. *"Religious truth is obstructed,"* writes Buber, *"by those who* demand obedience to all the *mitzvot* without actually believing the law to be directly revealed by God. The relation to the absolute is a relation of the whole man. To cut off the actions that express this relation from the affirmation of the whole human mind—as do those who advocate the observance of law as a means of preserving Jewish tradition and furthering Jewish civilization—is a profanation of those actions."

To Buber Zionism represents the opportunity of the people to continue its ancient existence on the land, an existence interrupted by the generations of exile. This implies that Jewish existence in the Diaspora from the time of the exile to the present cannot be understood as Judaism in the full sense of the term. The religious observances developed in exile have the character, in Buber's opinion, of conserving what was realized in the Jewish state before the exile. Following Moses Hess, he holds that the spirit of the old Jewish institutions which is preserved by these observances will have the power to create new laws in accordance with the needs of the time and the people, once it is able to develop freely again on the soil of Palestine.

In Franz Rosenzweig's famous essay, *The Builders*, he reproaches Buber for not accepting the Law as a universal, to be performed according to one's ability to do so. Buber replies that he cannot accept the laws and statutes blindly, but only as an embodiment of a real address by God to particular individuals. "Is this particular law addressed to me and rightly so?" Buber asks. On this basis, he writes, "At one time I may include myself in this Israel to whom a particular law is addressed and at times, many times, I cannot. And if there is anything I could with undivided heart call a *mitzvah* in my own life, it is just this, and I thus do and thus leave undone. . . . For me the one question which is sounded in my soul from abyss is: Is the Law God's Law?"

To understand Buber's relation to law and ritual, it is not sufficient to come to it with such ready-made categories as "How does he in fact observe?" or "How often does he go to synagogue?" One must approach these categories themselves in the light of this philosopher's understanding of revelation and of sacrament. For Buber the question is rather: "To what extent are these rituals, through our inner intention, through our participation and commitment, through our response to what God asks of us in the present, a part of the Biblical dialogue between God and man, of the *Hasidic* hallowing of the everyday?"

"If the answer were 'Yes,' I would not meditate on whether the Law is a force making for the wholeness of Life, for such would then be immaterial. On the other hand, no other 'Yes' can replace the missing affirmation. This missing 'Yes' is not quietly absent: its absence is noted with terror."

Buber has criticized severely those who see in Judaism only a one-time revelation of laws:

> O you secure and safe ones who hide yourselves behind the defense-works of the law so that you will not have to look into God's abyss! Yes, you have secure ground under your feet while we hang suspended, looking out over the endless deeps. But we would not exchange our dizzy insecurity and our poverty for your security and abundance. For to you God is one who created once and not again; but to us God is He who 'renews the work of creation every day.' To you God is One who revealed Himself once and no more; but to us He speaks out of the burning thornbush of the present . . . in the revelations of our innermost hearts—greater than words.

To accept the Law as a separate objective reality would be opposed to *emunah*—that unconditional trust in the relation with God which Buber feels to be the essence of Judaism. The Torah includes laws, yet is it not essentially law but God's instruction in His way. "A vestige of the actual speaking always adheres to the commanding word; the directing voice is always present or at least its sound is heard fading away." The conception of the Law as an objective possession of Israel constantly tends to supplant the vital contact with the ever-living revelation and instruction. The struggle against this tendency runs through the whole history of Israelite-Jewish faith—from the prophet's protest against sacrifice without inner intention to its peculiarly modern form in *Hasidism*, in which every action gains validity only by a specific devotion of the whole man turning immediately to God.

Buber the Teacher

Buber's philosophy of dialogue also is clearly reflected in his views on education. He is above all a teacher, and he elevates every activity to a work of education. Not only in his formal academic lectures at Frankfurt and at the Hebrew University, and in his adult education activities in Germany and Israel, but also in innumerable discussions with individuals and small groups and in the question periods after lectures, he has remained the teacher, interested not merely in the ideas of his pupils or partners but in those pupils and partners themselves. What is most essential in the teacher's meeting with the student, according to Buber, is that he see with the eyes of the student; that he experience the relationship from the other side without losing sight of his own. Only if the teacher makes the student present to his imagination in a real and concrete way can be avoid the danger that his will to educate will degenerate into arbitrariness and the desire to dominate and enjoy his students. Through discovering the "otherness" of the pupil, the teacher discovers his own real limits; but through this discovery he also recognizes the forces of the world which the pupil needs in order to grow, and he draws these forces into himself. Thus he makes himself the living selection of the world which comes in his person to meet, draw out, and form the pupil.

The teacher is able to educate his pupils only if he is able to build real mutuality between himself and them. This mutuality can only come into existence if the child trusts the teacher and knows that he is really there for him. "Trust, trust in the world, because this human being exists—that is the most inward achievement of the relation in education," writes Buber. The teacher who interferes, divides the soul into an obedient and a rebellious part, but the teacher who has integrity integrates the pupils through his actions and attitudes. The teacher must be "wholly alive and able to communicate himself directly to his fellow beings," but he must do this, as far as possible, without any arbitrariness or conscious striving for effectiveness. The teacher wishes to help his student, but he cannot desire to impose on him the product of his own struggle for actualization, for he believes that the right and the truth must be realized in each man in a unique, personal way. The real distinction between propaganda and education, accordingly, is not between a teacher's having values (or having the wrong values) and not having them, but between his imposing those values on the student and his allowing them to come to flower in the student in a way that is appropriate to the student's personality.

This means in Jewish education, as in education in general, that we betray a lack of real faith in the student and lose sight of what is really happening to him when we lay our sole stress on the content of Jewish education and lose sight of the unique personal relation that develops between student and teacher, student and book, if a genuine relationship to Judaism is to result. Adult education, in particular, is not conceived by Buber as an extension of the professional training of the universities, but as a means of creating a certain type of man demanded by a certain historical situation. "Adult education is concerned with character," says Buber, "and character is not above situation, but is attached to the cruel, hard demand of this hour." This means, ideally, individual instruction, real contact between teacher and student, "a truly reciprocal conversation in which both sides are full partners." It even means the readiness to deal with the personal lives of the students when these same students must, as in Buber's adult education institute in Israel, go forth to live with the people in the immigration camps in all situations of their lives. This concern with the students' personal lives does not mean that they should not learn the classics, Jewish and otherwise, but that they should do so not for the knowledge itself but in order to become whole persons able to influence others.

Influence of Buber

Today, in the third generation of his writing, speaking and teaching, Martin Buber is a representative figure for western European Jewry and world Jewry as well. He has done much to bring about a rebirth of Judaism, and his works will undoubtedly affect generations of thinking religious Jews to come.

Buber's philosophy of dialogue is a new and profound view

of human existence whose decisive implications for psychology, education, ethics and social thought are already widely recognized, as are its implications for religious philosophy. His influence on European Judaism has been far greater than on Judaism in Israel, where the division between Orthodox and secular has provided poor ground for his approach.

Nor is his influence in America comparable as yet to what it was in Germany and Central Europe. It is only in the last fifteen years that Buber's works have been published in America, but the great number of his works that have been appearing in recent years give evidence of the growing influence of his thought. Buber's early recreations of *Hasidism* can have no such vogue here as they had in Germany fifty years ago, even though they may increasingly be taken up as a part of the general interest in Jewish culture that is spreading in America.

Buber is unique among his contemporaries in the fact that his influence among Protestants has been as great as that among Jews, and he has had a significant impact on Catholics and Eastern Orthodox Christians as well. "To listen to Martin Buber," writes one Christian thinker, "means to advance out of the tumult and twilight of the secular into the eternal and to bow oneself before his, before our God, whom he proclaims with an impressiveness such as is seldom witnessed in Christian pulpits."

"Professor Buber," writes an Old Testament theologian, "is in a unique way the agent through whom, in our day, Judaism and Christianity have met and enriched one another."

Buber's existential "I-Thou" philosophy challenged "both orthodox and liberal theology," writes the theologian Paul Tillich, and "points a way beyond their alternatives."

American Judaism has on the whole been slower to assimilate Buber's thought than has American Protestantism, owing perhaps to the greater time-lag in the dissemination of European thought among American Jewish communities than among the Protestant. Also, while his thought has the virtue of preserving a rich, positive relationship to Judaism, the personal nature of his approach to religion makes it difficult to apply to many institutionalized programs in American Jewish life.

While an increasing number of American rabbis and Jewish lay leaders have come to a serious concern with Buber's thought, others reject all that Buber stands for with a vehemence often based on typical misunderstandings: that he must be too "Christian" since he has had such a strong influence on Christian thought; that, like the neo-Orthodox Protestants, he emphasizes God's grace at the expense of man's action; or that, like the atheistic existentialists, he emphasizes the dark and pessimistic aspects of human existence. There are also informed criticisms of Buber's philosophy of Judaism that have made it difficult for some to accept his views without serious qualifications. Some feel that he has presented a one-sided and too idealized picture of *Hasidism.* Others feel that he has emphasized the prophets at the expense of the patriarchs, or biblical Judaism at the expense of the talmudic and rabbinic; some that he does not himself take sufficient part in communal worship. The most serious objection to Buber, of course, is that he does not himself observe the traditional law and that he does not make the Law a cornerstone of his thinking. These questions are all serious, and for many, decisive.

If Buber refuses to make an abstract universal out of the Law but insists instead on the concrete dialogue with God in the particular situation, he also refuses, in the name of the dialogue, to follow liberal Judaism in treating moral values as a universal "essence" that can be abstracted from the body of Jewish tradition. One area of American Judaism to which Buber offers an especial challenge is that of social and personal ethics, which is in need of an honest and deep reassessment that will bring it into integral relation with the concrete daily life of American Jews. The universal ideal of justice and peace at the end of days must be converted into steps toward real community in the here and now. The "Covenant" must be reaffirmed as the task of becoming *a holy people,* a community of justice and loving-kindness, and not just a collection of well-meaning individuals.

On the basis of his understanding of the covenant and the Kingship of God, Buber criticizes the separation of nation and faith in modern Judaism. Reform Judaism has tended to look on Judaism as a religious creed, Conservative Judaism as a "civilization," and Orthodox Judaism as a set of religious laws. American Zionists view Judaism as a national destiny and perhaps also as a culture, but, for the most part, not as a people embodying an essential relationship to God in the life of the community. There is an ever-present danger in American Judaism of a dualism between "spiritual" values and everyday life. Only the overcoming of this dualism can make real the affirmation of the oneness of God that stands at the center of all Judaism. It is this that Martin Buber has emphasized in all his works.

FOR FURTHER READING

Books by Martin Buber

On Judaism (New York: Schocken Books, 1967). A collection, edited by Nahum Glatzer, of some of Buber's classic statements on Judaism.

The Knowledge of Man translated by Maurice Friedman (New York: Harper & Row, 1965). A collection of some of Buber's most important and difficult, later philosophical essays.

Books about Martin Buber

DIAMOND, Malcolm, *Martin Buber, Jewish Existentialist* (New York: Oxford University Press, 1960). A useful introduction to Buber's existentialist philosophy and Jewish concerns. Very readable.

FRIEDMAN, Maurice, *Martin Buber's Life and Work* (New York: Dutton, 1981–1985), 3 volumes. The definitive biography of Buber by his leading American disciple. Not too technical, a good starting point for study.

KATZ, Steven, *Post Holocaust Dialogues: Critical Studies in Contemporary Jewish Thought* (New York: New York University Press, 1983). Contains lengthy, detailed, technical criticism of Buber's philosophical and Hasidic corpus.

SCHAEDER, Grete, *The Hebrew Humanism of Martin Buber* (Detroit: Wayne State University Press, 1973). A broad, uncritical, introduction to Buber's philosophical and theological writings. Very much the work of a disciple.

SCHILPP, Paul Arthur and Maurice Friedman, editors, *The Philosophy of Martin Buber* (LaSalle [Il.]: Open Court Publishing Company, 1967). This collection of critical essays on all aspects of Buber's work remains the most wide-ranging and important of the secondary studies of Buber's work in its totality.

AMERICAN JEWISH
THINKERS

Until the Second World War, Jewish thought in the United States had neither the passion and fire of that of Russian Jewry, nor the profundity and depth of German Jewry's intellectual spokesmen. Aside from Solomon Schechter, Mordecai M. Kaplan and Kaufmann Kohler, there were few original theological thinkers in American Jewry. Nor were there any attempts to develop comprehensive systems of thought in the manner of Ahad Ha-am, Simon Dubnow or Martin Buber to serve as a guide to the perplexed of our generation.

There were diverse reasons for this neglect of Jewish philosophy and theology in the United States. First, the pragmatic character of the American environment has always stressed activity rather than introspection, in contrast to the German tendency toward abstract theorizing and philosophical speculation. In America, empirical research based on an accumulation of concrete facts has always been of more interest than conceptual philosophy. Throughout American history, there has existed an aversion for intellectual system and a lack of consistency in social and political thought.[1] In general, the scale of values in America has given less status and encouragement to the intellectual interested in religious or political theory than has been given to the intellectual in most European countries. This pragmatism is reflected in the American synagogue and in the sermons of American rabbis, who until recently, carefully avoided theological themes.

Secondly, during the early decades of the century, American Jewry was primarily an immigrant generation, absorbed in the problems of economic security and integration in its new environment. Even where there was interest, little time or energy was available for theoretical speculation and only today, in the 1960's, is Jewish culture in America beginning to receive the attention it deserves.[2]

Concern with the problems of Jewish survival, the emergency needs of world Jewry, and the intensified participation of American Jews in philanthropy have been additional causes for the deficit in original Jewish thought in this country. For the past generation, the psychic energy of American Jewish leadership has been directed toward raising funds for overseas relief as well as for local needs. The general public has been more interested in hearing about the problems of the Jewish people than in speculations on the nature of God or the concept of man. Finally, the restricted number of academic positions available in the American Jewish community has allowed relatively few scholars to devote themselves to the problems of Jewish culture and of Jewish thought.[3]

To these reasons must be added the fact that, as we have indicated earlier, Judaism throughout its history has not put great emphasis on theology. Rabbinic authorities have been wary about theological speculation, regarding *Halakhah* and the practice of the Jewish way of life as more important. Consequently the contribution of American Jewry to religious thought during the first four decades of the century was not commensurate with its potentialities.

However, beginning in the 1940's and particularly since the Second World War, there has been an increasing concern about the meaning of life, a revival of interest in Judaism and in the problems of Jewish religion and education. As a significant part of this trend, more attention is now being given to Jewish theology in academic circles, and at various rabbinical seminaries, on college campuses and in Jewish intellectual circles. Several new magazines and journals which contain an increasing number of articles on theological themes have made their appearance in the post-war period such as *Judaism, CCAR Journal, Conservative Judaism, Jewish Heritage* and *Tradition*. Also, the annual *Proceedings of the Rabbinical Assembly of America* (Conservative) and particularly of the *Central Conference of American Rabbis* (Reform) reveal this concern for the theoretical bases of religious faith. The American Jewish public has also shown an increasing interest in books and lectures on theological subjects.

In part, this is caused by the influence of Christian theology. The writings of Reinhold Niebuhr, Paul Tillich and also of Karl Barth and Emil Brunner have influenced a number of American Jewish thinkers in the post-war world.[4] But aside from such external influences, the anxieties of our time and the tragedies which befell the Jewish people have brought about a reevaluation of accepted approaches. And from the German Jewish philosophical heritage have come in recent years, translations of the writings of Martin Buber and Franz Rosenzweig and these, also, contributed to the new interest.

The immediacy of the period and the partisan feelings concerning many of the thinkers make it difficult to evaluate these current religious trends. No attempt to classify present-day theologians can do justice to the variety of approaches and to the nuances of difference among them. In this survey, we describe briefly the view of the existentialists, the religious naturalists and the liberals or modernists. Several of the thinkers, however, could be included in more than one category.

Some scholars describe the new interest in religious theory as a "theological renaissance" and emphasize the "seriousness and the passion of the theological quest in our day." [5] Others, however, are less optimistic in their appraisal and feel that we are merely at the beginning of the development of a Jewish theological literature. They point to the "paucity of Jewish theological achievement as contrasted with that of Catholicism and Protestantism . . . the insignificant recognition of the significance of theology and of its role in Jewish life," and the "fewness of Jewish scholars in general and of theologies in particular as compared with those of our neighbors." [6] Whatever the extent of this new concern with ultimate religious issues, a new and searching state of mind clearly exists and American Jewish thinkers are evidencing a sincere desire to cope with the intellectual hunger of our time.

One of those who helped to create this new spiritual climate was Milton Steinberg (1903-1950), whose brilliantly written theological essays in the 1940's pointed to the growing need in our generation for theological speculation. In Steinberg's view, religion caters to four distinct human needs: the need for a philosophy or theology, ritual, a system of ethics and religious emotion and associations.[7] While all of these elements are important for a "balanced religion," theology, or the search for an interpretation of reality as a whole, was considered by Steinberg the most important. Human beings, as Steinberg saw them, were "insatiably curious about metaphysics," and needed a religious *Weltanschauung* (one of his favorite words) to illuminate the nature of things and to live morally in the world.[8]

Although Milton Steinberg was a disciple of Mordecai Kaplan in his approach to Jewish culture and community and throughout his life remained a Reconstructionist, he did not share Kaplan's conviction of the futility of metaphysical speculation. For Steinberg, the riddle of the universe was not so readily dismissed. To him it made "a great deal of difference whether God is an Entity, a Being in Himself or whether He is an aspect of reality." [9] The purpose of religion was to throw a beam of light into the obscurity of the universe and in this light derive hope for the destiny of man.

Steinberg took a common-sense approach to the Jewish religion.

The God faith, to him, met the tests of practicality, plausibility and simplicity much better than did any mechanistic interpretation. He was among the first of American Jewish thinkers to become thoroughly familiar with Christian theological thought. He was well versed in the new existentialist and revelationist doctrines which dominated Protestant thought in the post-war period. He recognized their value as protests against those modern philosophies which rarified the living God into an abstract idea. However, he opposed their rejection of intellect as an instrument for attaining truth and found their pessimistic view of human nature as uncongenial to normative Judaism. To him, reason, though perhaps a limited instrument, remained the only means by which decisions could be made among conflicting "truths" and was "the sole pipeline for the communication of ideas." [10]

In spite of Steinberg's opposition, during the decade or more since his death, the existentialist approach has been applied to Judaism with increasing frequency by Jewish thinkers. Although the new thinking has not been adopted by the Jewish educators and social workers, as some of its exponents would have liked [11] and there has been resistance on the part of many rabbis to this orientation, a number of the younger Jewish theologians are now writing from this point of view.

Many existentialists shun the use of the word. They make clear that there is no existentialist system or school of thought; they do not want to be identified as "existentialists" since they disagree with other thinkers who share this label. [12] But they are united in repudiating the method and attitude of religious liberalism with its emphasis on reason, optimism and faith in man. Their point of departure is not the problem of faith and reason but that of the individual and his situation. For some Jewish existentialists this "situation" is the "dread and anxiety" of life and its ultimate meaning and purpose; for others it is the "joy and exultation" of the religious life.

To the Jewish existentialist there is only one form of authentic existence and that is existence under the covenant as described in Biblical and rabbinic Judaism. This covenant is an objective, supernatural fact designed by God to save man from isolation and meaninglessness. The current naturalistic and liberal orientations with their emphasis on the "idea of God" are inadequate. To the existentialist the "idea of God" is meaningless. God is important only if there is a personal relationship to him. [13]

Will Herberg was one of the first American Jewish thinkers to present this point of view in systematic form. Beginning as a "thoroughgoing Marxist," Herberg, like Hermann Cohen and Franz

Rosenzweig, came to Judaism from the outside. In a moment of crisis in his personal life, he encountered Niebuhr and felt his "whole being . . . shifted to a new center." [14]

Herberg's central concern, as he describes it in *Judaism and Modern Man* (1951), is the plight of modern man, his frustration and despair, his fragmentary existence and lack of orientation. One by one, Herberg examines the various "substitute faiths" in which modern man has put his hopes, such as science, psychoanalysis, Marxism and liberalism and finds that each is a way of evading ultimate theological issues. Man requires belief in an absolute God. But God can be deduced neither from history nor from the inner depths of human consciousness, as many modern thinkers would do. Intellectual affirmation is not enough. A "leap of faith" is called for, a return to the living God and a total commitment to him. [15]

Herberg's anti-rationalism, his preoccupation with sin—including the notion of original sin—his readiness to use Christian categories in his writings and his deep and overwhelming sense of crisis, led to considerable criticism of him in the Jewish community, and in recent years his influence has Waned. [16]

The neo-*Hasidic* writings of Abraham Heschel, professor at the Jewish Theological Seminary and descendant of a *Hasidic* dynasty, however, are much more authentic and have attracted a wide circle of readers. Schooled in contemporary thought, Heschel is an exponent of neo-mysticism and reaffirms the values of religious experience. His books which include *Man Is Not Alone* (1951), *The Sabbath: Its Meaning for Modern Man* (1951), *Man's Quest for God* (1954) and *God in Search of Man* (1955) contain many insights written with vivid word images and often in ecstatic language.

Heschel agrees with Herberg that man's intellect is insufficient to furnish the truth about God and the world. How then does one become aware of God's presence? According to Heschel, there are three starting points of contemplation about God; three trails that lead to Him. The first is the way of sensing the presence of God in the world. Viewing the world as power, beauty or grandeur will not result in the discovery of God. But by becoming aware of the ineffable, by responding with radical amazement to the sublimity of experience, we achieve new insights into the unknown. Second is the way of sensing His presence in the Bible, which to Heschel is the "repository of God's will." It came into our possession through divine revelation and is an answer to the question: what does God require of us? The third way of sensing His presence is in sacred deeds or *mitzvot*. These three ways do not enable us to comprehend God's nature, but they help us to apprehend Him, to establish a link with Him. Heschel calls this form of relation-ship a "leap of action" in distinction to Herberg's "leap of faith." [17]

Some present-day writers do not classify Heschel as a theologian but as a "poetical, mystical expositor of Jewish teaching and way of life." [18] Whatever the classification, his books on the meaning of prayer and the values of the Sabbath, and his strong religious fervor have helped to establish him in religious circles as a thinker of note.

Aside from Herberg and Heschel, several younger Jewish theo-logians are now using the existentialist approach as a framework for interpreting Judaism. Emil Fackenheim, professor at the University of Toronto, also draws from Niebuhr and is opposed to the "secular beliefs of the enlightenment" as reflected in liberal and naturalistic approaches. To him, also, the brutal facts of the past fifty years have demonstrated conclusively man's inability to save himself. "Moral progress is exposed to tragic frustration. Man can mitigate the tragic and evil in history, but cannot eliminate it." [19]

Fackenheim sees modern man facing a fundamental decision: is human existence closed or open to the Divine? Can we return from the shallow beliefs in "ideals" and "cosmic principles, remote and indifferent" to a faith in the "living God" of Biblical times? We can doubt whether Abraham or Moses existed, but it is not pos-sible to doubt that the biblical account reflects something which did take place—a succession of overwhelming experiences. In the Hebrew experience, the presence of God manifested itself in the form of a divine human encounter, and the Jew made a total com-mitment. Being a Jew today also means an acceptance of a religious commitment similar to that of our ancestors. If Judaism was not a divine human encounter, but merely the product of Jewish genius, the whole question of Jewish survival is called into question.[20]

Jakob Petuchowski associate professor at Hebrew Union Col-lege, has also been described as a religious existentialist. Author of many articles on various phases of Jewish theology and of the recent volume *Ever Since Sinai: A Modern View of Torah* (1961), he deals particularly with the doctrine of revelation and with the prob-lems which it poses to a modern-minded person. Accepting the findings of biblical criticism, Petuchowsky does not subscribe to the literalist interpretation of revelation at Sinai. Nor does he assent to the liberal view that the Torah represents the human record of man's search for the Divine. For him as for Franz Rosenzweig, the uniqueness and sanctity of the Torah is not dependent on its literary composition. What is essential is that its documents are the witnesses of revelation. Through the Torah we plumb the depths of our Jewish self-awareness. It is the vehicle for the expression and communication of God's commandments.

Like Rosenzweig, Petuchowski distinguishes between Torah as "legislation," that is, something written in a book and therefore impersonal, and "commandment," which is addressed personally to the individual. The modern Jew must be willing to listen to the commandment, ready to shape his whole life according to the pattern of the Torah. In the final chapter of the book, Petuchowsky stresses that by study and experimentation the Jew must "try out" those practices and observances which might contain God's commandment to him.[21]

The application of the existentialist approach to Judaism has not gone without opposition among contemporary Jewish thinkers. Most vehement in their antagonism have been the Jewish religious naturalists, a small but articulate group, disciples of Mordecai Kaplan, who have risen to the defense of human reason, the possibility for goodness in man, and for a Jewish orientation without supernaturalism. The naturalist theologians are critical of the "exaggerated pessimism of the existentialists with regard to man's natural endowments" and of their concept of God.

Impressed by the success of science and the scientific direction of American philosophy, they deny the existence of any "realm of human knowledge beyond that apprehensible through men's faculties of mind." In their view "there is no conscious force outside the universe acting upon it." [22] Their viewpoint is similar to that of Henry N. Wieman among the Protestants, who conceives of God as a process rather than as an entity or being.[23] Religion to the naturalists is a manifestation of man's struggle to make the most of himself, which is, to achieve salvation.

The leading disciple of Kaplan is Ira Eisenstein, President of the Reconstructionist Foundation, who has authored a series of works popularizing his teacher's major ideas. These include *Creative Judaism* (1935) and *What We Mean By Religion* (1938). In addition, Eisenstein has published *Judaism Under Freedom* (1955) which reveals a catholicity of interest in many phases of Jewish culture and community living. He is editor of the Foundation's magazine *The Reconstructionist* which, long before the current revival, frequently featured theological discussions. Eisenstein distinguishes between belief in God, which has remained constant among Jews, and conceptions of God which, in his view, have varied through the centuries. To him, belief in God means believing that the ideals we cherish are real, that these values emerge out of the very structure of the universe, and will win out in the end.[24]

Eugene Kohn has also been associated with the Reconstructionist Foundation from its inception. In *Religion and Humanity* (1953), which contains his theological position, and in his more recent work *Good To Be A Jew* (1959), he deals with the role of religion in civilization. Kohn is opposed to the current retreat from rationalism. He recognizes the need for religious faith, but that faith, he is convinced, cannot afford to ignore the experiences of men who in recent years have explored the realms of science and philosophy in search of truth.

Like Kaplan, he does not believe that a metaphysical explanation of the nature of the universe is necessary for belief in God. Such thinking, to Kohn, may be edifying to the human spirit as poetry, but it does not add to our knowledge. We cannot define God, but only those experiences which we identify with the divine. Kohn, therefore, begins his study of religion with human nature and man's ethical personality. For him, as for Eisenstein and Kaplan, to believe that our ethical impulses are as much a part of the universe as the laws of cause and effect, is to believe in God.[25]

Kohn disagrees with Heschel on the role of prayer. In his view when Jews don't pray, it is not because they haven't learned the "inner life and soul of the words," but because the traditional prayers often assume a conception of God incongruous with life today and with the scientific outlook on nature.[26] Together with Eisenstein and Kaplan, he has therefore been in the forefront in revising the liturgy, to make it consonant with the changed status of the Jew and the realities of the world we live in.

Jack J. Cohen shares this naturalistic outlook on religion. In his *The Case for Religious Naturalism* (1958) he applies this theory to the problems of Jewish life as they exist today. Cohen regards "the efforts currently being made to restore faith in a personal God by stressing the limitations of science" as an indication of the decline of a sense of security in the post-war world. The mistake of the "theologically directed religionists" is their failure to see the "close relationship between ideas and experience." There are questions to which man cannot find satisfying answers, such as, how the universe came into being, or how a good God can countenance evil. Man should rather devote himself to an understanding of the orderly processes of the universe and the power of human reason to understand reality. To Jack J. Cohen, God is "that quality of the universe expressed in its order and its openness to purpose, which man is constantly discovering and upon which he relies to give meaning to his life." [27]

Probably the largest number of American Jewish theologians

can be described as liberals or modernists. Though differing among themselves in outlook, they are nevertheless united in recognizing the challenge of modern science and in wanting to reconcile Judaism with modern culture. They believe that truth can best win over error in the open arena of honest, critical examination. They accept the findings of the more moderate Biblical and historical criticism, but they take the Bible seriously as a storehouse of divinely inspired wisdom. Many of the liberals recognize the crisis through which we are living, but feel the answer does not lie in what they describe as "irrational philosophies." They hold on to a belief in reason, though most of them are not ready to give up what the naturalists call "supernaturalism in religion."

One of the most prolific of contemporary liberal theologians is Jacob Agus, a rabbi in Baltimore and the author of a series of works on Jewish thought. These include: *Modern Philosophies of Judaism* (1940), *Banner of Jerusalem, Guideposts in Modern Judaism* (1954) and *Evolution of Jewish Thought* (1960). Agus aims to offer a tenable ground for faith in a God who is an "absolute personality." In this effort he follows "the broad highway of reason and universal experience" rather than that of "sudden illumination or the pale detachment of mystical wonderment."

Agus sees a basic distinction between fundamentalism and liberalism. Faith to him is liberal when it is characterized by "openness of soul" and derives from "the inner life of the soul in its growth." It examines all truth by reference to "the living values of man's intelligence," while fundamentalism relies on an "extra-human source of truth."

Agus describes the fundamentalist view of revelation as "simple and naive." To him, beliefs must be rooted in the laws of truth implicit in the structure of nature and human nature.[28]

Another present day expression of religious liberalism from a rational Jewish standpoint is that of Robert Gordis. In *A Faith for Moderns* (1960) Gordis presents the "distillation of his insights and attitudes on God and man, life and death, the individual and society." He makes clear at the outset that he is not writing for the "untroubled believer" who finds no difficulty with traditional religion or for those opposed to organized religion. Nor is he writing for the existentialists to whom, in Gordis' opinion, subjective commitment is more important than objective truth. He cannot accept their surrender of reason, their lack of confidence in man's efforts to rebuild the world, and their lack of respect for man's intellect. If religion consists principally of indescribable experiences of the ineffable, there can be no community of belief and of action linking men together. Gordis is interested in reaching those "who are unwilling to withdraw from the world or resign from the twentieth century," people who are in search of a "rational basis for religion." To him reason and faith are not antagonists, but partners in comprehending the world.[29]

Expositions of a liberal religious faith have also been put forth by the late Samuel Cohon and by Louis Finklestein, Max Kadushin, Levi Olan, Abba Hillel Silver,[30] and other spokesmen for contemporary Reform and Conservative Judaism.

Alongside the views of individual thinkers who are trying to show the relevance of Judaism for the modern world, a renewed interest has emerged during the past decade within each of the major religious groupings in its own ideology and in formulating its point of view. During the period between the two wars the major concern of Reform Judaism was with the practical problems of Jewish life—assimilation, anti-Semitism and the great debate over Zionism. At that time, theology was looked upon with skepticism. But the post-war period and the crisis of our time brought with it a growing recognition of the need for a restatement of the liberal religious faith. Thus an institute on Reform Jewish theology was held at the Hebrew Union College in the spring of 1950, attended by a large representation of Reform rabbis. Among the questions dealt with were: is the belief in God as an objective Divine reality indispensable to modern Judaism? Is it possible for man to believe that an existing God is active in the world? To what extent is there authority within Reform Judaism? Can we still believe in progress as salvation? As a result of the institute a permanent commission on Jewish theology has been established under the chairmanship of Bernard Heller, with Eugene Borowitz, Jakob Petuchowski and Emil Fackenheim as members.[31] Conventions of the Central Conference of American Rabbis during the 1950's have witnessed lively discussions on such questions as the mission idea in Judaism and the importance of the "poetry and drama of observance."

Undoubtedly, the most hotly debated issue has been the question of a guide for Reform Jews—an official pronouncement on the way in which Reform Jews might or should act. Some Reform spokesmen have felt that a guide is needed to overcome the "chaos in the ranks of Reform Judaism," particularly among the laity, and to develop a positive approach to Judaism. This guide would furnish a "definition of the ideals, values, principles and practices of Reform Jews." Others insist that the lack of any normative philosophical or theological climate in the present Reform movement makes such a guide impossible. Moreover, they fear that a guide will become in time an unchangeable and inflexible code, which is alien to the spirit of Reform Judaism.[32] Though no action has been taken, the possibility for a "Reform *Halakhah*" is still under discussion. The point of view of Eugene Mihali that "there is no Judaism without *Halakhah*" is echoed by other Reform thinkers. For Mihali this means the need "to select, modify and apply *Halakhah* in some harmony with the conditions of today's living." [33]

The role of *Halakhah* in Judaism has been very much under discussion in Conservative Judaism as part of a general effort to define its position. Since the end of the 1920's repeated calls have been heard in the ranks of the Rabbinical Assembly for a clarification of program and a greater preoccupation with the positive tenets of Conservative ideology. During the 1930's and 1940's, the naturalistic orientation of Mordecai Kaplan was subscribed to by many of the graduates of the Jewish Theological Seminary where he served as professor of homiletics. But in the years since the war, the "center" or moderate group, which adheres more closely to the traditional outlook, has grown and now has the largest number of adherents among Conservative leaders.

The turning point in the post-war development of Conservative Judaism came in the fall of 1948. As a result of criticisms that the Law Committee of the Rabbinical Assembly did not go beyond what an Orthodox body would permit, the Committee was enlarged to include representatives of the varied points of view in the movement.

The members of the new Committee on Law and Standards, for the most part, agreed that Jewish law is a prerequisite for a full Jewish life and that wherever possible the *Halakhah* should be respected. They recognized, however, that to deal with the "realities of present-day Jewish life," amendment of some laws would be necessary. A decision was promulgated permitting the local rabbi to lift or modify the ban against driving to the synagogue on the Sabbath. Another decision permitted the turning on of electricity on the Sabbath on the ground that *Halakhically* and scientifically there was no identification between electricity and fire. The use of the organ at Sabbath Services was allowed. The Committee also considered the proposal to call women to the Torah. The majority, while acknowledging the *Halakhic* basis for this innovation, opposed it primarily because of the psychological conditioning of the people.

In 1953 a National *Bet Din* (court) was established composed of members of the Committee on Law and Standards and of the faculty of the Jewish Theological Seminary to deal with problems of marriage and domestic relations. A clause was inserted in the Jewish marriage contract (*Ketubbah*) under which the bride and groom agree in advance to accept the authority of a Jewish religious court which can compel a recalcitrant partner to grant or submit to a divorce.

The Reconstructionists in the Conservative movement are critical of the present approach of the Committee. They argue that modern life has rendered *Halakhah* as law invalid and that a way must be found to restore the richness of the tradition through spiritual insight rather than by the authority of law. The moderates, however, insist that *Halakhah* must retain its central place in Jewish life.[34]

In addition to *Halakhic* questions, the Conservative movement during the past decade has concerned itself with goals and standards for Jewish education and with the revitalization of prayer for the modern Jew. The relationship between America and the new State of Israel has also been the topic of many stimulating sessions at the annual conventions of the Rabbinical Assembly.

Orthodoxy also has experienced a revival on the American Jewish scene during the post-war period. The development of Yeshiva College from a small institution in the 1930's to a large university, the newly established network of smaller *yeshivot*, the remarkable growth of Jewish Day Schools, the emergence of a new type of Orthodox Rabbi conversant with the culture of our day, the contemporary revival of interest in *Hasidism*—all indicate that traditionalism is a growing force in American Jewish life.

Several Orthodox spokesmen are developing interpretations of Judaism based on traditional categories or on the existentialist framework. Samuel Belkin, president of Yeshiva University, in his *Essays in Traditional Jewish Thought* (1956) and in his most recent volume, *In His Image* (1961), applies traditional Jewish attitudes to several contemporary problems and shows how "*Halakhic* resources can be tapped for the development of an authentical Jewish *Weltanschauung*." Emanuel Rackman, assistant to Dr. Belkin, is the author of a series of provocative articles in various Jewish journals in which he puts forth a philosophic interpretation of Judaism within the general framework of religious existentialism.[35] Eliezer Berkovits, professor at the Chicago Theological Seminary, is an original theologian and the author of a series of works which include *Toward Historic Judaism* (1943), *Judaism: Ferment or Fossil* (1956) and critical essays on the philosophy of Mordecai M. Kaplan (1957) and Martin Buber (1962). Marvin Fox, professor at Ohio State University, fills an important role as critic in evaluating contemporary trends in Jewish religious thought. *Tradition* magazine, established in 1958 as a "forum for the interpretation of the heritage of Torah and *mitzvot* in a manner the educated Jew can understand" introduces a growing number of younger Orthodox writers on theological questions such as Norman Lamm, David S. Shapiro and Walter S. Wurzburger.

American Orthodoxy has yet to meet the challenge of modern thought and to develop a philosophy of Judaism as Samson Raphael Hirsch and Isaac Breuer did for German Orthodox Jewry. But the movement is gradually articulating its point of view based on "absolute faith in the Divine origin of tradition."

The theological trends outlined in this survey began after the last war and the tragedies which befell the Jewish people. They are, however, related to earlier intellectual developments in American Judaism, as reflected in the writings of Kaufmann Kohler, Mordecai M. Kaplan and more recently Joseph Soloveichik—the three thinkers included in the final section of this book. Kohler represents the period until the end of the first World War when classical reform was dominant. Mordecai M. Kaplan developed his theories during the 1920's and 1930's when rationalism was still the mood in American thought. Joseph Soloveitchik is one of the outstanding Jewish minds of the post-war generation. Each is associated with one of the major religious institutions in American Judaism—Kohler with the Hebrew Union College, Kaplan with the Jewish Theological Seminary, and Soloveitchik with Yeshiva University. Though these men differ in their viewpoints on many of the basic issues in Jewish life, they are united in their efforts to find a framework of meaning for Jews in the modern world. Alongside the intellectual figures who arose in twentieth-century Russia and Germany they deserve a place. It is to these outstanding American Jewish thinkers of the twentieth century that we now turn.

8. Kaufmann Kohler

[1843-1926]

SAMUEL M. COHON

K A U F M A N N Kohler stands in the forefront of the creative scholars and thinkers who have shaped and directed the development of American Judaism. He courageously wrestled with the problems of Jewish faith and destiny. As rabbi of leading congregations in Chicago and New York and as President of the Hebrew Union College, he vigorously championed the cause of progress in Judaism and raised hosts of disciples who spread his message from hundreds of pulpits. As a prolific and erudite contributor to Jewish periodicals and scientific publications, as one of the chief editors of the *Jewish Encyclopedia*, and as author of a comprehensive textbook of Jewish theology, he deeply affected the thinking of Jews as well as Christians on the nature of Judaism in the Old and New Worlds. He enriched the religious thinking of his time, bequeathing a rich legacy, which, despite the changing cultural and intellectual climate, has remained significant for Jewish religious life today.

Early Years

Kaufmann Kohler was born on May 10, 1843, in Fuerth, Bavaria, a city famed for its Jewish traditions and culture. In his *Personal Reminiscences*, an intimate account of his early years, Kohler lovingly recalled the atmosphere of learning and piety in which he was reared. His home, like so many in Fuerth, was marked by genuine devotion to Jewish Orthodoxy. His father

Moritz studied Talmud day and night. His mother, Babette Lowenmayer, who was descended from a rabbinical family, was also pious, despite her fondness for Lessing and Schiller, the German poets.

At the age of five, Kaufmann was initiated into the Torah by his father, who taught him *Humash*. At six he entered the day-school of Simon Bamberger, who combined instruction in Bible with lessons in secular subjects. After a conflict between the modernist trends and tradition, this school was closed by the government in the interest of "enlightenment." The ten-year-old lad was then sent to the nearby town of Hassfurt to study under the Talmudist Eisle Michael Schueler. Four years later he was enrolled in Markus Lehmann's new rabbinical seminary at Mayence, where, in addition to Jewish studies, he received instruction in Greek and Latin. At the same time he attended the Talmud classes of Simon Bondi. In his nineteenth year he entered the *yeshivah* at Altona, headed by Jakob Ettlinger, one of the most prominent exponents of Orthodoxy among academically trained German rabbis. A pronounced mystic, Ettlinger spent hours in prayer before entering the lecture room, where he dwelt chiefly on *Halakhic* questions.

Influence of Samson Raphael Hirsch

It was Samson Raphael Hirsch of Frankfurt-Am-Main who exerted the greatest influence upon young Kohler and fired him with "the divine ardor of true idealism." Kohler was always proud to call this romantic protagonist of neo-Orthodoxy his teacher and to acknowledge indebtedness to him for the best part of his innermost life. "It may sound paradoxical," he testified, "and yet it is true, that without knowing it, Samson Raphael Hirsch liberated me from the thraldom of blind authority-worship, and led me imperceptibly away from the old mode of thinking, or rather of not thinking, into the realm of free reason and research. His method of harmonizing modern culture with ancient thought, however fanciful, fascinated me. He made me, the *yeshivah bahur* from Mayence and Altona, a modern man. The spirit of his teaching electrified me and became a lifelong influence to me."

Hirsch's universalism, optimism, and conception of Judaism as "a religion of joy, of hope, of faith in humanity and humanity's future" became part of Kohler's thinking. Hirsch was "proud of his German nationality, declared himself a product of modern culture, imbued with the spirit of German idealism, and blessed the emancipation of the Jew as the dawn of the new era of universalism, the final goal of Judaism." During the year and a half that he studied under Hirsch, Kohler attended the *gymnasium* at Frankfurt in company with the two sons of Abraham Geiger, the leader of Reform, without ever asking them to introduce him to their distinguished father. Nor would he enter a Reform synagogue, having been taught to regard it as a *tiflah*, "a perversion of a house of worship."

Later, when he attended the universities of Munich and Berlin, the pious *bahur* tasted the forbidden fruit of knowledge and was banished from the garden of innocence. Hirsch's naive exegetical system, based on the traditional belief that Hebrew was the original language of man, crashed in Professor Mueller's courses in Arabic; and the bottom of his artificial theology was knocked out by the philosophical and historical lectures which Kohler attended. He wrote: "I passed days and weeks of indescribable woe and despondency; the heavens seemed to fall down upon me and to crush me." He traveled to Frankfurt to lay his doubts and scruples before his revered teacher, but instead of having them resolved, he received the remarkable answer: "My dear Kohler, he who wants to journey around the world must also pass the torrid zone; proceed and you will come back safely." He proceeded, but never returned to the position from which he started. The disciple of Hirsch soon found himself in Geiger's opposing camp.

Days of "Anxiety and Trial"

At the University of Berlin, too, Kohler met with one disappointment after another. The renowned Zunz was inaccessible to visitors, especially to theological students. Aaron Bernstein, the author of *Voegele der Maggid* and leader of the Reform congregation, greeted him with the words: "You have come here to study theology, but will turn out to be a hypocrite like the rest." Moritz Steinschneider's lectures offered him "only the husks of Jewish learning, lists of names and dates of authors and

of manuscripts, with all sorts of attacks on other bibliographers."
To keep up with his Talmudic studies, Kohler attended daily
lessons of Michael Landsberg, "a man of singular naivete." Jewish life in the city appeared to him "frosty and uncongenial."
He threw himself into his Biblical, philosophical, and historical
studies at the university, where he came under the influence of
Hermann Steinthal, whose mythological and ethnological ideas
strongly affected Kohler, for they dissolved the life and law of
Moses, the Bible, and theology into myth and fable. Kohler
wrote:

> It was the crisis of my life that I passed, while new ideas crowded
> upon my mind, driving it more and more from the old moorings
> . . . and I had no friend of prominence in the big city to confide
> in during these days of anxiety and trial. Nor did I have a real
> Jewish home to keep the cherished memories of old fresh in me.
> Still while wrestling with my God and my own past, I never lost
> hold upon my ancestral faith, nor did I become a skeptic . . . I
> only felt that I had outgrown the romanticism and conservatism
> of those who adhered to the Breslau Seminary. So in solitary
> strength of faith I followed my own ideal of progressive liberal
> Judaism.

The existing Reform forces offered Kohler but little help in
his spiritual struggles. He recognized the constructive and laud-
able efforts of the Reform pioneers, Jacobsohn, Kley, and Salomon, in checking the tide of apostasy by removing the "repul-
sive features" of the old synagogue and "putting the venerable
matron in a more attractive attire borrowed from the Church,
by introducing innovations, such as confirmation, the organ and
choir, and the sermon in the vernacular." But such esthetic measures could not save the thinking Jew from his inner discords.
The entire structure of Jewish life was faltering; the whole Law,
Mosaic and rabbinic, the dietary and purity laws, the Sabbath
itself, were being discarded.

In his confused state, only the teachings of Abraham Geiger
held out some help to the perplexed idealist. This historian and
critic of genius, who "gave Reform its scientific basis," accentuated the principle of historic continuity, believing in evolution
rather than in revolution; and seeking the wholesome growth of
the whole, not the breaking away of the part. Kohler was attracted to Geiger's genial and kindly personality, his intellectual

integrity and courage in marshalling the forces of Reform against what he considered hypocrisy and hollow formalism. The reforms which Geiger introduced and proposed, however, appeared to Kohler as half-measures which failed to satisfy the hunger of his heart.

First Concept of Reform Judaism

Kohler's quest after spiritual harmony and truth is reflected in the first fruit of his scientific labors. In the introduction to his doctoral dissertation, *Der Segen Jacobs*, which he wrote under the inspiration of Steinthal and submitted to the University of Erlangen (1867), he sketched the religious problem facing the young intellectual. He deplored the tendency to regard as holy everything that was old and to denounce everything that was new, denying men, in the name of religion, the right to think and to gain maturity and independence. The harshness and cruelty of this folly tended to drive the young generation to seek freedom through frivolity. Should not the educational system, he demanded, aim from the beginning to transform external religious forms into inward spirituality, customs into conscious morality? "Is it not imperative that children be taught nothing in the name of religion, which in the next years would be contradicted or nullified by the teachers of natural sciences?" In opposition to the apathy in some circles and the materialistic nihilism of others, he argued that religion is not something that can be displaced by philosophical or ethical abstractions. Religion "must try to adopt the forms in which it can best serve the struggle of the age toward truth and ethical freedom, and thus connect the traditions of the past with the ideals of the future." These ideals he identified with the prophetic dream of a future "when men, united by a love of peace and truth, would regard and love one another as children of one God."

To be effective, he insisted, the religion of the prophets must be presented as the product of history. By gradually reshaping the legal institutions and historical traditions, prophetism raised the ancestral religion to a higher level. "For the Alpha and Omega of Judaism is not the Law, but the eternal moral idea."

In this first draft of Kohler's concept of Judaism and of Reform, he found the answer to his own perplexities and those of his age by viewing religion as an ethical discipline. Applying the principle of historical development to the Pentateuch itself, he found the key to the solution of the conflict between religion and science and the promise of a sounder and more satisfying religious life. Evolution was the masterword of this new view of Judaism, to which he resorted throughout his career.

The Turning Point

The publication of *Der Segen Jacobs* became the turning point in Kohler's career. In his *Zeitschrift* and in private letters, Abraham Geiger welcomed the outspoken author and co-worker in the field of Biblical research, and became his warm friend. On the other hand, Lehmann, one of Kohler's former teachers, attacked him in his journal *Der Israelit*, bringing consternation to his pious parents. Loewi, who had planned to place him in charge of the rising congregation of Nuremberg, expressed sorrow at seeing Kohler's rabbinical career blocked by what he had written. "Must a man tell all he knows to people who will hardly understand him?" he asked. To which Kohler replied: "He did not realize that there was in me something of that fire of which the prophet Jeremiah says that it cannot be quenched."

At Geiger's suggestion, Kohler enrolled in a course of Oriental studies at Leipzig under the eminent Arabist, Professor Fleischer, with the intent of preparing for a professorship in the history of religion. But, as he wrote, he "felt so little at home in the camel-charged atmosphere of Arabic desert poetry" that he was drawn constantly to Biblical themes. Geiger now counseled him to go to America, "the land of promise for progressive Judaism," and paved the way for him by warm letters of recommendation to Samuel Adler, David Einhorn, Bernhard Felsenthal, and Max Lilienthal. Through Lilienthal an invitation was extended to Kohler by Temple Beth-El of Detroit to become its rabbi.

Before leaving for America, Kohler attended the Jewish Synod at Leipzig, where he came under the spell of Moritz Lazarus. "Never as long as I live," he wrote some years later, "will I forget the deep impression made on me when, on that memorable 4th of July, 1869, he, as president of the Jewish Synod at Leipzig, at the concluding session, addressed a large and distinguished assembly of rabbis and laymen . . . in language as classical in form as it was prophetical in spirit, every word thrilling with fervor and zeal for the Jewish religion." The harmony of mind and soul which Kohler sought in vain in others he found in this philosopher and proponent of Judaism. "While others listened to him as if a prophet had spoken, I heard the voice of a new revelation . . . It was an inspiration of a lifetime." Lazarus' fusion of Judaism with German idealism fascinated Kohler. To Lazarus Jewish faith was not a matter of ancestral piety or racial heritage, "not creed and ceremony, but ideality, the spirit that lifts men towards the highest ideal." His aim was not to abolish the old forms, but to remove the indifference and materialism of the new age.

The New World

On arriving in New York, Kohler was met by David Einhorn, who took him to his home and to his heart. In this intrepid Reformer, who had suffered much for his progressive convictions and anti-slavery views, Kohler found a kindred spirit. He became Einhorn's son-in-law as well as his spiritual son. Throughout his career, he reverently cherished the character and teaching of this passionate lover of truth and justice, and esteemed him as "the theologian *par excellence* among the Reform pioneers."

A few months after assuming his rabbinical duties at Temple Beth-El in Detroit, where he remained from 1869 to 1871, he attended the Rabbinical Conference at Philadelphia, where he met representatives of all wings of American Reform Judaism. The conference, called by Einhorn and Samuel Adler, was held at the home of Samuel Hirsch. Among the participants were Isaac M. Wise, "the leader of the West," and Max Lilienthal. Einhorn submitted a set of principles as the basis of Reform Judaism, defining its distinguishing ideas and divergent lines of practice. The sessions formed a striking contrast to those of Leipzig. Instead of half-measures and compromise with Orthodoxy, the deliberations, marked by broad and independent thought and the application of the principles of Reform to life, held out to the enthusiastic radical the promise of unhampered progress in building up "American Reform Judaism, the religion of the future."

The conference was held in order to bring together the Reform parties of the East and the West. While an agreement on principles was attained, the hoped-for union remained a goal to be attained in the future. The personal rivalry between the leaders soon broke out into open conflict; a fighter by nature, Kohler was drawn into the conflict on the side of Einhorn against Wise. The differences between the two, while partly personal, concerned the nature of American Reform which no agreement in principles could compose. Wise, as a practical leader of men, was content to advance slowly in his religious reforms in the hope of winning over the German element, which then predominated, to his ideas of an American Reform which claimed the support of *Halakhah* for its innovations. Einhorn, on the other hand, stood uncompromisingly by his views of Reform as developed in Germany and would not sacrifice an iota of his principles no matter how few were his followers. Kohler threw himself into the fray and lustily fought for clear-cut principles of Reform in the press and from his pulpit.

Kohler's ideas of Reform came to full light when he accepted the post of rabbi of Sinai Congregation in Chicago, a position he held from 1871 to 1879. From its inception under Bernhard Felsenthal, Sinai Congregation had used Einhorn's prayer book. Kohler's preaching and teaching were devoted to showing the positive relation of science and philosophy to religion in general and to Judaism in particular. He espoused the doctrine of evolution, which Darwin had demonstrated in the realm of biology, as the key to open the secrets of the spiritual world. With the further aid of Bible criticism and the sciences of comparative religion and folklore, which were generally shunned by other Reformers, he unfolded the uninterrupted growth of Judaism, its independence of particular rites and ceremonies, in which it is embodied at any period of time, and its place among the religions of the world. Placing the Bible among the sacred books of other religions, he tried to show its true character as the great treasure of the spiritual life, uniting religion with morality. Israel's role among the nations, he stressed, was to serve as witness to the ever-living God, to maintain its "nationality pure and unalloyed, whilst claiming our full share in the duties and rights the state devolves upon all its citizens."

If in his efforts at the "complete harmonization of modern thought with the ancient faith," Kohler followed Geiger's "theoretical radicalism," he was impatient with the latter's "conservatism in practice." Samuel Holdheim now loomed for him as the ideal leader of radical Reform. In the name of Israel's Messianic mission to mankind, Holdheim discarded all ceremonial laws as obsolete outside of Palestine and no longer obligatory in an age of Jewish naturalization among the nations of the world. For a time Kohler followed the lead of Holdheim and of Samuel Hirsch in advocating the transfer of the Sabbath to Sunday, the actual day of rest for most Jews in America. In 1874, he introduced supplementary Sunday services with the understanding that the Sabbath worship would be continued. The services consisted of an abbreviated ritual and sermon. The experiment proved abortive and was discontinued soon after he left the congregation, only to be reintroduced years later by his successor, Emil G. Hirsch.

Reform vs. Conservative Judaism

It was as Einhorn's successor as rabbi of Temple Beth-El in New York (1879-1903) that Kohler came to the fore as chief spokesman of Reform Judaism. Here, too, he introduced Sunday services to supplement Sabbath worship. By his eloquent preaching and scientific writing, he vigorously championed the cause of Reform Judaism against the inroads of Felix Adler's ethical culture, on the one hand, and of Conservative Judaism, which was gathering strength, on the other.

Kohler's aggressive Reform was bound to clash with the growing Conservatism and Orthodoxy in New York. It came to a head when the Reform congregation of Ahavat Hesed (now Central Synagogue) invited the famous Talmudic lexicographer Alexander Kohut to its pulpit. With the arrival of this scholar, the Conservative elements found their voice, speaking with power and erudition. In his inaugural sermon, delivered in May, 1885, he defined his religious standpoint as "Mosaicorabbinical Judaism" freshened with the spirit of progress. He followed with a series of expositions of *Pirke Avot*, in which he attacked "Radical, and in my opinion unauthorized Radical, Reform, which has gained such dominion among our coreligionists in this new world," and read the Reformers out of Judaism.

Kohler, despite his admiration of Kohut, took up the challenge. In a series of pulpit discussions entitled "Backward or Forward," he dealt with the questions raised by the redoubtable exponent of middle-of-the-road Judaism. Significantly, he did not justify Reform by advancing Talmudic grounds to deny the authority of the rabbinic system, as was done by other Reformers. Instead, he appealed to his critical position regarding the evolutionary character of Judaism.

> Can we believe (he asked) exactly what our fathers believed concerning Revelation, Law, Resurrection and the Messianic future? Must we, or can we, believe that the tablets were expressly made and the Ten Words engraved on them by the very hand of God, and that the entire Pentateuch was dictated to the very letter by God? Suppose we have, through scientific study, arrived at the conclusion that its traditions and legends were transmitted by men of primitive culture and that they contain "traces of rude barbarism," which our reverential love of God forbids us to ascribe to Him as author. Ought we on this account no longer consider ourselves as standing within the pale of Judaism? No. I do not believe that the Mosaic statues about sacrifices, the incense, and the priestly apparel, or the sanitary and criminal laws, are unchangeable ordinances of God dictated from heaven. I distinguish in the Bible the kernel from the husk, the grain from the chaff, the spirit from the form.

In the heat of the discussion, Kohler permitted himself to say some sharp things about Orthodoxy. He referred to it as "fanatical; inconsistent and anachronistical," and declared that "Orientalism on our free American soil will not stand the test of time." He called for "a Bible purified from all its offensive and obnoxious elements," and complained that "we dwelt too long upon the rubbish of the past."

Kohut would not let these slurring remarks pass without strong rebuke as being unworthy of one who was proud of his rabbinical title. The battle between the Conservatives and the Reformers was on. Pereira Mendes and Sabato Morais came to the aid of Kohut. Emil G. Hirsch, I. M. Wise, and others joined on Kohler's side. The discussion extended to the entire Jewish press and pulpit.

Pittsburgh Platform of 1885

Smarting from the effects of his encounter with Kohut and other Conservative leaders and seeking support for his position, Kohler issued a call to the Reform rabbis of the country to meet in conference "for the purpose of discussing the present state of American Judaism, its pending issues and requirements, and of uniting upon such plans and practical measures as seem demanded by the hour." Nineteen rabbis responded and met in November, 1885, in Pittsburgh, under the presidency of I. M. Wise. Kohler was the guiding spirit of the conference. In his opening paper, he set forth a ten-point program for Reform:

1. Adoption of a platform that would "declare to the world what Judaism is and what Reform means and aims at."
2. Organization of a Jewish mission to work with the entire Jewish population and particularly with Jewish laborers by means of Sunday services and other educational measures.
3. Creation of a well-organized literature and press to carry the Jewish message to every Jewish household throughout the land.
4. Creation of a plan for effective religious instruction for Jewish children.
5. Improving the mode of worship by means of a uniform ritual, especially for weddings and funerals.
6. Revision of the readings from the Law and the Prophets for the Sabbath and the Holy Days, omitting all such passages that might, when translated, give offense to the congregation.
7. Revision or new translation of the Bible together with the Apocryphal books.
8. Popularization of Jewish literature among the people.
9. Redefinition of the position of Judaism in relation to the Gentile world, toward proselytism, circumcision, and intermarriage.
10. Reintroduction of worship and religious observance into Jewish homes.

Only the first of these points was acted upon at the conference. The draft of the platform, which Kohler presented, likewise contained ten articles, to which he later added a statement on immortality. Its wording was considerably revised by the conference without altering its content and spirit. Its publication called forth a storm of opposition from the Orthodox and Conservative camps, and indirectly contributed to the creation of the Jewish Theological Seminary. The nationalistic elements were vehemently hostile to its universalistic tone. Dr. Wise, who presided at its adoption and hailed it as a "declaration of independence," soon dissociated himself from it under the pressure of some constituents of the Union of American Hebrew Congregations and of the Hebrew Union College who regarded it as too radical. Consequently, while many Reform leaders recognized it as an authentic expression of Reform Judaism, it was never officially adopted by the Central Conference of American Rabbis, which was called into being by Dr. Wise and his disciples in 1889. On the occasion of its fiftieth anniversary, the C.C.A.R. reevaluated those principles and adopted them officially as the Guiding Principles of Reform Judaism.

With the creation of the C.C.A.R., Kohler found a new sphere for his Reform activities. He could now pursue some of the practical goals which he had set for the Pittsburgh meeting in the larger and more representative permanent rabbinical body. Here his efforts to create a uniform liturgy for the Reform congregations of the country were crowned with success. On the basis of his reworking of Einhorn's *Olat Tamid* and of Wise's *Minhag America*, the C.C.A.R. adopted the second volume of the Union Prayerbook (for the New Year and Day of Atonement) in 1894. The first volume (for the Sabbath and the Festivals), which appeared the following year, was the creation of Kohler in collaboration with Gustav Gottheil and the assistance of Maurice Harris. The two volumes came to be used in virtually all Reform congregations in the country. In the first revision of the Union Prayerbook, about a quarter of a century later, Kohler again played a leading part, composing some of its most stirring prayers.

Gradual Moderation of His Views

In numerous learned papers presented before the C.C.A.R., Kohler elucidated the meaning of Reform Judaism and its relation to the vexing problems of the day. The former radical gradually moderated his opinions and policies. In a paper entitled, *Is Reform Destructive or Constructive?* (1892), he affirmed that "the banner of Reform at all times does, did and shall stand for *Judaism one and inseparable*, for a Judaism broad, comprehensive and large-hearted enough to allow wide divergence of opinion, of belief and practice; and yet solid, firm, strong and uncompromising in the maintenance and defense of its eternal principles of faith and its time-honored institutions."

While Reform had served the cause of Judaism well, Kohler pleaded that we should not be blind to its defects. "We have reformed Judaism, but not the Jew." Agnosticism, indifference, and disregard for the claims of Judaism are characteristic of the young Jew of America as of Europe, whether he regards himself Orthodox or Reform. "Reform, with no other principle than that of progress and enlightenment, has created a tendency to treat the past with irreverence and to trifle with the time-honored institutions and the venerable sources of Judaism." This, he observed, is especially true of the Sunday services. On the basis of his experience, he, the former advocate, felt "conscience-bound to abandon the Sunday substitute for the Sabbath. The Sunday service is, in my judgment, a patricide. . . . It destroys or undermines the Sabbath, but it fails to build up a Judaism loyal to its ancient institutions." In our efforts at Reform, we have been energetic in abrogating and pulling down. "Let us now unite and cooperate in building up Judaism and render it the object of love, of pride and joy for all, the source of comfort and peace for every thirsting soul, a fount of life and inspiration to Jew and Gentile alike."

In a lecture before the C.C.A.R. in 1898, he pleaded for a united Israel, free from "wrangling and bickering between Reform and Orthodoxy, between Conservative and Radical, between East and West." Unwavering in his belief in the constructive power of Reform, he urged: "We need a power to counteract the arbitrary individualism, conservative forces to counteract the tide of unrestrained progress which ends in Nirvana, if not in cowardly surrender to the majority."

The growing Russian element in America, he noted, was undergoing the same process that the German element had, only at a faster pace. "With their brighter intellects and lesser emotional powers, they incline to swing with one stroke from superstitious and mystic Orthodoxy to a rationalism which comes

quite near to skepticism and nihilism. Wise and moderate conservative methods alone can exert a wholesome influence upon
them to mold their future . . . Reform to them means not
Judaism spiritualized, but, as it did to Graetz and others, Judaism
Christianized." To meet the situation, Kohler surprisingly suggested dropping the name of Reform and substituting for it the
more positive term 'Progressive.' "Progressive" Jews we all are,
the one advancing hastily, the other more slowly. . . . Today,
not Reform, but Judaism, must be the sole object of our solici-
tude."

Opposition to Political Zionism

Kohler's hope for Jewish unity crashed against the rising tide
of secular nationalism and political Zionism, which swept
through Jewry at the end of the nineteenth century. In a paper
on Zionism, prepared and delivered soon after the Basle Congress,
he voiced his opposition to the movement, taking a stand
from which he did not depart to the end of his life. "We
need a union of forces," social and religious, he insisted, but
not political. He heartily endorsed the colonization efforts of
the *Hoveve Zion* in Palestine, but the political program of Herzl
and Nordau appeared dangerous to him on two scores. First, it
implied that the Jews everywhere, including the free lands, are
"foreigners, aliens and exiles," thus playing into the hands of the
enemies of the Jewish people. Second, Zionism exchanges the
religious character of the Jew for a political one. "Judaism," he
stated, "is a religious truth entrusted to a nation destined to inter-
link all nations and sects, classes and races of men. It is a historical mission, not a national life." While he conceded that Zionism
succeeded in awakening the national sentiment in many a Jew,
"long alienated from his race and his faith," and imbued the
timid with self-respect, he expected no real good from the movement. "The spiritual and the religious mission of the Jew," he
declared, "would never be fulfilled by the creation of a Jewish
state."

Rabbi and Scholar

Kohler's was a creative ministry of public service and education. He took an active part in developing religious instruction

among immigrants on the lower East Side of New York and in providing the Sabbath Schools with curricular aids. He published a *Guide to Instruction in Judaism* and an elaborate essay on methods of teaching Bible history. He participated in the "Jewish Chautauqua" movement, founded by Henry Berkowitz, and edited the *Sabbath Visitor* (1881-1882). He contributed widely to the Jewish press and to scientific journals, American and German, on Judaism, Jewish ethics, comparative religion, Hellenistic literature, and related themes, and issued large numbers of sermons, lectures, and studies. In 1880, he published a volume of Einhorn's sermons in German; and, in 1886, he edited *The Jewish Reformer*. And, as has been stated, he was one of the moving spirits in launching the *Jewish Encyclopedia*, and served as editor of its departments of theology and philosophy, writing some of its basic articles on various phases of Judaism. (The total number of his articles was 288.) He translated the *Book of Psalms* for the Jewish Publication Society, and subsequently served on the Board of Editors which prepared the new translation of The Holy Scriptures (1908-1916).

President of the Hebrew Union College

The greatest challenge of Kohler's career came in 1903 when, at the age of sixty, he was elected to succeed I. M. Wise and Moses Mielziner as president of the Hebrew Union College in Cincinnati. Shortly before leaving New York, he welcomed the arrival of his friend Solomon Schechter to preside over the reorganized Jewish Theological Seminary. In 1903 also, he delivered an address at the dedication of the new building of the Seminary, and, at Schechter's invitation, lectured to the students on apocryphal literature.

His strenuous career as rabbi and as scholar had not equipped him with knowledge of academic procedure and with administrative skill. What he lacked in experience, however, he made up in his single-hearted devotion to the cause of progressive Judaism. Only his flaming zeal and enthusiasm enabled him to weather the storms that he encountered in his new office.

A former critic of the college, Kohler set himself to correcting some of its defects and to raising its standards. First of all, he resolved to make its religious position clear and unmistakable.

He made it a condition of accepting the presidency that the Hebrew Union College should definitely be committed to the Reform viewpoint. He also proceeded to intensify the academic program of the college by extending the period of instruction and by introducing courses that would enable students to fuse their Jewish heritage with knowledge of the new age. To the classic Jewish studies of Bible, Talmud, history, and philosophy, he added instruction which, for the most part, he himself offered—in Bible criticism, apocryphal and Hellenistic literature, New Testament, and historical systematic theology. For the study of modern Hebrew he substituted *Midrashic* literature as being of greater value for the rabbi. He subsequently added courses in practical theology, Jewish ethics, pedagogy, and applied sociology.

Much as he valued scientific knowledge, Kohler stressed even more the qualities of spirituality, sincerity, and moral integrity in both students and faculty. His rigid devotion to Reform principles and especially his anti-Zionism involved him in conflicts with professors, members of the alumni, and students. Although concentration on his own studies prevented him from achieving a warm relationship with most students, the more advanced among them revered him for his vast erudition, his preaching skill, and his depth of conviction.

Major Work on Jewish Theology

Kohler's signal achievement during his presidency of the college was his pioneer work on Jewish theology. It was undertaken at the suggestion of Gustav Karpeles, president of the *Gesellschaft zur Voerderung der Wissenschaft des Judentums*, and was published in German in 1910. The work met with a warm response in the scholarly journals of Germany, France, England, and America, both Jewish and Christian. Urged to make it accessible to English readers, Kohler thoroughly revised and enlarged the book which was published in 1918 under the title *Jewish Theology, Systematically and Historically Considered*.

Last Years

After eighteen and a half years as president of the Hebrew Union College (1903-1922), Kohler retired to private life with

his family in New York. He liked to cite the Talmudic statement, "The righteous find rest neither in this world, nor in the
world to come"; as Scripture says, "They go from strength to
strength, until they appear before God in Zion." In his retirement he continued his unfinished tasks. In 1923 he published his
*Heaven and Hell, with Special Reference to Dante's Divine
Comedy*, a contribution to his favorite study of comparative
religion and folklore. He wrote articles for a number of periodicals as well as a learned essay, *The Origin and Composition of
the Eighteen Benedictions* (1924), and contributed to the sym-
posium, *A Re-evaluation of Reform Judaism* (1924). He devoted himself especially to the completion of a work which had
engaged his interest for decades, *The Origins of the Synagogue
and the Church*. He finished the volume and had revised half
of it when death came on January 26, 1926. His *Studies, Addresses and Personal Papers*, edited by Enelow appeared in 1931,
and *A Living Faith: Selected Sermons and Addresses from the
Literary Remains of Dr. Kaufmann Kohler*, edited by the present
writer was published in 1958.

THEOLOGICAL IDEAS

Kohler's *Jewish Theology* marked the climax of his vast research and mature thinking on all phases of Judaism. He properly
presented it as a pioneer labor. While outstanding creations in
theology and philosophy came from the Middle Ages, few attempts to rethink the subject in terms of the new world-view
were made in modern times. Kohler undertook to supply the
need. His interest in the evolution of Judaism and in the variety
of its expressions naturally predisposed him to treat the subject historically. This method enabled him to take cognizance
of all phases of Judaism, of synagogue, church, and mosque.
The central themes of the book were God, man, Israel, and
the Kingdom of God.

Character of Jewish Theology

Kohler sharply distinguished between theology and philosophy. The one starts with the premises and data of the specific
religion, its "positive beliefs in a divine revelation and in the

continued working of the divine spirit." The other, while covering the same ground, is not so conditioned. Submitting the contents of religion in general to an impartial investigation, philosophy recognizes no divine revelation nor the superior claims of any one religion above any other; it is concerned only with discovering "how far the universal laws of human reason agree or disagree with the assertions of faith." Curiously, Kohler considered it just as incorrect to speak of a Jewish religious philosophy as it is to speak of Jewish metaphysics or of Jewish mathematics, and he negated the Jewish character of medieval Jewish philosophy.

The object of Jewish theology is to enable the modern Jew to comprehend his own religious truths in the light of present thought and to defend them against misconceptions and misrepresentations. However, it must not assume the character of apologetics. It cannot ignore the results of the sciences, however they may clash with biblical or rabbinic views. Apologetics has its legitimate place in defending Judaism against hostile attacks, but it cannot properly defend statements that are incompatible with scientifically established results. "Judaism," he wrote, "is a religion of historical growth which, far from claiming to be the final truth, is ever regenerated anew at each turning point of history. The fall of the leaves in autumn requires no apology, for each successive spring testifies anew the power of resurrection."

Jewish theology differs from Christian theology just as Judaism differs from Christianity. The latter rests on a creed or articles of faith, formulated by the founders of the Church as conditions of salvation. Judaism, on the other hand, "recognizes only such articles of faith as were adopted by the Jewish people voluntarily as expressions of religious consciousness, both without external compulsion and without doing violence to the dictates of reason." It knows no "salvation by faith" in the Pauline sense. Consequently, disbelief in the creed of the Church amounts to cutting oneself loose from its membership. Not so in Judaism. "It is birth, not confession" that makes the Jew. Renunciation of the faith only renders one an apostate Jew.

Nature of Judaism

Judaism, in Kohler's definition, combines two widely differing elements, race and religion, related to each other as the body is to the soul. Judaism is the vital force which has united the Jewish people, preserving and regenerating it ever anew. It is neither "the Jewish nationality with its cultural achievements and aspirations" as the secularists claim, nor nomistic or legalistic religion, as some Christians contend. Neither is it a pure theism, aiming to unite all believers in God into a universal church, of which certain visionaries dream. "Judaism is nothing less than a message concerning the *One and holy God* and *one undivided humanity* with a world-uniting messianic *goal*, a message entrusted by divine revelation to the Jewish people."

This twofold nature of Judaism—"a universal religious truth and at the same time a mission entrusted to a specially selected nation or race," has rendered it "an enigma to the student of religion and history." Two opposing forces are at work in Judaism, one centripetal, the other centrifugal, the spirit of separateness which concerns itself with the Jewish people, and the spirit of universalism which transcends that group and reaches out to the whole of humanity. Despite their seemingly contradictory character, the two combine into a perfect unity so that one is incomplete without the other.

Judaism has manifested a wondrous power of assimilation by continuously renewing itself to meet the demands of the time, first under the influence of the ancient civilizations and finally of the Occidental powers, molding its beliefs and customs into ever new forms, "but in consonance with its own genius." Instead of being fixed and closed for all time, it is as "multifarious and manifold in its aspects as life itself."

Like Judah Halevi, Kohler stressed the corporate character of Judaism. It is not the creation of a single person, either prophet or man with a divine claim, but of the God of Abraham, Isaac and Jacob, the fathers of the Jewish people. Accordingly, the name "Judaism" fittingly expresses its character. As the religion of the people, it has kept in touch with life and has escaped being reduced to a shadowy form of other-worldliness, asceticism, and pessimism. It is not a religion of redemption, condemning this earthly life as evil, but an ethical faith looking to the ultimate triumph of good, truth and justice over the powers of evil, falsehood and wrong.

Judaism, Christianity and Mohammedanism

In his defense of Judaism, Kohler often reacted vehemently against Pauline Christianity, which sought to reduce Judaism to an inferior legalistic faith and to deprive Israel of the right to exist. He also opposed both Ethical Culture, which ignores Israel, Torah, and God, and secular Jewish nationalism, which divests Israel of its religious character. He placed the mission of Israel at the center of his theology.

Kohler's attitude toward Christianity and Islam approximated that of Halevi and Maimonides. Despite their alienation from Judaism, Christianity and Islam are its daughter religions, divinely appointed to sow the seeds of Jewish truth over the globe. "Christianity in the West and Islam in the East have aided in leading mankind ever nearer to the pure monotheistic truth." At the same time Kohler emphasized the superior character of the mother faith in upholding God's unity, life's holiness and social ethics over Christianity, and in stressing the love of God and freedom of man against Islam's demands of "blind submission to the stern decrees of inexorable fate."

The Nature of God

Kohler took a negative attitude to philosophy and this affected his treatment of the doctrine of God. "Where God is felt as a living power," he insisted, "all philosophical arguments about His existence seem to be strange fires on the altar of religion. The believer can do without them, and the unbeliever will hardly be convinced by them." The God deduced by philosophical arguments was for Kohler "a mere abstraction, incapable of satisfying the emotional craving of the heart." "Reason alone will not lead to God, except where religious intuition forms, so to speak, the ladder of heaven, leading to the realm of the unknowable. Philosophy, at best, can only demonstrate the existence of a final cause, or of a Supreme Intelligence working toward sublime purposes. Religion alone, founded upon divine revelation, can teach man to find God, to whom he can appeal and whom he can trust in moments of woe, and whose will he can see in the dictates of conscience and the destinies of nature. Reason must serve as a corrective for the contents of revelation, scrutinizing ever anew the truths received through intuition, but it can never be the final source of truth." Accordingly, Kohler praised Judah Halevi for making "the historical fact of the divine revelation the foundation of the Jewish religion and the chief testimony of the existence of God."

Ultimately, however, it was not Halevi's traditional conception of God that Kohler adopted but the moral God of Kant. "God," he wrote, "is a postulate of men's moral consciousness." We can know His existence only through ethics. "The inner consciousness of our moral obligation, or duty, implies a moral order of life, or moral law; and this, in turn, postulates the existence of God, the Ruler of life, who assigns to each of us his task and his destiny."

In his chapter on "The Essence of God," Kohler stressed the practical need of the religious man to know what God is, at least to himself. This he finds in the opening work of the Decalogue. God is *Anokhi*, "I." This word lifts Him above all other existence, expressing "His unique self-consciousness." As man towers above all other creatures by his will and self-conscious action, so God "rules over all as the one completely self-conscious Mind and Will. In both the visible and the invisible realms, He manifests Himself as the absolutely free personality, moral and spiritual, who allots to everything its existence, form and purpose." In the words of Scripture, He is "the living God and the everlasting King." In relation to the world, His work and workshop, He is the self-conscious Master; "in relation to man, who is akin to Him as a self-conscious rational and moral being, He is the living Fountain of all that knowledge and spirituality for which men long, and in which alone they may find contentment and bliss."

Jewish Ethics

The soul of the Jewish religion is its ethics. The kingdom of God for whose coming the Jew longs "does not rest in a world beyond the grave, but (in consonance with the ideal of Israel's sages and prophets) in a complete moral order on earth, the reign

of truth, righteousness and holiness among all men and nations."
Deriving its sanction from God, Jewish ethics aims at hallowing
all of life, individual and social. Its motive is the splendid conception that man, with his finite ends, is linked to the infinite God
with His infinite ends; or, as the rabbis express it, "Man is a
co-worker of God in the work of creation."

Revelation and Prayer

The gap between God and man is bridged by revelation, on
the one hand, and by prayer, on the other. Kohler's conception
of revelation combined naturalistic with supernaturalistic elements, and was based on Biblical criticism as well as on ethnic
psychology. An element of mystery underlies the phenomenon.
The flash of genius manifested in the select individual or nation
brings them into contact with the divine. In the religious genius
"all the forces of the age seem to be energized and set in motion,
then to burst forth into a new religious consciousness, which is
to revolutionize religious thought and feeling." The appearance
of the divine upon the background of the prophetic soul, "which
reflects it like a mirror, is revelation." The Jewish prophet is
distinguished from others not by his capacity to receive a revelation, but rather by the intrinsic nature of the revelation which
he receives.

> His vision comes from a moral God. The form expressed by
> Abraham, Moses, Elijah, or by the literary prophets. . . . In
> speaking through them, God appeared actually to have stepped
> into the sphere of human life as its moral ruler. This self-revelation
> of God as the Ruler of man in righteousness, which must be
> viewed in the life of a prophet as a providential act, forms the
> great sequence in the history of Israel, upon which rests the
> Jewish religion.

Prophecy in the Bible is associated with dreams and visions.
Yet it is not the imagery but the divine truth itself which seized
the prophet with irresistible force, "so that he is carried away
by the divine power and speaks as the mouthpiece of God, using
lofty poetic diction while in a state of ecstasy. He speaks of God
in the first person. The highest stage of all is that where the
prophet receives the divine truth in the form of pure thought

and with complete self-consciousness." Revelation and prophecy are thus reduced to a form of reason, as in the Maimonidean system. Kohler would not limit them to the Biblical period. "Divine influence cannot be measured by the yardstick or the calendar. Where it is felt, it bursts forth as from a higher world, creating for itself its proper organs and forms."

Kohler agreed with Halevi that "the Jewish people, on account of its peculiar bent, was predestined to be the people of revelation." The story of the giving of the Law at Sinai represents "the consecration of the Jewish people at the outset of its history to be a nation of prophets and priests."

If revelation brings God down to man, prayer lifts man up to God. Prayer is the communion of the human soul and the creator. It is the expression of man's longing and yearning for God in times of dire need and of overflowing joy, an outflow of the emotions of man in his dependence upon the eternal source of his being. "Springing from the deepest necessity of human weakness, the expression of a momentary wish, prayer is felt to be the proud prerogative of man as a child of God, and at last it becomes adoration of the Most High, whose wisdom and whose paternal love and goodness inspire man with confidence and love." Modern thought rules out the possible influence of finite man upon the infinite God by means of any words which he may utter.

> Prayer can exert power only over the relation of man to God, not over God Himself. . . . The religious spirit experiences in prayer the soaring up of the soul toward union with God in consecrated moments of our pilgrimage. . . . The essence of every prayer of supplication is that one should be in unison with the divine will. Enriching as is the practice of personal prayer, still more effective is public worship, for through it one realizes that he is a member of a greater whole, and he prays only for that which advances the welfare of all. . . . In the ardor of communal worship, the traditional words of the prayerbook obtain invigorating power; the heart is newly strengthened; the covenant with heaven sealed anew.

The Bible and Israel's Mission

As the repository of the divine revelation to Israel, the Bible has served as the source of instruction concerning God and the world, and, through new methods of interpretation, has grown ever richer as a fountainspring of religious and ethical knowledge. The Bible, Kohler wrote in an earlier work, "is holy, not because it is inspired, but because and in so far as it does still, inspire. No book in the world enraptures the heart, responding to the innermost needs of the soul as much as does this venerable Bible." It gives virtue a finer mold and morality a deeper ring and resonance. He found the true genius of Judaism in the doctrinal side of the Torah, which impresses ethical and human idealism upon people, lifting them far above the narrow confines of nationality, and making them a nation of thinkers.

To preserve this heritage of truth as the light of the world is the abiding mission of the Jew. To carry out its world mission, "the Jewish people must guard against absorption by the multitude of nations as much as against isolation from them." It must continue its separateness and "avoid inter-marriage with members of other sects, unless they espouse the Jewish faith." For Kohler, as for the founders of the Reform movement, the idea of the mission of Israel replaced the traditional hope of the advent of a Davidic Messiah and the return of the Jewish people to the Holy Land. Through their dispersion, the Jews are to give witness to God and ultimately win the entire Gentile world to the recognition of God as the Father of all men and to the establishment of His kingdom of universal justice and truth, the Messianic Age.

Ritual and Institutions in Reform Judaism

While interpreting the theological content of Judaism, historically and systematically, Kohler pointed out that "the maintenance of a religion does not rest upon its doctrines, which must differ according to the intellectual capacity of the people and the prevailing views of each age. Its stability is based upon the forms and institutions which lend it a peculiar character and which express symbolically or otherwise, definite ideas, religious, ethical, and historical." The synagogue and its institutions of worship, study, and benevolence, the Sabbath and the holy days, and the rites and symbols of personal and communal character have served throughout history as forces that have preserved Jewish life and shaped it in patterns of holiness. As a Reformer, Kohler insisted that "the synagogue must revitalize its time-honored institutions and ceremonies" by freeing them from the elements of Orientalism and formalism which cling to some of them, and adjusting them to the Occidental climate in which we live, and thus "render religion again the deepest and strongest force of life."

Kohler stressed the doctrinal side of the Torah. "As law," he wrote, the Torah has "contributed to the marvelous endurance of the Jewish people, it permeated Judaism with a keen sense of duty and imprinted the idea of holiness upon the whole of life." But it also gave rise to "ritualistic piety and fostered hair-splitting casuistry, and caused the petrifaction of religion in the codified *Halakhah*." Beyond critical observations of this character, Kohler did not evaluate in *Jewish Theology* the significance of *Halakhah* for the modern Jew. However, as chairman of the Committee on Responsa of the Central Conference of American Rabbis, he sought to derive guidance from it for modern times. "We must in all matters of Reform and progress," he wrote, "agree upon leading principles and not allow them to become arbitrary and individualistic." In defining the position of Reform on questions of liturgy, marriage laws, burial rites, and mourning customs he explored the teaching of the Bible and rabbinic literature on these matters, and arrived at decisions for modern practice. "We should enlighten our people, working for a gradual advancement, following evolutionary not revolutionary methods," aiming to build up, not to destroy. In a paper on *The Harmonization of the Jewish and Civil Laws of Marriage and Divorce*, he coped with the problems that arise from the inferior status of woman in traditional Judaism. He insisted that "we cannot consistently tolerate practices which have the low Oriental view of woman as their basis." We must insist on the equality of man and woman both in the marriage ceremony and as witnesses at the ceremony.

Polarity of His Thought

An inner conflict may be noted between the romantic and the rationalist in Kohler, between the warmhearted pious believer and the radical critic of the Bible and tradition, and between the universalist and the particularist. An ardent idealist, he firmly believed in the advance of the forces of right in the world, despite temporary lapses into barbarism and hatred. "This very collapse of our boasted civilization," he affirmed during World War I, "this utter failure of all our progress betokens the molding of a new heaven and a new earth by the hand of God, and here lies Judaism's great opportunity, if we but realize it."

The idea of mission made him look beyond the painful present to the ultimate triumph of Israel's Messianic goal. He wanted the Jewish people to be ever mindful of their religious heritage and of the obligations which it imposed upon them. His career as scholar, reformer, and theologian was one continuous effort to awaken the Jewish people to renewed religious life. Reform to him meant no break with the past, but the affirmation of progress in Judaism and a mandate for further growth in ethical and spiritual perfection.

FOR FURTHER READING

JACOB, W., "Assessment of Christianity, One Historical Setting," in *Central Conference of American Rabbis Journal,* Volume 21 (New York: Winter, 1974). An evaluation of Kohler's attitude towards Christianity in light of his own Reform theological position.

KOHLER, Kaufmann, "Sinai Congregation and the Chicago Fire," in *Central Conference of American Rabbis Journal,* Volume 19 (New York: January, 1972). A translation by Shalom A. Singer of Kohler's Inaugural Address.

MARTIN, Bernard, "The Americanization of Reform Judaism'" in *Journal of Reform Judaism,* Volume 27 (New York: Winter, 1980). Includes a discussion of Kohler's role in this transformative process.

OLITSKY, K., "The Sunday—Sabbath Movement in American Reform Judaism," in *American Jewish Archives,* Volume 34 (New York: April, 1982). An assessment of Kohler's position, among others, on this controversial, ill-conceived religious innovation.

BLAU, Joseph, Editor Kaufmann Kohler's Jewish Theology (Hoboken, NJ: Ktav Publishing, 1978). A reprint of the original edition with a new introduction by Professor Joseph Blau.

9. *Mordecai M. Kaplan*

[1881-1983]

IRA EISENSTEIN

No twentieth-century thinker has understood better than Mordecai Kaplan the enormous challenges confronting Judaism and the Jewish people in this era of turbulence and vast social and cultural change. As rabbi, teacher, philosopher, and founder of the Reconstructionist movement in American Judaism, he has been a central figure on the American Jewish scene for more than fifty years. In the eyes of many, he has most successfully synthesized Jewish thought with the best of contemporary thought. His conception of Judaism for this age not only brings it into greater harmony with the values and conditions of democracy, but he also offers a program of Jewish living best calculated to make Judaism a powerful and meaningful force in the lives of American Jews.

From the Old World to the New

Mordecai Kaplan was born in a little town in the Jewish Pale of Russia in the year 1881. His father was a distinguished Talmudic scholar, gentle, idealistic, with unusually liberal tendencies for a man whose background and training were entirely traditional. Rabbi Israel Kaplan became the *Rosh Yeshivah* of sereral rabbinical academies, but his honesty and undeviating integrity brought him into conflict with the Russian authorities. Therefore, when he was invited to join Jacob Joseph, who had been elected Chief Rabbi of the New York *Kehillah*, he accepted the post of *dayan* (rabbinical judge) in the Chief Rabbi's office and set off for the new world.

Anna Kaplan, Mordecai's mother, was a strong-minded and intellectually gifted woman. She remained with her daughter and young Mordecai for a year in Paris, where relatives were close by, awaiting the summons to join Rabbi Israel in New York.

Mordecai still recalls the move to Paris and the subsequent voyage to America as symbolic of the problems with which he would have to deal in later years.

> The first occasion when being a Jew became a problem to me, (he wrote) was, when as a child of seven, I migrated with my mother and sister to Paris, at the same time that father, whose long rabbinical training had qualified him for a Jewish academic or rabbinic post, migrated to America. On the second Sabbath after our arrival, I remember attending school, and being asked to write out some lesson. In order not to transgress the prohibition of the Sabbath, I told a fib. I said my hand hurt me. The next Sabbath I stayed away from school. My predicament was solved during the week following. My mother found a small apartment in the Jewish section of Paris. There children were free from school on Saturday and Sunday instead of Thursday and Sunday as in the schools of the rest of the city.
>
> The second occasion, when being a Jew became a problem, was about a year later, when my mother, sister and I were on board a French steamer bound for New York. We were in steerage. It was Friday night. Announcement had been made that there would be fireworks on deck in honor of Bastille Day. I was eager to join the crowd to see the fireworks. But my mother would not permit me to go before reciting my Sabbath eve prayers. By the time I was through the fireworks were over and I was left heartbroken. Since then I have been living in two civilizations, the Jewish and the non-Jewish.

How to accomplish this happily and creatively has been the theme of Kaplan's life's work.

Kaplan as Student

In New York, Mordecai attended *heder* as well as public school. His father was not content with this regime, however, and a private tutor was engaged to come to the house at six o'clock every morning for two hours of Hebrew studies. Mordecai also received instruction from his father when their respective schedules permitted. In addition, distinguished scholars were frequent visitors to the Kaplan home, and Mordecai never missed an opportunity to listen in on the conversations that took place.

At the age of twelve, Mordecai was enrolled by his father in the Jewish Theological Seminary. In those days (1893), the Seminary was a modest little school and was not yet identified as "Conservative." Indeed, the faculty was made up of traditional Jews, but they did have secular learning and differed in this respect from the teachers at the *yeshivot*. The curriculum, too, was somewhat broader than that offered at a traditional *yeshivah* so that Biblical exegesis and Jewish history were included in Mordecai's program. For some years, all went well. Then Kaplan began to experience doubts about the authenticity of the Jewish tradition. He could not believe in the historic truth of the miracles; he doubted the Mosaic authorship of the Bible. Frequent visits to his home by the great Bible critic Arnold B. Ehrlich further undermined his beliefs. No wonder his mother tried to discourage him from listening to the scholarly discussions and from reading the manuscript of Ehrlich's commentary. Studying Maimonides' *Guide for the Perplexed* under a more traditional-minded teacher, Joseph Sossnitz, did not improve his state of mind. When at the age of twenty-one he was graduated from the Seminary and accepted his first pulpit, he was perplexed and troubled about Judaism and his own relation to it.

From "Minister" to Rabbi

Congregation Kehillat Yeshurun in the Yorkville section of New York did not recognize Kaplan's rabbinical degree as sufficient to entitle him to be called "rabbi." He was named "minister." In 1908 he married Lena Rubin, a member of one of the staunchest synagogue families, and they went to Europe for their honeymoon. Through his father's old contacts, he was able to obtain a *semikhah* or rabbinic ordination after being examined by a leading European rabbi. On his return, he was recognized as a full-fledged rabbi, and became, in fact, the first English-speaking Orthodox rabbi in the United States. Whatever his inner doubts, he maintained strict observance of the rituals and he preached non-controversial sermons. But this did not last long. Mordecai Kaplan was too keenly aware of the questions raised by modern science and too sensitive to the rapid deterioration that was taking place in the religious and cultural life of Jewry to remain silent. When he began to propose programs for Jewish living which took into account the new circumstances under which Jews lived, a clash occurred with his congregation. "The moment . . . I ventured beyond the domain of edification and attempted to advocate some specific policy as to how one can and should live as a Jew in a modern environment, I got myself into trouble."

Dean and Professor

The final separation from Kehillat Yeshurun came about when Kaplan was appointed the first dean of the newly organized Teachers Institute of the Jewish Theological Seminary. He had delivered an address to the alumni of the Seminary in the presence of Solomon Schechter, the president. Having come from Cambridge to reorganize the Seminary, Schechter realized the need for a teachers' training institution; he now saw in Mordecai Kaplan the right person to take charge. This post gave Kaplan the opportunity to withdraw from the rabbinate and devote himself to an academic career. Shortly thereafter the Chair in Homiletics was vacated, and Kaplan became professor of homiletics, a position he was to occupy for more than fifty years.

In this twofold role, as dean of the Teachers Institute and as professor of homiletics, Kaplan became the teacher of hundreds of rabbis and educators. His former students remember with great vividness the days spent in his classes. They recall his sturdy stride, his large and penetrating blue eyes, his fierce black beard (later to turn pure white), his monumental temper which flared up when he encountered stupidity or fuzzy thinking, his benign smile when the storm blew over, his warmth and friendliness which were not easily apparent behind the stern exterior, and, most of all, his constant insistence upon honesty and clear thinking. Students coming from traditional homes and schools went through traumatic experiences on first exposure to his relentless logic. But they were ever thankful to him because he made them think. And while they did not always come to agree with him, they never ceased to praise him for his courage, his deep insights, and his ever-youthful hospitality to new ideas.

Kaplan's teaching career was not to be confined to the Seminary. When the Graduate School for Jewish Social Work was organized, he was invited to join its faculty. From 1935 to 1937, he occupied the Chair in the Principles of Education at the Hebrew University in Jerusalem. He lectured at various other institutions, including the University of Chicago, and Teachers College, Columbia University.

Jewish Center and the SAJ

But at no time was Kaplan merely an academician. He had the highest regard for the kind of scholarship which threw light upon the past; but he believed that such knowledge had to be put to use to enable Jews to live as Jews in the present. He therefore kept putting aside scholarly projects upon which he had embarked in order to plunge into the arena of Jewish life that surrounded him. Even while in his first pulpit, Kaplan took an active role in Jewish education. He had worked with Judah L. Magnes, later to become president of the Hebrew University. With the emergence of the Bureau of Jewish Education, he was thrown together with Samson Benderly, one of the most creative personalities in the field of Jewish education. Thinking always of how to make Judaism meaningful and relevant for the average Jew, Kaplan outlined a plan for a new kind of congregation, one which would function as a "Jewish Center." By this he meant that it was to be not merely a place of worship but one in which leisure activities of all kinds were to be conducted —an unheard of idea in those days. He was asked to lead such a new institution and found himself once again in the active rabbinate. He was content to involve himself in a practical project because, in this instance, he was given the chance to try out a new idea. The Jewish Center put in a swimming pool and a gym, club rooms and library, and meeting rooms, and was really very different from the usual *shul*, which had consisted up till then of a sanctuary and a few classrooms. Kaplan wanted to broaden the functions of the synagogue so that social and cultural activities would take place there. (Subsequently, hundreds of institutions called "centers" were organized along similar lines.)

The Jewish Center, located on West 86th Street in New York,

would have been an ideal instrument through which Kaplan might have carried out some of his newly formulated concepts; but once again his insistence upon taking his own views seriously brought him into conflict with some of the lay leaders. In 1917, when the Center was built, American society was undergoing some basic changes. The war had produced many *nouveaux riches*, who still regarded labor as a commodity; and in those pre-New Deal days, labor unions were identified as radical and subversive. Kaplan did not hesitate to speak out against some employers who, he believed, were unfair to their workers.

This application of Jewish religious ethics to everyday life was the straw that broke the camel's back. Certain members of the Center had already begun to weary of Kaplan's unorthodox views—his critical approach to the Bible, to miracles, and to the whole concept of supernatural revelation. A split in the congregation ensued, and although the majority voted for Kaplan, he resigned. A small group of families resigned with him and organized, under his leadership, the Society for the Advancement of Judaism. In 1922, with twenty-two families, the institution which has come to be known as the SAJ, began its career, one destined to be of great significance in the life of Mordecai Kaplan, for out of this small group emerged the Reconstructionist movement with which his name is identified.

Establishment of the Reconstructionist Movement

When the SAJ was organized, it was not intended to be an ordinary congregation. Kaplan insisted that he be called "leader," possibly under the influence of the Society for the Advancement of Ethical Culture, whose name he paraphrased and which also used "leader." He felt that "rabbi" was merely a title, but not descriptive of the function; he agreed to serve as its leader on condition that the services performed for its members formed only a part of the larger program, that of disseminating his views and encouraging the formation of other societies of the same kind. The first step taken was the creation of the *SAJ Review*, a little magazine which immediately attracted as readers many of the alert and intellectual Jews of the country. Published at first in mimeographed form, it was later issued in print. But with the depression in 1929, the money ran out and the magazine ceased to appear.

In the meantime, Kaplan had been working for some years on the manuscript of a large work setting forth his views on the problem of Judaism in our time, surveying the current versions of Judaism (Reform, Orthodoxy, Conservatism, and secular nationalism), analyzing their weaknesses, and offering his own conception of Judaism as an evolving religious civilization. Kaplan's manuscript received first prize for the best book on the subject of American Judaism, an award offered by Julius Rosenwald, the well-known philanthropist.

Judaism as a Civilization, Kaplan's first major work, appeared in 1934. Its impact was great and immediate: it was hailed as a masterpiece by those who agreed with Kaplan, and was denounced as a menace by those who disagreed. But few could be indifferent to it. Prior to this, Kaplan had published only a few articles in the *Menorah Journal*. He was almost fifty-three years of age when this first volume was offered to the world.

He had waited a long time for this literary debut mainly because he knew that his first book would be carefully scrutinized by those who had already learned of his heterodoxies. He wanted it to be perfect. It is interesting to speculate upon the effect his philosophy might have had on American Jewry had it appeared, full-fledged, some fifteen or twenty years before. There are those who contend that the book came upon the scene too late, and that, had it come sooner, it might have won over many Jewish intellectuals who, in the interval, had become alienated from Jewish life and Jewish religion.

In any case, Kaplan's close disciples lost no time in rallying to his side when he proposed the creation of a magazine to carry on where the *SAJ Review* had left off. The writer, who had come to the SAJ in 1929 to serve as associate leader, assisted him in bringing together the first editorial board. Milton Steinberg, Leon Lang, Ben Zion Bokser, Israel Goldstein, and Eugene Kohn made up the first board, with Barnett R. Brickner, Edward L. Israel, Alexander M. Dushkin, Jacob S. Golub, and Max Kadushin as contributing editors.

The name *"Reconstructionist"* was given to the new magazine. As early as January, 1928, in the *SAJ Review*, Kaplan had written that the main task before American Jewry was to "reconstruct the Jewish civilization," and hence "the SAJ prefers to be considered a branch of the Reconstructionist movement in Jewish life." Though the editors at their first meeting considered the name awkward and cumbersome, Milton Steinberg defended it warmly and won over the board.

The SAJ was in no position to subsidize this new venture; but its lay leaders agreed to lend the name of the Society as publisher, provided that no funds of the congregation's budget were to be used to pay for its publication. For five years, this arrangement continued, until, in 1940, the Jewish Reconstructionist Foundation was established for the express purpose of issuing the magazine and otherwise supporting the movement.

In those five years, Kaplan was stimulated to prepare for publication a great deal of material which he had accumulated. Apparently, with the appearance of *Judaism as a Civilization* and the magazine, his reluctance to publish was overcome. Soon thereafter he published *Judaism in Transition*, a volume of essays which had been delivered at various times and which dealt with a variety of themes: the challenge of both Fascism and Communism, Maimonides, Moses Mendelssohn, and the rabbinic training for our day. Actually, it is the one book which he published in all the years which had no very clear structure. Next came *The Meaning of God in Modern Jewish Religion*, an interpretation of the Sabbath and festivals in modern terms bringing together a large number of sermons he had delivered at the SAJ. He wove them into coherent treatments of each of the major holidays. In these works, Kaplan laid down the broad lines of his thinking, and he was prepared to translate some of his ideas into practical form.

Worship Texts Revised

In 1941, Kaplan's *New Haggadah*, edited jointly with Ira Eisenstein and Eugene Kohn, came out. This was the first attempt to apply the principles of Reconstructionism to a liturgical text. Kaplan had been in Palestine from 1937 to 1939, and he had been very much impressed with the *Haggadot* which were being created continually there. He came back with several samples and thought he might be able to use them as a basis for a *Haggadah* here. The old *Haggadah* is built around the miracles, the plagues, and the Passover sacrifice. The *New Haggadah* makes freedom the central theme. It also introduces the personality of Moses, and brings in *Midrashim* which did not appear in the original, and leaves out quite a number which did. Until this time, Kaplan had met with only minor opposition from his colleagues at the Seminary, perhaps because his philosophy was still couched in theoretical terms. Because the *New Haggadah* put the theory into practice, a storm now broke out. He had tampered with a sacred text, and this was to be furiously resisted. However, the reception given to this *Haggadah* was mild compared to that which the *Sabbath Prayerbook* received in 1945.

For years Kaplan had regarded the SAJ as a laboratory for experimentation in religious services. The new *Sabbath Prayerbook* was the result of three years of experimenting with a loose-leaf notebook-prayerbook. When Kaplan and his associates (Eugene Kohn, Ira Eisenstein, and Milton Steinberg) felt that they had finally worked out the type of service which they deemed most meaningful for the modern Jew, they issued it in final form. Its purpose was to revise the text in such a way that the worshipper would not be called upon to pray for what he did not believe in. This involved certain changes in the passages dealing with resurrection, the personal Messiah, the chosen people, and the passage in which it is stated that the rainfall is influenced by the observance of the *mitzvot*. The other major purpose of the book was to include a large anthology of prayers, readings and poems which would enable the synagogue service to vary from week to week, so that any monotony which might creep in would be obviated. An introduction to the *Sabbath Prayerbook* was written originally by the editors, and a shorter version was prepared by Rabbi Milton Steinberg for the second printing. The Reconstructionist service follows the traditional pattern, rather than the skeletal pattern of the service as it has been conducted throughout the years, with the exception that on *Shabbat* morning the *musaf* service does not have the regular form of the *amidah*.

Once this prayerbook appeared, the Orthodox rabbis gathered in the McAlpin Hotel in New York and formally pronounced the ban of *herem* or excommunication upon the chief editor, Mordecai M. Kaplan. At this same sensational meeting, a copy of the offending prayerbook was burned. The Orthodox were not, however, the only protestants. Two of Kaplan's fellow-faculty members wrote a letter to the *Ha-Doar*, the weekly Hebrew magazine, dissociating themselves from Kaplan's views.

When questioned by the press about the *herem*, Kaplan stated that since he was not Orthodox himself, the Orthodox rabbis had no jurisdiction over him. Despite the criticism directed against him by his colleagues, he decided to proceed with even greater determination. Soon thereafter, 1947, the *High Holiday Prayerbook* was issued; the *Festival Prayerbook*, completing the cycle, was published in 1958.

Reconstructionism as a Movement

Kaplan is, par excellence, the thinker, the teacher, the writer, and the lecturer. When conditions required, he could be the organizer as well. The SAJ was certainly the product of his organizing talents; and so were the Teachers Institute, the Jewish Center, and the Reconstructionist movement. But one must concede that his greatest strength lay in formulating the idea and the purpose; the more prosaic tasks of creating the institutions were left to others.

In the instance of the Reconstructionist movement, all the weaknesses of the leader as organizer seemed to operate. A philosophic approach, at best a school of thought, Reconstructionism was never able to organize itself in a way that did not involve complicated relationships with other organizations. Most of the leaders, like Kaplan himself, were affiliated with the Conservative group; some came from the Reform wing, others from the secular groups. The philosophy seemed to attract Jews of all denominations, serving as a sort of umbrella under which people of varying interest could gather.

At the same time, however, Kaplan wanted the movement to do more than serve as a unifying force. He wanted Reconstructionism to be the spokesman for a specific set of ideas which were to serve as answers to those who did not find themselves spiritually at home in any of the existing groups. In order to function in both ways, Kaplan conceived of a twofold program—overall and sectional—the first for the purpose of uniting, the second for the purpose of adding a new force to the existing ones.

The sectional program was never to be separated from the overall, lest the charge be made that he was creating a new denomination, and hence further fragmenting Jewish life. As a result, the movement has captured more sympathy and admiration than concrete support. Compared to other movements on the American scene, its adherents are few. This, however, is understandable, since one cannot be a player and an umpire at the same time; and one is rejected as an umpire even though one disclaims any intention of playing. In spite of these organizational obstacles, Kaplan and his brand of Judaism are reckoned with wherever Judaism is discussed.

With unflagging zeal, Kaplan, now more than eighty, goads his fellow Jews to make ever more strenuous efforts to reorganize the Jewish community, to re-think the relationship of the Diaspora to the land of Israel, to reinterpret Jewish religion, to replenish Jewish culture—in short, to reinvigorate Judaism so that it may once again become a potent factor in the world.

In 1957, at Kaplan's instigation, a conference was held in Jerusalem to discuss the future status of world Jewry. Other "ideological conferences" are being planned as a result of his proddings. The Zionist Organization of America is considering the program for a "New Zionism" (the title of a book published by Kaplan), or, as it has come to be known, a Greater Zionism. The Jewish Theological Seminary has called upon him to head a new project dealing with the relation of Judaism to ethics.

Philosophy and Program

What, specifically, is the philosophy and program which Mordecai Kaplan has developed, which makes him so controversial a figure, and at the same time the highly respected and honored spiritual leader? What is the essence of Reconstructionism?

Kaplan believes that if Judaism is to survive it must be reconstructed. That is to say, it must adapt itself to the new conditions resulting from the political, economic, cultural, and social changes that have taken place in the world since the beginning of the nineteenth century.

Judaism has, of course, undergone "reconstructions" in the past; at the great turning points in Jewish history, fundamental changes had to be made in order that the Jewish people might survive. In the past, however, people did not have a sense of history, and therefore their innovations were to them merely the process of making explicit what was already implicit in the tradition. They could not imagine that their way of life or belief actually needed to be revised, and they therefore honestly thought that they were merely interpreting, not introducing anything new. But as we look back we realize that unconsciously they did, quite basically, reconstruct Judaism.

For example, when the Israelite tribes settled in Canaan, they had to transform themselves from a nomadic to an agricultural nation. Again the challenge was faced and met when they were transformed from a loose confederation of tribes into a united monarchy. Once again, when Nebuchadnezzar led their leaders away captive to Babylon, they were compelled to reconstruct their form of organization, their theology, and their way of life. Upon their return to Palestine, they became a theocracy. When the Romans destroyed the Temple in the year 70 C.E., they had to remake themselves once again, this time into an *ecclesia* or church form of community.

In modern times, dating from about the end of the eighteenth century, the Jewish people have had to face new and unprecedented challenges created by the twin forces of nationalism and naturalism. Emancipation offered Jews the opportunity, for the first time, to become citizens on an equal, legal basis with non-Jews. This meant that they were to be not only *in* the various lands of the dispersion, but *of* them, part and parcel of new nations. At the same time, exposure to the intellectual currents of the modern world shook many of their long-cherished beliefs about God and themselves as a people. The scientific approach to the study of the past particularly rocked the foundations of their inherited notions regarding the authenticity of the Biblical account of their origins and of the origins of the Torah.

Reform, Orthodox, and Conservative Judaism

Kaplan was of course familiar with the attempts already made to meet these challenges by the three major religious movements in Jewish life, Reform, Orthodoxy, and Conservatism, and by the secular movements, particularly Zionism. In *Judaism as a*

Civilization, Kaplan discusses the strengths and weaknesses of each of those approaches to Judaism. Reform properly takes into account the fact that Judaism has evolved and changed and must continue to do so. Reform also contributed a re-emphasis upon the ethical message of the prophets. But the mistake that Reform made, Kaplan states, was in assuming that religion could be detached from the culture that gave rise to it, that it could function, so to speak, in a vacuum. Reform repudiated Jewish peoplehood, cut off all ties to the land of Israel and to the rituals and folkways that made Jews a distinctive ethnic group. Reform reduced Judaism exclusively to a religion, in the Protestant sense of the term, that is, a communion of believers united by a common conception of God, and nothing else.

The second movement to attempt to adjust the Jew to the conditions of modern life is Orthodoxy (which Kaplan distinguishes from traditional Judaism), which he describes as that Judaism which came down from the past, represented by those who had virtually no contact with the outside world, whose education was confined to the Jewish texts, and who were not called upon to meet the intellectual challenge of the non-Jewish civilization. Modern or neo-Orthodoxy is represented by those who, having been exposed to a secular education, reaffirm their loyalty to Judaism, reconciling it with what they have learned from non-Jewish sources.

This type of neo-Orthodoxy, first formulated by Samson Raphael Hirsch in Germany, Kaplan says, has since become the viewpoint, for the most part, of the so-called Orthodox or traditionalists. Their strength, he believes, lies in their adherence to a maximalist program of Judaism; that is, they recognize the importance of approaching Judaism as a total way of life, permeating every aspect of their existence. They are also to be commended for the seriousness with which they treat the process of education. Of all the groups on the American scene, Kaplan feels, they alone have insisted upon an intensive education for their children.

But the Orthodox fail in reckoning with the intellectual challenge of modern times. They are the supernaturalists, *par excellence.* In the face of modern science, they stoutly maintain their belief in the existence of a supernatural order beyond the natural. They reaffirm their belief in the literal revelation of the Torah at Mount Sinai; they believe in the miracles recorded in the Bible; and they consider *Halakhah* or Jewish law as possessed of divine authority and hence not subject to change. Even interpretation of the law is permitted only to those who possess true rabbinical authority, that is, ordination granted by an Orthodox rabbi. Because the Orthodox shun the natural and adhere to the supernatural view, Kaplan states, they cannot make their religion and civilization a force for freedom, justice, and peace.

Conservatism, the third major force in Judaism, has also failed to meet the challenge of our time. Although Kaplan has been affiliated with the Conservative movement throughout his life, he has never hesitated to write or speak about its shortcomings. Indeed, he has said that if Conservatism had lived up to his hopes for it as the instrument through which the Jewish people would be made the focus of Judaism there would have been no need for launching the Reconstructionist movement.

Conservatism grew out of the "historical school," that group of scholars in Europe who concerned themselves with scientific study of the Jewish past. In this country, Solomon Schechter had developed the idea of "Catholic Israel," that it was the Jewish people which established, in every age, what Judaism should mean to it in that age, that Judaism was indeed the product of the people. The obvious inference from this approach was that Judaism would be understood as the evolving religious civilization of the Jewish people.

But unfortunately, says Kaplan, the leaders lacked either the insight or the courage to draw that inference fully. In one respect, to be sure, Conservatism carried out the implication of the approach by wholeheartedly supporting Zionism. Unlike the Reformers, who at first disapproved altogether of Zionism, and the Orthodox, who at one time insisted upon waiting for the Messiah, the Conservative rabbis saw in Zionism the indispensable opportunity to revive the Jewish people, and their religion and culture. They recognized that Judaism cannot exist without a Jewish people.

But in other respects, Conservatism followed either Reform or Orthodoxy. It followed Reform by introducing late Friday evening services, confirmation, and other practices which added to the decorum and dignity of public worship. It adhered to the Orthodox emphasis upon the *Halakhah*, except that the Conservatives felt free to put to use the instruments for legal interpretation available in the tradition itself. However, neither in theory nor in practice have the Conservatives accepted the theory that genuine innovation is legitimate.

Concept of Religion: Living in Two Civilizations

In place of these contemporary versions of Judaism, Kaplan presents his own view of Judaism as an evolving civilization. For him, religion is the highest expression of a civilization, the beliefs, institutions and forms which grow out of the attempt to give expression to its idea of salvation. Salvation is another term for the highest good, fulfillment, the ultimate purpose of life. Every people develops its own distinctive idea of the highest good when it translates that idea into sacred literature, sacred commemorations, or identifies that idea with revered heroes and sanctified places—these become the religion of the group. For that people, God is the power that makes for salvation. He is the source of that salvation and the assurance that salvation so understood is attainable, provided the people live up to the requirements of God, His "law" or "will."

Different groups have distinctive conceptions of salvation and God, which they represent by their unique *sancta*, the books, holidays, places, and heroes which emerge out of their respective histories. Thus the Jewish people's *sancta* include the Bible, *Yom Kippur* and *Pesah*, Jerusalem and Moses. We see then that religion is organically bound up with the civilization, which in turn is given its highest expression through religion.

The challenge of nationalism to modern Judaism arose when Jews, who had formerly lived exclusively in the Jewish civilization, were offered emancipation, the opportunity to become participants in the civilizations of their respective nations. In most European countries, this meant exchanging the Jewish culture for the French, the English, or the German. For this reason, Reform theoreticians believed that they could solve the problem by becoming Germans by culture and remaining Jews by religion alone.

In America, however, says Kaplan, under the conditions of democracy properly understood, no such choice is required. In the past, Jews had to choose between being Jews and being citizens of the lands they lived in, because Christianity and Judaism were mutually exclusive. But today, one can be an American and a Jew at the same time. This means that one can and should live in two civilizations, sharing to the fullest the culture and the religion of both.

Naturalism and the Concept of God

In Kaplan's thinking there is no room for the distinction between natural and supernatural. In former times, when men could not understand some phenomenon of nature, they ascribed it to the intervention of the deity in the affairs of the world. When some great truth dawned upon them, when some extraordinary event took place in the life of their nation, they attributed the event to their god. But science has shown that in the realm of physical nature, laws operate which are not subject to suspension or interference. If there is a drought, certain meteorological conditions explain it; it is not punishment for sins. When disease strikes, medical science understands the cause—or assumes a cause, though it may not be understood—but disease is no longer considered a punishment for sin.

Where, then, in such a natural order, can God be found? Kaplan's answer is that God is to be found in the moral law, which is as integral a part of the cosmos as any physical law. God is to be identified with that force in the universe that makes for goodness, justice, mercy, and truth. That force in the universe which spells creativity appears in man in the form of moral responsibility and moral courage. Wherever men display such responsibility and courage, they are manifesting the presence of God. When men strive to know the moral law and live up to it, they achieve salvation.

How do they know the moral law? They know it from experience, from intuition, and from reason. When all three achieve a consensus, men know that they have come upon a truth. Discovery rather than revelation is the means by which such truth becomes available to men. If men are honest with themselves and humble, they will recognize that the glimpse of truth they perceive at any given time is only part of what there is to be known. Each generation strives to expand the knowledge of truth, to refine what it has received from the past and transmit it to posterity. Religious naturalism contends that man's highest duty is to "seek God," that is, to dedicate himself to the striving after truth, for the purpose of knowing how best to live with himself and with his fellow man. The divine is to be found, therefore, within nature, operating through it to make man truly and fully human.

Concept of Prayer

Where does prayer fit into this concept of God? If God is not personal, not a being but a process, a force, how can one address prayer to Him? How does one achieve dialogue, as Buber describes it, with that which is not personal? Kaplan explains that prayer must resort to "reification," which means ascribing personality to that which is abstract or non-personal. The impulse to pray is human and cannot be abolished. The human being needs to give vent to his thoughts, feelings, aspirations, and fears. The sum total of a man's prayers represents his conception of salvation, of that which he needs to fulfill himself.

But he often finds that he must address himself to impersonal forces and intangibles. The poet frequently addresses "justice," "death," or "duty" or the "spring." These are obviously not persons; yet the limitations of the human mind and human expression are such that inevitably the word "Thou" is used. There is no other way of putting into words what one strongly feels without, at the moment of praying or waxing poetic, resorting to the dialogue form.

This conception of prayer implies, of course, that it is only subjectively efficacious, not objectively. This means that it affects the one who prays, giving him faith, courage, or hope— or merely relieves the pressure of his mood. Prayer will not change the weather or any other external condition.

Concept of the Chosen People

In rejecting supernaturalism with regard to the Torah, Kaplan at the same time finds it necessary to reject the corresponding supernaturalism of the Jewish people. The doctrine of the "chosen people" is the form in which the idea is conveyed that Jews belong to a people with supernatural status. The history of the Jews, according to this doctrine, is not to be understood in terms of the history of any other people. No generalizations about political, economic, and social forces apply to Jews because their history is, so to speak, above history.

The Reform group retains this doctrine, though they do not hold to the Orthodox interpretation of it. Reform expresses the concept of chosenness through the idea of the "mission of Israel," meaning that God has selected Israel to teach the world the idea of ethical monotheism. The Orthodox claim that Israel is chosen by virtue of the revelation at Sinai, when the Jewish people accepted the responsibility to live by the entire Torah both written and oral.

Kaplan's naturalism obviously prevents him from taking the Orthodox position. As for the Reform attitude, he finds it untenable on several counts. If Jews were to claim that they possess "hereditary traits which qualify them to be superior to the rest of the world in the realm of the religious and the ethical," then they would be assenting "to the most pernicious theory of racial heredity." Second, "for Jews to claim credit for having given to mankind those religious and ethical concepts which hold out promise for a better world smacks of arrogance." Third, "for Jews to maintain that they possess the truest form of truth would be understandable, if they still believed that the teachings of their religion are immutable and infallible." Finally, the attempt to interpret "chosenness" as referring to the fact "that the Western world is indebted to Israel for its fundamental religious ideas and institutions" is to confuse the historical fact with a theological doctrine. It may or may not be true that the Jews influenced the course of Western civilization. But to raise that fact to the level of a divine manifestation is to open the door to identify any and every historical event with God's will. This can have disastrous results, especially when the wicked prosper.

Kaplan is aware of the fact that the doctrine of "chosenness" is the traditional mode of expressing some profound psychological truth, namely, that a people has no right to live for itself alone, that the only worthwhile life is the one dedicated to a cause beyond itself, and that the Jewish people in particular has always been imbued with the ambition to perform some great service for the welfare of humanity, for the advancement of the kingdom of God. This urge to assume responsibility for the realization of a divine plan for mankind was couched for centuries in the concept of chosenness.

Some alternative to this doctrine must therefore be offered if the "baby is not to be thrown out with the bath water." The alternative to the supernaturalist conception of the Jewish people cannot be the secularist notion that history is meaningless. "Fortunately," writes Kaplan, "the Jewish tradition abounds in affirmations concerning the meaning of God, the destiny of man, the uses of the world and the vocation of the Jewish people, the relevance of which to the modern naturalist world-outlook can be easily explored." It is best in the interests of truth and enlightened religion to omit all reference to chosenness, and

> to put in its place the doctrine of vocation, of divine calling, in which all peoples can have a share. The vocation of each society, or people, is to enable all who belong to it to foster their freedom and responsibility in such a way as to become as fully human as their potentialities warrant. Likewise, in relation to other societies and peoples, the vocation consists in so regulating its own group activities—its economic, political and religious institutions—as to further the ultimate outlawing of war and the universal establishment of peace based on justice and freedom.

So seriously does Kaplan regard the concept of vocation that he urges Jews to take some dramatic and symbolic step to renew the "covenant," that is, to restate, in terms of modern experience the ideals, that plus which Jews must add to their desire for mere survival. The renewal of the covenant is closely related to his call for a clarification of the status of the Jewish people throughout the world.

Concept of Jewish Law

Kaplan believes that no Jewish life can function wholesomely without law. Indeed, he regards the Jewish emphasis upon law as one of Judaism's most distinctive contributions to civilization. Judaism was never satisfied with mere exhortation or maxim. If an ethical idea was not translated into legislation, it had no effective existence at all. In view of the fact that Jews in the Western world have learned the values of democracy, however, they should recognize that the authoritarianism of the past has no place in today's society. As Kaplan puts it, the past should have a vote but not a veto. If people are to live under law, they must give their consent to that law; they must be assured that the law is being laid down by those who have been elected to represent them, and that, in the final analysis, lawmakers are responsible to their constituents.

This democratic concept of law implies, of course, a prior fundamental concept, namely, that the "constitution" may be amended. Legislators must be limited; that is the function of a constitution. But unless the constitution itself can be adjusted to the needs and the wishes of the people, no basic changes are possible. Obviously, neither the Orthodox nor the Conservatives would countenance the doctrine that the Torah might be amended.

Concept of Ritual

In addition, says Kaplan, a distinction must be made in our time between ritual practice and law. In the past, every Jewish act was determined by the *Halakhah*, whether it had to do with the observance of the Sabbath or the issuing of a divorce. In the future, however, ritual should be conceived in altogether different terms. It should serve essentially as symbols of the basic values which Jews seek to articulate. If a particular ritual symbolizes a value no longer held sacred by Jews, it should either be revised or set aside. And since new values are constantly emerging, new rituals should be devised to symbolize them. Thus creativity in ritual is imperative. New forms must be created and old ones adapted and improved.

For this purpose, Jews must enjoy a wider latitude than is provided by the legalistic approach. In all creativity, trial and error play an important role. Jews must have faith that in time the beautiful and meaningful rituals will persist, while irrelevant or unesthetic ones will fall by the way. So long as the purpose is kept clearly in mind, there is no danger that the continuity with the past will be lost, or that Jews will devise such varied rituals that they will no longer be able to recognize one another. Rituals that grow out of the ancient *sancta* will always be identified as Jewish.

Kaplan is well aware of the fact that Jews want and need to be guided in their choice of rituals; but he opposes the authoritarian outlook which relies entirely upon a *Shulhan Arukh*, a fixed set of rules handed down from above. He believes that mature people should participate in thinking through some of the ritual problems that have arisen as a result of modern living and the changed attitude toward the authority of the past. They will not obtain from Kaplan any set of rules or observances dealing with *kashrut* or any phase of ritual; he may offer suggestions, but he will not lay down rules. This is sometimes frustrating to those who think they will receive a new code, neatly packaged, from the Reconstructionist movement.

Concept of Community

Any discussion of law, says Kaplan, is meaningless, however, unless it presupposes the existence of a community in which that law can function. In the past, the Jewish community was physically segregated and legally recognized. It was imposed upon Jews in the sense that they had to belong to it. A Jewish community in the United States differs in a number of vital respects. It can not be based upon geographical segregation; it has no legal status; it has to be entirely voluntary. But so far as possible it should have cohesion, mutual responsibility, and a sense of Jewish peoplehood.

American Jewry has grown "like Topsy." Organizations operate without regard for the general welfare. Each is concerned about pursuing its own ends. As a result, Jews experience the sense of belonging, not to the Jewish people, but to some institution or organization. There is no organic unity, and without such unity, law and what now prevails, are mutually contradictory.

First steps have been taken in the right direction, Kaplan points out. Many localities have set up community councils, some of which are functioning well. But these are only first steps because the purpose behind them is limited. They are intended to avoid waste and duplication, but they are not yet conceived as instruments for the advancement of Judaism as a civilization. Only when disparate groups move beyond the stage of mutual consultation to mutual responsibility, will they create the organic Jewish communities.

Zionism and the Concept of the Trans-National Jewish Community

Kaplan's emphasis upon Judaism as a civilization led him to recognize that the land of Israel had always played a vital role in the life and consciousness of the Jews. Every culture or civilization is the fruit of some soil. If Judaism was to flourish once again, it would have to be rooted in the land, where Jewish civilization would be the majority civilization, where the language would be that of the masses of people, where the calendar would be Jewish, and the schools, courts and theatres conducted in the Hebrew language and in the spirit of the tradition. That is why Kaplan's philosophy of Judaism places Israel at the center.

Zionism was, for Kaplan, the great revolutionary movement which carried the Jewish people over the threshold from medievalism to modernism because it interpreted the ancient yearning of Jews to "return" and their millennial Messianic aspirations in naturalist instead of supernaturalist terms. Thus, rather than wait for the Messiah to redeem them from exile, the Jews themselves undertook the task. What would have seemed heresy to their forebears—the appropriation to themselves of the prerogatives of divinity—now became the accepted norm for Jewish collective endeavor.

With Zionism, Judaism reentered the stage of history as a modern civilization. The Zionism of Herzl unfortunately became identified in the minds of Jews with refugee aid and nothing more. Actually, says Kaplan, Herzl and the early Zionist saw in Zionism the drive for the renaissance of the spirit and culture of the Jewish people, so seriously threatened by the emancipation which opened the doors wide to assimilation. With the establishment of the State of Israel, Jewish culture took on a new lease on life.

But with it have also come problems and confusion. One example is the mistaken notion that all Jews must go to live in Israel, that Judaism cannot survive outside the Land. This might be the case, says Kaplan, if there were no Israel and Jewish culture had no home. But with Israel as the core and focus of world Jewry, the Diaspora can be inspired and replenished. The fact that Jews yearned for centuries to return to the Land does not call for the complete ingathering of the exiles in our time. With free nations offering Jews equality, "exile" no longer carries the same connotation.

However, if some Jews live in Israel and become Israelis, and other Jews live in the Diaspora and become Americans, Englishmen, and so on, is there not the danger that Jews may be divided into two unrelated peoples? What shall the common bond be between them? Indeed, how shall Jews be designated, and what shall their status be in this new setting? They are obviously no longer to be regarded, as they were for centuries, as a nation in exile. Those who are living as a nation are not in exile; and those who live outside the nation also do not consider themselves in exile. Besides, they no longer share in common the conception of the Torah as the supernaturally revealed will of God. "Jews who wish to normalize their relationship to other Jews, whether in Israel or outside, cannot escape the necessity of having their unity redefined, and their status as a people with a common history and a common destiny reaffirmed."

This can only be accomplished by calling together the Jews of the world, through their representatives, to adopt a formal "covenant" similar to that which Jews adopted on previous occasions at momentous turning points in their history. Kaplan proposes that Jews adopt the concept of the "trans-national Jewish community, through the expansion of the Zionist ideal into a 'Greater Zionism.' " The purposes of the Greater Zionism should be to reinstate the spiritual unity of the Jewish people through the reclamation of *Eretz Yisrael* as the homeland of its tradition, culture and religion. To attain this objective, world Jewry should seek to preserve the State of Israel and endeavor to render it autonomous and self-sustaining.

Secondly, all Jews should recognize in their peoplehood the indispensable source of their religious or spiritual unity and personal salvation. The core of the Jewish people should be in *Eretz Yisrael,* and the rest of its body should consist of organic communities, organically correlated, throughout the Diaspora. Jews outside *Eretz Yisrael* owe their political allegiance to the various countries of which they are citizens. Thirdly, in view of the new development in the conception of Jewish unity, it is essential that this conception be clearly formulated and spelled out in its implications for Jews in their relations to one another and to the rest of the world, and become morally binding upon all Jews through a reaffirmation of the covenant which has kept them united hitherto.

It might seem, at first glance, that Kaplan is begging the question by calling upon all Jews to see in the Jewish people the basis for their "religious" unity. The very problem of unity arises out of the fact that they do not seem to have been able to retain their *religious* unity. What Kaplan is asking is that Jews unite—whatever their specific interpretations of Torah, *Halakhah*, or supernaturalism—upon the spiritual interests which they share as a result of their being members of the same culture or civilization.

For Kaplan believes that nationhood (as it used to be called when it referred not to sovereign states but to common cultures) generates its own spiritual values through a consensus which arises out of a common history and civilization. The religion of a group (as we have seen) is conveyed through the *sancta* which it creates, and the feelings of reverence which those *sancta* arouse, and the common ethical and spiritual values which they symbolize. In reality, the Zionist movement has been strongly tinged with religious fervor.

Zionists themselves have not recognized that the movement to revive the people was really religious. Certainly, it has been dubbed secular by those who are supposed to represent "religion." This has been due to the fact that few people understand what really happened with the rise of Zionism. The old supernaturalism was replaced by naturalism. That is what made Zionism the revolutionary movement it became. Somehow, even Orthodox Jews (except for the Neturai Karta, who still await the Messiah, and preserve their consistency complete) sensed that in the common effort to revive the Jewish people spiritual forces were unleashed which could become—and indeed have become—the inheritance of the whole community of Israel.

Religion of Democracy

Kaplan's efforts to understand Judaism and to reconstruct it for the new age led him to understand better the spiritual dilemma of America—and indeed of all the free nations in their struggle to combat totalitarianism. He has been deeply disturbed by the failure of democracy to meet the challenges of Fascism and Communism, which threaten to destroy all the values of the humanistic tradition and unloose dark powers of destruction, captivating men's minds and engaging their fanatic loyalty. Democracy continues to be paid lip service by those who enjoy its blessings without understanding its real commitments.

Unless democracy itself is raised to the level of a religious faith, it will not be able successfully to cope with the seductive claims of totalitarianism. Kaplan believes that such a faith, the religion of democracy, is already emerging in America. Basing his approach to American religion on his recognition of the role of *sancta*, he identifies the American attitude toward the flag, the Fourth of July, Thanksgiving Day, Memorial Day, as the *sancta* through which Americans are expressing their affirmation of the American creed.

That creed "asserts the sacredness of the human soul and its dignity, as a responsible creative moral agent. It regards all men as 'endowed by their Creator with . . . inalienable rights . . . among these . . . life, liberty, and the pursuit of happiness.' "

> Democratic religion would be universal in its reference; however, in order to avoid being merely a congeries of "vague generalities," it would have to be based—for America—on the "particularity of the life, the strivings, the experience, the travails, the hopes and the ideals of the American people at its best." The values of American democratic religion would be universal; its specific practices, rites and ceremonies, its *sancta*, would be particular.

To indicate how this religion of American democracy might be translated into the forms of liturgy, Kaplan (in collaboration with Eugene Kohn and J. Paul Williams) published *The Faith of America*, which contains suggested "services" for the major American holidays of the year, from New Year's Day to Election Day. Drawing upon the writings of outstanding spokesmen of the American ideal, these readings, prayers, poems, and songs constitute the rudiments of an American prayerbook.

"If democracy were thus regarded as a faith . . . a scheme of salvation that implies belief in a Power that makes for salvation," many of the troublesome problems of "religion in the public schools could be solved very simply." That is to say, "if the churches would concede to the public school the right to teach religion, the religion of democracy. The churches should realize that to instill in the child the yearning to achieve the ethical and spiritual implications of democracy and the faith that democracy is worth living for and dying for is to teach religion of a high order. Surely any sincere believer in God must recognize that a system of education which would inculcate in our youth that attitude toward democracy would make of the American people an instrument of divine revelation."

Kaplan and His Critics

Though virtually every rabbi, educator, social worker, and lay leader acknowledges his debt to Mordecai Kaplan, they have not necessarily accepted his philosophy. His critics range from the Orthodox, who consider him the mentor of the atheists, to those who share his theology but cannot understand why one has to be a Jew in order to believe in a naturalistic God.

Among Zionist leaders he is regarded as unrealistic for believing that Jewish life can thrive in the Diaspora; among the non-Zionists and anti-Zionists he is accused of setting up Israel as the authoritative center of a theocratic realm. Among social workers he is considered too much of a theologian; among theologians he is charged with being nothing more than a sociologist. Among those who call for the integration of Jews into American life, his blueprint for the organic community seems like a plan for a new ghetto; while those who worry about assimilation cannot reconcile themselves to his insistence that Jews live in two civilizations. Those who are acquainted with his personal habits of Jewish observance confuse him with the Orthodox; while the Orthodox rail at his suggestion that ritual should be removed from the category of *Halakhah*. Finally, he himself reports that he has been taken "for a thinker among men of action, and for a man of action among thinkers."

But all agree that, right or wrong, Mordecai M. Kaplan must be recognized as one of the foremost philosophers of Judaism in the twentieth century.

FOR FURTHER READING

Books by Mordecai M. Kaplan

The Religion of Ethical Nationhood (New York: Macmillian, 1970). A mature statement of Kaplan's Zionism.

Kaplan, Mordecai and Arthur Cohen, *If Not Now, When?* (New York: Schocken Publications, 1973). An interesting dialogue between two significant, and very different, Jewish thinkers on many fundamental matters.

Books about Mordecai M. Kaplan

BERKOVITS, Eliezer, *Major Themes in Modern Philosophies of Judaism* (New York: Ktav Publishing Company, 1974). A frontal, and in many ways correct, attack upon Kaplan's reconstructionist position. But there is more to the issues than Berkovits allows.

BOROWITZ, Eugene, *Choices in Modern Jewish Thought* (New York: Behrman House, 1983). A balanced introduction to Kaplan's main concerns, with criticism.

COHEN, Jack J., *The Case for Religious Naturalism* (Reconstructionist Press, New York, 1958). An informed defense of Kaplan's theology by a close disciple.

Judaism: A Journal devoted a special number (Number 117, Volume 30, 1981, No. 1) to Kaplan's life and thought on the 100th anniversary of his birth. Contains some good things on diverse topics.

10. R. Joseph Soloveitchik

[1903-]

AHARON LICHTENSTEIN[1]

J U D A I S M traditionally constitutes a distinctive way of life. To be a Jew is to be a member of a community, committed to a specific regimen. It means thinking, feeling, acting in accordance with a particular normative pattern, trying to govern oneself through every walk of life by a complex detail of comprehensive laws. In his personal and in his collective life the Jew recognizes the authority of law and strives to adhere to its precepts. As creed and code, *Halakhah* consists of a set of principles revealed through a written and an oral Torah at Sinai and of the details elicited from them by subsequent rabbinic exegesis and analysis. Dating from Sinai, and yet ever abreast of contemporary conditions, *Halakhah* has been a corpus of canon law which has set the standard for Jewish life. It is the mainstream of Jewish thought and action.

The *Halakhic* way of life thus constitutes our central Jewish heritage. What is its meaning in everyday life? How does it meet man's basic spiritual needs? What do its laws reveal of God's purposes for Israel? How is it related to the conditions of modern life? The contemporary thinker who has done the most to answer these questions is R.[2] Joseph Soloveitchik. His life has been devoted to an understanding of the relation of *Halakhah* to daily life and the development of a Torah-*Halakhic* world-outlook.

He was singularly equipped by nature and training for this task. As a Talmudic scholar he is perhaps the most eminent of contemporary rabbinic authorities with a masterful grasp of *Halakhah* proper. On the other hand, his wide knowledge of general and religious philosophy combined with personal insight into human nature and the condition of man has given him a sensitive awareness of man and his problems. Fusing technical *Halakhic* knowledge with psychological and philosophical perception, he has related the ideal *Halakhic* system to the basic realities of human life. Based on his staunch commitment to our central religious heritage, he has interpreted both its significance and its substance. He has formulated a creative philosophy, conservative and progressive, keeping intact our Jewish tradition even as he was developing it further. It is as the scholar and philosopher of *Halakhah* that he is significant.

Early Years and Studies

Joseph Soloveitchik was born into a family with a tradition of Jewish scholarship, on February 27, 1903 (12 Adar, 5665) in Pruzhan, Poland. His grandfather, Rav Haym Soloveitchik ("the Brisker Rav"), had revitalized Talmudic study through his emphasis on scientific classification and rigorous analysis; his father, Rav Mosheh, pursued the "Brisker" method as rabbi-scholar in various Eastern European communities.

Most of R. Joseph Soloveitchik's early years were spent in the White Russian town of Khoslavitch, where his father served as rabbi. Although the town traditionally elected a *Mitnagged* as rabbi, its Jewish populace consisted largely of Lubavitcher *Hasidim*. When the seven-year-old Joseph was sent to study Talmud at the local *heder*, he came under the tutelage of an elderly devotee of *Habad*. This *Hasid* was dominated by the interesting notion that although studying the Talmud was fine, the study of *Tanya*, the central classic of *Habad Hasidut*, was still better, and he conducted his classes accordingly. While ostensibly teaching Talmud he devoted most of the study time to introducing his tyros generally, and often surreptitiously— to the mysteries of *Habad*. For the better part of a year, young Soloveitchik's Talmudic progress was impeded while the study of *Tanya* accompanied by enthralling stories of *Hasidic* lore proceeded merrily apace!

While Rav Mosheh was somewhat slow to detect the true

state of affairs, his wife—herself the learned daughter of an outstanding rabbinic scholar—was more perceptive. Detecting the slow rate of growth in her son's Talmudic knowledge, she prodded Rav Mosheh to remedy the situation. Failing to obtain proper satisfaction, she finally complained to Rav Haym and upon the family's next visit to Brisk, the budding scholar was duly examined and found wanting. The result was that Rav Haym recommended that Rav Mosheh henceforth take personal charge of his son's Talmudic education; and it was from that day that the period of rigorous, mutual study dated.

During the next twelve years, young Soloveitchik dedicated himself almost exclusively to the study of Jewish law. Under Rav Mosheh's tutelage he was trained in the "Brisker" method with its insistence on incisive analysis, exact definition, precise classification and critical independence. Gradually, the acute dialectic of *Halakhic* logic—so rigorous and yet so subtle; so flexible and still so firm—became second nature, and Soloveitchik emerged from this period thoroughly imbued with the religious and intellectual discipline of *Halakhah*.

As a result of the youth's absorption in his *Halakhic* studies, his secular education took second place. To be sure, this does not mean that his training was narrow. Talmudic study, while technical and difficult, is more than an intellectual training ground. It is a total, intellectual, moral and religious discipline. *Halakhah* is not a "subject"; it is a way of life. Furthermore, in purely intellectual terms we must recognize the depth and range of Talmudic material. Only in his later years did he achieve the equivalent of a secular education. However, he acquired a lifelong taste for literature from his mother, who led him from fairy tales to Ibsen, Pushkin, Lermontov, and Bialik. When he reached his latter teens, R. Soloveitchik attained the equivalent of a "*gymnasium*" (i.e., high school and junior college) education from a series of tutors.

During this period he had studied little, if any, formal philosophy. Even the central classics of medieval Jewish thought had not entered into the curriculum he had pursued under the tutelage of his father. Despite a consuming interest in Maimonides' strictly *Halakhic* magnum opus, *Mishneh Torah*, Rav Mosheh had never so much as opened the *Moreh Nevukhim* (*Guide for the Perplexed*); and although father and son had often informally explored the rich vein of ethical, social, political, and even metaphysical thought which lies just beneath the surface of technical *Halakhic* minutiae, there had been no systematic, much less intensive, study of problems of general philosophy.

University of Berlin

When he was twenty-two, R. Soloveitchik entered the University of Berlin and for the first time approached the serious study of a secular discipline. His chosen field was philosophy. At the University, he plunged into the more abstract and abstruse aspects of philosophy, focusing his interest on a study of logic, metaphysics and epistemology. In all these areas—particularly the last two—the current approach was influenced by the thought and philosophy of Kant, and Soloveitchik steeped himself in Kantianism and its dicta.

The nineteenth century had produced innumerable heirs and disciples of Kant and now, early in the twentieth century there developed the powerful current of neo-Kantianism. This school was represented at Berlin by Heinrich Maier, but its acknowledged leaders were George Natorp and Hermann Cohen of Marburg; hence the name *"die Marburg Schule."* Neo-Kantianism was centrally, even radically idealist. With Kant, it held the mind, with its *a priori* categories, to be the true source of knowledge. But, unlike Kant, who also recognized at least secondarily, *a posteriori* empirical knowledge, it insisted first, that the mind was the *sole* source of truth, and secondly, that it was the foundation of reality as well as of knowledge. Above all, its leaders—Cohen in particular—recognized the supremacy of the mathematical and scientific—especially physical—interpretation of reality. On the one hand, declared Cohen, "Thought forms the ground of Being," and, on the other hand, pure thought is to be identified with mathematics and science. Hence, his characterization of his own system as a mathematico-scientific idealism, which equated ultimate Being with mathematic-scientific laws as developed by the mind.

R. Soloveitchik was especially attracted to this school of thought and to this day maintains considerable interest in mathematics and physics. He studied under the direction of Heinrich

Maier and in 1931 wrote his doctoral dissertation on the subject of Hermann Cohen's epistemology and metaphysics. He had planned a different dissertation, which might have better indicated the future course of Soloveitchik's intellectual interests. Its topic was to have been "Maimonides and Plato," and its thesis that general Maimonidean scholarship had erred in seeing Maimonides as a confirmed Aristotelian. However, since no one in the department of philosophy at the University was qualified to supervise such a work, it never went beyond the planning stage.

After receiving his doctorate in 1931, R. Soloveitchik married Dr. Tonya Lewit (herself the recipient of a Ph.D. in education from Jena) and, a year later with his wife and first-born child, emigrated to the United States. A few months after his arrival, R. Soloveitchik accepted the post of Chief Rabbi of Boston, the city which has since been his home.

Spiritual Mentor

Bred in a tradition that emphasized the intellectual, rather than the pastoral function of the rabbinate, it was R. Soloveitchik's conception that the rabbi is above all a student, scholar and teacher. Soloveitchik, therefore, dedicated himself to the task of disseminating a deeper knowledge of Torah Judaism. He set out to encourage a general awareness of the values of traditional Judaism and their relevance to modern life. Thus, periodic *derashot*—lengthy public discourses combining *Halakhic*, homiletic, and philosophic material—his weekly *Halakhic shiurim* (lectures) on the lay level, and his own, richly philosophic understanding of human nature, won for him an ever growing reputation for wisdom and scholarship.

Turning his attention from the older to the younger generation, R. Soloveitchik founded the first Hebrew day school in New England, The Maimonides School, and to this day continues his active interest in its administration. Shortly thereafter, he gathered around him a small group of young Talmudic scholars and organized an informal institute which he guided. He delivered regular *shiurim* to the members. The institute was disbanded in 1941, however, when Soloveitchik accepted the position which has done the most to project him into prominence upon the Jewish scene. Succeeding his father, R. Soloveitchik became and is today professor of Talmud at the Rabbi Isaac Elchanan Theological Seminary, today part of Yeshiva University.

In this capacity, he has become the spiritual mentor of the majority of today's younger Orthodox rabbis. Although his activities at the Yeshiva became more and more time-consuming, R. Soloveitchik did not give up his home in Boston, but commuted weekly to New York. He began by teaching Talmud and *Halakhah*, delivering two to four two-hour *shiurim* weekly, but he has also gone on to lecture in related fields. For many years he has offered courses in Jewish philosophy at the University's graduate school. For the past three years he has been the principal Jewish participant in a project sponsored by the National Institute of Mental Health undertaken jointly by Harvard University, Loyola and Yeshiva, with the purpose of studying religious attitudes toward psychological problems. In 1957-1959 he gave a series of lectures on Jewish social philosophy to a group of social workers in New York. Since 1952 he has been the chairman of the *Halakhah* Commission of the Rabbinical Council of America, the principal American Orthodox rabbinical organization. Since 1946 R. Soloveitchik has been honorary president of the Religious Zionists of America (formerly *Mizrachi*) and more recently he has represented the entire American Jewish community as a member of the Advisory Committee on Humane Methods of Slaughter, set up by the Secretary of Agriculture. Currently he has been in the public eye as the outstanding candidate for the vacant Chief Rabbinate of Israel. Although this office has been offered to him, up to now R. Soloveitchik has declined to accept it.

R. Soloveitchik's prominence is not accidental. It is the result of considerable exposure to an educated public. Prior to his arrival at Yeshiva, his life had been primarily "an epoch of concentration," characterized by intensive study, and in a sense, by isolation. During the last two decades, however, his activities have shifted their emphasis. But R. Soloveitchik himself has remained essentially a lonely figure, although he has many loyal students and some devoted associates.

Most of his time, R. Soloveitchik has devoted to expounding his ideas to others. Particularly when speaking in his native Yiddish, he is an orator of note—and of the old school. His public *derashot*, tinged with a flair for the dramatic and the rhetorical, captivate his audience for at least two hours and, on his father's *Yahrzeit*, for four! As a *Halakhic* expositor who is endowed with an unusual facility for explaining difficult technical problems, R. Soloveitchik is without a contemporary peer. His philosophic lectures, delivered in Hebrew, or more frequently in English, tend to be more technical in nature, and are sometimes characterized by a predilection for abstract and over-intellectualized language.

It is evident, from all this, that the spoken word has been paramount in R. Soloveitchik's approach. When we turn to consider the list of his publications, we find it meager indeed. There is no full-length book included, and the major item is a weighty essay *The Halakhic Personality*, which appeared in the first volume of the scholarly Hebrew quarterly, *Talpioth* (1944). This, together with a few scattered articles on a variety of subjects in various learned journals, *Festschriften* and newspapers, comprise virtually his entire bibliography. The fact is, that although R. Soloveitchik has published very little, he has written a great deal. This reluctance to appear in print has been noted by all observers, lamented by most, and explained by very few. R. Soloveitchik himself once described it as a "family malady." His grandfather published only a single, posthumous volume, his father only a few articles, and his uncle published none at all. Yet all three were world-renowned *Halakhic* scholars with a great deal of material in manuscript. R. Soloveitchik attributes this familial reluctance to the demands of perfectionism. No matter how clearly a problem is formulated, or how soundly its solution is expounded, a gnawing fear persists that perhaps it can be done better.

CONCEPT OF HALAKHAH

R. Soloveitchik's thought has always focused on assessing the human situation. Man is viewed from two aspects: he is both passive and active, cause and effect. Philosophically, man is both object and subject, thing and person. Man is acted upon by external forces, but man also acts himself. Rolling down a hill, he exists in one capacity; walking up the hill, in quite another. The surgeon is the master craftsman, his patient is his object. Conversely, the man as patient seeks the surgeon as object. The subject exists as an individual, a man who is first and foremost a single, unitary entity, different from any other creature. As object, however, man is merely a quantitative element, one part of a collective whole. In his capacity as subject, man is not only individual, but is a spiritually self-determined individual. The demagogue is a subject, his captive audience puppets. Only the singular and free personality truly exists as subject.

Dual Character of Man

This awareness of man's dual character, which is fundamental to traditional Judaism, is a cornerstone of R. Soloveitchik's thought. To him, religion begins with recognition of self as subject and social ethics as affording the same status to others. Borrowing from Kierkegaard, R. Soloveitchik goes so far as to suggest that if we must single out one definitive key to man's essential personality, that key is his "loneliness"—not the emotion of wretched forlornness, but the state of being alone, a distinct self-contained entity. The concept of the "human face divine," the creation of man in the image of God of which the Torah speaks, refers, according to Soloveitchik's interpretation, to man's free and singular personality, his individual aloneness and not to his rational or emotional faculties. The religious life, then, is literally a process of spiritual *self*-awareness, self-assertion, and self-creation. The freedom inherent in the divinely ordained dual nature of man includes the freedom to abdicate. If he chooses, man may be reduced from subject to object. It is only through strenuous effort that the subject status is developed and maintained. The spiritual life is a process whereby a free agent breaks the bonds of external controls and establishes the seat of power within his inner personality. Existence as subject is clearly a prerequisite for religious life. As object, man is simply part of the herd, and the herd itself just so much cosmic dust.

At the apex of religious development, man simultaneously issues a call to God, and responds to God's call to him. God and man are drawn into a community of existence, into what

R. Soloveitchik calls "a covenantal community." This community brings God and man together in an intimate, person-to-person relationship.

Premises of Torah-Halakhic Life

It is in the attainment of this goal that *Halakhah* is important. "Nearness to God" is reached through a life of total dedication to the apprehension and fulfillment of His will. It is this which *Halakhah* offers, and imposes upon the Jew.

The Torah-*Halakhic* life rests upon three central premises. The first is the recognition—at once knowledge and acknowledgement—that God exists as the sole, absolute end, all else being ancillary and relative. Only God constitutes pure and complete Good, and only He can be an absolute *desideratum*. All other values, social, political, personal or even intellectual, are inferior and secondary and derive their worth only from their ultimate advancement of man's religious existence.

The second premise is man's total commitment, unconditional and unqualified, to the service of God. He recognizes that he must direct all his efforts to the greater glory of his Creator. His own desires must be completely subordinated, if not effaced; all his resources are to be utilized for the enactment of what is simultaneously God's will and man's destiny. Third, is the conviction of Torah and *Halakhah* as truth. Faith in their essential revealed character lies at the heart of traditional Judaism and *Halakhic* laws are part of a divinely ordered discipline.

In the *Halakhic* life, existence for the Jew is filled with meaning; he is a conscious, spiritual personality, acting in accordance with divine norms and toward a divine purpose. *Halakhah* as a way of life is eminently practical, intimately concerned with the pragmatic exigencies of day-to-day living. As a religious system, *Halakhah* governs a Jew's attitude and behavior in virtually every area of his life. It addresses him as producer and consumer, as worshipper and thinker, as husband and father, artist and scholar. Its laws require some actions, permit others, and proscribe still others. As the regimen of heightened religious life which Israel sought, and God imposed, *Halakhah* commits the Jew to a divinely ordained discipline and presents a blueprint for an idealized existence within the realities of life.

Insisting that God must be served with the head, as well as with the hands and heart, *Halakhah* views intellection as integral to individual religious life and posits a minimum of personal study as one of man's fundamental daily obligations.

Role of Intellect

The role of intellection is threefold: Study is a necessary prerequisite to fulfill religious observance. The maintenance of moral and ritual norms requires clear and accurate knowledge of their general nature and specific details. Secondly, intellectual activity has its own value. Torah study gives the Jew insight —as direct and profound as man is privileged to attain—into the revealed will of his Creator. Through the study of *Halakhah*— the immanent expression of God's transcendent rational will— man's knowledge of God gains depth and scope. Further, religious study is a stimulus to the total spiritual personality. Faith can be neither profound nor enduring unless the intellect is fully and actively engaged in the quest for God.

Finally, human intellect is crucial as the partial creator of *Halakhah* itself, in that collective Torah scholarship half perceives and half creates the blueprint of the ideal temporal life. It is, and from the beginning was intended to be, partly divine and partly human handiwork. Its basic design consists of a body of general principles which were divinely ordained and hence immutable and incontrovertible. These were given to Moses through a written Torah—the Pentateuchal text—and a companion oral Torah, which consists of dicta clarifying Biblical statements, filling in details concerning laws set forth only generally in the written Torah, and establishing additional, independent laws. It prescribes the methods and procedures for subsequent interpretation by man for the development of *Halakhah*, Such interpretation of *Halakhic* law, and it is here that the human element enters, is indispensable since the fundamental laws as they were delivered to Moses could not cover the infinite array of specific instances which, in the kaleidoscopic circumstances of human life, might some day arise.

Thus, *Halakhah* declares initially that meat is neither to be cooked nor eaten with milk. The question arises, then, whether fowl is included as "meat," or whey in "milk," or frying and steaming in "cooking." Or, it may require that a grain *matzah* be eaten on *Pesah*, and one might question whether whole-wheat or rice *matzah* qualifies. In the same manner, referring to the injunction against profiteering, one might ask whether this applies to luxuries as well as to necessities—to corporations as well as to individuals. Through analysis and exegesis, creative *Halakhic* scholarship elicits what is implicit in axiomatic revealed principles, subsumes the concrete instance under the relevant category, and ultimately resolves the problem by rendering authoritative decision. This, in turn, provides a basis for future application and development.

Implementation of Halakhah

The apprehension of *Halakhah* is one side of the *Halakhic* life; its implementation is the other. R. Soloveitchik's exposition of this aspect of *Halakhah* centers around two principal concepts. The first is *kedushah*, which may best be translated as "sanctity" and understood to refer to the Torah's attitude on man's internal and external relation to nature. Again and again Soloveitchik has emphasized that Judaism is not content to speak of the dignity of man; it insists on the *sanctity* of man, and sees this sanctity manifest itself within man's natural life. *Halakhah's* attitude seeks to transmute the natural—or rather, it demands that man transmute it. *Halakhah* recognizes man's physical, social and economic needs and does not permit him to deny them. It demands, however, that human effort be exerted unstintingly so that man's total existence and experience be consecrated to God. Through its comprehensive norms, *Halakhah* guides man along the road to sanctification of himself and his environment. It accomplishes this in two ways: first, it posits specific *desiderata* and prescribes required means for their minimum attainment and the direction of creative effort for their maximum achievement. Second, it impresses upon the Jew that divine will has expressed itself in every area of human activity and that there is a right and a wrong way for man to act in every sphere of his existence. It emphasizes that man must always act with a conscious awareness of his relationship to God. Thus, *Halakhah* extends to seemingly neutral areas. What does God care, asked the rabbis, whether an animal is slit at the throat or at the nape?

The point is, they answered, that He wants *man* to care, wants him to be aware of His commanding presence in every area of life. By forbidding one type of behavior, permitting a second and requiring a third, *Halakhah* engages man's conscious mind and will at every point. A man who sits down to a steak dinner is merely a carnivorous biped; the same man insisting upon a kosher steak involves his spiritual personality in the exercise of a purely physical action. *Halakhah* makes the service of God part of a total life which is suffused with religious significance, harmoniously organized into a divinely ordained whole and gives man a sense of purpose and a sense of the divine purpose.

Clearly, R. Soloveitchik's concept of the *Halakhic* regimen is positive, dynamic and comprehensive. His approach emphasizes the integration of all parts of living into a unified, religious framework. It knows no dualism and recognizes no dichotomy between the religious and the secular. Each is distinct, but by no means disjunct. As *Halakhah* condemns secular moralism, so does it reject narrow ritualism. While liberal Judaism has developed around the Temple, "*Halakhah*, which draws divinity into the physical world, does not revolve around congregations and synagogues. They are its minor sanctuaries; its true sanctuary is the realm of daily life within which the realization of *Halakhah* takes place." *Halakhah* does not permit the Jew to secularize life; it enjoins him from escaping it. The *Halakhic* figure neither ignores the transcendental nor flees to it; he seeks to incorporate it within his own temporal existence. *Halakhah*, therefore, sees man attaining his highest felicity by establishing the Kingdom of Heaven on earth—"not by transforming the finite into the infinite, but by introducing the infinite into the finite."

Thus, while God alone can be recognized as an absolute good, all aspects of human activity attain vital significance as segments of a life committed in its totality to God. Within a total religious context, intellectual activity is invaluable; but to divorce it from ultimate spiritual purpose is to commit the grievous sin of intellectual pride.

Attitude to State of Israel

In this context, R. Soloveitchik has firmly resisted any apotheosis of an independent State of Israel as such. As a purely political element, it leaves the moral and religious conscience cold. The state is meaningful only insofar as it helps fulfill the historical destiny of the people, the universal and timeless "community of the committed." It is the common commitment to a divinely ordained way of life that makes us a people, bound as subjects, by spiritual destiny and not only as objects, by inexorable historical fate. However, a State of Israel, consecrated to God and aware of its unique, historical and political position, is an indispensable instrument of national religious fulfillment.

Of such a state, R. Soloveitchik has much to say. He sees the character, structure and development of the State of Israel as one of the major challenges to contemporary Jewry. He accepts the present state warmly, but only as a means. The challenge is to direct the means to its proper end, which can be attained only through the religious life. The path of Torah is not an easy one, and R. Soloveitchik is careful to point out that it does not pretend to be. The Torah life begins with a sense of crisis and a call for sacrifice. It concludes with the profoundest sense of serenity and security. Initially, however, it makes demands rather than promises. "Commitment" in heart and action is a God-centered, rather than a self-centered life, dedicated to the sanctification of man.

Sources of Sanctity

In *Halakhah* nothing is sacred but man literally makes it so. No object, no place is holy unless so designated by man. The very dates of holidays within limits must be determined by man's manipulation of the lunar calendar, and time itself must be sanctified. Unless the scribe intends to sanctify it, a Torah scroll is no more holy than a newspaper. Even the Temple and all its appurtenances remain profane unless they are specifically dedicated by human word and thought, until the Jew declares: "This vessel is consecrated to God."

Perhaps the most striking example of this is a single phenomenon which R. Soloveitchik has often pointed out: Mount Sinai, which God sanctified by his descent to man, has retained no trace of sanctity, its very location being a matter of archaeological dispute. But Mount Moriah, which Abraham sanctified by his ascent to meet God, became the site of the Temple, and remains *Halakhically* eternally sacred. Nothing could indicate more clearly the significance of the inner spiritual element with reference to objective action. While the regimen of *Halakhah* provides the necessary forms, it leaves to the initiative of man's creative spirit the vital task of infusing these forms with meaningful content. Objects designated by divine command, and hallowed by time and collective usage, evoke a powerful, emotional response.

Halakhah and Jewish Identity

With its pervasive psychological realism, *Halakhah* has recognized that ordinary mortals need to be jogged out of their spiritual lethargy, and that unless they are prodded to specific action, many will be quite content to neglect the religious life completely. Habitual observance ingrains moral and religious sensibility into the very fiber of the personality. It strengthens the inner power of spirit and, at a deeper level, human emotion is profoundly affected by the very process of externalization. The objective *Halakhic* mold helps man avoid emotional extremes. It restrains excesses; it curbs violence and turbulence, it channels religious feeling into "the depth, and not the tumult, of the soul." If religion is to leave a profound and lasting imprint, it must relate to action as well as to emotion; neither tepid sermons nor evangelical fervor will suffice. Both within the individual, and within the community, the *Halakhic* regimen adds an element of permanence to religion.

We should keep in mind, however, what we sometimes tend to forget: the most legalistic ritualism is better than no worship whatever; and the individual who, within *Halakhah*, lapses into a formalistic rut, would very likely be bereft of religious awareness completely were he without it. At the very least, ritual establishes a floor for religion; at most, it leads man toward the scaling—and holding—of the loftiest spiritual heights.

The objective character of *Halakhah* helps the Jew transcend his own subjective existence. In one sense, the *Halakhic* way of life serves as a distinctive mark of identification. As a minimal, uniform tradition, it helps weld the organic whole of the community of Israel. *Halakhah* places the Jew's life in a total perspective; he can see his isolated efforts as part of Israel's timeless and universal enterprise. It links him with a heroic past and a glorious future. His Jewish solidarity is expressed in fulfilling a common destiny, not merely in suffering a common fate.

To the usual division of *mitzvot* into physical and spiritual duties, e.g., eating *matzah* and fearing God respectively—R. Soloveitchik has added a third category whose significance he has particularly underscored. This includes *mitzvot* in which an inner and outer moment are both directly involved. He has distinguished, for instance, between the rituals of eating *matzah* and of mourning. With respect to the former, its spiritual ends are attained outside the framework of the *mitzvah* itself. The command is simply *to eat matzah*, and it is fulfilled by the physical act. All other results are ancillary. For example: a doctor tells me to exercise *in order* to lose weight. But to lose weight and to exercise are two very different things, and if I exercise, I have obeyed the doctor's order, though I lose nary an ounce. As long as I consciously eat *matzah*, I have obeyed the divine command —in itself significant. With respect to the ritual of mourning, however, the situation is different. Here, the actual command is to undergo an emotional experience and the ritual is merely a concomitant procedure. The latter is the *act* required by the *mitzvah* and a means *to* and symbol *of* its fulfillment, but the fulfillment itself is purely internal. Though the mourner should observe the ritual in its minutest detail, if there is no emotional participation he has not observed the *mitzvah* at all.

Prayer and Repentance

Thus R. Soloveitchik has emphasized an essentially experiential and practical approach to the *mitzvot*. Working from the foundations of *Halakhic* scholarship, he has been able to apply this concept to a number of commandments, above all, to those most crucial of religious duties—prayer and repentance. *Halakhically*, both require outward manifestation. Yet, R. Soloveitchik has shown that the essential *Halakhic* fulfillment is wholly internal. Prayer consists of an inner religious experience—of a sense of crisis, a feeling of dependence, a yearning for communion with God. Repentance, likewise, is fulfilled internally and the human element, which the *Halakhah* has emphasized, R. Soloveitchik sees as deriving its motivating force from man's creative spirit. To him, repentance represents the supreme example of man's redeeming, sanctifying, and even creative powers which are rooted in the inner personality. Here, as elsewhere, conduct is important as an expression of the religious character and as the means to its formation.

The essence of Judaism lies in prayer and repentance, in Soloveitchik's view and in recent years he has placed increasing emphasis on the emotional element in Judaism. He has done this referring both to fact and value, holding that it *is* important and that it *ought* to be important. In the first place, and here both *Hasidic* and contemporary influences are clearly discernible, at the profoundest depths of his personality, man is not the orderly, rational being he imagines. He is subject to powerful emotional stresses; he is ravaged by inner conflict and crisis. Filled with a tragic awareness of his own weakness, he is overwhelmed by the mystery of divinity which simultaneously attracts and repels him, and is resentful of his own impotence. Conversely, he is animated by the most naive faith. In the inner sanctum of his personality, man is reduced to child-like innocence. Stripped of his rebellious armor, he is suffused with religious love and his sense of weakness translates itself into a feeling of dependence which draws him ever closer to the sole source of absolute strength and solace. It is at this fundamental level, and through the dialectic interplay of these emotions that Soloveitchik sees religious life at its most intense. And again, he holds not only that it *is* so, but that it *should* be so. Only by admitting his childish innocence can man open his heart to God.

R. Soloveitchik's emphasis upon religious experience is reflected in some recent writings dealing with the relation of intellect and emotion. They must be interanimate; there is no false opposition between thought and experience. "The study of *Halakhah*," he wrote last year, "bears two aspects. It begins as the cognition of an idea, and it concludes as the experience of a presence." The faith of the Torah scholar is itself "sustained by the truth he discovers." At a deeper level, his cognition of *Halakhah* leads him beyond intellect to an "existential consciousness into which it merges." At this level, *Halakhic* ideas are no longer abstract concepts, but living realities, not merely perceived, but experienced. He confronts *Halakhic* situations not as a clear, confident thinker, but as a pulsating, vibrant soul and reacts to

it as to an immediate presence. Above all, he reacts to the presence of its Giver, toward whom, now with fear, now with love,
he is inexorably drawn. Hence, as R. Soloveitchik points out, the
greatest Jewish personalities have always combined remarkable
critical power with profoundly naive faith. However, R. Soloveitchik does not reject the intellect within religious life. But, in
stressing that the most profound awareness comes beyond cognition at the level of experiential consciousness, he indicates where
his primary emphasis lies. It is upon *avodah she-be-lev*—innermost worship.

Such, in broad outline, is Soloveitchik's thought. Essentially,
he views all aspects of life from the framework of *Halakhah* and
in this sense, his concepts are not, of course, wholly original.
Halakhic raw materials date, after all, from Sinai. R. Soloveitchik,
therefore, attempts to understand and interpret the aims of *Halakhah* through the religious and philosophic principles which are
embedded in its welter of legal detail. He relates the ideal *Halakhic* system to the conditions which bear upon the modern
Jew's existence and experience. He understands and utilizes tradition so well because of his own historical tradition and ex-
pounds upon it with his own, original approach. His thought, as
part of his life, is devoted to the timeless truth of *Halakhah*.

FOR FURTHER READING

Books by Joseph B. Soloveitchik

Shiurei Harav (New York: Yeshiva University Press, 1974). Contains an
English translation of a number of Soloveitchik's "sermons."

"The Lonely Man of Faith," *Tradition*, Vol 7, Number 2 (Summer,
1965), pp. 5–67. Solveitchik's famous English essay presenting, in
summary, much of his religious philosophy. A must.

Books about Joseph B. Soloveitchik

BESDIN, Abraham, editor, *Reflections of The Rav* (Jerusalem: World
Zionist Organization, 1980). A collection of a number of Soloveitchik's recent discourses and essays.

BOROWITZ, Eugene, *Choices in Modern Jewish Thought* (New York:
Behrman House, 1983). Especially interesting because Borowitz is a
major Reform theologian who is nonetheless a sympathic critic of
Soloveitchik's orthodox formulations.

KAPLAN, Lawrence, "The Religious Philosophy of Rabbi Joseph
Soloveitchik," *Tradition*, (Fall, 1973), pp. 43–64. A valuable introduction by a student and disciple.

KAPLAN, Lawrence, translator and editor of Joseph B. Soloveitchik's *Halachic Man* (Philadelphia: Jewish Publication Society, 1984). An outstanding English translation and edition of Soloveitchik's classic, and most famous, Hebrew essay of 1944.

PELI, Pinchas H., editor, *On Repentance* (Jerusalem: Oroth Press, 1980). An English translation of Soloveitchik's brilliant discourses on the theme of repentance. Peli provides a helpful, context setting, introduction.

SINGER, David, *Joseph B. Soloveitchik* (New York: New York University Press, scheduled for 1986). The best, most comprehensive, study of Soloveitchik that is available.

Tradition: A Journal of Orthodox Opinion, published a special number (Spring, 1978) which contained five essays by Soloveitchik.

Notes

Foreword

1. Salo Baron, *A Social and Religious History of the Jews*, Volume I, Part I, pp. 195-196. See also Victor T. Cherikover, *Hellenistic Civilization and the Jews*, p. 377.
2. *Great Ages and Ideas of the Jewish People*, edited by Leo Schwarz, pp. 244-246.
3. "My Double Life and Excommunication" in *Memoirs of My People*, edited by Leo Schwarz, pp. 84-94. For scholarly works on Acosta see Baron, *op. cit.*, Volume III, p. 140.
4. Meyer Waxman, *A History of Jewish Literature*, Volume II, p. 260. Jacob Agus, however, in his *Evolution of Jewish Thought* includes Spinoza "in the total panorama of Judaism for his sentiments as well as his thoughts derived from the philosophical tradition in Judaism and reflected the exigencies and experiences of Jewish life." (p. 300). Also, Joseph L. Blau in *The Story of Jewish Philosophy*, p. 259, regards Spinoza's doctrine of God as "an extension of the idea of the immanence of God which is repeatedly defended among Jewish writers." For a bibliography on this subject see Salo Baron, *op. cit.*, Volume III, p. 140.
5. Waxman, *op. cit.*, pp. 516-522.
6. See essay on Moses Mendelssohn by Alfred Jospe in *Great Jewish Personalities in Modern Times*, edited by Simon Noveck, pp. 30-32.
7. Solomon Schechter, *Studies in Judaism*, Chapter 2. See also Shalom Spiegel, *Hebrew Reborn*, Chapter 5.
8. For a brief description of the views of Geiger and Frankel see *Great Jewish Personalities*, *op. cit.*, pp. 63-66; on Samson Raphael Hirsch see Chapter 3 by Edward Jelenko in *ibid.* and Steven S. Schwarzschild in *Conservative Judaism*, Winter, 1959, pp. 26-45.
9. Waxman, *op. cit.*, Volume III, Chapter 10, deals with the work of Zunz, Rappaport and Steinschneider. For the new attitude towards the science of Judaism in the twentieth century see introduction by Nahum Glatzer to *Franz Rosenzweig: On Jewish Learning*, pp. 12-13.

10. *Dubnow: Nationalism and History*, edited by Koppel S. Pinson, Jewish Publication Society of America, Philadelphia, 1958.

11. *Between God and Man: An Interpretation of Judaism*, selected, edited and introduced by Fritz A. Rothschild, Harper and Brothers, New York, 1959.

12. In addition, several other twentieth-century Jewish thinkers deserve systematic treatment. These include Chaim Zhitlovsky (1865-1943), socialist theoretician and exponent of Jewish secularism both in Russia and in the United States; Nathan Birnbaum (1864-1937), Russian Jewish nationalist, who later became a founder of the *Agudat;* Claude Montefiore (1858-1938), British Jewish liberal thinker; Horace Kallen (born 1882), American Jewish philosopher and Zionist thinker; Hayim Greenberg (1889-1952), American Labor Zionist thinker and leader; and Isaac Breuer (1833-1948), disciple of Samson Raphael Hirsch and spokesman for Orthodox Jewry in Germany and later in Palestine.

The Idea of Jewish Nationalism

1. Hillel Bavli, "Zion in Modern Literature" in *Zion in Jewish Literature*, edited by Abraham S. Halkin, p. 102.

2. Simon Halkin, *Modern Hebrew Literature*, Chapter 2.

3. Salo Baron, "The Impact of Nationalism" in *Great Ages and Ideas of the Jewish People*, p. 355. See also Ernst Renan, *Qu'est-ce que c'est une Nation?*

4. Quoted by Baron, *op. cit.*, p. 355.

5. Louis Greenberg, *The Jews in Russia*, Volume I, Chapter 11.

6. Dubnow, *op. cit.*, First and Second Letters, pp. 73-115. See also pp. 48-51 and pp. 137-139.

7. *Ibid.*, p. 56.

8. Israel Knox, "Zhitlovsky's Philosophy of Jewish Life" in *Contemporary Jewish Record*, April, 1945, pp. 172-182.

9. *The Jewish People Past and Present*, Volume I, pp. 369-388. See especially Section 6, "Nationalism in the Bund," pp. 381 ff.

10. *Great Jewish Personalities in Modern Times*, pp. 233-235.

11. Maurice Samuel, *Harvest in the Desert*, Chapter 7. On Edmond de Rothschild see Frederic Morton, *The Rothschilds, a Family Portrait*, pp. 197-209, and Isaac Naiditch, *Edmond de Rothschild*.

12. Theodor Herzl, "The Jewish State" in *The Zionist Idea*, edited by Arthur Herzberg, pp. 204-261. See especially pp. 204, 215, 221, 222. See also "First Congress Address" in *ibid.*, p. 229.

13. Marie Syrkin, *Nachman Syrkin, Socialist Zionist, A Biographical Memoir and Selected Essays*, pp. 283-284.

14. Simon Federbush, "Religious Zionism" in *Struggle for Tomorrow*, edited by Feliks Gross and Basil J. Vlavianos, p. 77.

15. Samuel Mohilever, "Message to the First Zionist Congress" in Herzberg, *op. cit.*, p. 402.

16. Herzberg, *op. cit.*, pp. 411-413.

17. Martin Buber, *Israel and Palestine*, pp. 143-161.

Ahad Ha-am

1. Max Raisin, *Great Jews I Have Known*, p. 3. See also, Shmaryah Levin, *The Arena*, p. 26. Levin wrote "one element was lacking in the make-up

of Ahad Ha-am. He was a great teacher but not a political leader, a guide but not an organizer." *The Arena*, p. 26. See also pp. 41 and 175.

2. Chaim Weizmann, *Trial and Error*, pp. 52-54, 85-86, 139-141.

3. For Ahad Ha-am's reaction to the invitation from Dropsie College see his letter to E. Lubarski in *Ahad Ha'am; Essays, Letters, Memoirs*, translated from the Hebrew and edited by Leon Simon (Oxford East and West Library), p. 306, hereafter entitled *East and West* to distinguish it from other volumes of essays edited by Leon Simon.

4. Ira Eisenstein, "Kaplan and His Teachers" in *Mordecai Kaplan—An Evaluation*, pp. 23-24. See also, "The Way I Have Come" in the same volume, p. 298. For Martin Buber's estimate of Ahad Ha-am see *Israel and Palestine*, pp. 143-147.

5. *Pirké Zichronot* (Reminiscences) in *Kol Kitvé Ahad Ha-am* (collected works—one volume edition), p. 466. An English translation of a large part of these reminiscences can be found in *East and West*, pp. 236-340 and in Leo Schwarz' *Memoirs of My People*, pp. 248-253. The Reminiscences and the Letters constitute the major source of the biographical part of this essay.

6. *East and West*, p. 327.

7. Although Asher Ginzberg, unlike Martin Buber, never returned to *Hasidism*, his early *Hasidic* training was not without influence on his later thought. See his essay "The People of the Book" in *East and West*, pp. 59-64. For *Hasidic* influences in the early life of Joseph Soloveitchik see Chapter 10 of this book.

8. *East and West*, p. 326.

9. See "The Supremacy of Reason" in *East and West*, pp. 139-182.

10. *Kol Kitvé*, p. 481.

11. Leon Simon and Joseph Heller, *Ahad Ha-am: The Man, His Work and Teaching* (Hebrew), pp. 134-135. Selections from Pisarev's writings are now available in English in Dimitri Pisarev, *Selected Philosophical, Social and Political Essays*. Little has been written on the influence of Pisarev on Russian Jewish thinkers. See Shalom Spiegel, *Hebrew Reborn*, pp. 192 and 196.

12. On Ahad Ha-am's lack of self-confidence see the story he tells of his father in *Kol Kitvé*, p. 468. This manifested itself in his relationship with the *Bene Mosheh* Society, his doubts about his trip to London in 1793 and his refusal to accept the post offered him at Dropsie College. Leon Simon, *Ahad Ha-am, a Biography*, p. 72.

13. For a description of this circle of writers see Chaim Tschernowitz, *Hkakme' Odessa* (New York 1948); on Mendele Mocher Sephorim in Odessa see "Grandfather Mendele As I Knew Him" in *Commentary*, March, 1956. The story of Dubnow's stay in Odessa will be found in Dubnow, *Nationalism and History*, pp. 14-20.

14. *Road to Freedom: Writings and Addresses* by Leon Pinsker, with an introduction by B. Netanyahu, contains the full text of *Auto-Emancipation* as well as a selection of Pinsker's correspondence. For Ahad Ha-am's estimate of Pinsker see his essay "Dr. Pinsker and His Brochure" which he published in 1892 after the death of Pinsker and particularly a second essay written on the occasion of his tenth *yahrzeit* in which Ahad Ha-am summarizes the contents of *Auto-Emancipation* in a clear and succinct fashion. The latter will be found in *East and West*, pp. 183-200.

15. "The Wrong Way" in *Ten Essays on Zionism and Judaism*, hereafter called *Ten Essays*, pp. 1-24. The original essay is in *Kol Kitvé*, pp. 469 ff.
16. *East and West*, p. 333.
17. *Kol Kitvé*, p. 440.
18. The story of Ahad Ha-am's relationship to the Ahiasaf Publishing Company is told in Shmarya Levin, *The Arena*. See also *Kol Kitvé*, pp. 327-330, where Ahad Ha-am evaluates the firm on the occasion of the tenth anniversary of its founding.
19. A brief diary of this first trip is to be found as part of the "Reminiscences" in *Kol Kitvé*, pp. 470-471. This is not included in the translation either in *East and West* or in Leo Schwarz' *Memoirs of My People*.
20. *Kol Kitvé*, p. 5.
21. *Ibid.*, pp. 127-128.
22. Some of his best letters about *Ha-Shiloah* will be found in *East and West*, pp. 236-260. See particularly his letters to Dr. S. Bernfeld, pp. 253, 254 and 258 and his letter to Eliezer Kaplan, p. 255.
23. Letter to Dr. J. Tchlenow, October 7, 8. *Ibid.*, p. 277.
24. "The First Zionist Congress," *Kol Kitvé*, p. 276.
25. *Ibid.*
26. *East and West*, p. 289.
27. Quoted in Alex Bein, *Theodor Herzl*, p. 259.
28. *East and West*, p. 283.
29. Ahad Ha-am's tribute to Herzl after his death is included in his introduction to Volume III, *Kol Kitvé*, p. 249.
30. Quoted in Glickson, p. 97.
31. Leon Simon biography, *op. cit.*, pp. 209-211.
32. To S. Dubnow in *East and West*, p. 309.
33. *East and West*, p. 314.
34. Translation of this essay under the title "Summa Summarum" will be found in *Ten Essays*.
35. Ahad Ha-am expressed his feelings about the intermarriage of his daughter in personal letters to Simon Dubnow and Moses Smilansky. See *Igrot Ahad Ha-am*, Volume IV, p. 289 and Volume V, p. 12.
36. *Igrot*, Volume V, pp. 246-320.
37. *Kol Kitvé*, pp. 8-10. A translation of most of this essay will be found in Leon Simon's introduction to *Ten Essays*.
38. Glickson, *op. cit.*, p. 132.
39. "Past and Future" in *Selected Essays by Ahad Ha-am* translated from the Hebrew by Leon Simon, p. 80.
40. "Many Inventions" in *ibid.*, pp. 159-160.
41. See his early essay "Discarded Manuscripts" in *Kol Kitvé*, pp. 115-121.
42. Quoted in Norman Bentwich, *Ahad Ha-am and His Philosophy*, p. 15.
43. "Past and Future" in *Selected Essays*, p. 82.
44. Yehezkel Kaufman in *Hatekufah*, Volume XXIV.
45. See "Rival Tongues" in *East and West*, pp. 222-230. Also Ahad Ha-am's letter in *ibid.*, pp. 267 and 268.
46. For Ahad Ha-am's theory of religion see Heller and Simon, pp. 180-183.
47. Letter to M. K. in *East and West*, p. 263.
48. The Hebrew word is "*Tivi'im.*" See "Rabbi Mordecai Eliasberg" in *Kol Kitvé*, pp. 41-43.
49. Personal interview by the writer with the aged rabbi of the Odessa Synagogue, June, 1958.

50. "A New Savior" in *Selected Essays*, p. 249.
51. "Sabbath and Zionism" in *Kol Kitvé*, p. 286.
52. "National Morality" in *Kol Kitvé*, p. 161.
53. *East and West*, p. 270.
54. Heller and Simon, pp. 174-180.
55. "Jewish and Christian Ethics" in *East and West*, p. 137.
56. "Priest and Prophet" in *Selected Essays*, p. 134.
57. "Judaism and Nietzsche" in *East and West*, p. 80.
58. "Moses" in *Selected Essays*, p. 313.
59. Y. Kaufman, *op. cit.*
60. "Language and Its Literature" in *Kol Kitvé*, pp. 93-97.
61. "The Spiritual Revival" in *Selected Essays*, pp. 253-296.
62. "Concerning the Hebrew Encyclopedia in the Hebrew Language" in *Kol Kitvé*, p. 104 ff.
63. "Words of Peace" in *op. cit.*, p. 59.
64. "Sacred and Profane" in *Selected Essays*, pp. 41-45.
65. "The People of the Book" in *East and West*, pp. 59-64.
66. "Slavery in Freedom" in *Selected Essays*, pp. 171-194.
67. "Imitation and Assimilation" in *East and West*, p. 122.
68. Sir Isaiah Berlin, *The Life and Opinions of Moses Hess*, p. 40. See also Martin Buber, *Israel and Palestine*, pp. 111-122.
69. *Road to Freedom*, *op. cit.*, pp. 94-95.
70. Glickson, *op. cit.*, Chapter 6.
71. "A Spiritual Center" in *East and West*, pp. 201-208. On this central idea see also Ahad Ha-am's letters in *East and West*, pp. 282-287, 290, 291.

Aaron David Gordon
I. Life of Gordon

1. Israel Cohen, *A Short History of Zionism*, p. 65. See also Maurice Samuel, *Harvest in the Desert*, Chapter 12.
2. S. H. Bergman, Introduction to *Ho-odom V'hatevah* (*Man and Nature-Writings of A. D. Gordon*), p. 9.
3. Aside from an occasional reference in his writings, the only adequate source for Gordon's early life before he left for Palestine is Joseph Aronovitch, *Biographical Notes*, which appears in *Ho-umah V'Ha-avodah*, pp. 55-72. This biographical sketch is also available in English in *Zionism Pamphlets No. 5*. It is the English version that we cite here.
4. S. M. Dubnow, *History of the Jews in Russia and Poland*, Volume II, pp. 414-421. See also Maurice Samuel, *op. cit.*, pp. 67-68.
5. Aronovitch, *op. cit.*, p. 17.
6. *Ibid.*, p. 18.
7. Maurice Samuel, *op. cit.*, p. 119.
8. On Petach Tikvah see *Sefer Ha-yovayl* (Jubilee Volume on the completion of fifty years since the founding of Petach Tikvah) which traces the story of the founders and the early years of that colony; on Rishon Le Zion see "Colonies, Agricultural" in *Universal Jewish Encyclopedia*, Volume III, pp. 270 and 286.
9. Aronovitch, *op. cit.*, p. 23.
10. A. D. Gordon, *Kaf Hay Shanah L'Ptirato*, edited by M. Kushner, p. 83.
11. Gordon, though an admirer of Ahad Ha-am, became very perturbed when Ahad Ha-am used his influence in the *Hovevei Zion* movement to have it withdraw support from a socialist Hebrew paper published in Tel Aviv,

because it had printed a radical article by Brenner, denying any relationship between Jewish nationalism and Judaism.

12. Joseph Baratz, *A Village by the Jordan, the Story of Degania.*
13. Kushner, *op. cit.*
14. *Ibid.*
15. See Baratz, *op. cit.,* pp. 85-95. The most recent account of the colony is *Darchah Shel Degania (The Way of Degania, The Story of the Kevutzah's Fifty Years)*, which includes a sketch of Gordon's personality and his impact on the colonists, pp. 109-125.
16. Baratz, *op. cit.,* p. 92.
17. Samuel Dayan, *Gordon in Degania* (pamphlet), p. 7.
18. Aronovitch, *op. cit.,* p. 28.

Jewish Thought in Twentieth Century Germany

1. *Great Jewish Personalities*, Volume I, pp. 157-160. See also Joseph Blau, *Story of Jewish Philosophy*, Chapters 5-7.
2. Solomon Schechter, *Studies in Judaism*, Third Series, pp. 47-83. See also *Great Jewish Personalities in Modern Times*, pp. 63-64.
3. Bernard Heller, *Odyssey of a Faith*, p. 178.
4. Max Gruenewald, "The Modern Rabbi" in *Yearbook II*, Leo Baeck Institute, 1957, pp. 85-97.
5. Kaufmann Kohler, *Jewish Theology Systematically and Historically Considered*, p. 8.
6. Howard Sachar, *The Course of Modern Jewish History*, pp. 224-227 and 233-235.
7. S. Spier, "Jewish History As We See It" in *Yearbook I*, Leo Baeck Institute, p. 13.
8. Max Mayer, "A German Jew Goes East" in *Yearbook III*, Leo Baeck Institute, pp. 344-360; and S. Adler-Rudel, "East-European Jewish Workers in Germany" in *Yearbook II*, *op. cit.,* pp. 136-140. See also *Yearbook II*, pp. 136-140.
9. *Franz Rosenzweig: On Jewish Learning*, edited by N. N. Glatzer, pp. 12-13. Leo Baeck also urged a reorientation of the *Wissenschaft des Judentums.* See *Yearbook I, op. cit.,* p. 201.
10. H. Graetz, *History of the Jews*, Volume V, Chapter 9, 1895.
11. N. Glatzer, "The Frankfort Lehrhaus" in *Yearbook I*, Leo Baeck Institute, pp. 105-122.

Leo Baeck

1. Samuel Baeck was a prolific writer. His most important books were *Erzählungen und Religionssätze der Heiligen Schrift*, Lissa 1875 and 1886, *Geschichte des Jüdischen Volkes und seiner Literatur vom Babylonischen Exile bis auf die Gegenwart.* Lissa 1878 and 1894 (Last edition published after the author's death by his son.) Also see article on Samuel Baeck in the *Universal Jewish Encyclopedia.*
2. It was certainly not by pure chance that Leo Baeck chose for his doctor's dissertation the topic *Spinoza's erste Einwirkungen auf Deutschland (Spinoza's First Effects on German Thought* (Published by Meyer & Mueller, Berlin, 1895). For Spinoza was that Jewish philosopher who, through Jacobi and especially Goethe, had a tremendous impact on German philosophy and literature in the 18th and 19th centuries. Hegel's philosophy was very much influenced by Spinoza, too. Baeck offers in his thesis (pp.

68-84) very valuable material on the linguist Johann Georg Wachter who was the first to defend most energetically what Leo Baeck calls the "Spinozism of the Kabbalah." He published the book *Elucidarius Cabalisticus sive reconditae Hebraeorum philosophiae brevis et succincta recencio* (sic), Halle, 1706. Wachter refutes the statements of Spinoza's detractors. He says (always according to Baeck's thesis) that it is erroneous to claim Spinoza has "deified" the world; on the contrary: God and nature could not be distinguished from each other in a more stringent manner than Spinoza had done. That God should have bodily properties was proved as a most absurd statement by Spinoza; rather, according to him, there is nothing but the spiritual, for a divisible substance would be an impossible concept (our translation from the German).

3. Professor Sigmund Maybaum (1844-1919), a pupil of Israel Hildesheimer, after serving as a rabbi in Hungary and Bohemia was called to Berlin in 1881, where, because of his unique oratorical powers, he quickly achieved a position of leadership. Despite his Orthodox beginnings, he accepted the concepts of modern Bible criticism. His major works include: *Die Entwicklung des Israelitischen Prophetentums, Methodik des jüdischen Religionsunterrichts und Anfänge der jüdischen Predigt*. See also—*Universal Jewish Encyclopedia*.

4. H. G. Adler's work on *Theresienstadt*, which has become a classic in its field, was published by J. C. B. Mohr in Tübingen in 1955. It contains a characterization of Dr. Leo Baeck on pp. 249 ff. and reports on his activities in the concentration camp on pp. 152 ff and 201 ff. In 1958 it was followed by a publication of the Theresienstadt documents, called *Die verheimlichte Wahrheit* (The Hidden Truth). Baeck is mentioned on pages 131, 135, 136, 143.

5. The titles of the lectures delivered by Baeck at the Hebrew Union College in Cincinnati during the school years of 1950-51, 1951-52 and 1952-53 were as follows: "Selected Texts from the New Testament and from Christian Apocryphal Literature"; "Documents of Jewish and Other Religious Faiths"; and "Midrashic Texts Illustrating the Problems of Judaism."

6. *The Essence of Judaism*, New York, Schocken, 1948, p. 16.

7. *Ibid.*, pp. 30 ff.

8. *Ibid.*, pp. 41 ff.

9. *Ibid.*, p. 83.

10. *Ibid.*, p. 84.

11. Baeck. *Judaism and Christianity*, Philadelphia, The Jewish Publication Society, 1958. Introduction by Walter A. Kaufmann, pp. 6-8.

12. In 1952 Baeck published an essay entitled "Israel und das Deutsche Volk" ("Israel and the German People") in the German periodical *Merkur*. He was deeply impressed by its reception. *Ibid.*, p. 17.

13. *Dieses Volk-Juedische Existenz* made a tremendous impression on the German people and German ministers. The *Merkur* said: "The day will come when this book, probably the last great Jewish message in the German language, will be prized as an important testimony of Jewish teaching in this age, and, no less as the enduring legacy of a Jew from Germany to the German people." *Ibid.*, pp. 17-18.

Recent Trends in American Jewish Theology

1. Joseph L. Blau, "What's American About American Jewry?," in *Judaism*, Summer 1958, pp. 209-210. See also Jacob Agus, *Guideposts in Modern*

Judaism, 1954. Norman Frimer in "The A-Theology of American Jewry" in *Judaism* also discusses the reasons for this lack of interest in theology.

2. *Survey Report: National Jewish Cultural Services*, A Study Conducted by Council of Federations and Welfare Funds, pp. 4-13.

3. Solomon Freehof, "Jewish Scholarship in America" in Friedman and Gordis' *Jewish Life in America*, p. 176.

4. Present-day Jewish writers take differing views on the desirability of this Christian influence. Levi Olan in "Niebuhr and the Hebraic Spirit" in *Judaism*, Spring 1956, laments this influence as does Judd Teller in "A Critique of the New Theology" in *Commentary*, March 1958. See also Trude Weiss-Rosmarin in *Jewish Spectator*, November 1960. Jakob Petuchowski is less disturbed by this influence; see *Jewish Spectator*, January 1961.

For Emil Fackenheim's defense of Niebuhr's interpretation of Judaism, see his article "Judaism, Christianity and Reinhold Niebuhr: A Reply to Levi Olan" in *Judaism*, Fall 1956.

5. David Silverman, "Current Theological Trends: A Survey and Analysis" in *Proceedings of Rabbinical Assembly of America*, 1959, pp. 71 ff.

6. Samuel Cohon, "The Future Task of Jewish Theology" in The *Reconstructionist*, Jan. 10, 1958, p. 21.

Steven Schwarzschild also contrasts the enviable kind of specialization in theological research and the specialized theological journals which are available to Christian thinkers with the "eclectic and necessarily superficial" thought among Jews. See *Judaism*, Fall, 1958, p. 363.

8. *Ibid.*, p. 75.

9. Official transcript of Adult Education Lectures on "New Currents in Religious Thought," Lecture II on religious pragmatism, p. 30. The additional phrase "a useful fiction" attributed in a recent book to Steinberg does not appear in the official transcript. See *Conservative Judaism*, Summer, 1960, p. 10 for a discussion of this point.

10. "Theological Issues of the Hour" in *Proceedings of Rabbinical Assembly of America*, 1949, pp. 356-408.

11. Eugene Borowitz, "Existentialism's Meaning for Judaism" in *Commentary*, November, 1959, pp. 414-420.

12. On the general view of existentialism see Simon Kaplan, *The New World of Philosophy*, Chapter 5.

13. Borowitz, "Towards the New Covenant Theology" in *Commentary*, June 1961, pp. 322-326; *Commentary*, and "An Existentialist View of God" in *Jewish Heritage*, Spring 1958.

14. Will Herberg, "From Marxism to Judaism" in *Commentary*, January, 1947, pp. 25-32.

15. *Ibid.*, *Judaism and Modern Man*, pp. 25-41. See also Herberg's comments on Steinberg in *Proceedings of Rabbinical Assembly*, op. cit., pp. 409-428.

16. For critiques of Herberg's philosophy see Eugene Kohn, "The Menace of Existentialist Religion" in the *Reconstructionist*, November, 1951; Joseph Narot, "Recent Jewish Existentialist Writing" in *Yearbook*, Central Conference of American Rabbis, Vol. LXII, 1953, pp. 436 ff. and Steven S. Schwarzschild "Judaism a la mode" in *Menorah Journal*, March 1952.

17. Abraham J. Heschel, *Between God and Man. From the Writings of Abraham J. Heschel*, edited with an introduction by Fritz Rothschild, pp. 35-36. See also Joseph Lookstein, "Neo Hasidism of Abraham Heschel" in *Judaism*, Summer, 1956. For other articles on Heschel's philosophy see:

Maurice Friedman, "Abraham J. Heschel: Toward a Philosophy of Judaism" in *Conservative Judaism*, Winter, 1956 and Marvin Fox's review of *God in Search of Man* in *Judaism*, Winter, 1957.

18. Trude Weiss-Rosmarin, op. cit., Jan. 1961.
19. Quoted by Israel Levinthal in "Judaism and Existentialism" in *Brooklyn Jewish Center Review*, October, 1961.
20. Emil Fackenheim, "Jewish Existence and the Living God" in *Commentary*, August, 1959, pp. 128-136.

    For other articles by Fackenheim see: "Can We Believe in Judaism Religiously" in *Commentary*, Dec. 1948; "The Modern Jew's Path to God," *Commentary*, May, 1950; "Can There Be Judaism Without Revelation," *Commentary*, December, 1951; "Self-Realization and the Search for God. A Critique of Modern Humanism and a Defense of Jewish Supernaturalism," *Judaism*, October, 1952.

21. Jakob Petuchowski, *Ever Since Sinai*, see especially pp. 78-80 and 109-112.

    In addition to the thinkers listed above several other men are writing on theological issues from the existentialist point of view. These include Samuel Dresner, editor, *Conservative Judaism* magazine, Steven S. Schwarzschild, Managing Editor, *Judaism* magazine and Maurice Friedman, Monford Harris, Fritz Rothschild and Seymour Siegel.

22. Jack J. Cohen, *The Case For Religious Naturalism*, pp. 21 and 25.
23. L. Harold De Wolf, *Present Trends in Christian Thought*, pp. 25-28. See also, Henry W. Wieman article in *Mordecai M. Kaplan, An Evaluation*, pp. 193-210.
24. Ira Eisenstein, *Judaism Under Freedom*, pp. 69-70.
25. Eugene Kohn, *Good to Be a Jew*, p. 104.
26. *Proceedings of the Rabbinical Assembly of America*, 1953, pp. 179-191.
27. Jack J. Cohen, *op. cit.*, pp. xiii-xiv; 121-122 and 130. For critical reviews of Cohen's book see, Henry N. Wieman, "Naturalistic Religion and the Future of the Jews" in the *Reconstructionist*, Oct. 17, 1958; and David W. Silverman in *Judaism*, Summer, 1958, pp. 282-4. Other religious naturalists include Ludwig Nadelmann and Harold Schulweis.
28. Jacob Agus, "The Nature and Task of Liberal Judaism" in *Judaism*, Fall, 1958, pp. 291-295.
29. Robert Gordis, *Faith For Moderns*, pp. 1-9.
30. Regrettably, limitations of space make it impossible to survey the viewpoints of these thinkers in this essay.
31. Eugene Borowitz, Theological Conference; Cincinnati, 1950 in *Commentary*, June, 1950, pp. 567-572. See also annual reports on the commission by Bernard Heller in *Proceedings of Central Conference of American Rabbis, 1959-1962.*
32. *Proceedings of Central Conference of American Rabbis*, 1959, pp. 263-264.
33. Quoted by Israel Knox, in *Commentary*, Dec. 1954, p. 446. On the relationship between Reform Judaism and *Halakhah* see Bernard Bamberger "Halakhah in Our Age: The Basic Problem" in *Judaism*, Spring 1957.
34. See Benjamin Kreitman's excellent summary of these developments and the ensuing discussion in *Proceedings of Rabbinical Assembly of America*, 1958. See also Fritz Rothschild "Conservative Judaism Faces the Need for Change" in *Commentary*, March, 1955 and Myron Fenster in *Reconstructionist*, March 20, 1959.
35. Rackman's most recent articles are "The Dialectic of the Halakkah" in

Tradition, Spring 1961, and "Israel and God: Reflections on Their Encounter" in *Judaism,* Summer 1962.

Joseph Soloveitchik

1. This essay is a condensation of a longer chapter submitted by the author and prepared with his permission during his absence from the country.
2. R stands for Hebrew word *Rav* which means "rabbi" and is used by the author to denote respect and reverence.

Glossary

ABRAMOWITZ, SHALOM JACOB (1836-1917): Pen-name MENDELE MOKHER SEFORIM ("Mendele the Bookseller"). Famed Hebrew and Yiddish writer of the *Haskalah* period whose realism and precise style in stories of the Pale of Settlement left a lasting mark on Hebrew and Yiddish literature.

ACOSTA, URIEL (c. 1585-1640): Portuguese-born Marrano religious skeptic who denounced Catholicism and fled to Holland where he converted to Judaism. His later attacks on the Oral Law and basic Jewish doctrines caused his excommunication by the rabbis.

AGUDAT ISRAEL (Heb., "union of Israel"): World organization of Orthodox Jews established in 1912. It opposed Zionism and drew its doctrines from the neo-Orthodoxy of Samson Raphael Hirsch.

ALIYAH (Heb., "ascent"): Refers here to the "waves" of immigrants coming to Palestine. First *Aliyah*, 1882-1903; Second *Aliyah*, 1904-1914 etc. Also, the "calling up" to the reading of the Torah.

AUTO-EMANCIPATION: Pamphlet by Dr. Leon Pinsker (1882) offering a searching analysis of anti-Semitism and calling for territorial independence and a revival of national consciousness as the solution to the "Jewish problem."

BAAL TESHUVAH (Heb., a "penitent returner or backslider."): Alienated Jew who returns to Judaism.

BAECK, SAMUEL (1834-1912): Father of Leo Baeck, rabbi, philosopher and author of a history of the Jewish people and its literature from the Babylonian Exile to his day.

BARTH, KARL (1886-   ): Eminent Calvinist theologian whose rigorous revelationist doctrines are set forth in such works as *The Word of God and the Word of Man* (1928), *Dogmatics in Outline* (1949).

BIALIK, HAYYIM NAHMAN (1872-1934): Poet laureate of the Jewish people. (GJP II)*

BILU, BILUIM: Name given to first idealistic pioneer group which in 1882 left Russia for Palestine. The word "Bilu" is made up of the first letters of their motto, from Isaiah: *Bet Jacob ekhu ve-nelkhah* ("O house of Jacob, come ye and let us go forth").

BIRNBAUM, NATHAN (1864-1937): Jewish philosophical writer in Vienna, formulator of the word "Zionism," supporter of Herzl. His views changed, however, to advocacy of Diaspora nationalism in 1899 and in 1912 to Orthodoxy. In 1919 he joined the *Agudat Israel* and became its chief secretary.

BRENNER, YOSEF HAYYIM (1881-1921): Hebrew writer and journalist who settled in Palestine in 1910 where he was a leader of the worker's movement and writer of novels depicting life in Palestine.

BUBER, SOLOMON (1827-1906): Grandfather of Martin Buber. Essayist and author of books dealing with *Midrashic* literature. Versed in classical languages and Aramaic, he enriched *Aggadic* literature by editing previously unknown *Midrashim* with scientific clarity.

DAYAN (Heb., "judge"): Judge of a rabbinic court.

DUBNOW, SIMON (1860-1941): Russian historian. Author of the ten-volume history: *Weltgeschichte des Jüdischen Volkes,* which emphasizes the eastern European and socio-economic aspects of Jewish history, and presents his theory of Spiritual Autonomism calling for social and cultural autonomy in the Diaspora rather than political, territorial autonomy. Also wrote, *History of the Jews in Russia and Poland* and *The History of Hasidism.*

ECKHART, MEISTER JOHANNES (c. 1260-1327): Called by Buber "the greatest thinker of Western mysticism." He taught that God is in every man; that complete self-abandonment to Him constitutes salvation.

EINHORN, DAVID (1809-1897): Rabbi and leader of extreme Reform segment of U.S. Jewry whose liturgy *Olat Tamid* ("Perpetual Offering") was adopted by Reform synagogues.

EXISTENTIALISM: Modern school of philosophy based on the proposition that "existence is prior to essence." It has gained wide popular acceptance particularly through the works of Jean Paul Sartre.

* *Great Jewish Personalities in Modern Times,* B'nai B'rith Great Books Series: Volume II.

FELSENTHAL, BERNHARD (1822-1908): German-born Reform rabbi of Sinai (1861-64) and Zion (1864-87) Temples in Chicago; a founder of the Jewish Publication Society of America.

FEUCHTWANGER, LION (1884-1958): Contemporary writer whose historical novels include, *Jew Süss, The Ugly Duchess, Success* and a work on the life of Josephus.

FRANKEL, ZECHARIAH (1801-75): Founder and chief exponent of historical Judaism in Germany and first director of the Breslau Rabbinical Seminary. His numerous scholarly works include *The Ways of the Mishnah.*

FRISCHMAN, DAVID (1861-1922): Distinguished Hebrew poet, editor and writer who introduced a new note of beauty to Hebrew literature.

GEIGER, ABRAHAM (1810-1874): Philosopher of Reform Judaism, founder of the *Hochschule für die Wissenschaft des Judentums* in Berlin and Bible scholar whose theories were brought to the United States by mid-nineteenth century German immigrants.

GOLAH (Heb., "the captivity"): Denotes Jewish peoples living outside Palestine, but originally those living in Babylonia during the period of the Second Temple.

GOTTLOBER, ABRAHAM (1810-1899): Russian *Haskalah* writer, editor of the monthly *Ha-Boker Or* and poet who translated Schiller and Herder into Hebrew. After 1881 he joined *Hoveve Zion* and became a Zionist poet.

GRAETZ, HEINRICH (1817-1891): German historian and scholar whose monumental 11-volume *History of the Jews* based on original sources and collating the work of many different branches of Jewish learning in the nineteenth century has had inestimable influence on Jewish historians.

GYMNASIUM (Ger.): School equivalent to U. S. high school and junior college.

HALAKHAH (Heb., "law"): From *halakh*: "go" or "follow." The legal portion of Talmudic and later literature. Refers largely to oral Law, the traditional interpretations of written law.

HALUKKAH (Heb., "division"): Ancient form of Jewish charity collected by emissaries for the support of Jews living in Palestine.

HA-MELITZ (Heb., "The Advocate"): Russian Hebrew periodical founded by Alexander Zederbaum which appeared first weekly and then daily from 1860 to 1904. First in Odessa and then in St. Petersburg; it was an influential voice of Russian Jewry.

HA-POEL HA-TZAIR (Heb., "The Young Worker"): Palestine's

Zionist Labor Party founded in 1905. Its members founded the first *kevutzah* at Degania.

HASIDISM: Mystical religious social movement founded by Israel Baal Shem Tov (1700-60). Preached the equality of all men, pantheism of God, central role of the *zaddik* or *rebbe* who through his connection with God brings life to the world.

HASKALAH (Heb., "enlightenment"): Movement (c. 1750-1880) for the enlightenment of the Jews through knowledge of the sciences, European languages and culture. The movement produced a literature which stressed knowledge, the value of manual labor, faith in human nature and social progress as well as aesthetics. It was hoped that the movement would result in the emancipation of the Jews.

HA-TZEFIRAH (Heb., "the dawn"): Warsaw Hebrew daily founded in 1862 by Hayyim Slonimsky and later edited by Nahum Sokolow from 1904.

HERBERG, WILL (1906-   ): Theologian, scholar and author of such works as *Judaism and Modern Man, Protestant, Catholic, Jew* and editor of *The Writings of Martin Buber.*

HESS, MOSES (1812-1875): German writer and precursor of Zionism whose *Rome and Jerusalem* (1862) was the first critical exposition of the bases of Jewish nationalism.

HIBBAT ZION (Heb., "Love of Zion"): Movement which began in Russia after the pogroms of 1881 for the establishment of colonies and settlement of Jews in Palestine.

HIRSCH, EMIL G. (1851-1923): Rabbi, educator and civic leader who succeeded Kaufmann Kohler at Sinai Congregation in Chicago. He was an opponent of Zionism.

HIRSCH, BARON MAURICE de (1831-1896): Banker, philanthropist, founder of the Jewish Colonisation Association (I.C.A.) in 1891 for the establishment of Jewish agricultural settlements in Argentina.

HIRSCH, SAMSON RAPHAEL: (1808-1888) Founder of German neo-Orthodoxy which sought to blend western culture with traditional Jewish observance. (GJP I)*

HISTADRUT: Jewish Labor Federation in Palestine founded in 1920.

HOCHSCHULE FÜR DIE WISSENSCHAFT DES JUDENTUMS: Berlin educational institution for advancement of Jewish studies, teacher and rabbinic training founded in 1870.

* *Great Jewish Personalities in Ancient and Modern Times,* B'nai B'rith Great Books Series: Volume I.

HOMILETICS: The art of preaching.

HONI HA-MEAGEL (Heb., "Honi the Circle Drawer"): First century C.E. legendary miracle worker and rain maker who slept for 70 years waking to find a completely different world.

HOVEVE ZION (Heb., "Lovers of Zion"): Societies of *Hibbat Zion.*

ILLUY (Heb.): child prodigy, genius, brilliant scholar.

JÜDISCHE WISSENSCHAFT (Ger., "Jewish science"): movement for the scientific study of Judaism (known as the Science of Judaism) which flourished in central and western Europe in the nineteenth century. Its systematic study of Jewish institutions and ideas laid the groundwork for twentieth-century Jewish scholarship.

KABBALAH (Heb., "tradition"): Ancient lore of Jewish mysticism of which the *Zohar,* a mystical 13th century Bible commentary, is the great classic.

KASHRUT (Heb., from *kasher* "fit"): Regulations of the Jewish Dietary laws.

KATZENELSON, BERL (1887-1944): Zionist leader and journalist who became a leader of the labor movement in Palestine.

KEHILLAH (Heb., "Jewish community"): Usually refers to type of organized community in Europe which had legal recognition of the State.

KIBBUTZ (Heb., "gathering in"): Israel collective settlement resembling *kevutzah.*

KIERKEGAARD, SØREN (1813-1855): Danish existentialist philosopher whose works include *The Sickness Unto Death, Either-Or,* etc. Only recently influential, he has had a marked effect on several thinkers in this volume.

KLATZKIN, JACOB (1882-1948): Hebrew publicist, philosopher of Zionism, founder of the Eshkol publishing house and chief editor of the fifteen volume *Encyclopaedia Judaica.*

KROCHMAL, NAHMAN (1785-1840): Galician Jewish philosopher and proponent of the theory of a "Jewish mission" based on the unique spirituality of the Jewish people. His *A Guide for the Perplexed of the Time* was published posthumously in 1851.

KUPAT HOLIM: Sick Benefit Society of the Jewish Labor Federation in Israel.

KEVUTZAH: A collective or cooperative form of settlement in Palestine in which all members share alike in work and profits go into the treasury for improvement of the settlement.

LANDAUER, GUSTAVE (1870-1919): German anarcho-socialist writer and educator. Buber edited his lectures on Shakespeare and his letters.

LAZARUS, MORITZ (1824-1903): German philosopher, educator and contributor to the field of *Völkerpsychologie* (national psychology); the theory of nations as spiritual individuals. His major work was the *Ethics of Judaism*. He opposed Jewish nationalism since he considered the Jewish people merely as a religious differentiation.

LEBENSOHN, ABRAHAM DOV (1794-1878): Poet, grammarian, reviver of Hebrew poetry in Russia and outstanding pioneer of *Haskalah*.

LEBENSOHN, MICHAL (1828-1852): Gifted Hebrew poet, son of Abraham Dov. He applied rules of modern prosody to Hebrew verse.

LILIENBLUM, MOSES LEIB (1843-1910): Early Jewish nationalist and pioneer who emphasized the practical aspects of Palestine settlement.

LILIENTHAL, MAX (1815-1882): German-born rabbi who tried unsuccessfully, at the behest of the Russian government, to introduce secular education into the Russian Pale of Settlement in 1840. Emigrated to the United States in 1844 and was one of the founders of the Union of American Hebrew Congregations and the Hebrew Union College.

LUZZATTO, SAMUEL DAVID (1800-1865): Italian founder of modern Jewish scholarship, defender of Orthodoxy and builder of Hebrew culture.

MATMID (Heb., "one who persists"): Unusually diligent person, "perpetual student."

MAY LAWS: Russian laws enacted May 3, 1882 which prohibited Jews from living outside Pale of Settlement.

MAZZINI, GIUSEPPE (1805-1872): Italian writer, philosopher of nationalism, and liberal leader of the Italian nationalist movement.

MELAMMED (Heb., "teacher"): Teacher in a *heder*, the traditional Jewish religious school.

MENDELSSOHN, MOSES (1729-1786): The first "modern Jew" to combine Jewish and modern culture. German philosopher, Bible translator. (GJP Vol. II)

MIDRASH: Homiletic and legendary embellishment of the Bible used by the ancient rabbis to interpret and teach Judaism by finding new meanings in addition to the literal ones in the text.

MITNAGGED (Heb., "opponent"): One who opposes *Hasidism.*
Term came into use after the ban against *Hasidism* issued by
the Vilna Gaon in 1772. (GJP II)

MITZVAH (Heb., "commandment"): Injunction of the Torah
(there are 613). Colloquially—a good deed.

MORAIS, SABATO (1832-1897): Sephardic rabbi who played a
leading role in 1886 in the organization of the Jewish Theological Seminary of America. Morais served as its first president
until his death.

NORDAU, MAX (1849-1923): Physician, world-renowned Zionist
leader. Ardent co-worker of Herzl's who actively participated
in the Zionist Congresses delivering major addresses. Brilliant
interpreter and critic of civilization. He was a "political Zionist"
and supporter of Uganda Jewish settlement plan.

PALE OF SETTLEMENT: System instituted in 1791 of restricted
Jewish residence in 25 provinces of Czarist Russia.

PHARISEES (Heb., *Perushim*—"separate"): Jewish religious party
during the Second Temple period which contributed to the
development of Jewish law and doctrine.

PILPUL (Heb., "debate"): Talmudic casuistry. Analytic method of
Talmud study involving intricate mental gymnastics.

PINSKER, JUDAH LOEB (LEON) (1821-1891): Pioneer Zionist,
Odessa physician, author of *Auto Emancipation* (1882), a
resounding call for the self-emancipation of the Jews by the
establishment of a home of their own. He became the president
of the *Hoveve Zion* (Lovers of Zion) societies.

PIRKE AVOT (Heb., "Chapters of the Fathers"): Teachings of
the sages from the third century B.C.E. to third century C.E.
which had been incorporated into the liturgy.

PISAREV, DIMITRI (1840-1868): Radical Russian writer whose
works influenced the Russian Jewish intelligentsia. He was a
Darwinian and positivist.

POALE ZION (Heb., "Workers of Zion"): Socialist Zionist Party.

POGROM (Russ., "destruction"): An organized massacre for the
devastation of a group usually with governmental approval—especially against the Jews, e.g., Russian pogroms of 1881 and 1905.

RAPOPORT, SOLOMON JUDAH (1790-1867): Galician rabbi
and scholar of *"Wissenschaft"* whose enlightened researches
formed a base for modern Jewish scholarship.

RAVNITZKI, JEHOSHUA HANA (1859-1944): Author, editor
and publisher and one of the first *Hoveve Zion.*

REINACH, SALOMON (1858-1932): French archaeologist and

prolific writer. Vice-president of the central committee of Alliance Israelite Universelle and member of the Jewish Colonisation Association Committee.

ROSSI, AZARIAH de (1514-1578): Italian physician, scholar and critical Jewish historian and commentator who used the scientific method in his studies. His great work was *Me'or 'Enayim* (1574).

ROTHSCHILD, BARON EDMOND de (1845-1934): Notable philanthropist who supported Palestine settlements, settled Galilee and Samaria and sent agricultural experts and officials to supervise his benefactions.

RUPPIN, ARTHUR (1876-1942): Zionist leader and sociologist in 1921 appointed director of the colonization department in Jerusalem. He wrote *The Sociology of the Jews.*

SCHOLEM, GERSHOM (1897-   ): Outstanding contemporary authority on *Kabbalah* and Jewish mysticism. Scholem gave Jewish mysticism a new standing in Jewish philosophy and history. He published numerous works including *Major Trends in Jewish Mysticism.*

SCHULMAN, KALMAN (1819-1899): Prolific writer of the *Haskalah* period. His translations are some of the first novels to appear in Hebrew. He helped to educate his generation with his varied writings.

SEMIKHAH (Heb., "placing"): The writ of ordination of a rabbi permitting him to render decisions in matters of ritual law. The conferring (placing) of leadership.

SHEKALIM (Heb., "shekels"): Old practice of levying a half-shekel "Temple Tax" revived in modern period by the Zionist Organization as a levy for World Zionist Congress participation and indication of support.

SHIMONOWITZ, DAVID (1886-1956): Russian-born Hebrew poet; often called *the* poet of modern Palestine, for his poems deal with all aspects of life in Palestine.

SHOMRIM (Heb., "The watchman"): Organization of mounted Jewish guards founded in 1909 to protect Jewish life and property in Palestine.

SHULHAN ARUKH (Heb., "The Prepared Table"): Work of Joseph Caro published in 1567 and accepted as the final authority on Jewish law and observance by Orthodox Jews.

SIMMEL, GEORG (1858-1918): Philosopher and sociologist who introduced the theories of Bergson and William James into German idealistic thought.

SMOLENSKIN, PERETZ (1842-1885): Writer of the *Haskalah*

period who criticized *Haskalah* assimilationism and advocated Jewish nationalism.

SOKOLOW, NAHUM (1860-1936): Versatile essayist, vital contributor to the modernization of the Hebrew language and Zionist leader. He wrote *A History of Zionism.*

STEINSCHNEIDER, MORITZ (1816-1907): Educator and brilliant "father of Jewish bibliography." Scholar and writer of such works as *A Catalogue of the Hebrew Books in the Oxford Library.*

STEEBEL (Yidd., "small room"): Prayer room of a synagogue, also room where *Hasidim* gather—viz. *Hasidic steebel.*

STRAUSS, LEO (1899-   ): Philosopher at *Akademie für die Wissenschaft des Judentums* before coming to the U.S. where he taught at the New School for Social Research and University of Chicago.

USSISHKIN, MENAHEM MENDEL (1863-1941): Noted Zionist leader, a founder of the Bilu (1882) and Bene Zion society (1884), supporter of Herzl and leader of the fight against the Uganda Jewish settlement proposal.

WISSOTSKY, KALONYMOS Z. (1824-1904): Head of Wissotsky Tea Firm, philanthropist sponsor and founder of *Ha-Shiloah,* financier of schools and Jewish charities in Russia and Palestine.

WOLF, LUCIEN (1857-1930): English journalist, historian and crusader against anti-Semitism. He was a territorialist strongly opposed to Zionism.

WOLFF, THEODOR (1868-1943): Author and editor of *Berliner Tageblatt.* Respected German columnist active in political affairs.

YESHIVAH (Heb.): Traditional Jewish school for study of Talmud and rabbinic literature.

YISHUV (Heb.): The Jewish settlement in Palestine. Jewish community.

ZADDIK (Heb., "righteous man"): *Hasidic* rabbi regarded as the intermediary between God and man, the spiritual leader and advisor on all matters.

ZEDERBAUM, ALEXANDER (1816-1893): Russian Hebrew and Yiddish writer and editor and founder of *Ha-Melitz.* Also founded the Yiddish periodical *Kol Mevasser.* He was an advocate of Jewish nationalism.

ZUNZ, LEOPOLD (1794-1886): Scholar, founder of the Science of Judaism and author of such works as: *Die gottesdienstlichen Vorträge der Juden,* a history of Jewish homiletics which has become a classic.

*About the Contributors

JACK COHEN (*Aaron David Gordon*) is Director of the B'nai B'rith Hillel Foundation at the Hebrew University, Jerusalem, and author of *The Case for Religious Naturalism* and *The Religion of the Jewish Prayer Book*.

JACOB B. AGUS (*Abraham Isaac Kuk*) is rabbi of Congregation Beth El in Baltimore, and author of *Modern Philosophies of Judaism, The Evolution of Jewish Thought, Guideposts in Judaism*, etc.

EPHRAIM FISCHOFF (*Hermann Cohen*) is rabbi of Congregation Agudath Sholom in Lynchburg, Va., and author of numerous articles, reviews and translations on sociological and Jewish subjects.

HENRY W. BRANN (*Leo Baeck*) is Washington correspondent of the *Jewish Forum*, subject analyst of the National Library of Medicine in Washington, and author of numerous essays and articles in the field of German philosophy and psychology.

NAHUM N. GLATZER (*Franz Rosenzweig*) is Professor of History and Chairman of the Department of Near Eastern and Judaic Studies at Brandeis University, and author of *In Time and Eternity, Language and Faith, A Midrash Reader, Life and Thought of Franz Rosenzweig*, etc.

MAURICE FRIEDMAN (*Martin Buber*) is Professor of Philosophy at Sarah Lawrence College, author of *Martin Buber: The Life of Dialogue*, and editor and translator of many of Buber's works, including *Pointing the Way, Hasidism and Modern Man, The Tales of Rabbi Nachman*, etc.

SAMUEL COHON (*Kaufmann Kohler*) was Professor of Jewish Theology at the Hebrew Union College in Cincinnati, and author of *Authority in Judaism, Saadia Gaon, Judaism—A Way of Life, The Unity of God*, etc.

IRA EISENSTEIN (*Mordecai M. Kaplan*) is President of the Reconstructionist Foundation, editor of *The Reconstructionist*, and author of *Creative Judaism, What We Mean by Religion, The Ethics of Tolerance, Judaism under Freedom*, etc.

AHARON LICHTENSTEIN (*Joseph Soloveitchik*) is Professor of English at Stern College, in New York.

The contributors are identified by their occupations at the time of the writing of the essays

Index